Spanish Grammar in Context

THIRD EDITION

'This is a well-conceived edition, which covers important grammatical areas clearly and methodically, while engaging students with topics of interest to their studies. I recommend it highly.'

Ronan Fitzsimons, *Nottingham Trent University, UK*

'Great use of authentic texts to introduce Spanish grammar and culture.'

Viviannette González-Barreto, *Indiana University, USA*

Spanish Grammar in Context provides an accessible and stimulating approach to learning grammar. Authentic texts are used to illustrate and explain the key areas of Spanish grammar, followed by a range of exercises to help students reinforce and test their understanding. An answer key is also presented at the back of the book.

Features include:

- A rich variety of texts sourced from all over the Spanish-speaking world, including excerpts from contemporary literature, magazines and newspapers
- Texts carefully selected to cover topical issues and themes relevant to contemporary Spain and Latin America
- Clear, user-friendly and comprehensive coverage of grammar, aided by a list of grammatical terms
- An abundance of exercises designed to build up grammatical understanding and effective comprehension and communication skills
- Free companion website at www.routledge.com/cw/Kattan-Ibarra featuring an assortment of extra exercises for additional practice.

This third edition has been revised and updated throughout and offers new exercises and fresh texts.

Spanish Grammar in Context will be an essential resource for intermediate to advanced students of Spanish. It is suitable for both classroom use and independent study.

Juan Kattán-Ibarra is a freelance author.

Angela Howkins was formerly Lecturer in Spanish at Dundee College, Scotland. She has taught widely in Spanish and has lectured on Spanish history and civilisation.

LANGUAGES IN CONTEXT

The *Languages in Context* series presents students with an engaging way of learning grammar while also acquiring cultural and topical knowledge. Each book in the series uses authentic texts, drawn from a generous variety of sources, as the starting point for the explanation of key areas of grammar. Grammar points are then consolidated with a wide range of exercises to test students' understanding.

Aimed at intermediate to advanced students, the *Languages in Context* series is suitable for both class use and independent study.

The following books are available in this series:

French Grammar in Context
Spanish Grammar in Context
German Grammar in Context

Spanish Grammar in Context

THIRD EDITION

JUAN KATTÁN-IBARRA AND ANGELA HOWKINS

LONDON AND NEW YORK

First published in Great Britain in 2003 by Hodder Arnold
Second edition published in 2008 by Hodder Education, part of Hachette UK Company
This third edition published in 2014 by Routledge
2 Park Square, Milton Park, Abingdon, Oxon OX14 4RN

and by Routledge
711 Third Avenue, New York, NY 10017

Routledge is an imprint of the Taylor & Francis Group, an informa business

British Library Cataloguing in Publication Data
A catalogue record for this book is available from the British Library

Library of Congress Cataloging in Publication Data
Kattán-Ibarra, Juan.
Spanish grammar in context / Juan Kattan Ibarra, Angela Howkins. – Third Edition.
pages cm. – (Languages in Context)
Previous ed.: London : Hodder Education, 2nd ed., 2008.
Includes bibliographical references and index.
1. Spanish language–Grammar. 2. Spanish language–Grammar–Problems, exercises, etc. 3. Spanish language–Textbooks for foreign speakers–English. I. Howkins, Angela. II. Title.
PC4112.K38 2014
468.2′421–dc23

2013031174

ISBN: 978-0-415-72348-0 (hbk)
ISBN: 978-0-415-72347-3 (pbk)
ISBN: 978-1-315-81746-0 (ebk)

Typeset in Minion
by Graphicraft Limited, Hong Kong

Printed and bound by CPI Group (UK) Ltd, Croydon, CR0 4YY

Contents

Preface

There comes a point in language study where an understanding of how a language functions is vital for progress to be made. *Spanish Grammar in Context* is designed to give students who are in the final years of school or the early stages of university study, and adult learners who are at an equivalent stage, an understanding of how Spanish functions in a practical and relevant way. More advanced students may also find the book both interesting and useful for review and revision purposes.

The starting point of each chapter is an authentic text in which a particular grammatical point is highlighted. This focuses the student's attention on this part of speech and how it functions in context. There then follows a clear and concise explanation of both form and usage, with examples from the text or from everyday language. Differences in usage between Peninsular and Latin American Spanish are noted. The subsequent exercises provide practice of the grammar points highlighted and explained in the text. Exercises vary from the practice of form and use within the context of a single sentence through gap-fill to more open-ended communicative types of exercises. Translation exercises are included, especially where usage differs considerably from English and so can cause problems for English speakers. Except for those exercises which are of a communicative nature, a key is provided for the exercises of each chapter, thus making the book ideal for self-study. In the classroom context, it can be used for the study of grammar and/or of a topic area, as the texts chosen lend themselves to exploitation beyond the study of the grammar point in question.

The texts are taken from authentic sources from all over the Spanish-speaking world. They include excerpts from contemporary literature, and from newspaper and magazine articles, including 'agony aunt' letters, and have a richness and variety which make them intrinsically interesting to read. Some exercises relate to the topic of the text, others simply practise the particular grammatical point, the aim of all types being to help students to achieve a greater understanding of function and a greater confidence when using the language for their own communicative purposes.

The book is divided into two main parts: one which deals with aspects of the verb, and the other which deals with nouns, adjectives, pronouns, prepositions and all other parts of speech which go to make up a sentence. Chapters can be studied sequentially, or in random order, according to whichever grammar point the student wishes to study, thus making it a useful and handy reference/revision tool. However, chapters which deal with related grammar points are grouped together (for example, the present and imperfect subjunctive). As each text is taken from an authentic source, it naturally produces examples of grammar not explicitly studied in that particular chapter. These are indicated in the chapter under the heading "Other points to note in the text", so that students may study the text beyond the confines of the grammatical point for which it has been chosen, or teachers may exploit it further in the classroom. The consolidation exercises found at the end of the book comprise six texts, three journalistic and three literary, each with questions which give students the opportunity to test their knowledge of grammar. A glossary of grammatical terms and a table of irregular verbs are also included to make the book as user-friendly as possible.

The book does not pretend to be exhaustive in its coverage but focuses on those areas of grammar which are important for effective communication. At all times grammar is presented not as an end in itself but as the necessary tool for effective communication. This approach encourages students not only to read for comprehension and pleasure, but also to have an awareness of how the language is used. By developing skills of observation and analysis in their studies, students will be able to enhance their productive skills and so reap the rewards that language study brings.

Note to the third edition

The format of the third edition of *Spanish Grammar in Context* remains the same as for the previous editions. However, additional texts have been included to give further illustration of specific points of grammar and some texts, which because of fast-moving technologies have become out-dated, have been replaced. The themes of the texts continue to be topical and relevant to students of Spanish. In certain chapters, exercises have been added. Students who are looking for more practice of specific grammar points are referred to the companion website at www.routledge.com/cw/Kattan-Ibarra where they will find exercises for all the chapters of the book except for Chapter 30, Word Order.

Acknowledgements

Thanks are due to the authors and publishers/media agents who kindly allowed us to make use of their texts. Every effort has been made to trace all copyright holders of material. Any rights not acknowledged here will be acknowledged in subsequent printings if sufficient notice is given to the publisher.

Spain: *Quo*, 'Trucos para hacer turismo sin arruinarte', July 1996, 'Cómo ponerse en forma en 30 días', 'Duele el sol', July 1997; *El País*, '364 días en automóvil', 23 September 2001; *El País Semanal*, 'Lo que aprendí en la escuela', 'Decálogo del ciudadano silencioso', 12 September 1999; *Expansión*, 'Un libro es más importante que un pan bien hecho: entrevista con Isabel Allende', 15 November 1997; *Blanco y Negro*, *ABC*, 'Entrevista: Montserrat Caballé', 29 May 1988, 'Veintiocho años, y en paro', 26 November 1995; *16*, 'A la caza del meteorito', 15 October 2000, 'Nacho Paunero: Maltratar a un animal es delito y es necesario denunciarlo', 9 July 2006; *CNR*, 'Nos estamos fumando el planeta', 20 October 1998; *Cambio 16*, 'Entrevista con Mario Molina', 15 July 1996, 'El sol, ¿amigo o enemigo?', 19 July 1998, 'La dieta mediterránea', 21 November 1988, 'La España beoda', 21 December 1987; *Tribuna*, 'Consejos para evitar incendios', 15 July 1996; *Prima*, 'Estrategias para encontrar empleo: la entrevista', October 1996; *Tiempo*, 'Retrato del nuevo español', 11 May 1987, 'Si usted quiere un hijo perfecto', 17 November 1997, 'El homo erectus, el primer balsero del estrecho de Gibraltar', 17 November 1997, 'El efecto invernadero', 14 July 1997; *El Mundo*, 'Estados Unidos está en el proceso de convertirse en un país hispano', 8 July 2006; excerpts from *Queda la noche* by Soledad Puértolas, Editorial Planeta-De Agostini, S.A.; **Chile:** *El Mercurio*, Valparaíso, 'Latinoamericanos, los más apasionados y belicosos del mundo', 26 November 2000; *El Metropolitano*, 'Al rescate de la Amazonia', 13 October 1999, 'Palabra de forjador ambiental', 30 October 1999; *La Tercera*, 'Dos tercios de la población mundial vivirá en ciudades en el año 2025', 6 July 2000, 'Alerta sobre alteración de costas del mundo', 24 April 2001, 'El futuro de la raza humana', 21 October 2006, 'Roberto Bolaño: inédito y final', 3 April 2010, 'El selecto club de las palabras que han sobrevivido por 15.000 años', 11 May 2013, 'Cómo viven y quiénes son la nueva oleada de españoles en Chile', 10 June 2012; *El Mercurio*, Santiago, '¿Qué habría sucedido si . . . ?', 24 February 2001, '¿Para esto estudié tanto?', 26 June 1999, 'Parece que maduré, aunque no quería', 15 October 1999, 'El barco donde estaba el paraíso', 17 April 1994, 'La escritura me ha dado poder', 13 December 2003, 'Lo que pesa (y lo que vale) el español hoy en el mundo', 29 March 2009; *Revista de El Sábado de El Mercurio*, 'El hombre digital', 28 January 2006, '*Volver* es mi película más terapéutica', 10 June 2006, 'Rosa Montero: El éxito es una luz que te dan los otros', 30 August 2008, 'Cómo viviremos en 2030', 2 February 2008 (Part 1), 26 February 2008 (Part 2);

La Nación, 'El amor es mi único discurso', 16 March 1995; **Venezuela:** *El Universal*, 'Automóviles y caminos inteligentes, la meta para dentro de 30 años', 9 May 1991; **Bolivia:** *Presencia*, 'Bosque más antiguo del planeta se encuentra en Chile', 12 March 1991; **Mexico:** *Este país*, Greenpeace, 'Ingeniería genética: Frankenstein o el moderno Prometeo', October 1995 (summary document 'Genetically engineered plants: releases and impacts on less developed countries', a Greenpeace International inventory prepared by Isabelle Meister and Dr Sue Mayer, November 1994); *El Universal*, 'Las quejas de las esposas modernas', 23 April 2000, 'Los incas realizaban sacrificios humanos', 26 October 2000; **Uruguay:** *El País*, 'Ejercicio físico es protector de la salud', 6 April 1991; **Argentina:** *Buena Salud*, 'El desmayo por estrés', 'Las conflictivas camas solares', 'La anemia y el deporte', No 26; *La Nación*, 'Hasta cuándo los padres "bancan" a sus hijos', 14 May 2006; Compañía Editora Espasa Calpe Argentina S.A., Buenos Aires, excerpt from the novel *Boquitas pintadas* by Manuel Puig, © Herederos de Manuel Puig, with kind permission from Guillermo Schavelzon & Asociados, Agencia Literaria, Barcelona, España; Excerpt from *La salud de los enfermos* (from the collection *Todos los fuegos el fuego*) by Julio Cortázar, © Herederos de Julio Cortázar, 2013.

Glossary of grammatical terms

Adjective A word which provides more information about a noun: *His/her house is very* ***big*** Su casa es muy **grande**. *It's a* ***real*** *pity* Es una **verdadera** lástima.

Adverb A word used to provide more information about a verb, an adjective or another adverb: *He/she treated me* ***badly*** Me trató **duramente**. *It was* ***extremely*** *difficult* Fue **extremadamente** difícil. *They behaved* ***incredibly*** *well* Se comportaron **increíblemente** bien.

Article There are two types of articles: ***definite*** and ***indefinite***. Definite articles in Spanish are **el**, **la**, **los**, **las** *the* in English. Indefinite articles are **un**, **una** *a*, *an* in English: ***the*** *boy* **el** chico; ***a*** *magazine* **una** revista.

Clause A group of words within a sentence which has its own verb. A ***main clause*** functions on its own; a ***subordinate clause*** is dependent on another clause. In *I'll tell her when she arrives* Se lo diré cuando llegue, '*I'll tell her*' 'Se lo diré', the main clause, can function on its own; '*when she arrives*' 'cuando llegue', the subordinate clause, is dependent on the main clause.

Conjunction A word like *and* **y**, *or* **o**, *but* **pero**, which joins words or groups of words.

Definite article See ***Article***.

Demonstrative Words like **este**, **esta** *this*, **esos**, **esas** *those*, are called demonstratives: ***this*** *book* **este** libro; ***those*** *ideas* **esas** ideas.

Direct object See ***Object***.

Finite verb A verb form such as the one in *They work hard* **Trabajan mucho**, is said to be ***finite*** because it indicates ***tense***, ***person*** and ***number***. Gerunds, infinitives and past participles are non-finite verb forms.

Gender In Spanish, all nouns are either masculine or feminine. For example, **el** colegio ***the*** *school*, is masculine, while **la** universidad ***the*** *university*, is feminine. Nouns referring to male people are masculine and those referring to female people are feminine.

Gerund Refers to the forms of the verb ending in -**ando** and -**iendo**, e.g. habl**ando**, com**iendo**, viv**iendo**. Some of its uses correspond to those of the verb form ending in *-ing* in English, e.g. *She is* ***eating*** Está **comiendo**.

Imperative See ***Mood***.

Indefinite article See ***Article***.

Indicative See ***Mood***.

Indirect object See ***Object***.

Infinitive The basic form of the verb, as found in the dictionary. In Spanish, infinitives end in -**ar**, -**er** and -**ir**, e.g. habl**ar** *to speak*, com**er** *to eat*, viv**ir** *to live*.

Irregular verb A verb which does not behave according to a set pattern.

Modal verb An auxiliary verb which is used with another verb to convey a certain mood or intention, e.g. *We **must** do it* **Debemos** hacerlo (obligation); *We **can't** help you* No **podemos** ayudarte (possibility). Among modal verbs in Spanish we find **poder** *to be able to, can*, **deber** *must*, **tener que** *to have to.*

Mood Refers to the forms verbs can take depending on how these are used. There are three moods of the verb: ***indicative***, normally associated with statements of fact, e.g. ***They are coming*** *tomorrow* **Vienen** mañana; ***imperative***, used for commands, directions and instructions, e.g. ***Come*** *here!* ¡**Ven** aquí!; and ***subjunctive***, normally associated with doubt, possibility, wishes, etc., e.g. *I don't think they'll **come*** No creo que **vengan**. See ***Subjunctive mood***.

Noun A word like *table* **mesa**, *cat* **gato**, *kindness* **bondad**.

Number Used to indicate whether something is ***singular*** or ***plural***, e.g. *the hotel* **el hotel** is singular, *the hotels* **los hoteles** is plural.

Object In the sentence *I gave **him the keys*** **Le** di **las llaves**, the phrase ***the keys***, which undergoes the action of the verb in a direct way, is said to be the direct object, while ***him***, the recipient of the giving, is the indirect object. An object can be a noun or noun phrase, e.g. *the keys*, or a pronoun, e.g. *him*.

Passive and active A sentence such as *The police caught the thief* **La policía atrapó al ladrón**, containing a subject (*the police*) carrying out the action expressed by the verb, is said to be an ***active*** sentence. In *The thief was caught by the police* **El ladrón fue atrapado por la policía**, the object of the active sentence (*the thief*), undergoing the action expressed by the verb, becomes the subject, and the agent carrying out the action (*the police*) is introduced by the preposition *by*, **por** in Spanish. This type of sentence is called ***passive***.

Personal pronoun As the name suggests, personal pronouns refer to persons, e.g. *I* **yo**, *he* **él**, *she* **ella**, *we* **nosotros**, *him* **lo**, **le**, *us* **nos**. See ***Pronoun***.

Possessive A word like *my* **mi**, *mine* **mío**, *her* **su**, *hers* **suyo**.

Preposition A word such as *to* **a**, *in* **en**, *between* **entre**, which provides information such as direction, location, time.

Pronoun A word that stands in place of a noun or noun phrase which has already been mentioned, e.g. *My brother is a teacher. **He** is a teacher.* Mi hermano es profesor. **Él** es profesor. *This hotel is much better. **This one** is much better.* Este hotel es mucho mejor. **Este** es mucho mejor. *My bedroom is small. **Hers** is big.* Mi habitación es pequeña. **La suya** es grande.

Reflexive pronoun A word such as *myself* **me**; *yourself* **te**, **se**; *ourselves* **nos**.

Reflexive verb When the subject and the object of a verb are one and the same, the verb is said to be reflexive, e.g. ***I** hurt **myself*** **Me herí**. ***We** hid **ourselves*** **Nos ocultamos**.

Relative clause A group of words which refers back to something previously mentioned in the sentence, a noun or a pronoun, known as the ***antecedent***. See also ***Relative pronoun***.

Relative pronoun A word like **que** *who, whom, that, which*, **el/la cual** *that, whom, which*, **cuyo** *whose*, which introduces a relative clause. See ***Relative clause***.

Subject In a sentence such as ***My wife** prepared a delicious meal* **Mi mujer** preparó una comida deliciosa, ***my wife***, the person performing the action denoted by the verb, is the subject of the sentence. A subject can be a single word or a group of words.

Subjunctive mood The subjunctive mood is used very rarely in modern English, but there are remnants of it in sentences such as the following: *I insist that he **come*** Insisto que **venga**. *I wish he **were** here* Ojalá **estuviera** aquí. Spanish uses the subjunctive much more frequently than English.

Subordinate clause See *Clause*.

Tense Changes in the verb which indicate aspects of time are referred to as tenses, for example, present tense, future tense, preterite tense. In *He **works** in a bank* **Trabaja** en un banco, the verb is in the present tense. In *He **worked** there for a long time* **Trabajó** allí durante mucho tiempo, the verb is in the preterite tense.

Verb A verb is a word such as *to speak* **hablar**, *to exist* **existir**, *to feel* **sentir**, which can denote actions, states, sensations, etc.

Part One: The verb

1 The present tense

Text

In an interview published after his death, the Chilean writer Roberto Bolaño (1953–2003) talked about his life in Blanes, in Catalonia, Spain. Read the interview for understanding first, then read it again and see how the present tense has been used.

Roberto Bolaño: inédito y final

– *Descríbame un día normal.*

– **Es** facilísimo. **Me levanto** a las siete de la mañana con un frío de perros. Yo **vivo** en una casa y mi mujer en otra, como a 10 metros de la mía, en otro edificio, pero en la misma calle.

– *¿**Viven** separados?*

– **Vivimos** cada uno en nuestra casa y **estamos** mucho mejor así. **Llevamos** 17 años juntos, y lo **recomiendo** vivamente, porque mi mujer **es** básicamente mi amiga. Entonces **hay** un respeto por las libertades del otro, absoluto. Bueno, **me levanto** a las siete de la mañana. Mi casa **es** una especie de covacha espartana. Lo primero que **hago** es encender el ordenador, luego **me dirijo** a la cocina, **pongo** agua a calentar, luego **voy** al baño. Después **voy** a la cocina y **me hago** una infusión de manzanilla, **vuelvo** al ordenador y **me pongo** a trabajar en el acto, inmediatamente. **Son** como las 7.10 y de ahí **trabajo** hasta las 10.00 de la mañana, 10.30 a lo más, que **es** cuando **voy** al correo, **veo** mi apartado, **veo** si hay cartas, **compro** el periódico, **vuelvo** a casa e **intento** trabajar un poco más. A las 11.10 u 11.20 **vuelvo** a salir y **me voy** a buscar a mi hijo al colegio, que **sale** a las 12.00. Siempre **soy** el primero en llegar. **Hay** una plaza al lado del colegio y **aprovecho** para leer el periódico, algún libro. Mi hijo **sale** a las 12.00 y **volvemos** a casa, esta vez a la casa de mi mujer. Le **hago** la comida al niño, **me hago** la comida a mí mismo y **estamos** hasta las 3.00 de la tarde. Entonces lo **vuelvo** a dejar al colegio, al turno de tarde, y generalmente **espero** a mi mujer en la misma plaza del colegio. Mi mujer **sale** a las 3.00 de trabajar y **nos volvemos** juntos a casa. Todo esto teniendo en cuenta que **vivo** en un pueblo pequeño, Blanes, a una

(*Continued*)

hora y cuarto de Barcelona. **Es** un
50 pueblo costero, un balneario,
pequeñito. Bueno, con mi mujer **nos volvemos** caminando, conversando,
a veces **nos metemos** en un bar a
comer un bocadillo o a tomar algo.
55 Ella **se va** a su casa, yo **me voy** a la
mía. Si **estoy** en pleno trabajo de
escritura **duermo** una siesta y
cuando **me despierto, sigo**
escribiendo. Mi hijo **sale** a las 5.00
60 de clases, lo **va** a buscar mi mujer, y
a eso de las 6.00 **voy** a casa de mi
mujer, **estamos** juntos, **hacemos** la
cena, luego tal vez **salimos**, pero
generalmente **alquilamos** un video.
65 **Nos cuesta** mucho ir al cine. Sólo
vemos películas infantiles en el cine,
pero películas de adultos pocas
veces, porque con quién **dejamos** al
niño. **Volvemos** a casa después de
70 alquilar un video y dar una vuelta
por Blanes. **Hacemos** la cena,
vemos el video, el niño **se acuesta** . . .

Diario *La Tercera*, Chile

The present tense

1 USAGE

The present tense is used:

a To refer to an action or a state of affairs which is valid in the present.

Vivimos cada uno en nuestra casa. (línea 8) *We each live in our own house.*
Estamos mucho mejor así. (l. 9) *We are much better like this.*

See also **llevamos** (l. 9), **son** (l. 24), **vivo** (l. 47), **estoy** (l. 56), **nos cuesta** (l. 65).

b To refer to something which is generally true or universal.

Hay una plaza al lado del colegio. (l. 34–35) *There's a square by the school.*
Es un pueblo costero. (l. 49–50) *It's a coastal town.*

c To refer to habitual actions.

Me levanto a las siete de la mañana. (l. 2–3) *I get up at 7.00 in the morning.*
Lo primero que **hago** es encender el ordenador. (l. 17–18) *The first thing I do is turn the computer on.*
Me dirijo a la cocina. (l. 18–19) *I go to the kitchen.*

There are a number of other examples of this use in the text. Consider for instance **pongo** (l. 19), **voy** (l. 20), **hago** (l. 21), **vuelvo** (l. 22), **me voy** (l. 31), **sale** (l. 36), **volvemos** (l. 37), **nos metemos** (l. 53), **hacemos** (l. 62), **alquilamos** (l. 64).

Habitual actions may also be expressed with the modal auxiliary verb **soler** '*to be accustomed to*' followed by the infinitive:

Suelo acostarme temprano. *I usually go to bed early.*
No **suele** llegar tarde. *He/she doesn't normally arrive late.*

A less frequent construction with the same meaning is that with **acostumbrar (a)** '*to be accustomed to*' with the infinitive:

Los sábados **acostumbran (a)** quedarse en casa. *On Saturdays they usually stay at home.*

d To refer to a timeless fact or situation.

Mi mujer **es** básicamente mi amiga. (l. 11–12) *My wife is basically my friend.*
Hay un respeto por las libertades del otro. (l. 13–14) *There's respect for the other's freedom.*

e To refer to actions taking place at the moment of speaking.

El niño **duerme**. (for 'Está durmiendo') *The child is sleeping.*
¿Qué **haces**? (for ¿Qué estás haciendo?) *What are you doing?*

f To express ability.

Toca el piano. *He/she plays the piano.*
Nadas muy bien. *You swim very well.*

g To refer to the future, especially to pre-arranged events and, generally, with verbs of movement.

En mayo **se elige** un nuevo presidente. *A new president will be elected in May.*
Mañana **llega** Antonio. *Antonio is arriving tomorrow.*

h To refer to the past (historic present).

La guerra **termina** en 1939. *The war ended in 1939.*
Miguel de Cervantes **nace** en Alcalá de Henares en 1547. *Miguel de Cervantes was born in Alcalá de Henares in 1547.*

i To refer to an action or state which began in the past and is still in progress.

Llevamos 17 años juntos. (l. 9–10) *We've been together for 17 years.*
Hace cinco años que **viven** allí. *They've been living there for five years.*

j As an imperative, especially in directions and instructions.

En la esquina **doblas** a la derecha. *You turn right at the corner.*
Si me llama Elena le **dices** que regreso pronto. *If Elena phones tell her I'll be back soon.*

k In requests, translating *will* in English.

¿Me **pasas** el pan? *Will you pass the bread?*
¿Nos **ayuda**, por favor? *Will you help us, please?*

2 FORMATION

Regular verbs

Spanish verbs fall into three categories according to the ending of the infinitive (the base or dictionary form of the verb): **-ar**, **-er** and **-ir**. Most verbs are 'regular', that is, they follow a fixed pattern in their conjugation. To form the present tense, remove the **-ar**, **-er** or **-ir** of the infinitive and add the endings for the present tense:

	tom**ar**	com**er**	viv**ir**
yo	tom**o**	com**o**	viv**o**
tú	tom**as**	com**es**	viv**es**
usted/él/ella	tom**a**	com**e**	viv**e**
nosotros/as	tom**amos**	com**emos**	viv**imos**
vosotros/as	tom**áis**	com**éis**	viv**ís**
ustedes/ellos/ellas	tom**an**	com**en**	viv**en**

Stem-changing verbs

A number of verbs change their stem (the infinitive, e.g. **tomar**, minus the ending: **tom-**) in the present tense, in all but the first and second person plural, but otherwise their endings are those of regular verbs. Verbs like **volver** (l. 22), *to return, come back*, **dormir** (l. 57) *to sleep*, **costar** (l. 65), *to be difficult, cost*, **acostarse** (l. 73) *to go to bed*, **recomendar** (l. 10) *to recommend*, **encender** (l. 17) *to turn on*, **tener** (l. 47) *to have*, **despertarse** (l. 58) *to wake up*, **seguir** (l. 58) *to continue, go on, follow*, are stem-changing. The model verbs which follow will show you the pattern of changes for the present tense.

o into **ue**

-ar: (acostarse) me ac**ue**sto, te ac**ue**stas, se ac**ue**sta, nos acostamos, os acostáis, se ac**ue**stan.
-er: (volver) v**ue**lvo, v**ue**lves, v**ue**lve, volvemos, volvéis, v**ue**lven.
-ir: (dormir) d**ue**rmo, d**ue**rmes, d**ue**rme, dormimos, dormís, d**ue**rmen.

jugar *to play* follows the same pattern, with the **u** of the stem changing into **ue**:

j**ue**go, j**ue**gas, j**ue**ga, jugamos, jugáis, j**ue**gan.

e into **i**

-ir: (seguir) s**i**go, s**i**gues, s**i**gue, seguimos, seguís, s**i**guen.

e into **ie**

-ar: (recomendar) recom**ie**ndo, recom**ie**ndas, recom**ie**nda, recomendamos, recomendáis, recom**ie**ndan.
-er: (encender) enc**ie**ndo, enc**ie**ndes, enc**ie**nde, encendemos, encendéis, enc**ie**nden.
-ir: (preferir) pref**ie**ro, pref**ie**res, pref**ie**re, preferimos, preferís, pref**ie**ren.

Stem changes occur not only in the present tense but also in other tenses, such as the preterite (Chapter 2), the present subjunctive (Chapter 14) and imperfect subjunctive (Chapter 15), and also in the imperative (Chapter 17) and the gerund (Chapter 9).

Spelling changes

A number of verbs, not considered irregular, undergo changes in the written form of the stem. The following examples illustrate spelling changes affecting some present tense forms, but note that spelling changes also occur in other tenses:

> **seguir** (l. 58) *to continue, go on, follow*: (yo) si**g**o; **dirigirse** (l. 18) *to go to, to make for*: (yo) me diri**j**o; **vencer** *to conquer*, (yo) ven**z**o; **coger** *to catch*, (yo) co**j**o; **conocer** *to know*, (yo) cono**zc**o; **construir** *to build*, (yo) constru**y**o, (tú) constru**y**es, (usted, él, ella) constru**y**e, (ustedes, ellos, ellas) constru**y**en.

Verbs derived from these, and most verbs with a similar spelling, undergo similar changes. For spelling rules affecting verbs, see page 283.

Irregular first person singular

Many verbs are irregular in the first person singular (**yo**) of the present tense. Among these we find:

caer *to fall*	**caigo**	**salir** *to go out*	**salgo**
hacer *to do, make*	**hago**	**traer** *to bring*	**traigo**
poner *to put, place*	**pongo**	**valer** *to be worth*	**valgo**

Some are also stem-changing: **decir** *to say, tell* (**dig**o, d**i**ces, d**i**ce . . .), **venir** *to come* (ven**g**o, v**ie**nes, v**ie**ne . . .), **tener** *to have* (ten**g**o, t**ie**nes, t**ie**ne . . .), etc.

Irregular verbs

A number of verbs are called 'irregular' because they do not follow a fixed pattern in their conjugation. Verbs like **ser** (l. 2) *to be*, **estar** (l. 9) *to be* and **ir** (l. 20) *to go*, fall within this category. The following are their present tense forms:

	ser	**estar**	**ir**
yo	**soy**	**estoy**	**voy**
tú	**eres**	**estás**	**vas**
usted/él/ella	**es**	**está**	**va**
nosotros/as	**somos**	**estamos**	**vamos**
vosotros	**sois**	**estáis**	**vais**
ustedes/ellos/ellas	**son**	**están**	**van**

See also **Irregular verbs** on pages 279–282.

OMISSION OF SUBJECT PRONOUNS

Subject pronouns (**yo**, **tú**, **él**, etc.) are often omitted in Spanish as these are normally made clear by the form of the verb. Thus **soy** means *I am*, while **somos** means *we are*. Generally, subject pronouns are used:

a For emphasis or contrast.

Ella se va a su casa, **yo** me voy a la mía. (l. 55–56) *She goes to her house, I go to mine.*

b To avoid possible ambiguity, as it may occur with the third person singular or plural of the verb.

Se levanta temprano. *He/she gets up/you get up early.* But:
Ella se levanta a las 6.30. *She gets up at 6.30.*

c When they stand on their own.

'¿Quién hace la comida?' *'Who makes dinner?'* – '**Yo**' *'I do'.*

Usted (abbreviated **Vd.**) and **ustedes** (abbreviated **Vds.**) are heard more often as a sign of politeness.

LATIN AMERICAN USAGE

The **vosotros/as** subject pronoun, used for familiar address in the plural, and the corresponding form of the verb, are not used in the Spanish-speaking countries of Latin America, where **ustedes** is used in both formal and familiar address.

In the Río de la Plata area (Argentina and Uruguay), **vos** is used instead of **tú**. Regular present tense forms for **vos** are different from those of **tú** above: **vos tomás**, **vos comés**, **vos vivís**. Stem changes affecting the **tú** form of the verb, e.g. **tú tienes**, do not apply to the **vos** forms, e.g. **vos tenés**. The irregular form **eres** (from **ser**) becomes **sos**: **vos sos** (see also Chapters 14, 17 and 25).

Other points to note in the text

- Reflexive or pronominal verbs: *me levanto a las 7.00* (l. 2), *me dirijo a la cocina* (l. 18–19), *me pongo a trabajar* (l. 23), *me hago una infusión* (l. 21), *me voy a buscar a mi hijo* (l. 31–32), *nos metemos en un bar* (l. 53), *se va a su casa* (l. 55), *me despierto* (l. 58), etc. (see Chapter 12)
- **Ser** and **estar**: *es facilísimo* (l. 2), *estamos mucho mejor así* (l. 9), *es básicamente mi amiga* (l. 11–12), *es una especie de covacha* (l. 15–16), *lo primero que hago es . . .* (l. 17), *son como las 7.10* (l. 24), *soy el primero* (l. 33), *estamos hasta las 3.00 de la tarde* (l. 40–41), *es un pueblo costero* (l. 49–50), etc. (see Chapter 13)
- Object pronouns: *lo recomiendo* (l. 10), *le hago la comida* (l. 38–39), *lo vuelvo a dejar al colegio* (l. 41–42), *lo va a buscar mi mujer* (l. 60) (see Chapter 25)

EXERCISES

1 Complete these sentences by putting the appropriate present tense ending to each verb.

a Mañana (yo) sac________ las entradas y luego te llam________ ¿vale?
b Si (tú) no estudi________, no aprend________ nada.
c Domingo y su mujer visit________ a su hija que viv________ en Acapulco.
d Usted escrib________ artículos para *La Vanguardia* ¿verdad?
e En la discoteca Rosario y yo bail________ y beb________ mucho.
f El Día de Reyes los niños españoles recib________ regalos.
g Ustedes habl________ muy bien inglés.
h Oye, Rafa, ¿tú y Pili sub________ en el ascensor?
i Hace diez años que (nosotros) viv________ en Santander.
j Antes de una función, los músicos intent________ no hacer nada.
k ¿Por qué no guard________ (vosotros) las cosas en el armario?
l De día Fernando trabaj________ como guía y de noche toc________ la guitarra en un bar. Lleg________ a casa agotado.
m Hoy día (nosotros) pas________ menos tiempo con la familia.
n Todos los días Begoña corr________ en el parque.
o (Yo) compr________ el periódico en el quiosco de la esquina y lo le________ mientras desayun________ en el bar.

2 Put the verb in brackets into the correct form of the present tense.

a Mi padre me (decir) ________ que yo no (conducir) ________ bien.
b ¿No ________ (conocer, tú) a la hermana de Enrique? Yo, sí que la ________.
c ¿A qué hora (empezar) ________ el partido?
d ¿Cuándo (pensar, vosotros) ________ volver a Guadalajara?
e En mis ratos libres (oír) ________ música, (leer) ________ o (salir) ________ con los amigos.
f Si (querer, tú) ________ tocar bien el piano, (tener) ________ que dedicarle muchas horas.
g Mariana (jugar) ________ bien al ajedrez.
h Todavía no (saber, yo) ________ a qué hora (volver, yo) ________ el jueves.
i ¿Me (dejar, tú) ________ tu diccionario un momento? No (tener, yo) ________ el mío.
j (Calentar, usted) ________ el aceite, (freír) ________ las patatas* y (añadir) ________ el jamón.
k ¡Cuánto ________ (llover) en este país!
l Y luego (venir, ellos) ________ y nos (decir) ________ que no lo (querer) ________.
m Como (saber, tú) ________ el camino, yo te (seguir) ________.
n No (ir, ellos) ________ a tomar la sopa, (preferir) ________ los entremeses. Y también (pedir) ________ más pan.
o En invierno (soler, yo) ________ dormir unas ocho horas por noche, pero en verano (dormir) ________ menos.

* *In Latin American Spanish:* ***las papas***.

3 Use one of the verbs below to complete each sentence.

pintar	**ir**	**mentir**	**empezar**	**servir**
nevar	**ser**	**perder**	**abrir**	**conseguir**
conducir	**asistir**	**dormir**	**comer**	**medir**

a Los vegetarianos no ________ carne.
b Un artista ________ cuadros.
c ________ mucho en la Sierra Nevada.
d Si ________ el pasaporte, tienes que ir a la comisaría.
e Las corridas de toros ________ a las cinco de la tarde.
f En días laborables Domingo ________ ocho horas.
g Ustedes ________ escoceses ¿verdad?
h La mayoría de la gente ________ de Nueva York a Miami en avión.
i La cena se ________ a partir de las nueve.
j Los británicos ________ por la izquierda.
k Esta habitación ________ 3 metros de ancho.
l Si no ________ entradas, no pueden ir al concierto.
m Ese grupo de estudiantes sólo ________ a clase por la mañana.
n ¡Qué mentiroso es Miguel! ________ tanto que nadie le cree cuando dice la verdad.
o Aquí los comercios no ________ hasta las diez.

4 Translate into Spanish using the present tense to refer to the future.

'On Friday, we'll be saying goodbye to María. What shall we give her as a present?'
'She likes jewellery. Shall we give her some earrings?'
'Yes, why not? I'll phone her tonight to tell her that there's a party at my house Thursday night.'
'And when will we buy the earrings?'
'Shall we leave it until Wednesday? I have to go to Paris and I'll not be back until Tuesday.'
'OK. Where shall we meet? Outside the jeweller's?'
'Yes. I'll see you there at ten.'

5 Roberto Bolaño describes an ordinary day in his life. Re-read the interview with him and then write as in a report, or tell a partner in Spanish, what such a day is like.

6 A Spanish film crew has come to your town and you have the chance to interview the director. Prepare questions to find out:

- what time s/he starts and finishes work
- whether s/he eats with the actors
- to relax, what books s/he reads
- what music s/he listens to
- what programmes s/he watches on television
- what sport s/he does to keep fit.

You may think of other questions you can formulate using the present tense to add to this list.

7 Imagining that you are the film director, make up answers to the questions in exercise **6**.

8 How similar and how different is your lifestyle to the one outlined here by Rafael? Discuss with a partner and/or write a response detailing the similarities and differences in lifestyle.

- Yo, normalmente, desayuno en un bar cerca del trabajo. Tomo un zumo de naranja, un café con leche y una tostada.
- A media mañana, vuelvo al bar con los compañeros de trabajo y tomo otro café.
- A la hora de comer, voy a casa y como con mi familia. Veo un poco de tele antes de volver a trabajar.
- Cuando termino de trabajar, no voy directamente a casa. Me reúno con los amigos en un bar al lado de casa.
- Dos veces a la semana, voy al gimnasio para mantenerme en forma.
- Los fines de semana, suelo ir al pueblo con la familia. Tenemos una casa allí y es donde siempre pasamos las vacaciones.

2 | The preterite

Text 1

The following passage comes from a novel by the late Argentinian writer Manuel Puig, better known for his work *El beso de la mujer araña* (*The Kiss of the Spider Woman*). The main grammatical point here is the preterite tense, known in English as the simple past. Read the text and study its use.

Boquitas pintadas

El ya mencionado jueves 23 de abril de 1937 Juan Carlos Jacinto Eusebio Etchepare **se despertó** a las 9:30 cuando su madre **golpeó** a la puerta y **entró** al cuarto. Juan Carlos no **contestó** a las palabras cariñosas de su madre. La taza de té **quedó** sobre la mesa de luz. Juan Carlos **se abrigó** con una bata y **fue**
5 a cepillarse los dientes. El mal gusto de la boca **desapareció**. **Volvió** a su habitación, el té estaba tibio, **llamó** a su madre y **pidió** que se lo calentara. A las 9:55 **tomó** en la cama una taza de té casi hirviente, con la convicción de que ese calor le haría bien al pecho. **Pensó** en la posibilidad de beber constantemente cosas muy calientes y envolverse en paños calientes, con los
10 pies junto a una bolsa de agua caliente, la cabeza envuelta en una bufanda de lana con únicamente la nariz y la boca descubiertas, para terminar con la debilidad de su aparato respiratorio.

Manuel Puig, *Boquitas pintadas*, © Herederos de Manuel Puig

Text 2

In an interview, the Spanish writer Rosa Montero remembers her childhood.

"El éxito es una luz que te dan los otros"

– *¿Cree en la suerte?*
– En la buena suerte no, esa se la hace uno, a punta de trabajo. Pero la mala suerte sí existe, ese momento . . . que
5 te destroza la vida. [. . .]

Rosa llama las cosas por su nombre. Al evocar su infancia, por ejemplo, es de un realismo estremecedor:

Vengo de una familia que no tenía
10 ni un duro. Hasta mis 16 años no

(*Continued*)

había agua caliente en casa.
Entonces **tuvimos**, porque
heredamos un calentador viejo y
pequeñito de cinco litros de un tío;
15 **fue** la primera vez que **pudimos**
tomar una ducha tibia. Mi infancia
no **fue** feliz. Yo no tenía un hogar:
mi madre, un ser muy libre, odiaba
lo doméstico. Cuando **nací**, mi padre
20 era un torero de renombre, pero a
mis cinco años **decidió** reciclarse
porque no se puede torear
eternamente y **se retiró** a los 45
para montar una modesta fábrica de
25 ladrillos en un terreno cerca de casa;
pero claro, se lo **comieron** los
créditos. Se marchaba a las 5.00 de
la mañana en mobilette, con el
pecho cubierto de diarios para pasar
30 el intenso frío, y volvía a las 12.00
de la noche, embarrado de pics a
cabeza y malhumorado. **Fui** a un
instituto público de niñas pobres.
Me acuerdo de haber visitado a una
35 compañera de clases que vivía en un
subterráneo y cuya madre era
conserje, y me maravillaba de ver
que en los brazos del sofá habían
colocado unos tapetitos de encaje
40 plástico. Ese mimo lo convertía
en un hogar. Mi madre, que se
sentía atrapada en el matrimonio
y en la maternidad, nunca **colocó**
una flor.

45 – *¿Le dolió la pobreza?*
– La pobreza es muy relativa. Yo sabía
que no teníamos dinero, pero **sufrí**
sobre todo porque en casa no había
buen rollo. No había dramas, pero
50 no era un hogar feliz. [. . .] Así y
todo, ¡**tuve** una suerte! Mi mamá
pintora y mi padre torero se movían
en el ambiente taurino, que es
completamente interclasista y más
55 bien bohemio. A los toros van desde
el duque hasta el gitano. Por eso **me
formé** en la total ignorancia de las
clases sociales y hasta hoy esas
diferencias no existen para mí. Es
60 un privilegio que le agradezco a mi
familia. Me **permitió** crecer sin
ningún tipo de complejos, en plena
libertad.

Revista *El Sábado*, Diario *El Mercurio, Chile*

The preterite

1 USAGE

a To refer to actions which took place and were completed at some point in the past. In this context it may be accompanied by time phrases such as **ayer** *yesterday*, **el lunes pasado** *last Monday*, **hace una semana** *a week ago*, **el verano pasado** *last summer*, **el ya mencionado jueves 23 de abril de 1937** (T. 1, l. 1).

A las 9:55 **tomó** en la cama una taza de té casi hirviente. (T. 1, l. 7) *At 9.55 he had an almost boiling cup of tea in bed.*

Fue la primera vez que **pudimos** tomar una ducha tibia. (T. 2, l. 15–16) *It was the first time we could take a lukewarm shower.*
Se retiró a los 45. (T. 2, l. 23) *He retired at 45.*

b In a narrative context it is often used alongside the imperfect tense (Chapter 3), with the preterite signalling a completed action or series of actions, and the imperfect providing a descriptive framework.

Volvió a su habitación, el té **estaba** tibio, **llamó** a su madre y **pidió** que se lo calentara. (T. 1, l. 5–6). *He returned to his room, the tea was lukewarm, he called his mother and asked her to heat it for him.*
Mi infancia no **fue** feliz. Yo no tenía un hogar. (T. 2, l. 16–17) *My childhood wasn't happy. – I didn't have a home.*
Cuando **nací**, mi padre era un torero de renombre. (T. 2, l. 19–20) *When I was born, my father was a well-known bullfighter.*

The description in the previous sentences is provided by the imperfect tense forms **estaba** *it was*, **no tenía** *I didn't have*, **era** *he was.*

c To refer to an action which was completed before another one took place or to one which was interrupted at some point in the past.

Después que **cenó**, **salió** a dar un paseo. *After he/she had dinner, he/she went out for a walk.*
Trabajó allí hasta que la **despidieron**. *She worked there until she was sacked.*

d To refer to actions which took place over a prolonged period of time but ended in the past.

A mis cinco años decidió reciclarse. (T. 2, l. 20–21) *When I was five he decided to change jobs.*
Vivieron en la Argentina durante quince años. *They lived in Argentina for fifteen years.*

Compare the use of the preterite **vivieron** in the second sentence with the imperfect **vivía** in the following one, in which the beginning or end of the action are not specified.

Vivía en un subterráneo. (T. 2, l. 35–36) *She lived in a basement (flat).*

THE PRETERITE AND THE IMPERFECT

The distinction Spanish makes between the preterite and the imperfect (Chapter 3) is very important, as this affects meaning. Note the difference between the following sentences:

Trabajé en un banco. *I worked in a bank.*
Trabajaba en un banco. *I worked/was working/used to work in a bank.*

Trabajé signals a completed past event, while **trabajaba** refers to an ongoing past action. A suitable time phrase for the first sentence might be **desde 1995 hasta 1999** *from 1995 till 1999.* To the second example one could add **en aquel tiempo** *at that time.*

2 FORMATION

Regular verbs

entrar	**volver**	**vivir**
entr**é**	volv**í**	viv**í**
entr**aste**	volv**iste**	viv**iste**
entr**ó**	volv**ió**	viv**ió**
entr**amos**	volv**imos**	viv**imos**
entr**asteis**	volv**isteis**	viv**isteis**
entr**aron**	volv**ieron**	viv**ieron**

Su madre **golpeó** a la puerta y **entró** al cuarto. (T. 1, l. 2–3) *His mother knocked on the door and entered the room.*

No **contestó . . .** (T. 1, l. 3) *He did not reply . . .*

Volvió a su habitación. (T. 1, l. 5–6) *He returned to his room.*

El mal gusto de la boca **desapareció**. (T. 1, l. 5) *The bad taste in his mouth disappeared.*

Heredamos un calentador viejo. (T. 2, l. 13) *We inherited an old heater.*

Me formé en la total ignorancia de . . . (T. 2, l. 56–57) *I grew up in total ignorance of . . .*

Stem-changing verbs

a Some **-ir** verbs, like **pedir** *to ask for*, in line 6, text 1, change the **e** of the stem into **i** in the third person singular (**Vd.**, **él**, **ella**) and plural (**Vds.**, **ellos**, **ellas**).

Pidió que se lo calentara. (T. 1, l. 6) *He asked her to heat it for him.*

¿Qué **pidieron**? *What did they ask for?*

Among other verbs like **pedir** we find **corregir** *to correct*, **despedir(se)** *to say goodbye*, **divertirse** *to have fun*, **elegir** *to choose*, **mentir** *to lie*, **preferir** *to prefer*, **sentir(se)** *to feel*, **reír(se)** *to laugh*, **servir** *to serve*, **vestir(se)** *to dress*, etc.

b **Dormir** *to sleep*, like **dormirse** *to fall asleep*, and **morir(se)** *to die*, change the **o** of the stem into **u** in the third person singular and plural.

Se **durmió** inmediatamente. *He/she fell asleep immediately.*

Durmieron toda la mañana. *They slept all morning.*

Irregular verbs

A number of very common verbs, like **ir** *to go*, in line 4, text 1, have irregular preterite forms.

Fue a cepillarse los dientes. (T. 1, l. 4–5) *He went to brush his teeth.*

The following list includes only the most common irregular verbs. For their forms, see the **Irregular verbs** on pages 279–282:

andar *to walk*, **caber** *to fit*, *to be contained*, **dar** *to give*, **decir** *to say*, **estar** *to be*, **haber** *to have* (auxiliary), **hacer** *to do*, *make*, **ir** *to go* (conjugated like **ser**), **poder** *to be able*, **poner** *to put*,

querer *to want*, **saber** *to know*, **ser** *to be* (conjugated like **ir**), **tener** *to have*, **traer** *to bring*, **venir** *to come*, **ver** *to see*.

Entonces **tuvimos** un calentador viejo. (T. 2, l. 12–13) *We then had an old heater.*
¡**Tuve** una suerte! (T. 2, l. 51) *I had such luck!*
Fue la primera vez. (T. 2, l. 15) *It was the first time.*
Fui a un instituto público. (T. 2, l. 32–33) *I went to a state secondary school.*

Compounds of these verbs, for example **componer** *to compose*, **contener** *to contain*, **deshacer** *to undo*, are also irregular.

Spelling changes

A few verbs undergo spelling changes in the first person singular (**yo**) only:

c changes to **qu** before **e**, e.g. **buscar** *to look for*, **busqué**; **tocar** *to touch, play* **toqué**.
g changes to **gu** before **e**, e.g. **llegar** *to arrive*, **llegué**; **pagar** *to pay*, **pagué**.
z changes to **c** before **e**, e.g. **comenzar** *to begin, start*, **comencé**; **empezar** *to begin, start*, **empecé**.

For other spelling rules affecting verbs see page 283.

Other points to note in the text

- Imperfect: *estaba* (T. 1, l. 6), *tenía* (T. 2, l. 9), *había* (T. 2, l. 11), *odiaba* (T. 2, l. 18), *era* (T. 2, l. 20), *se marchaba* (T. 2, l. 27), *volvía* (T. 2, l. 30), etc.
- Prepositions: *a* (T. 1, l. 2), *sobre* (T. 1, l. 4), *con* (T. 1, l. 4), *en* (T. 1, l. 7), *para* (T. 1, l. 11), *por* (T. 2, l. 6), *hasta* (T. 2, l. 10), etc. (see Chapter 28)
- Reflexive verbs: *se despertó* (T. 1, l. 2), *se abrigó* (T. 1, l. 4), *cepillarse* (T. 1, l. 5), *envolverse* (T. 1, l. 9), *reciclarse* (T. 2, l. 21), *se retiró* (T. 2, l. 23), *se marchaba* (T. 2, l. 27), *me maravillaba* (T. 2, l. 37), *se sentía* (T. 2, l. 41–42), *se movían* (T. 2, l. 52), *me formé* (T. 2, l. 56–57). (see Chapter 12).

EXERCISES

1 Complete these sentences by putting the appropriate preterite tense ending to each verb.

a (yo) Pas________ dos horas viendo la tele y luego sal________ a dar un paseo.
b ¿(tú) Estudi________ castellano en la universidad y no le________ *El Quijote*?
c La madre de Juan Carlos le prepar________ una taza de té pero él no la beb________.
d ¿A qué hora (usted) entr________ y por qué no cog________ * los papeles?
e (nosotros) Viaj________ a Córdoba en autocar y de allí sali________ para Resistencia.
f ¿(vosotros) Mand________ los informes pero no recib________ ninguna respuesta? ¡Qué raro!
g Los amigos de Juan Carlos le llam________ y luego sub________ a visitarle.
h Ustedes encontr________ el sitio sin dificultad ¿verdad? ¿Volv________ en taxi o en autobús?

i Su hijo no les escrib________ ni les llam________ una sola vez.

j Decid________ quedarnos la noche en Santo Domingo.

k Los dos jóvenes intent________ aprender quechua antes de emprender su viaje a los Andes.

l (Ellos) no lo encontr________ nada fácil y no aprend________ mucho.

m ¿Dónde (tú) conoc________ a tu mujer?

n El tren lleg________ con dos horas de retraso y por eso Marisol perd________ el último autobús.

o (Yo) Alquil________ un coche en Guadalajara y recorr________ toda la provincia.

* *In some Latin American countries, notably Argentina,* ***tomar*** *should be used rather than* ***coger****, which has sexual connotations.*

2 Put the verb in brackets into the correct form of the preterite.

a El verano pasado (ir, yo) ________ por primera vez a Cuba. (Ser) ________ una experiencia maravillosa.

b Carmen no (saber) ________ qué hacer y por eso no (hacer) ________ nada.

c (Andar, nosotros) ________ y (andar) ________ pero estábamos completamente perdidos y no (poder) ________ encontrar la casa.

d ¿Dónde (estar, vosotros) ________ ayer? ¿Por qué no (venir) ________ a clase?

e No nos (servir, ellos) ________ la paella como era debido así que (ir, nosotros) ________ a pedir el libro de reclamaciones pero nos (decir, ellos) ________ que no existía.

f ¿Y esto lo (traducir, ustedes) ________ cuando (estar) ________ en Bolivia?

g – Me encanta tu poncho. ¿Dónde lo (comprar, tú) ________?
– No lo (comprar) ________ yo. Me lo (traer) ________ Carlos de Argentina.

h No (tocar, yo) ________ nada. (Entrar) ________, (poner) ________ los papeles en el escritorio pero no (tocar) ________ nada.

i – El jueves (empezar, yo) ________ a trabajar a las ocho.
– No. Usted (empezar) ________ más tarde.
– No, no es verdad. (Llegar, yo) ________ a las ocho menos cuarto, (tomar) ________ un café y (ponerme) ________ a trabajar. Luego (venir) ________ Carlos y entre una cosa y otra no (tener, yo) ________ tiempo para terminarlo.

j Cuando ella (ver) ________ a dos ladrones salir por la ventana de su casa, (coger)* ________ una piedra, (ponerse) ________ a gritar y a seguirlos, y (conseguir) ________ retenerlos.

* *See note above about the use of* ***coger****.*

3 The following text is written using the historic present. Rewrite it using the preterite tense.

Carlos Gardel, el famoso cantante de tango, nace con el nombre de Charles Gardes en Francia a finales de 1890. Sus padres deciden probar fortuna en Argentina y el 9 de marzo de 1893 llegan a Buenos Aires. Es aquí donde nace su interés por la música y donde adopta el nombre de Carlos Gardel. Recibe clases de solfeo de algunos de los cantantes más conocidos de la época y en 1917 incorpora el tango a su repertorio y se convierte en cantor de tangos. Escribe canciones, sale en películas y llega a ser uno de los intérpretes de tango más famosos del mundo. Muere el 24 de junio de 1935 en Medellín, Colombia, cuando su avión se estrella contra otro.

4 Put the verb in brackets into the correct form of the preterite, then imagine and recount in Spanish what Juan Carlos did for the rest of that day, after he finally got up.

Esa mañana Juan Carlos no se sentía bien cuando (despertarse) ________ y por eso no (querer) ________ levantarse. Su madre le (dar) ________ un té pero en vez de beberlo (ir) ________ al cuarto de baño. El té (enfriarse) ________ y su madre (tener) ________ que prepararle otro. Después de beberlo, Juan Carlos (dormirse) ________ y (dormir) ________ hasta la hora del almuerzo cuando (levantarse) ________.

5 You lead such a busy life that you note down everything in your diary. Using this extract from last Friday, give an account of what you did that day. You may wish to add information to this bare outline.

mañana

7,30	gimnasio
9,00	desayuno
9,30	hora con el dentista
10,00	reunión con jefe de sección
1,30	Bar La Flor – aperitivos con Jaime y Susana

tarde

2,30	Restaurante La Oficina – almuerzo con Nacho
4,30	preparar informe para semana que viene
7,30	casa, llamar a Adolfo – su cumpleaños
8,30	Bar Gregorio – copas con la pandilla
9,30	cena y cine con M

6 Read these answers that Antonio gave you about his latest holidays. Then write the questions you asked him to elicit these answers.

a Bueno, fui a La Habana, Cuba.
b Estuve una semana allí.
c No, no viajé solo. Fui con unos amigos.
d Viajamos primero en autobús hasta el aeropuerto y allí tomamos un avión que nos llevó a La Habana.
e Nos alojamos en un hotel en un complejo turístico bastante alejado del centro.
f El primer día dimos un paseo por la parte vieja de la ciudad.
g Visitamos el Museo de la Revolución y también una fábrica de tabacos.
h Por la noche no salimos, no.
i Hizo un tiempo espléndido – sol y calor todos los días.
j Compré lo típico – unas maracas, unos CDs de son cubano y habanos, por supuesto.
k Me lo pasé estupendamente bien.

7 Write an account of a real or imaginary holiday, saying where you went, with whom, how you travelled, what you did there, etc.

8 Complete the text by putting the verbs in brackets into the correct form of the preterite or the imperfect tense.

Cuando Manuel Puig (nacer) ________ el 28 de diciembre de 1932, nadie (sospechar) ________ que (ir) ________ a ser un ilustre escritor argentino. (Pasar) ________ su niñez en General Villegas, su pueblo natal, en la Provincia de Buenos Aires. Su padre (dedicarse) ________ a la vinicultura y su madre (trabajar) ________ en el hospital regional. Ella (ser) ________ quien le (transmitir) ________ a Manuel su afición al cine. (Tener) ________ tres años cuando sus padres lo (llevar) ________ por primera vez a una función, y a partir de entonces, él y su madre (ir) ________ con regularidad.

Para cursar secundaria, Manuel (trasladarse) ________ a Buenos Aires. Allí, por su afán de adentrarse en el cine europeo (no le (gustar) ________ el cine nacional), (aprender) ________ francés, alemán e italiano. A los 23 años, (conseguir) ________ una beca para estudiar en el Centro Sperimentale di Cinematografía de Roma. Pero pronto (darse cuenta) ________ de que no (tener) ________ el carácter como para ser director de cine. (Dejar) ________ Roma para Londres y luego Estocolmo, y (empezar) ________ a escribir guiones.

Entre 1961 y 1962, mientras (trabajar) ________ como asistente de dirección de cine en Buenos Aires y Roma, (decidir) ________ seguir el consejo de un buen amigo y (convertir) ________ un guión en su primera novela *La traición de Rita Hayworth.* Ya (vivir) ________ en Nueva York. Por las mañanas (trabajar) ________ y por las tardes, después de echarse la siesta, (escribir) ________. A las once, (acostarse) ________.

En 1967, Manuel Puig (volver) ________ a Buenos Aires, y al año siguiente, la novela (salir) ________ a la venta, seguida en 1968 por *Boquitas Pintadas.* Las traducciones de la novela (aparecer) ________ en las listas de los libros más vendidos, pero la novela que le (otorgar) ________ verdadero reconocimiento internacional (ser) ________ *El beso de la mujer araña* (1976) que él mismo (adaptar) ________ para el cine en 1985.

Manuel Puig (seguir) ________ escribiendo hasta su muerte en México en 1990.

3 The imperfect

Text 1

The Spanish film director Pedro Almodóvar was asked why he left his parents' home when he was young. As you read this, and the interviews which follow, focus your attention on the use of the imperfect tense.

"Parece que maduré, aunque no quería"

– *¿Por qué huir?*

– Porque tanto ella como mi padre habían decidido un futuro inmediato para mí que no **era** el que yo **quería**, aunque fuera un niño. Yo ya **sabía** algunas cosas de mi vida y no **coincidían** con el futuro que ellos **proyectaban**: me habían buscado trabajo en un banco del pueblo y les dije que no **quería.** Pero no me **dejaban** partir. Amenazaron con mandarme incluso a la Guardia Civil, pero les dije que no, que me **iba**. Después vieron que **era** en serio, que no **era** un capricho, que **estaba** dispuesto a irme a Madrid a seguir estudiando, a ser dueño de mi vida y a crear mi futuro. Entonces, como muchos chicos, me fui dándole una patada a la puerta y estuve separado de ellos.

Revista *Wikén*, Diario *El Mercurio*, Chile

Text 2

The Chilean writer Isabel Allende talks about her childhood.

"Un libro es más importante que un pan bien hecho"

– *¿De dónde nace su rebeldía contra la autoridad masculina?*

– De muy, muy pequeña. Yo me crié en una casa de hombres, en una familia muy severa. La vida **era** austeridad, esfuerzo, disciplina, sufrimiento. No se **discutía** nunca una decisión de mi abuelo. Después **venían** mis tíos,

(*Continued*)

que **eran** unos bárbaros. Ellos **tenían** la libertad y la autoridad que mi madre nunca tuvo. Creo que de muy chica me di cuenta de eso y me rebelé contra esa autoridad. Yo **vivía** en una sociedad donde lo que **mandaba era** siempre masculino, y para colmo, me tocó un golpe militar. Y no hay nada más autoritario, más masculino que eso.

Diario *Expansión*, España

Text 3

Gabriel García Márquez, the Colombian writer, remembers his grandparents.

El barco donde estaba el paraíso

– *¿Qué tanta influencia tuvo tu abuela en tu formación?*

– El esposo de mi abuela, mi abuelo, **era** un coronel de las guerras civiles de fines de siglo pasado, que tuvo actuaciones verdaderamente notables de valor, dc arrojo, de determinación. Así lo recuerdo ahora. En aquel momento no lo **podía** juzgar: él **era** el jefe, el coronel de la casa. Yo **vivía** en el mundo de las mujeres; él **era** el único hombre en una casa llena de mujeres. Cuando llegué, yo **era** el segundo hombre, pero **estaba** entre las mujeres, y lo **veía** a él desde el punto de vista de las mujeres y me **daba** cuenta de que nadie le **hacía** caso. El mundo aquél y el mundo entero **giraban** alrededor del sol por la determinación de las mujeres. Y, claro, el centro de ese universo de mujeres **era** la abuela. La abuela, que se **llamaba** Tranquilina y que **era** la persona más intranquila y más móvil que yo recuerde.

Diario *El Mercurio*, Chile

The imperfect

1 USAGE

The imperfect tense is used:

a Generally, to refer to an ongoing state or action in the past, whose beginning or end is not specified. In this context, English normally uses the simple past or, depending on the meaning, a construction with *used to*. Most imperfect tense forms in the texts correspond to this usage.

Yo ya **sabía** algunas cosas . . . (T. 1, l. 5–6) *I already knew a few things . . .*
Yo **vivía** en el mundo . . . (T. 3, l. 11) *I lived in a world . . .*

Consider also **era, quería** (T. 1, l. 4), **venían**, **eran** (T. 2, l. 8, 9), **podía** (T. 3, l. 9).

b In narrative contexts, in conjunction with the preterite, where the imperfect provides the background description for the actions expressed by the preterite. In English, both correspond to the simple past.

Yo me crié en una casa de hombres . . . (T. 2, l. 3–4) *I was brought up in a house full of men.*
La vida **era** austeridad . . . (T. 2, l. 5) *Life was austerity . . .*

c To refer to past habitual actions, expressed in English through the simple past or the *used to* form.

Giraban alrededor del sol. (T. 3, l. 19–20) *They revolved around the sun.*

Similarly, **se discutía** (T. 2, l. 7), **mandaba** (T. 2, l. 14), **veía** (T. 3, l. 16).

Past habitual actions may also be expressed with the imperfect form of **soler** '*to be accustomed to*', '*to be in the habit of*' followed by the infinitive:

Solían pasar las vacaciones en el campo. *They used to spend their holidays in the country.*
Solíamos vernos todos los domingos. *We used to see each other every Sunday.*

d In place of the imperfect progressive.

No **coincidían** con el futuro que ellos **proyectaban**. (T. 1, l. 6–8) *They didn't agree with the future that they were planning.*

e To refer to an action which was in progress in the past when something else happened.

Dormíamos cuando sucedió. *We were sleeping when it happened.*

Here, **dormíamos** is equivalent to the continuous form **estábamos durmiendo**.

f In place of the present tense, to request something in a polite way.

Quería hablar con usted. *I wanted to speak to you.*

g Instead of the conditional, in colloquial speech.

Yo que tú lo **hacía** (for **haría**). *If I were you I'd do it.*

2 FORMATION

Regular verbs

The imperfect of **-ar** verbs is formed by adding **-aba** to the stem. The endings for **-er** and **-ir** verbs have **-ía** in all their forms.

estar	**saber**	**vivir**
est**aba**	sab**ía**	viv**ía**
est**abas**	sab**ías**	viv**ías**
est**aba**	sab**ía**	viv**ía**
est**ábamos**	sab**íamos**	viv**íamos**
est**abais**	sab**íais**	viv**íais**
est**aban**	sab**ían**	viv**ían**

Estaba dispuesto a irme a . . . (T. 1, l. 15–16) *I was ready to leave for . . .*
Yo ya **sabía** algunas cosas . . . (T. 1, l. 5–6) *I already knew a few things . . .*
Yo **vivía** en una sociedad . . . (T. 2, l. 13–14) *I lived in a society . . .*

Irregular verbs

There are only three irregular verbs in the imperfect. They are **ir** *to go*, **ser** *to be* and **ver** *to see*:

ir:	iba, ibas, iba, íbamos, ibais, iban.
ser:	era, eras, era, éramos, erais, eran.
ver:	veía, veías, veía, veíamos, veíais, veían.

Les dije que . . . me **iba**. (T. 1, l. 13) *I told them . . . I was leaving.*
Era un coronel . . . (T. 3, l. 3–4) *He was a colonel . . .*
Lo **veía** a él . . . (T. 3, l. 15–16) *I used to see him . . .*

Other points to note in the texts

- Pluperfect tense: Text 1: *habían decidido* (l. 3), *me habían buscado* (l. 8) (see Chapter 5)
- Preterite tense: Text 1: *dije* (l. 10), *amenazaron* (l. 11), *vieron* (l. 14), *me fui* (l. 19), etc. Text 2: *crié* (l. 3), *tuvo* (l. 11), *di* (l. 12), etc. (see Chapter 2)
- Personal pronouns: The texts contain numerous examples of different types of pronouns, among these *ella, mí, me, les* (Text 1, l. 2, 4, 10, 9); *yo, me, ellos* (Text 2, l. 3, 3, 9); *lo, me, le* (Text 3, l. 9, 17, 18) (see Chapter 25)

EXERCISES

1 Put the verbs in brackets into the correct form of the imperfect tense.

Mis abuelos (ser) ________ campesinos que (vivir) ________ en una casa pequeña que no (tener) ________ ni agua ni electricidad. Mi abuelo (cultivar) ________ sus tierras mientras mi abuela (ocuparse) ________ de la casa y también (hacer) ________ encaje. Todos los martes mi abuelo (cargar) ________ el carro y con el burro que (llamarse) ________ Sancho, (ir) ________ al mercado donde (vender) ________ sus cultivos. De vez en cuando mi abuela lo (acompañar) ________ para vender sus encajes. Los dos (estar) ________ contentos a pesar de la vida tan dura que (llevar) ________.

2 Change the verbs in the following sentences from the present tense to the imperfect tense.

a Los domingos si hace buen tiempo doy un paseo en el parque.
b Es baja y lleva un abrigo que le toca los pies.
c Mientras los demás trabajan, tú charlas.
d Estudiamos una hora cada día.
e Cada vez que vamos a la costa llueve sin cesar.
f Por la noche ven la tele y se acuestan tarde.

g Sabe muy bien que no podemos hacerlo.
h Mi padre es una persona autoritaria que no me deja hacer lo que quiero.
i Por la mañana Antonio da clases de francés y por la tarde se reúne con los amigos en el casino.
j Vamos al mercado que es en la plaza los martes.
k Nada más levantarme, pongo la radio y oigo las noticias mientras me visto.
l ¿Qué haces en el tiempo libre? ¿Practicas algún deporte?
m Los niños siempre están jugando: unas veces van al parque, otras veces bajan al río a pescar.
n El chico no es muy guapo y lleva gafas pero sabe vestir.
o El camping adonde voy de vacaciones es enorme y cuenta con dos piscinas, una climatizada.

3 How much has your life changed?

i) Think of and write down things that were part of your life but are no longer, and vice versa, things which are now part of your life but used not to be, e.g.:
Antes iba a la piscina dos veces a la semana pero ahora no tengo tiempo.
Fumaba veinte cigarrillos al día.
Antes no podía hacer la compra los domingos porque los supermercados no se abrían.

ii) Write questions you can ask members of your group to find out what their lives were like when they were younger, e.g.:
Cuando eras pequeño/a, ¿dónde vivías?
Cuando eras más joven, ¿hacías deporte?
¿qué te gustaba comer/beber?

4 Complete these sentences using the imperfect tense to describe what the person was doing or what was happening.

a Cuando sonó el teléfono, Juan ________.
b Cuando llegaron sus amigos, Elena ________.
c María vio el coche atropellar al ciclista mientras ________.
d Laura se durmió mientras ________.
e No abrimos la ventana porque ________.
f Consuelo no pudo dormir porque ________.
g Los turistas no visitaron el castillo porque ________.
h Cuando llegó la noticia, el señor Martín ________.
i Cuando murió su padre, ella ________.
j Cuando me encontré con Alfonso, él ________.

5 Form complete sentences from these phrases, adding link words where necessary and putting the verbs into the appropriate past tenses, imperfect or preterite.

a La última vez que (yo) ver a Fernando • él estar buscando trabajo.
b (Nosotros) entrar en el museo • llover.
c (Yo) conocer a Isabel • tener el pelo largo y rubio.

d Pedro y yo ir por la calle • toparnos con Ana.
e Ser las once de la mañana • (ellos) partir para Santiago.
f (Yo) no ir a trabajar • tener resaca • dolerme la cabeza.
g Marisa bajar por la escalera • resbalarse • torcerse el tobillo.
h Llegar a la fiesta Jorge • todos estar borrachos.
i Ducharme con agua fría • hacer mucho calor.
j Inés estudiar derecho • compartir piso con tres chicos.

6 Translate into Spanish using the imperfect tense where appropriate.

a In those days girls didn't go out after ten at night.
b While he was waiting, he chatted with me.
c We were very tired when we arrived.
d I didn't realise that he was ill.
e We used to live in a small village where everyone knew one another.
f Everything was going well until it started to rain.
g We were expecting my uncle in the morning but he didn't arrive till mid afternoon.
h We were beginning to get worried about him so we phoned his daughter.
i They got out of the taxi and, as the door was open, went into the house without knocking.
j Vicente brought us a bottle of wine whenever he visited.

7 While on holiday, you were lucky enough to meet an octogenarian who talked to you about his life. Now write an account of your conversation which uses the imperfect tense and includes details of: his physical appearance, what he was wearing and what he said about his work, his family life and his leisure activities when he was a younger man.

8 Write or discuss with a partner the arguments you would use to defend or oppose these propositions:

- Antes la vida era más difícil.
- Antes la mujer no tenía tanta libertad.
- Antes la vida para los estudiantes no era tan dura.

4 | The perfect

Text

Isabel Allende, the Chilean writer, talks about her experience as an author and the way in which writing has helped her own personal growth. The grammar focuses on the use of the perfect tense, a construction which is particularly suitable for relating past experiences which bear some relationship with the present.

La escritura me ha dado poder

Llevo más de 20 años escribiendo y **he aprendido** poco de literatura, pero algo **he aprendido** sobre mí misma, porque cada libro es un viaje hacia el alma y la memoria. Ahora conozco mis limitaciones y, aunque sigo cometiendo muchos errores, los perdono con más facilidad, porque **he tomado** cariño a mis viejos defectos. La edad no nos hace más sabios ni mejores, sólo acentúa lo que ya somos. Siempre fui hiperactiva, desafiante, enamoradiza y un poco escandalosa. La edad no me **ha dado** calma, tampoco me **ha hecho** más sumisa o menos enamorada ni me **ha quitado** el gusto por llamar la atención. Sé que no tengo control sobre nada, las cosas realmente importantes nos suceden sin ser planeadas, de modo que más vale relajarse y vivir al día. Eso me hace desprendida y me da una gran libertad para existir y para escribir.

Me gusta la vida que **he llevado** y sólo me arrepiento del dolor que **he causado** a otros. Si pudiera vivir de nuevo, haría más o menos el mismo camino, aunque trataría de empezar a escribir más temprano. Esperé 39 años para hacerlo. Si hubiera sido hombre, tal vez habría escrito mis memorias a los 19. Si volviera a empezar daría las mismas batallas, sobre todo aquellas contra el machismo. Esas batallas son las que me **han aportado** mayores satisfacciones, por cada golpe recibido **he dado** dos.

La escritura me **ha dado** una voz, me **ha conectado** con lectores en muchas lenguas, me **ha obligado** a ser consecuente con mis ideas, creencias y acciones. La escritura me **ha dado** poder.

Estoy en edad de dar (. . .) Mi papel es proteger a las mujeres jóvenes y a los niños; me toca nutrir y en lo posible multiplicar la asombrosa belleza de este planeta. La tierra y sus criaturas necesitan de mis cuidados y también de mi espada. A nosotras, las viejas poderosas que ya nada tenemos que

(*Continued*)

perder, nos corresponde guiar, combatir.
50 Vamos a cambiar lo que no funciona. La civilización **se ha disparado** en una carrera de consumo y materialismo insostenible, hay un abismo entre los ricos y la mayoría cada vez más
55 numerosa de los pobres. La violencia se **ha institucionalizado** entre naciones y entre individuos. ¡Basta!

Revista de Libros, *El Mercurio*, Chile

The perfect

1 USAGE

Spanish, like English, makes a distinction between the perfect tense (e.g. *He has gone out*) and the simple past (e.g. *He went out*). Use varies from region to region, especially in the Spanish-speaking countries of Latin America, where the perfect is overall much less frequent than in Peninsular Spanish. Generally, the perfect tense is used:

a To describe past events which bear some relationship with the present.

Note that most instances of the perfect tense in the text correspond to this usage.

Llevo más de veinte años escribiendo y **he aprendido** poco de literatura. (l. 1–2) *I've been writing for more than twenty years and I have learned little about literature.*

. . . pero algo **he aprendido** sobre mí misma . . . (l. 2–3) *. . . but I have learned something about myself . . .*

La edad no me **ha dado** calma . . . (l. 13–14) *Age has not calmed me down . . .*

. . . tampoco me **ha hecho** más sumisa . . . (l. 14) *it hasn't made me more submissive either . . .*

Me gusta la vida que **he llevado** . . . (l. 23) *I like the life that I have led . . .*

. . . sólo me arrepiento del dolor que **he causado** a otros. (l. 23–25) *. . . I only regret the pain that I have caused to others.*

¿**Has leído** la carta de Daniel? Está sobre la mesa. *Have you read Daniel's letter? It's on the table.*

¿Quién **ha abierto** la ventana? Hay una corriente de aire. *Who has opened the window? There's a draught.*

In the last two examples, Latin American Spanish, just like English, may use the preterite tense or simple past: ¿**Leíste** . . . ? *Did you read . . . ?*, ¿Quién **abrió** . . . ? *Who opened . . . ?*

b To refer to past events or actions which continue into the present.

La escritura me **ha dado** una voz, me **ha conectado** con lectores en muchas lenguas, me **ha obligado** a ser consecuente con mis ideas . . . (l. 36–39) *Writing has given me a voice, has connected me with readers in many languages, has forced me to be consistent with my ideas . . .*

La civilización **se ha disparado** en una carrera de consumo y materialismo insostenible . . . (l. 50–53) *Civilisation has careered off in a mad rush of unsustainable consumerism and materialism . . .*

La violencia **se ha institucionalizado** entre naciones y entre individuos . . . (l. 55–57) *Violence among nations and individuals has become institutionalised . . .*

The continuity of the action into the present can be made more specific through the continuous form:

He estado tratando de encontrar una solución. *I've been trying to find a solution.*
Ha estado lloviendo toda la mañana. *It has been raining all morning.*

c To refer to the immediate or recent past, often with adverbs such as *hoy*, *esta tarde*. Here, English may use the simple past rather than the perfect tense.

There are no examples of this use in the text.

Esta tarde **he visto** a María. *I saw Maria this afternoon.*
He desayunado muy bien. *I had a good breakfast.*

In Spain, you may also hear the preterite in this context, especially if the event is seen as more distant. Latin Americans, on the whole, will show preference for the preterite:

Esta mañana **vi** a María. **Desayuné** muy bien.

d The perfect tense is not normally used with reference to events which were completed in a more distant past, for which you need to use the preterite (Chapter 2). In parts of Spain, however, you may hear sentences such as:

¿Dónde **ha nacido**? *Where were you born?*
He nacido en Sevilla. *I was born in Seville.*

In this context, though, most speakers show preference for the preterite:

¿Dónde **nació**? *Where were you born?*
Nací en Burgos. *I was born in Burgos.*

2 FORMATION

The perfect tense, like all compound tenses, is formed from the auxiliary verb **haber** *to have*, followed by the past participle. To form the past participle remove the -**ar**, -**er** or -**ir** ending and add -**ado** to the stem of -**ar** verbs, and -**ido** to that of -**er** and -**ir** verbs. Here are three examples:

	tomar	aprender	vivir
yo	he tom**ado**	he aprend**ido**	he viv**ido**
tú	has tom**ado**	has aprend**ido**	has viv**ido**
Vd./él/ella	ha tom**ado**	ha aprend**ido**	ha viv**ido**
nosotros/as	hemos tom**ado**	hemos aprend**ido**	hemos viv**ido**
vosotros/as	habéis tom**ado**	habéis aprend**ido**	habéis viv**ido**
Vds./ellos/ellas	han tom**ado**	han aprend**ido**	han viv**ido**

The past participle of **ir** *to go* is **ido** and that of **ser** *to be* is **sido**:

¿Dónde **ha ido**? *Where have you/has he/she gone?*
Han sido muy felices. *They've been very happy.*

IRREGULAR PAST PARTICIPLES

There are a number of common verbs whose past participle is irregular. The main ones are:

abrir	**abierto**	*opened*	morir	**muerto**	*died*
cubrir	**cubierto**	*covered*	poner	**puesto**	*put*
decir	**dicho**	*said*	romper	**roto**	*broken*
escribir	**escrito**	*written*	ver	**visto**	*seen*
hacer	**hecho**	*made/done*	volver	**vuelto**	*returned*

. . . tampoco me **ha hecho** más sumisa . . . (l. 14) *. . . it hasn't made me more submissive either . . .*
Ha escrito varias novelas. *She/he has written several novels.*
¿Quién te lo **ha dicho**? *Who told you?*
No la **hemos visto** desde hace mucho tiempo. *We haven't seen her for a very long time.*
¿Dónde lo **habéis puesto**? *Where have/did you put it?*

Compounds of the above verbs have similar forms, e.g. **predecir** *to predict*, **predicho** *predicted*; **componer** *to compose*, **compuesto** *composed*; **deshacer** *to undo*, **deshecho** *undone.*

Other points to note in the text

- Gerund: *Llevo más de 20 años escribiendo* (l. 1), *sigo cometiendo muchos errores* (l. 6–7) (see Chapter 9)
- Subjunctive: *Si pudiera vivir de nuevo* (l. 25), *Si hubiera sido hombre* (l. 29), *Si volviera a empezar* (l. 30–31) (see Chapters 15 and 16)
- Conditional: *haría más o menos el mismo camino, aunque trataría de empezar a escribir más temprano* (l. 25–28), *daría las mismas batallas* (l. 31–32) (see Chapter 7)
- Prepositions *por* and *para*: *el gusto por llamar la atención* (l. 15–16), *me da una gran libertad para existir y para escribir* (l. 21–22), *Esperé 39 años para hacerlo* (l. 28), *por cada golpe recibido* (l. 35) (see Chapter 28)

EXERCISES

1 Change the verb in the perfect tense according to the new subject given in brackets.

a No he entendido bien su explicación. (nosotros)
b ¿Habéis visto las fotos? (ustedes)
c ¿Has visitado Escocia alguna vez? (Carmen)
d Todavía no han llegado. (el señor Botín)
e ¿Cómo sabes que María ha recibido el paquete? (Javier y María)
f No te ha podido ayudar. (yo)
g ¿Por qué no me lo has dicho ? (vosotros)
h ¿A qué hora has quedado con Juan? (usted)
i No me he esforzado en absoluto. (tú)
j Esta mañana nos hemos despertado muy pronto. (los niños)

2 Change the verb in these sentences from the present to the perfect tense.

a Aprendo mucho aquí.
b ¿Vas al centro?
c Ya sale el tren.
d Vendemos la casa.
e ¿Usted llama al despacho?
f Se me cae todo.
g Ustedes tienen mucha suerte.
h ¿Entendéis?

3 Translate into Spanish.

a We have always gone on holiday to Spain.
b They haven't said anything to Pili because they haven't seen her.
c Why haven't you (**tú**) done this?
d Where have you (**ustedes**) put the bags?
e Gonzalo still hasn't come back from Paris.
f I haven't written to Isabel because I haven't had time.
g Carlos is very upset because his dog has died.
h The neighbours say you **(vosotros)** have broken the fence.

4 Tomorrow you are going to visit a friend but now, unable to get to sleep, you are lying in bed going through your mental check list. Choosing an appropriate verb from the list below, fill in the gaps using the **yo** form of the perfect tense.

olvidar	**cambiar**	**hacer**	**poner**	**poder**	**comprar**
envolver	**dar**	**decir**	**leer**	**escribir**	

A ver si ________ todos los preparativos necesarios para el viaje. ________ el billete* y ________ a Otilia para decirle la hora de mi llegada. ________ los regalos que le voy a dar y los ________ en la maleta. ________ libras a dólares. ________ todas las guías que ________ sobre los sitios que voy a visitar. Le ________ a la vecina que voy a estar fuera quince días y le ________ la llave de la casa. Seguro que ________ hacer algo.

* *In Latin American Spanish:* ***el boleto***.

5 Complete the questions to these answers using the verbs in brackets.

a – ¿ ________ (dormir) bien?
– No. No he pegado ojo en toda la noche.

b – ¿ ________ (comer)?
– Todavía no. Van a comer dentro de poco.

c – ¿ ________ (visitar, vosotros) Benidorm alguna vez?
– Muchas veces. Visitamos Benidorm por primera vez hace más de diez años.

d – ¿Por qué no ________ (ir) Susana de vacaciones este año?
– Porque su madre está enferma.

e – ¿Qué tal lo ________ (pasar, ustedes)?
– Mal. Todo nos ha salido muy mal hoy.

f – ¿ ________ (abrir) ya el banco?
– No. No abre hasta las diez.

g – ¿Qué ________ (hacer, usted) esta mañana?
– Nada de interés.

h – ¿ ________ (llover) mucho?
– No, al contrario. Ha hecho muy buen tiempo todo el día.

i – ¿Si yo ________ (perder) alguna vez mi pasaporte? Perderlo no, pero el año pasado en Italia me lo robaron.

6 You have some Spanish-speaking visitors staying with you and want to plan their stay to be as pleasant as possible, e.g. have they slept well, have they eaten, have they bought any souvenirs, have they been to/visited the local attractions . . .

Imagine the situation, think of and write down as many questions as you can of the kind that you would ask your visitors, using the perfect tense.

7 **i)** Think of and write down in Spanish three things that you have done and three things that you have not done in your life, e.g. climbed a mountain, written to someone famous.

ii) Think of other deeds/feats which you can add to this list to draw up a questionnaire to use to find out if anyone in your group has done any of these things.

iii) Use your questionnaire to interview other people in your group.

iv) Write a report giving the results of your survey.

8 Think about and write down and/or discuss with a partner what you have got so far out of learning Spanish: what you have learned, what friendships you have made, what new horizons have opened up.

5 | The pluperfect

Text 1

Text 1, like Text 2 below, both from a novel by the Spanish author Soledad Puértolas, contains a number of examples of the use of the pluperfect tense, the Spanish equivalent of *had* + past participle, as in *I had seen it.*

Queda la noche

Gisela tenía una extraña historia a sus espaldas que nunca me **había sido** contada con precisión, tal vez porque nadie la conocía muy bien. Su padre, un alemán que **había venido** a instalarse en España, le debía a mi abuelo un gran favor, aunque nunca supe qué clase de favor. El caso es que la familia Von Rotten
5 estaba en deuda con la nuestra. Pero el misterio no era ése, sino un oscuro episodio que **había ocurrido** en su juventud. Al parecer, su mejor amigo de infancia **había sido** un chico vecino suyo, sordo mudo, con quien pasaba las tardes. Cuando más adelante dijeron a sus padres que querían casarse se encontraron con una prohibición tajante. Lo que no era seguro era lo que **había sucedido** después:
10 una fuga o un acto de fuerza, pero el padre de Gisela reaccionó con inapelable firmeza y la familia del chico se esfumó. Más tarde corrió el rumor de que el chico se **había muerto** y que su muerte no **había sido** enteramente natural. Podía haberse tratado de un suicidio, de un dejarse morir. Sea como fuere, este episodio verdadero, falso o exagerado, no resultaba incongruente con la personalidad de
15 Gisela. Su vida consistía en prestar ayuda a los demás y su conversación giraba siempre alrededor de los grandes problemas de la humanidad y del egoísmo y miserias de los poderosos.

Text 2

Text 2, from the same novel, contains further examples of the use of the pluperfect tense.

A mi vuelta de Madrid, me esperaba malas noticias. De nuevo, más o menos unidas a las complicaciones. Mario me **había llamado** y me **había dejado** el recado urgente de que lo llamara. Cuando al fin pude hablar con él me comunicó una noticia dramática. Un coche **había atropellado** a Ángela en medio de la
5 calle. Ángela, la funcionaria que, de vuelta de un congreso en Sri Lanka, **había decidido** pasar unos días en Delhi, donde la **habíamos conocido** aquel verano. **Había muerto**. Pero debía haber algo extraño en aquella muerte, algo más extraño que la muerte misma, porque la policía **había abierto** una investigación. A Mario ya le **había interrogado**. Seguramente, de un momento a otro, me
10 llamarían a mí. Debían de haber encontrado nuestras direcciones anotadas en alguna parte. Recordé que Ángela **había sacado** una agenda en el restaurante del hotel y que nos **había pedido** nuestros teléfonos.

The pluperfect

1 USAGE

Spanish uses the pluperfect tense in much the same way as English does, that is, to refer to past events or actions which occurred before another past event or situation, in this case, the situation referred to by the narrator. There are several examples of the pluperfect in the passages, among them the following:

Nunca me **había sido** contada . . . (T. 1, l. 1–2) *It had never been told to me . . .*
. . . **había venido** a instalarse en España . . . (T. 1, l. 3) *. . . he'd come to settle in Spain . . .*
. . . un oscuro episodio que **había ocurrido** en su juventud. (T. 1, l. 5–6) *. . . an obscure episode which had happened when she was young.*
Más tarde corrió el rumor de que el chico se **había muerto** . . . (T. 1, l. 11–12) *Later on there was a rumour going round that the boy had died . . .*
Mario me **había llamado** y me **había dejado** el recado urgente . . . (T. 2, l. 2–3) *Mario had called me and had left me an urgent message . . .*
Un coche **había atropellado** a Ángela . . . (T. 2, l. 4) *Angela had been run over by a car . . .*
. . . **había decidido** pasar unos días en Delhi . . . (T. 2, l. 5–6) *. . . she had decided to spend a few days in Delhi . . .*
. . . la **habíamos conocido** aquel verano. (T. 2, l. 6) *. . . we had met her that summer.*

A clear example of the use of the pluperfect to refer to a past action which took place before another past event is in sentences like the following:

Habían cenado cuando llegamos. *They had had dinner when we arrived.*
Ya **había salido** cuando la llamé. *She had already gone out when I called her.*

2 FORMATION

The pluperfect indicative is formed with the imperfect of the auxiliary verb **haber** *to have* followed by the past participle. The past participle of -**ar** verbs ends in -**ado**, and that of -**er** and -**ir** verbs ends in -**ido**. For irregular past participles, see Chapter 4 or **Irregular verbs** on pages 279–282.

tomar	vivir
había tomado	había vivido
habías tomado	habías vivido
había tomado	había vivido
habíamos tomado	habíamos vivido
habíais tomado	habíais vivido
habían tomado	habían vivido

Other points to note in the texts

- Imperfect and preterite tenses: Text 1: *Gisela tenía una extraña historia* (l. 1), *nadie la conocía* (l. 2), *le debía . . . un gran favor, aunque nunca supe* (l. 3–4), *estaba en deuda* (l. 5), etc. Text 2: *me esperaba* (l. 1), *Cuando al fin pude hablar con él me comunicó* (l. 3), *debía haber algo extraño . . .* (l. 7), etc. (see Chapters 2 and 3)
- Possessives: Text 1: *sus espaldas* (l. 1), *su padre* (l. 2), *mi abuelo* (l. 3), *la nuestra* (l. 5), *su juventud* (l. 6), *vecino suyo* (l. 7), etc. Text 2: *A mi vuelta de Madrid* (l. 1), *nuestras direcciones* (l. 10), *nuestros teléfonos* (l. 12). (see Chapter 24)
- Object pronouns: Text 1: *me había sido contada* (l. 1), *nadie la conocía* (l. 2), *le debía a mi abuelo un gran favor* (l. 3). Text 2 *me esperaba* (l. 1), *me había llamado y me había dejado el recado urgente de que lo llamara* (l. 2), *me comunicó una noticia dramática* (l. 3), *donde la habíamos conocido* (l. 6), *nos había pedido nuestros teléfonos* (l. 12), etc. (see Chapter 25)

EXERCISES

1 Put the verb in brackets into the correct form of the pluperfect, then read the sentence and study the use of the verb tenses.

a Federico fue a Marbella porque sus tíos lo (invitar).
b Mina y yo (repetir) los versos tantas veces que los sabíamos de memoria.
c Me pidió ayuda porque tú lo (echar) de casa.
d Cuando nos avisaron del accidente, ya (salir, vosotros).
e Ya te lo (decir, yo) mil veces pero tú no querías creerme.
f (Ver, él) la película la semana anterior pero tenía ganas de verla de nuevo.
g Todavía no (terminar, él) de construir la casa cuando murió.
h Sus hijos le (prometer) su ayuda pero al final no se la dieron.
i Reconocí a Jesús en seguida por lo que sus amigos me (contar) de él.
j Era obvio que los presentes no (entender) nada del discurso.

k ¿Y esa fue tu primera visita a Roma o (estar) antes?

l Apenas (terminar) su interpretación, el público aplaudió largamente.

m Cuando fuimos a visitarla, ella aún no (levantarse).

n Cuando se decidieron a comprar la casa, ya se (vender).

o Cuando entré en el cine, por suerte la película no (empezar).

2 Rewrite the sentences using the pluperfect tense as in the example.

Example: No le escribió. Confesé que . . .
Confesé que no le había escrito.

a Cerraron el castillo antes de la hora indicada.
Descubrimos que . . .

b Carmen fue al centro.
La madre de Carmen me dijo que . . .

c No visitamos El Prado y por lo tanto no vimos *Las Meninas* de Velázquez.
Les explicamos que . . .

d No dije la verdad.
Tuve que confesar que . . .

e Los ladrones entraron por la ventana del comedor.
Les dijimos a los guardias que . . .

f Le robaron la cartera en la Plaza Mayor.
Le contó al policía que . . .

g Se encontró con unos amigos allí.
Me contó que . . .

h No me dieron ninguna explicación por sus acciones.
Me di cuenta de que . . .

i No leyeron el informe.
Confesaron que . . .

j Vino a la capital en busca de empleo.
Nos contó que . . .

k Margarita no trajo nada y por eso no le dimos nada.
Expliqué que . . .

l Su hija se casó en Nueva Zelanda.
Se enteraron de que . . .

m Se metió las llaves en el bolsillo.
Estaba seguro de que . . .

n Nadie le comunicó las buenas noticias.
Pronto supo que . . .

o Los niños vieron un DVD y después cenaron.
Le dije a su madre que . . .

3 Translate into Spanish:

a I was happy because Roberto had given me a present.
b He had wrapped it up and left it on my seat.
c I hadn't told him that it was my birthday.
d Later he told me that he had bought the bracelet because he had liked it.
e He hadn't thought about the price.
f When I got home, Amelia had already gone to bed.
g She had turned everything off and left me a note on the table.
h She hadn't got in touch with Eduardo as she had been out all evening as well.
i However, she had received the news that Aunt Silvia had died.
j Víctor had inherited everything and Aunt Silvia had left us nothing.

4 Just after Christmas you went shopping in the sales and when you got home you found that thieves had broken into your house. Recount this incident in Spanish using the pluperfect where possible, for example to explain how the thieves had gained entry, the rooms they had gone into, how you realised what they had taken.

6 The future

Text 1

The article which follows makes some interesting predictions about the world population in the year 2025. As in Text 2 below, the style is journalistic, the future tense being common in this type of context. Read the two texts to find out what predictions are being made, then go back through them and study the language, especially the use of the future tense.

Dos tercios de la población mundial vivirá en ciudades en el año 2025

En el año 2025, alrededor de 5 mil millones de personas, es decir, dos tercios de la población mundial, **vivirán** en ciudades. La mayoría de ellas **habitará** en suburbios hacinados, con lo que se prevé la formación de muchos cordones de pobreza.

En un plazo de 25 años **existirán** ciudades con más de 30 millones de habitantes, **habrá** 100 ciudades con más de cinco millones de personas y **serán** 300 las urbes con más de un millón de residentes.

La mayor parte de este crecimiento **se producirá** en los países en desarrollo, especialmente en Africa, Asia y América Latina y el Caribe, que en conjunto **duplicarán** su población urbana. El incremento **se registrará** especialmente en Africa, que **duplicará** su población urbana en sólo 13 años. Para Peter Marcuse, profesor de la Universidad de Columbia, el siglo XXI **traerá** una gran división en las ciudades. "De este crecimiento, los únicos beneficiados **serán** quienes pertenecen al tercio más rico de la sociedad. La diferencia entre ricos y pobres **crecerá** aún más."

Diario *La Tercera*, Chile

Text 2

What will the world be like in 2030? The following are some of the predictions made by the *Forum of Young Global Leaders*, of the *World Economic Forum* in Davos, Switzerland.

Cómo viviremos en 2030

Internet en todo el planeta. En dos décadas, la mayoría de los medios **convergirán** hacia la plataforma internet (y la televisión interactiva). Las personas **ocuparán** más horas en la red y **crecerá** como soporte publicitario.

Internet **será** accesible casi en cualquier punto de la Tierra, pero los contenidos de primer nivel **serán** reducidos a los suscriptores, es decir, **habrá** más control de parte de los proveedores de la información.

La interactividad **aumentará**, igual que la tendencia a que el usuario arme su propio paquete de contenidos para sí mismo o para otros. Debido al superávit de información la gente **demandará** crecientemente entretenimiento. [. . .]

Los retos del medio ambiente. La temperatura **subirá** entre 0,5 y 1,5 grados Celsius de aquí a 2030. Mientras, el nivel de los océanos **se elevará** entre 6 y 11 centímetros como consecuencia del calentamiento global. **Veremos** más tormentas, ciclones, tornados y huracanes, severas sequías e inundaciones frecuentes.

La destrucción de los ecosistemas **seguirá** y **habrá** menos especies sobre la Tierra. El creciente uso del suelo y el cambio climático **producirán** la extinción de entre 21 por ciento y 24 por ciento de los organismos en Asia, y entre 16 por ciento y 35 por ciento en África. Los mamíferos y las aves **desaparecerán** a una velocidad cien veces mayor que la de la naturaleza.

Pero mientras hoy hay más de 100 mil áreas protegidas alrededor del mundo, lo que equivale al 12 por ciento de la superficie terrestre, se espera que en las próximas dos décadas se multipliquen los esfuerzos de protección y que la legislación se haga mucho más estricta, tanto a nivel nacional como global. [. . .]

A su vez la demanda por agua de uso agrícola, industrial y doméstico **crecerá** un 16 por ciento en las próximas dos décadas, en particular en los países en desarrollo, lo que se **sumará** a las crecientes sequías que se **vivirán** en Medio Oriente, el Magreb, norte de China y amplios sectores de India y Sudáfrica. [. . .] El agua **se transformará** en foco de conflicto, dado el aumento de la demanda. [. . .]

Dado el crecimiento de la población y la consecuente necesidad de alimentos, cada día **veremos** más tierras deforestadas para convertirse en terrenos cultivables.

Comida inteligente. La mayoría de los alimentos y bebidas ya no sólo le **quitará** el hambre o la sed; además, lo **ayudarán** a quedarse dormido, a concentrarse más o a mejorar su sistema digestivo.

Si tiene poco tiempo, no **tendrá** para qué recurrir a la comida chatarra, porque ésta, además de rápida, **será** orgánica y saludable.

(*Continued*)

75 Para comprobar las propiedades de sus alimentos, basta que revise el empaque; ahí **encontrará** un chip que le **dirá** cuánto tiempo toma en digerir, sus posibles efectos 80 secundarios y qué recursos – además de los ingredientes – se han ocupado en su producción.

No más colegios. Despídase de la sala de clases. En 2030, éstas **podrán** 85 hacerse en su propia casa, porque los mejores profesores a lo largo del mundo **dictarán** cursos virtuales usando telepresencia y tecnologías 3D.

Podrá aprender durante toda su 90 vida: agentes tecnológicos **producirán** planes educativos diseñados especialmente para usted. A diferencia de cómo se desarrolla hoy, el aprendizaje virtual **será** en comunidad, 95 no en solitario.

Hay cosas que nunca cambian: nunca **podrá** saber más de tecnología que sus hijos. Éstos **vivirán** simultáneamente en el mundo real y 100 virtual, interactuando con la misma facilidad en uno y otro.

Trabajo ideal. No **pasará** más de 5 a 8 horas a la semana en la oficina, porque desde cualquier lugar del 105 planeta, incluso arriba de un avión, **podrá** acceder a ésta. La mayoría de las reuniones **serán** virtuales.

Usted **será** un adulto mayor, pero no se desanime: este grupo **será** más 110 capaz y poderoso que nunca. Todos **podrán** trabajar más allá de los 65 años, aunque **serán** especialmente las mujeres las que prefieran hacerlo. Además, **aumentará** en varios años la 115 esperanza de vida, y la mayoría de los niños **conocerá** a sus bisabuelas. [. . .]

Revista *El Sábado*, *El Mercurio*, Chile.

The future

1 USAGE

The future in English can be expressed in a number of ways. Consider for instance *They will go to Spain. She's leaving tomorrow. We are going to do it.* Spanish also uses different forms to talk about future events:

Irán a España. **Sale** mañana. **Vamos a hacerlo.**

This chapter deals with the equivalent of the *will* form, known as the future tense, which is used:

a Generally, with future meaning, to refer to future events, including predictions. This use is much more common in writing, especially in formal registers, for example the press, as in the two texts above. Most of the examples of the future tense in the texts correspond to this one. Here are a few of them:

Vivirán en ciudades. (T. 1, l. 3–4) *They will live in cities.*
Duplicarán su población. (T. 1, l. 18) *They will double their population.*
. . . el siglo XXI **traerá** una gran división . . . (T. 1, l. 23–24) *. . . the twenty-first century will bring a great division . . .*
Internet **será** accesible casi en cualquier punto de la Tierra. (T. 2, l. 8–9) *Internet will be accessible almost anywhere in the world.*
La temperatura **subirá** entre 0,5 y 1,5 grados Celsius. (T. 2, l. 21–23) *Temperatures will rise between 0.5 and 1.5 degrees Celsius.*
Veremos más tormentas . . . (T. 2, l. 27) *We'll see more storms . . .*
Lo **ayudarán** a quedarse dormido. (T. 2, l. 68) *They'll help you to sleep.*
Podrá aprender durante toda su vida. (T. 2, l. 89–90) *You'll be able to learn throughout your life.*
No **pasará** más de 5 a 8 horas en la oficina. (T. 2, l. 102–103) *You won't spend more than 5 to 8 hours in the office.*

In the spoken language, especially in informal registers, reference to future actions is usually expressed with forms other than the future tense, for example with the construction **ir a** + infinitive:

Vamos a viajar en avión. *We're going to travel by plane.*
Van a volver en junio. *They're going to come back in June.*

The present tense is also frequent in this context, especially with pre-arranged actions and with verbs of movement:

Se van mañana. *They're leaving tomorrow.*
Elsa **llega** el próximo lunes. *Elsa is arriving next Monday.*

b To express probability and supposition.

A esta hora **estarán** en casa. *They will/must be at home at this time.*
Tendrá tu edad. *He/she must be your age.*

c To express uncertainty in relation to a future action.

No sé si la situación **cambiará.** *I don't know whether the situation will change.*
Supongo que lo **harán.** *I suppose they'll do it.*

d In interrogative sentences, to express the idea of *I wonder.*

¿Cómo **será** la vida en el 2030? *I wonder what life will be like in 2030.*
¿Qué hora **será**? *I wonder what time it is.*
¿**Volveremos** a verlos? *I wonder whether we'll see them again.*

e To express promises.

Te prometo que se lo **diré.** *I promise you I will tell him/her/them.*
Te juro que no **volverá** a suceder. *I swear it won't happen again.*

OTHER WAYS OF TRANSLATING '*WILL*' IN SPANISH

Note that certain constructions with *will* in English, which do not refer to future time, are normally expressed through forms other than the future in Spanish.

¿Me ayudas, por favor? (present tense) *Will you help me, please?*
¿Quieres pasar? (**querer** + infinitive) *Will you come in?*
No quieren escucharme. (**querer** + infinitive) *They won't listen to me.*

2 FORMATION

Regular verbs

The future tense is formed with the whole infinitive, to which the endings are added. Verbs in **-ar**, **-er** and **-ir** all share the same endings. Here are three examples:

encontrar *to find*	encontrar**é**, encontrar**ás**, encontrar**á**, encontrar**emos**, encontrar**éis**, encontrar**án**
ser *to be*	ser**é**, ser**ás**, ser**á**, ser**emos**, ser**éis**, ser**án**
vivir *to live*	vivir**é**, vivir**ás**, vivir**á**, vivir**emos**, vivir**éis**, vivir**án**

Ahí **encontrará** un chip . . . (T. 2, l. 77) *There you'll find a chip . . .*
. . . los únicos beneficiados **serán** quienes **pertenecen** al . . . (T. 1, l. 25–26) *. . . the only ones who will benefit from this will be those who belong to . . .*
. . . **vivirán** en ciudades. (T. 1, l. 3–4) *. . . they will live in cities.*
Ocuparán más horas en la red. (T. 2, l. 5–6) *They'll spend more time on the net.*
La destrucción de los ecosistemas **seguirá.** (T. 2, l. 30–31) *Destruction of ecosystems will continue.*

Irregular verbs

Some verbs have an irregular stem in the future tense, but the endings are the same as those of regular verbs. Note the following examples in the texts:

. . . **habrá** 100 ciudades . . . (T. 1, l. 10) *. . . there will be a hundred cities . . .*
No **tendrá** para qué recurrir a la comida chatarra. (T. 2, l. 71–72) *You won't have to resort to junk food.*
Le **dirá** cuánto tiempo toma digerir. (T. 2, l. 78–79) *It will tell you how long it takes to digest.*
Podrá acceder a ésta. (T. 2, l. 106) *You'll be able to acess this.*

The following are the most common irregular future forms:

caber *to be contained* **cabré, cabrás** . . .	**querer** *to want* **querré, querrás** . . .
decir *to say, tell* **diré, dirás** . . .	**saber** *to know* **sabré, sabrás** . . .
haber *to have* (auxiliary) **habré, habrás** . . .	**salir** *to go out* **saldré, saldrás** . . .
hacer *to do, make* **haré, harás** . . .	**tener** *to have* **tendré, tendrás** . . .
poder *to be able* **podré, podrás** . . .	**valer** *to be worth* **valdré, valdrás** . . .
poner *to put* **pondré, pondrás** . . .	**venir** *to come* **vendré, vendrás** . . .

Compounds of the above verbs are conjugated in the same way, e.g. **reponer** *to replace*, **repondré, repondrás** . . . ; **retener** *to retain*, **retendré, retendrás** . . . See also **Irregular verbs** on pages 279–282.

Other points to note in the texts

- Adjective agreement and position: Text 1: *población mundial* (l. 3), *suburbios hacinados* (l. 5), *población urbana* (l. 18), *una gran división* (1. 23–24); Text 2: *televisión interactiva* (l. 4), *soporte publicitario* (l. 6–7), *calentamiento global* (l. 26), *cambio climático* (l. 33), *áreas protegidas* (l. 41), *comida chatarra* (l. 72), etc. (see Chapter 20)
- Prepositions: There are numerous prepositions in both texts, among them *a, con, de, en, entre, hacia, para, por, sobre* (see Chapter 28).
- Reflexive verbs: Text 1: *se producirá* (l. 15), *se registrará* (l. 19); Text 2: *se elevará* (l. 24–25), *se multipliquen* (l. 45), *se haga mucho más estricta* (l. 46–47), *se transformará* (l. 57–58), *despídase* (l. 83), *podrán hacerse* (l. 84–85), *no se desanime* (l. 109). (see Chapter 12).

EXERCISES

1 Put the verb in brackets into the correct form of the future tense.

a (Estar, yo) ________ libre este fin de semana, de eso no cabe duda.
b Cuando vayas a su casa, (ver, tú) ________ su colección de miniaturas.
c Rogelio ha dicho que no (salir) ________ hasta el jueves.
d Vamos a hacer esto ahora y después (hablar) ________ de eso.
e Los equipos (jugar) ________ dos partidos.
f ¿(Venir, tú) ________ solo o con tu novia?
g Si seguís trabajando a ese ritmo, pronto (agotaros) ________.
h Si todo me sale bien, (poder, yo) ________ pasar unos días contigo en Madrid.
i (Tener, ellos) ________ que prestar mucho más atención si quieren aprobar el examen.
j Dicen que en los próximos años (haber) ________ una explosión de estrés y para liberar este estrés, (practicar, nosotros) ________ más deportes de riesgo.
k Según el parte meteorológico, la mitad sur peninsular (ser) ________ la más afectada por las nubes y por los chubascos. En Canarias también (haber) ________ nubes y las temperaturas (subir) ________ un poco.
l Aquí en el itinerario pone que (hacer, nosotros) ________ una parada en San Agustín.

2 The Camino de Santiago is a famous pilgrim route in the north of Spain which every year attracts thousands of pilgrims, some of whom use less traditional ways of reaching Santiago. One such pilgrim was interviewed recently and below is what he said. Change the underlined verbs to appropriate forms of the future tense.

a <u>Voy a hacer</u> el Camino en globo. Para mí, <u>es</u> la primera vez.
b Me <u>va a acompañar</u> mi amigo Eduardo. Para él, <u>es</u> la tercera vez.
c En el globo <u>vamos a llevar</u> lo mínimo. Así no <u>voy a tener</u> problemas con el peso. Yo <u>voy a guiar</u> el globo y Eduardo <u>va a sacar</u> las fotos.

d Como todos los peregrinos, vamos a alojarnos en los albergues. Bueno, lo vamos a intentar. También vamos a bajar en otros sitios – eso, seguro.

e ¿Qué voy a hacer una vez en Santiago? Hombre, voy a seguir las tradiciones: primero, voy a ir a la catedral, voy a entrar por la puerta del Obradoiro, voy a rezar un Padre Nuestro, voy a subir al camarín del Apóstol y lo voy a abrazar. Y muy importante, voy a golpear la cabeza tres veces contra la imagen del santo. Esto me va a dar sabiduría y prudencia.

f No vamos a volver en seguida. Vamos a quedarnos unos días. Pero una vez de vuelta, Eduardo va a revelar sus fotos, yo voy a escribir el texto y vamos a publicar un libro sobre nuestra aventura.

g El libro va a salir dentro de un año. Vamos a ponerle por título "*A Santiago en globo*". Le va a gustar.

3 Complete the questions that were asked in this interview in the future tense. Use the formal form of address: *usted* or *ustedes*.

a ¿Cómo .... ?

b ¿Quién ....?

c ¿Qué ....?

d ¿Dónde ....?

e ¿Qué ....?

f ¿Cuánto tiempo ....?

g ¿Cuándo ....?

4 Here is an outline itinerary for a group of students who are visiting an educational establishment in a Spanish-speaking country to discuss a joint project. Rewrite the itinerary as a piece of continuous prose using the future tense.

Miércoles

9,00 Llegada al Instituto. Recibimiento por parte del director. Visita de las instalaciones.
11,15 Presentación del grupo de alumnos del Instituto.
12,30 Salida del Centro. Visita al Ayuntamiento. Comida en el Ayuntamiento.

Jueves

8,30 Trabajo en el aula.
11,50 Trabajo en el aula con el grupo de alumnos del Instituto.
14,00 Almuerzo en la cantina del Instituto.
16,00 Visita turístico-cultural del centro de la ciudad.

Viernes

10,00 Revisión del proyecto.
11,30 Café.
12,00 Planes futuros: actividades a realizar durante el resto del año hasta la próxima reunión.
14,00 Comida. Tarde libre.

Sábado

Día libre para visitas y compras.

Domingo

8,30 Salida al aeropuerto. Vuelo de regreso.

5 Put each verb in brackets into the first person singular of the future tense to form your ten-point plan to be environmentally friendly.

DECÁLOGO

Palabra de forjador ambiental

1. **El respeto ayuda a construir un mundo mejor.** (Ejercer) ________ mi rol de forjador, procurando que todos cuidemos el planeta que compartimos.
2. **El aire limpio es fundamental para una vida sana.** (Procurar) ________ caminar o andar en bicicleta*, en lugar de usar medios de transporte motorizados y contaminantes.
3. **El agua es la cuna de toda forma de vida.** (Ahorrar) ________ la cantidad que uso al ducharme, al lavarme los dientes y la que se pierde en las llaves* que gotean.
4. **Los animales y las plantas tienen derecho a vivir mejor.** (Plantar) ________ nuevos árboles y (cuidar) ________ todos los que hay a mi alrededor, en las plazas, parques y calles.
5. **Un ambiente sano está libre de basura.** (Elegir) ________ productos biodegradables y en envases retornables, procurando reducir la cantidad de desechos que genero.
6. **La energía que cuido y ahorro hoy, me será útil mañana.** (Apagar) ________ las luces y televisor que nadie esté usando.
7. **El silencio es valioso y sano.** (Evitar) ________ que se toque la bocina sin necesidad, las alarmas que hacen mucho ruido y el volumen excesivo cuando escucho música.
8. **Mi casa también es parte del planeta.** (Cuidar) ________ que nadie fume dentro de la casa y que usemos combustibles limpios.
9. **La tierra seguirá siendo generosa si sabemos cuidarla.** (Cuidar) ________ los bosques, no (contaminar) ________ las aguas y (proteger) ________ la vida silvestre.
10. **La atmósfera hace posible la vida en la tierra.** (Preferir) ________ siempre los productos que no dañen la capa de ozono.

Diario *El Metropolitano*, Chile

* *In Peninsular Spanish* andar en bicicleta = ir en bicicleta, la llave = el grifo

6 What does the future hold for us?

The two texts you have read have given you some indications. Write down your thoughts on the following questions:

¿Cómo será la ciudad del futuro en cuanto a:
- la vivienda
- los medios de transporte
- el comercio / las compras
- la seguridad?

¿Qué cambios habrá en nuestras vidas en cuanto a:
- la familia
- la alimentación
- el ocio
- el trabajo?

Discuss your views with a partner. Do you agree in your visions of the future?

7 The conditional

Text 1

The article which follows looks at the future of mankind and the division of human beings into two species. The main grammatical point in this and in Text 2 below is the conditional tense, usually associated with *would* in English.

El futuro de la raza humana

Al igual que las dos especies humanas que el escritor H.G. Wells describe en su novela *La máquina del tiempo*, nuestra raza **podría** dividirse en dos subespecies dentro de 100 mil años. Así lo cree el teórico de la evolución del London School of Economics Oliver Curry quien, tras analizar diversos escenarios, proyectó los cambios que **afectarían** al hombre en el futuro.

Según explicó, la evolución de nuestra apariencia física **estaría** guiada por factores como la "mayor selectividad a la hora de elegir pareja" y la "excesiva dependencia tecnológica," que **degradaría** algunas capacidades del hombre.

El momento cumbre para la raza humana **llegaría** dentro de mil años, cuando la ciencia y la tecnología tengan el potencial de crear un hábitat ideal para la humanidad. Curry explica que "la mejor dieta y nutrición **haría** que la población sea más alta, superando los dos metros de estatura como promedio. También alcanzaremos los 120 años de vida." La ingeniería genética, implantes cibernéticos y avances tecnológicos nos **convertirían** en seres casi perfectos.

Pero, tras este auge **podría** llegar la degradación. La excesiva dependencia de la tecnología y los avances en medicina **reducirían** la habilidad natural del hombre para luchar contra enfermedades o, incluso, la capacidad para llevarse bien con los demás.

Finalmente, en el curso de los próximos 100 mil años, los humanos **se volverían** más selectivos a la hora de elegir pareja, provocando que la especie se divida en dos subespecies, una clase alta genética de hombres altos, delgados, sanos, atractivos, inteligentes y creativos. En contraste **existiría** una subclase humana más bien "tonta, fea y parecida a los duendes."

Diario *La Tercera*, Chile

Text 2

On an entirely different theme, Text 2 considers the damage caused by civilisation to the Earth's forests.

Nos estamos fumando el planeta

La Tierra ha perdido casi la mitad de sus bosques en los últimos 10.000 años, el tiempo que hace que el hombre aprendió a cultivar y dejó de recolectar su alimento. Entonces nacieron la agricultura y la ganadería, consideradas por los antropólogos como las llaves que pusieron en marcha el motor de la civilización.

A partir de ese momento, el ser humano **comprobaría** que era capaz de transformar su entorno. Fue un primer paso que lo **diferenciaría** para siempre del resto de los animales, pero que también **iniciaría** el camino hacia la deforestación. La agricultura no sólo mejoró su dieta y su esperanza de vida. De paso, también cambió su forma de vivir proporcionándole más tiempo para actividades que **incrementarían** su calidad de vida.

Esa situación **favorecería** la aparición de la artesanía – germen de la futura industria – que, junto a la cultura, **acabaría** por poner en marcha un aumento demográfico que no iba a retroceder jamás y que **sería** imparable. De los cinco o diez millones de habitantes que los biólogos calculan que había hace 10.000 años, el planeta ha pasado a acoger a toda una población de cerca de 6.000 millones de seres humanos estimados en la actualidad.

Revista *CNR*, España

The conditional

1 USAGE

a Like the English *would*, in *I would do it, but I can't*, the Spanish conditional is used for expressing conditions.

... los cambios que **afectarían** al hombre en el futuro. (T. 1, l. 9–10) *... the changes that would affect mankind in the future.*

... nuestra apariencia física **estaría** guiada por ... (T. 1, l. 11–12) *... our physical appearance would be determined by ...*

El momento cumbre para la raza humana **llegaría** dentro de mil años ... (T. 1, l. 18–19) *The culminating moment for the human race would come within a thousand years ...*

... los humanos **se volverían** más selectivos ... (T. 1, l. 38–39) *... humans would become more selective ...*

b To express the future in the past.
This use of the conditional is common in journalistic style. Text 2 is a good example, where all the forms of the conditional correspond to this usage.

A partir de ese momento, el ser humano **comprobaría . . .** (T. 2, l. 10–11) *From that moment onwards human beings were to discover . . .*
Esa situación **favorecería . . .** (T. 2, l. 22) *That situation was to favour . . .*
. . . **sería** imparable (T. 2, l. 27) *. . . it was to be unstoppable.*

Another context for this use of the conditional is indirect speech.

Dijeron que este verano **irían** a Los Ángeles. *They said this summer they'd go to Los Angeles.*
Álvaro me prometió que me **escribiría**, pero no lo hizo. *Alvaro promised me he would write to me, but he didn't.*

The original statements in the examples above might be:

'Este verano **iremos** a Los Ángeles.' '(Te prometo que) te **escribiré**.'

c With modal verbs like **deber**, **poder**.

. . . nuestra raza **podría** dividirse en dos subespecies . . . (T. 1, l. 3–4) *. . . the human race might become divided into two subspecies . . .*
No **debería** suceder. *It shouldn't happen.*

d For politeness, in sentences like the following:

¿Te **importaría** cerrar la ventana? *Would you mind closing the window?*
¿Le **molestaría** que lo deje aquí? *Would you mind if I leave it here?*
¿Me **harías** un favor? *Would you do me a favour?*

e To express supposition and uncertainty with regard to something in the past.

En aquel tiempo él **tendría** veinte años. *At that time he must have been twenty.*
Serían las dos cuando ocurrió. *It could have been two o'clock when it happened.*
¿Lo **sabría** Julia? *I wonder whether Julia knew about it.*

2 FORMATION

Regular verbs

As with the future tense, the conditional is formed with the whole infinitive, to which the endings are added. The endings, which are those of the imperfect tense of **-er** and **-ir** verbs (**-ía**), are the same for **-ar**, **-er** and **-ir** verbs. Here are three examples:

estar *to be*	estar**ía**, estar**ías**, estar**ía**, estar**íamos**, estar**íais**, estar**ían**
ser *to be*	ser**ía**, ser**ías**, ser**ía**, ser**íamos**, ser**íais**, ser**ían**
vivir *to live*	vivir**ía**, vivir**ías**, vivir**ía**, vivir**íamos**, vivir**íais**, vivir**ían**

La tierra **estaría** habitada por dos subespecies. *The earth would be inhabited by two subspecies.*
Los seres humanos **serían** casi perfectos. *Human beings would be almost perfect.*
Viviríamos hasta los 120 años. *We would live to 120.*

Irregular verbs

Some verbs, like **hacer** *to do, make,* and **poder** *to be able to, can,* have the same irregular stem in the conditional as in the future tense (Chapter 6), but the endings are the same as those of regular verbs. Note the following examples in Text 1:

Pero, tras este auge **podría** llegar la degradación. (T. 1, l. 30–31) *But after this peak there might come a decline.*

. . . la mejor dieta y nutrición **haría** que la población sea más alta . . . (T. 1, l. 22–24) *. . . a better diet and nutrition would result in a taller population . . .*

The following are the most common irregular conditional forms:

caber *to be contained* **cabría, cabrías** . . .	**querer** *to want* **querría, querrías** . . .
decir *to say, tell* **diría, dirías** . . .	**saber** *to know* **sabría, sabrías** . . .
haber *to have* (auxiliary) **habría, habrías** . . .	**salir** *to go out* **saldría, saldrías** . . .
hacer *to do, make* **haría, harías** . . .	**tener** *to have* **tendría, tendrías** . . .
poder *to be able to* **podría, podrías** . . .	**valer** *to be worth* **valdría, valdrías** . . .
poner *to put* **pondría, pondrías** . . .	**venir** *to come* **vendría, vendrías** . . .

Compound forms of the verbs above are irregular in the same way. For example:

proponer *to propose* **propondría, propondrías** . . .
detener *to detain* **detendría, detendrías** . . .

See also **Irregular verbs** on pages 279–282.

Other points to note in the texts

- Adjective agreement and position: Text 1: *las dos especies humanas* (l. 1), *diversos escenarios* (l. 8), *nuestra apariencia física* (l. 11–12), *excesiva dependencia tecnológica* (l. 14–15), *el momento cumbre* (l. 18), etc. Text 2: *los últimos 10.000 años* (l. 2–3), *un primer paso* (l. 12–13), *la futura industria* (l. 24), etc. (see Chapter 20)
- Adverbs: Text 1: *Así* (l. 5), *cuando* (l. 20), *como* (l. 25), *casi* (l. 29), *incluso* (l. 35), etc. Text 2: *casi* (l. 1), *Entonces* (l. 5), *siempre* (l. 13), *también* (l. 15), *jamás* (l. 27), etc. (see Chapter 21)
- Definite article: There are numerous examples of the use of the definite article in the texts, among these the following: Text 1: *las dos especies humanas* (l. 1), *el teórico* (l. 5–6), *la evolución* (l. 6), *los cambios* (l. 9), *los 120 años de vida* (l. 26–27), etc. Text 2: *la Tierra* (l. 1), *la mitad* (l. 1), *los últimos 10.000 años* (l. 2–3), *la agricultura y la ganadería* (l. 5–6), etc. (see Chapter 18)
- Preterite tense: Text 2: *dejó* (l. 4), *nacieron* (l. 5), *pusieron* (l. 8), *Fue* (l. 12), *mejoró* (l. 17), *cambió* (l. 18) (see Chapter 2)

EXERCISES

1 Make these requests sound more polite by changing the verb to the conditional form.

a ¿Puedes pasarme el agua?
b ¿Puedo hablar con la señorita Blanco?
c ¿Me hace el favor de subir el equipaje?
d ¿Le importa esperar un momento?
e ¿Puede decirme dónde está Correos?
f ¿Me permiten explicarles el problema?

2 Use the conditional to rewrite and express the supposition or probability in these sentences.

a Probablemente eran las once de la noche cuando entraron.
b Seguramente compraba la ropa en el Rastro.
c Probablemente había como mil personas en la manifestación.
d Seguramente eran jóvenes los que lo hacían.
e Seguro que al anciano le dolía la pierna, por su modo de andar.

3 When the first phase of the International Space Station was launched, a spokesperson gave out the following information.

a 16 países participarán en el proyecto que costará más de 200.000 millones de dólares.
b Un español tomará parte en la misión.
c La estación espacial medirá lo equivalente a dos campos de fútbol y será un enorme laboratorio en el que vivirán y trabajarán siete astronautas.
d Su labor pondrá al alcance del hombre la exploración de Marte y también por medio de sus investigaciones encontraremos vida más allá de nuestro planeta.

Use the conditional to turn what the spokesperson said into indirect speech, beginning each point in the following way:

a Dijo que . . .
b Aseguró que . . .
c Afirmó que . . .
d Añadió que . . .

4 Rewrite these sentences putting the first verb in brackets into a past tense and the subsequent verb(s) into the conditional form.

a Pedro (estar) ________ seguro de que sus padres no le (dejar) ________ salir esa noche.
b Pilar (saber) ________ muy bien que Joaquín se lo (contar) ________ todo a su novio.
c Marta me (prometer) ________ que (venir) ________ a tiempo y que (traer) ________ su carné de conducir.
d Nos (advertir, ellos) ________ de que nos (poner) ________ pegas y así ha sido.
e El profesor les (explicar) ________ a los estudiantes que (tener) ________ que hacer otra evaluación.
f Los técnicos (decir) ________ que no (tardar) ________ en hacer los análisis.

5 This extract is taken from a longer article profiling the modern Spanish male. Put the verbs below into the third person singular of the conditional and insert them into the text in the order given.

(**a**) **volver** (**b**) **comprender** (**c**) **asombrarse** (**d**) **sufrir** (**e**) **llegar**

Si el bisabuelo de cualquier nuevo español levantara la cabeza es seguro que, a fuerza de sobresaltos, (**a**) ________ a postrarla eternamente. No (**b**) ________ el comportamiento en casa del bisnieto varón, distribuyéndose, más o menos a la par, las tareas domésticas con la mujer. (**c**) ________ ante el afán de su descendiente por trabajar, por hacer dinero y gastar, que es la religión consumista del tiempo presente.

El bisabuelo (**d**) ________ el definitivo impacto mortal al contemplar, por ejemplo, el culto al cuerpo de su bisnieto, el armario lleno de ropas con colores de dudosa hombría, las colonias para oler bien, los aceites para poner tersa la piel, las lámparas de rayos para mantener un sempiterno bronceado . . . En fin, (**e**) ________ a la conclusión de que España había degenerado y caído en un relajamiento afeminado de las buenas costumbres.

Revista *Tiempo*, España

6 How would our great-grandparents react to our lives today? What changes would they notice and make to their lives to adapt to today's world?

Discuss with a partner or write down your thoughts using the conditional tense to express what they would do.

7 Text 2 suggests that evolutionary forces will make us all taller. Answer the following question using the conditional tense to express your ideas.

¿Cómo cambiaría tu vida si fueras más alto/a: qué cosas podrías hacer que ahora no puedes y vice versa?

8 In what way would your life change if you lived in your ideal world?

- ¿Dónde vivirías?
- ¿A qué te dedicarías?
- ¿Adónde irías de vacaciones?

Consider these questions and add more to discuss with a partner, and/or write an account of what changes your ideal world would bring to your life.

For more practice using the conditional in 'if' constructions, see Chapters 15 and 16.

8 | The infinitive

Text

The article which follows gives general guidelines on how to get fit in 30 days. You may be unfamiliar with some of the words in the text, so try to get the gist of what it says in your first reading, then go back through it, looking up some of the new words. Finally, read it again paying attention to the grammar and the ways in which infinitives have been used.

Cómo ponerse en forma en 30 días

Antes de **iniciar** un plan regular de entrenamiento, hay que **tener** en cuenta la condición física de la que partimos. Obviamente no puede **hacerlo** de la misma manera una persona que nunca ha hecho ejercicio que otra habituada a **hacer** deporte. Es imposible **compensar** en 30 días lo que no se ha hecho en toda la vida. Lo esencial es **tener** un buen estado de salud, **comenzar** con sesiones de baja intensidad, **ir** aumentando progresivamente los ejercicios y, una vez finalizado el plan, **seguir** practicando ejercicio regularmente. La regularidad es el secreto de la forma física. La duración más recomendable debe **ser** de entre 20 y 30 minutos de ejercicio aeróbico, dado que las sesiones de menor duración no suponen una mejora de la forma física. En cuanto a la intensidad, es muy importante **hacer** el ejercicio de tal manera que nos permita **completar** la sesión de entrenamiento. Si nos cansamos pronto, la solución no es otra que **hacerlo** más despacio. Entre las recomendaciones que hacen los expertos está el **mantener**, al **comenzar** un programa de entrenamiento, un nivel de ejercicio aeróbico, es decir, a una intensidad en que la energía para el trabajo realizado se obtenga en mayor proporción de la respiración. Una buena manera de **controlar** que se mantiene un ritmo adecuado consiste en que el ejercicio nos haga **sudar**, pero nos permita **hablar** al mismo tiempo. **Entrenar** muy intensamente – sobre todo durante las primeras sesiones – tendrá más inconvenientes que ventajas, ya que existe un mayor

(*Continued*)

45 riesgo de lesiones, cansancio crónico y disminución del rendimiento en el trabajo o en los estudios, lo que nos puede **conducir** a **abandonar** el deporte. Antes de **comenzar** a practicar
50 cualquier deporte es recomendable **someterse** a un reconocimiento médico para **comprobar** que estás en perfecto estado físico. La práctica deportiva, de manera especial para
55 aquellas personas que no están excesivamente habituadas, obliga a un esfuerzo que puede **causar** serios inconvenientes en organismos con algún tipo de problema físico. Los
60 resultados de las pruebas médicas nos ayudarán a **determinar** la forma, la cantidad y la intensidad de la actividad deportiva que tenemos la intención de **practicar**.

Revista *Quo*, España

The infinitive

1 USAGE

The infinitive is the full form or 'dictionary' form of the verb, which in Spanish is expressed by a single word ending in **-ar**, **-er** or **-ir** (e.g. **hablar**, **comer**, **vivir**). In English, this is made up of two words, *to* + verb (e.g. *to speak*). There are a number of infinitives in the text, but their usage varies, as you will see from the notes below. Extra examples have been given in order to illustrate points not found in the article.

a As a noun, sometimes preceded by **el**, the masculine singular form of the definite article. Note here the use of the *-ing* form in English for the Spanish infinitive.

Entre las recomendaciones . . . está **el mantener** . . . (l. 28–30) *Among the recommendations . . . is maintaining . . .*
Entrenar muy intensamente (l. 43) *Training very intensively . . .*

b After prepositions and prepositional phrases.

Antes de iniciar un plan . . . (l. 1) *Before starting a programme . . .*
. . . **para comprobar** . . . (l. 52) *. . . in order to check . . .*

Similarly, **a hacer** (l. 7), **de controlar** (l. 37), **de practicar** (l. 63–64).
Note again the use of the *-ing* form in English to translate most of these examples.

c After modal verbs such as **poder** *to be able*, *can*, *may*, **deber** *must*, **tener que** *to have to*, **haber que** *to be necessary* (Chapter 10).

. . . **hay que tener** en cuenta la condición física . . . (l. 2–3) *. . . it's necessary to take into account the physical condition . . .*
. . . **debe ser** de entre 20 y 30 minutos . . . (l. 18–19) *. . . it must be between 20 and 30 minutes . . .*
. . . **puede causar** . . . (l. 57) *. . . it may cause . . .*

d After a number of verbs, many of which may require a preposition.

> . . . consiste en que el ejercicio nos **haga sudar**, pero nos **permita hablar** . . . (l. 38–40)
> *. . . it consists of the exercise making us sweat, but allowing us to speak . . .*
> . . . nos **ayudarán a determinar** . . . (l. 60–61) *. . . they'll allow us to determine . . .*

Note, however, that with the exception of a few verbs (e.g. **permitir** *to allow*, **prohibir** *to forbid*, **ordenar**, **mandar**, *to order*) the infinitive cannot be used when the subject of the first verb is different from that of the second verb. In this case you need the construction **que** + subjunctive. Compare: **Conseguí hacerlo** *I managed to do it*, **Conseguí que lo hiciera** *I got him/her to do it* (see Chapters 14 and 15).

e After adjectives, in phrases such as **es imposible** *it's impossible*, **es importante** *it's important*, **es difícil** *it's difficult*, **parece fácil** *it seems easy*, **resulta caro** *it's expensive.*

> **Es imposible compensar** en 30 días . . . (l. 8) *It's impossible to make up in 30 days . . .*
> . . . **es muy importante hacer** el ejercicio . . . (l. 23–24) *. . . it's very important to do the exercise . . .*

f Preceded by **al**, usually expressed in English with ***on*** + ***-ing***.

> . . . **al comenzar** un programa . . . (l. 30–31) *. . . on starting a programme . . .*

g After **ver** *to see*, and **oír** *to hear.*

> Los **vi salir** hace un rato. *I saw them go out a while ago.*
> Jamás la **he oído cantar**. *I've never heard her sing.*

h After verbs which express some kind of feeling, when the subject of both verbs is the same.

> **Siento llegar** tarde. *I'm sorry to be late.*
> **Temo** no **ser** capaz. *I'm afraid not to be able.*

If the subjects are different, you must use the subjunctive:

> Siento que él no **esté** aquí. *I'm sorry he's not here.*
> Temo que no **vengan**. *I'm afraid they may not come.*

i In place of the imperative for giving directions and instructions.

> **Seguir** hasta el próximo semáforo. *Continue as far as the next traffic lights.*
> No **adelantar**. *Do not overtake.*

j As an informal command or exhortation, often preceded by the preposition **a**.

> ¡**Dejar** todo aquí! *Leave everything here!*
> ¡**A levantarse**! Es muy tarde. *Get up/Let's get up! It's very late.*
> Y ahora, ¡**a callarse**! *And now, keep quiet/let's keep quiet!*

k Preceded by **de**, to express conditions.

> **De ser** así tendremos que decírselo. *If it's like that we'll have to tell him/her.*
> **De haberlo** sabido lo hubiese comprado. *If I had known I would have bought it.*

Other points to note in the text

- Modal verbs: *hay que tener* (l. 2), *no puede hacerlo* (l. 4–5), *debe ser* (l. 18), *nos puede conducir* (l. 47–48), *puede causar* (l. 57) (see Chapter 10)
- Adjective agreement and position: *un plan regular* (l. 1), *la condición física* (l. 3), *la misma manera* (l. 5), *un buen estado* (l. 10), *baja intensidad* (l. 12), etc. (see Chapter 20)
- Adverbs: *obviamente* (l. 4), *nunca* (l. 6), *progresivamente* (l. 13), *regularmente* (l. 15), *pronto* (l. 27), *despacio* (l. 28), etc. (see Chapter 21)

EXERCISES

1 Make a sentence from the two parts using the preposition in brackets and making any necessary changes. Then translate the sentences into English.

Example: Salió del cuarto – no hizo ruido. (sin)
Salió del cuarto sin hacer ruido. (*S/he went out of the room without making a noise.*)

a Fueron a Salamanca – aprendieron español. (para)
b Estoy aquí – no hago nada. (sin)
c Entró en el salón – encendió la luz. (al)
d Primero cenamos – luego salimos. (después de)
e Llegaron – llamaron a sus amigos. (al)
f Se fue – no dijo nada. (sin)
g Iniciaron el programa – primero acudieron al médico. (antes de)
h Marta compró media docena de huevos – hizo una tortilla. (para)
i Primero visitaron el castillo – luego compraron recuerdos. (después de)
j Habló con Juan – primero leyó la carta. (antes de)

2 Put these words into the correct order to make meaningful sentences.

a poder • no • ayudarte • siento.
b a • espera • Madrid • ir.
c con • Inés • seguir • no • los • quiso • ejercicios.
d ejercicio • es • hacer • importante • muy.
e escuchar • aprender • que • hay • para.
f ir • porque • no • al • tengo • gimnasio • puedo • trabajar • que.
g ponerse • imposible • sin • es • ejercicio • en forma • hacer.
h comprar • para • coche • quieren • España • a • un • ir.
i bajó • aceite • a • supermercado • al • Marta • comprar
j tener • poder • Ignacio • debe • tanto • mucho • soportar • aguante • para

3 Translate into Spanish – take care to use the infinitive with or without a preposition where necessary.

- **a** As they went in, they began singing.
- **b** I heard them singing.
- **c** The best thing about living here is being able to go to the theatre.
- **d** The worst thing about living in the metropolis is being so far from the countryside.
- **e** Life in the country is opening the window and seeing, hearing and smelling Nature.
- **f** Going to the gym is a good way of getting fit.
- **g** She is incapable of giving up smoking.
- **h** He denies having helped the thieves.
- **i** Being able to talk to her daughter is her only consolation.
- **j** They got bored doing the same thing over and over again.

4 Put these hostel rules into Spanish using the infinitive.

- **a** No smoking.
- **b** Do not use.
- **c** No showers before 7 o'clock.
- **d** Do not leave clothes in the changing rooms.
- **e** Put the lights out before midnight.
- **f** Clear the table after eating.
- **g** Wash up.
- **h** Beds must be made on arrival.

9 The gerund

Text

This article considers the main reasons for the *greenhouse effect* and its consequences. The grammar focuses on the use of verb forms such as **incrementando** *increasing*, **produciendo** *producing*, which are known as gerunds. Read the text and note how these have been used.

El efecto invernadero

La principal causa del *efecto invernadero* es la acción del hombre. Desde los inicios de la Revolución Industrial, a finales del siglo XVIII, se han estado **produciendo** y **liberando** millones de toneladas de gases y partículas, parte de las cuales se han ido **acumulando** en la atmósfera que rodea el planeta, **agudizando** así el llamado *efecto invernadero*.

Es la atmósfera que recubre el planeta la que permite la existencia de formas superiores de vida en la Tierra merced a una doble acción: por un lado, filtra aquella parte de los rayos solares que son dañinos para las formas vivas, **impidiendo** que lleguen hasta la superficie; por el otro, evita que los rayos del sol reboten en la corteza terrestre y se pierdan en el espacio. Gracias a la atmósfera, hasta 60 por 100 de la energía solar que llega a la Tierra queda atrapada aquí, **elevando** así la temperatura media del planeta del mismo modo que lo hacen los vidrios o los plásticos transparentes dentro de un invernadero.

Si no fuera por la atmósfera, la Tierra sería un gigantesco sorbete de hielo, con una temperatura media inferior en 33 grados centígrados a la temperatura media actual, donde sólo formas de vida muy simples y primitivas podrían existir.

Pero toneladas y toneladas de gases y partículas producidas por la quema de combustibles fósiles, incendios de bosques y otras fuentes de contaminación lanzadas a la atmósfera están **incrementando** notablemente el *efecto invernadero* **ocasionando** el recalentamiento generalizado, que ya se ha producido y seguirá **produciéndose** en los años sucesivos.

Revista *Tiempo*, España

The gerund

1 USAGE

Verb forms such as **hablando** *speaking*, **comiendo** *eating*, **saliendo** *going out*, are known as ***gerunds***. Some of the uses of the gerund correspond to that of the *-ing* verb form in English, while others are different.

a The gerund may function as a kind of adverb to refer to:

i An action which is simultaneous with or complementary to the action expressed by the main verb.

. . . se han ido **acumulando** . . . **agudizando** así . . . (l. 8–9) *. . . they have been building up . . . thus worsening . . .*

. . . filtra . . . los rayos solares . . . **impidiendo** que . . . (l. 15–17) *. . . it filters the sun's rays . . . preventing them from . . .*

ii Cause.

Viendo que era tan tarde, decidí irme. (Como era tan tarde . . .) *Seeing that it was so late, I decided to leave.*

iii Manner.

Se acercó a mí **sonriendo**. (con una sonrisa) *He/she approached me smiling.*

iv A condition.

Trabajando así llegarás muy lejos. (Si trabajas así . . .) *Working like that, you'll go far.*

v Concession.

Insistió en hacerlo, **sabiendo** lo difícil que era. (aunque sabía . . .) *He/she insisted on doing it, knowing how difficult it was.*

b With **estar**, in the continuous tenses.

. . . se han **estado produciendo** y **liberando** . . . (l. 5–6) *. . . they are being produced and released . . .*

. . . **están incrementando** . . . (l. 40) *. . . they are increasing . . .*

c With **ir**, to indicate that the action expressed by the verb occurs gradually.

. . . se han **ido acumulando** . . . (l. 8) *. . . they have been accumulating . . .*

d With **seguir** and **continuar** to denote continuity.

. . . **seguirá** (or **continuará**) **produciéndose** . . . (l. 43–44) *. . . it will continue occurring . . .*

e With **venir**, to denote duration or repetition.

Esto **viene pasando** desde hace mucho tiempo. *This has been going on for a long time.*

f With **acabar** and **terminar** to indicate a result.

Acabaron/Terminaron divorciándose. *They ended up getting divorced.*

g With **llevar** and an expression of time, to express continuity.

Llevo dos años viviendo aquí. *I have been living here for two years.*

h With **quedarse**, to indicate duration in the action expressed by the verb.

Se quedó mirándome fijamente. *He/she carried on staring at me.*

i With **andar**, to express the idea of going around doing something.

Anda buscando trabajo. *He/she's (going round) looking for work.*

SPANISH GERUND AND ENGLISH *-ING*: DIFFERENCES

There are important differences in use between the Spanish gerund and the English *-ing* form:

a The Spanish equivalent of the English *-ing* form used as a noun is normally the infinitive.

Telling him will not help at all. El **decírselo** no ayudará en nada.

b The Spanish gerund is not normally used as an adjective.

A swimming costume. Un traje de baño.
The falling leaves. Las hojas que caen.

c After a preposition, Spanish uses the infinitive, not the gerund (see Chapter 8).

After having lunch . . . Después de **haber** almorzado . . .
She left without saying goodbye. Se fue sin **despedirse**.

d Actions involving different subjects, often expressed with *-ing* in English, require different constructions in Spanish.

I love being sent flowers. Me encanta que me manden flores.
We like her dancing. Nos gusta su forma de bailar.

e Different actions performed by a single subject are usually expressed in Spanish with an infinitive, not with the gerund.

I hate going to bed late. Odio **acostarme** tarde.
We enjoy taking a walk in the evening. Nos agrada **salir** de paseo por la tarde.

2 FORMATION

To form the gerund, remove the ending of the infinitive and add **-ando** to the stem of **-ar** verbs and **-iendo** to that of **-er** and **-ir** verbs, e.g. **habl*ando***, **com*iendo***, **viv*iendo***. A few verbs form the gerund in a slightly different way:

a **-iendo** becomes **-yendo** when the stem of the verb ends in a vowel. Common examples are: **caer** – **cayendo** (*to fall – falling*), **creer** – **creyendo** (*to believe – believing*), **leer** – **leyendo** (*to read – reading*), **oír** – **oyendo** (*to hear – hearing*). The gerund of **ir** is **yendo**.

b Most verbs in **-ir**, which change the stem in the third person of the preterite, have a similar change in the gerund. Among them we find the following:

Infinitive	*3rd persons, preterite*	*gerund*	
dormir	**durmió, durmieron**	**durmiendo**	*sleeping*
morir	**murió, murieron**	**muriendo**	*dying*
pedir	**pidió, pidieron**	**pidiendo**	*asking for*
sentir	**sintió, sintieron**	**sintiendo**	*feeling*
venir	**vino, vinieron**	**viniendo**	*coming*

c The gerund of **decir** is **diciendo**, *saying*, and that of **poder** is **pudiendo**, *being able to.*

d The gerund has a past form made up of the gerund of **haber** and the past participle, e.g. **habiendo terminado**, *having finished.*

POSITION OF PRONOUNS WITH THE GERUND

Pronouns are normally added to the gerund, unless this is preceded by a finite verb, in which case the pronoun can either go before the finite verb or be attached to the end of the gerund. If the pronoun is added to the gerund, you need to place a written accent on the **a** in **-ando** or the **e** in **-iendo**.

Viéndola así, preferí no hablarle. *Seeing her like that, I preferred not to speak to her.*
Estoy **terminándolo** *or* Lo estoy **terminando**. *I am finishing it.*

Other points to note in the text

- Relative pronouns: *las cuales* (l. 7), *que* (l. 9 and 11), *la que* (l. 12) (see Chapter 26)
- *Por* and *para*: *por un lado . . . por el otro* (l. 14–18), *para las formas* (l. 16), *si no fuera por* (l. 28), *producidas por* (l. 36) (see Chapter 28)
- Subjunctive, present and imperfect: *impidiendo que lleguen* (l. 17), *evita que . . . reboten . . . y se pierdan* (l. 18–19), *si no fuera por* (l. 28) (see Chapters 14 and 15)

EXERCISES

1 Choose a verb from the list and put it into the gerund form to complete the sentences.

usar **dormir** **estudiar** **sustituir** **bailar** **trabajar** **correr** **viajar**

a – ¿Los niños están en el jardín?
– No, están en su cuarto, ________.

b – ¿Cómo va a pasar el verano Rosario?
– ________ en un bar.

c – ¿Qué le dijiste al policía?
– Que vi a dos jóvenes que salieron ________ de la tienda.

d – ¿Cómo puedo ahorrar energía?
– ________ estas bombillas por unas de bajo consumo.

e – Y ¿cómo puedo ahorrar agua?
– ________ la ducha en lugar de la bañera.

f – ¿Y Margarita?
– ________ tangos con Ernesto.

g – ¿Por qué hizo tal viaje?
– Porque ________ a la luna tendría experiencias únicas.

h – ¿Cómo conseguiste notas tan buenas?
– ________.

2 Put the verb in brackets into the correct form of the continuous tense.

a – ¿Por qué no vinieron tus amigos?
– Porque (trabajar) ________.

b – ¿Se puede hablar con la señora Calvo?
– En este momento (atender) ________ a un cliente.

c – ¿Qué pasa?
– No sé. (seguir, nosotros) ________ las instrucciones y de repente la máquina estalló.

d – ¿Fuisteis a esquiar el fin de semana?
– Sí, pero la nieve (derretirse) ________.

e – ¿Llegamos tarde?
– Bueno, un poco; ya (servir, ellos) ________ la cena.

f – ¿Has visto a Esteban y su familia últimamente?
– Los vi en agosto; (prepararse, ellos) ________ para la mudanza.

g – ¿Qué hacéis ahora?
– Nada. (Descansar) ________.

h – ¿Por qué has puesto esa cara?
– (Reírse, ellos) ________ de mí.

i – ¿Has entregado el informe?
– Sí, pero (beber) ________ café toda la noche para terminarlo.

j – ¿Y Teresa?
– Todavía (vestirse) ________.

k – ¿Nos vamos ya?
– Espera un momentito; (ponerse, yo) ________ las botas.

l – ¿Has visto las nuevas urbanizaciones?
– Sí, (construir, ellos) ________ casas por toda la costa.

3 Replace the underlined words with gerunds, making other adjustments where necessary.

a El Presidente salió al balcón y saludó a las masas.

b Si me escribes a esta dirección, la carta llegará.

c Al mismo tiempo que nos ayudas, aprenderás.
d Seguimos utilizando nuestros coches, aunque sabemos del daño que esto causa al entorno.
e Pasó la noche en el tren y leyó *La muerte de Artemio Cruz*.
f Mientras descansaba en el Pirineo, se olvidó de todos sus problemas.
g Encontró a su madre que lloraba.
h Si mientes así, no llegarás a ninguna parte.
i Al salir de casa, dimos con Alejandro y su mujer.
j Mientras caminaba todo le parecía más fácil.
k Va por la calle y al mismo tiempo escucha música.
l Solo si trabajas, realizarás tus sueños.

4 Form sentences from the constituent parts as in the example, then translate into English.

Example: Elvira • un año • reformar su casa.
Elvira lleva un año reformando su casa.
(*Elvira has been renovating her house for a year.*)

a Los agricultores • dos años • plantar bosques.
b Sofía • seis meses • ir al trabajo en autobús.
c Los oficinistas • año y medio • reciclar el papel.
d Nosotros • mucho tiempo • reducir nuestro consumo de electricidad.
e Los ecologistas • más de treinta años • crear conciencia sobre los peligros que corre el planeta.
f Carlos • seis años • enseñar francés en la Escuela de Idiomas.
g Los campesinos • siglos • cultivar estas tierras.
h Gloria • un año ya • investigar la desaparición de la abeja.
i Pepe • no mucho tiempo • vender relojes.
j Este grupo de jóvenes • varios años • ir a Guatemala de voluntarios.

5 Rewrite these sentences using the bracketed verb to make a gerund construction. Then study each one, thinking about the meaning.

a La suciedad se acumula en el fondo del mar. (estar)
b La situación mejora. (ir)
c Notamos un aumento del nivel del mar desde hace varios años. (venir)
d Según los ecologistas, el hombre destruirá el planeta. (acabar)
e El hombre contamina la atmósfera desde los inicios de la Revolución Industrial. (venir)
f Los municipios instalan contenedores específicos para los distintos tipos de basura. (estar)
g Los fabricantes de vidrio apoyarán el reciclado como una medida activa a favor del medio ambiente. (seguir)
h Poco a poco estamos cambiando nuestros hábitos al tirar la basura. (ir)
i Con el creciente número de viajes turísticos, se dañará la naturaleza de las Islas Galápagos. (acabar)

- **j** Si los glaciares y parte de los polos se derriten al mismo ritmo que ahora, el nivel del mar aumentará en las zonas costeras. (seguir)
- **k** El cambio climático se intensifica a medida que la contaminación recalienta el planeta. (estar)
- **l** Ya cambian de opinión los políticos ante todos los indicios y pronósticos. (ir)

6 Rewrite these sentences using **andar, ir, seguir, quedarse** or **venir** + gerund, according to which seems the most appropriate to the context.

- **a** Mi hermano dice a todo el mundo que soy tonta.
- **b** Poco a poco estamos aprendiendo.
- **c** Todavía estás fumando a pesar de lo que te ha dicho el médico.
- **d** Fernando y Javier buscan un apartamento.
- **e** Estuvimos charlando hasta altas horas de la noche.
- **f** Poco a poco estoy conociendo la ciudad.
- **g** Todavía tiramos la basura sin separarla.
- **h** Escribía todo lo que oía.
- **i** Ese alcalde busca excusas para justificar la corrupción.
- **j** Todavía piensan lo mismo a pesar de lo que acaban de ver.
- **k** Desde hacía tiempo, Pablo notaba un dolor sordo en la espalda.
- **l** Miramos los cuadros totalmente conmovidos.

7 Translate the English into Spanish to complete these sentences.

- **a** Por efecto del calentamiento global los polos *will end up melting.*
- **b** Muchos científicos desmienten el pésimo estado de salud de la Tierra, *accusing the environmentalists of sensationalism.*
- **c** Se sabe que si la emisión de gases de efecto invernadero no se limita, las temperaturas *will carry on increasing.*
- **d** Ahora tenemos que separar la basura, *depositing plastics and tins in one bag and throwing organic material into another bag.*
- **e** Las lavadoras de alta tecnología detectan automáticamente la cantidad y tipo de ropa a lavar, *consuming only the necessary water and electricity.*
- **f** *By recycling glass* se ahorra la materia prima con que se fabrica el cristal.
- **g** En las selvas tropicales la deforestación *is threatening the indigenous populations.*
- **h** En los más de 150 años que *temperatures have been recorded* los años más calurosos corresponden a los años más recientes.

See also Chapter 8, **The infinitive**, for ways that English *-ing* can be rendered in Spanish.
See Chapter 13, ***Ser* and *estar***, for more practice of the gerund with *estar*.

10 | Modal verbs

Text 1

A reader whose husband fainted due to stress wrote to a health magazine seeking advice. This letter, and Texts 2 and 3 below, contain several examples of modal verbs, such as **soler** *to be accustomed to*, **deber** *must*, **tener que** *to have to*, which are followed by an infinitive. Read the letters and study the ways in which they have been used.

El desmayo por estrés

Desde hace un mes mi marido tiene un nuevo trabajo que le exige mucho desgaste tanto físico como psicológico. Llega todas las noches cansado, y por la mañana ***suele levantarse*** *sin fuerzas, pero sigue adelante con todo. Hace una semana estábamos desayunando y de*
5 *repente, cuando* ***quiso pararse**** *se cayó. El médico dijo que fue un simple desmayo y que* ***se tenía que relajar***, *pero yo no quedé muy conforme con esta respuesta. ¿Me* ***podrían aclarar*** *qué fue lo que pasó y qué* ***debe hacer***?

Graciela Pérez, Revista *Buena Salud*, Argentina

* *Peninsular Spanish* **levantarse**.

Text 2

This text presents a letter from someone asking for advice on sunbeds.

Las conflictivas camas solares

Estoy muy asustada porque todo el invierno fui a la cama solar y hace un tiempo leí que era muy malo y que ***podía provocar*** *algunas enfermedades en la piel.* ***Quisiera saber*** *si esta información es real y qué opinan los médicos con respecto al tema de las camas solares.*
5 *Además, quisiera que me digan cuánto tiempo* ***se puede tomar*** *sol así y qué cuidados* ***hay que tener***.

Florencia Massini, Revista *Buena Salud*, Argentina

Text 3

The letter in Text 3 comes from a professional volleyball player seeking a second opinion about a medical condition.

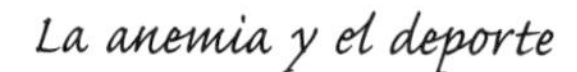
La anemia y el deporte

Soy deportista – juego al voleibol desde hace cinco años – y tengo una exigencia física muy grande porque ***suelo entrenar*** *todos los días dos horas y los fines de semana siempre* ***debo jugar*** *algún partido. Hace unos días me sentí muy mal, como si estuviera débil, y el médico*
5 *me dijo que* ***tenía que hacerme*** *un análisis de sangre y de orina. Allí salió que tenía los glóbulos rojos muy bajos y que me faltaba hierro (anemia). El médico me indicó que* ***debía seguir*** *un tratamiento muy completo de vitaminas y que no* ***podía hacer*** *deporte hasta que mi organismo se equilibrara. ¿Esto* ***debe ser*** *así? ¿No* ***puedo seguir***
10 *entrenando?*

Jorge Martínez, Revista *Buena Salud*, Argentina

Modal verbs

1 USAGE

Modal auxiliary verbs are used with the infinitive to express a certain intention or mood with regard to the accompanying infinitive. Below are the main Spanish modal verbs and their specific usage. Extra examples have been given to illustrate usage not found in the texts.

a **Soler** (**o** changes into **ue**) *to be accustomed to, usually*, is used for expressing habitual actions in relation to the present (in the present tense, see Chapter 1) or the past (in the imperfect tense, see Chapter 3), as an alternative to using the present and the imperfect. This modal verb is generally infrequent in Latin America.

. . . **suele levantarse** sin fuerzas. (T. 1, l. 3) (for **se levanta . . .**) *. . . he usually gets up without energy.*

. . . **suelo entrenar** todos los días dos horas . . . (T. 3, l. 2) *. . . I usually train for two hours every day . . .*

Solían visitarnos a menudo. (for **Nos visitaban . . .**) *They used to visit us often.*

b **Querer** (**e** changes into **ie**) normally translates *to want*, but depending on the context it can have other meanings as well. The forms **quisiera** and **querría** *I'd like*, are common in polite offers and requests, while the imperfect tense form **quería** *wanted to*, is also used in polite address. The preterite form **quiso** normally translates *tried to*.

. . . cuando **quiso pararse** se cayó. (T. 1, l. 5) *. . . when he tried to get up he fell.*

Quisiera (o **Quería**) **saber** si . . . (T. 2, l. 3) *I'd like to know if . . .*

c **Tener que** *to have to*, expresses obligation and strong need.

. . . **se tenía que relajar** . . . (T. 1, l. 6) *. . . he had to relax . . .*
. . . **tenía que hacerme** un análisis de sangre y de orina. (T. 3, l. 5) *. . . I had to have a blood and urine test.*

d **Poder** *to be able to, to manage, can, may*, is used to express:

i Requests which, when used in the conditional, convey more formality and politeness, the equivalent of *could you . . . ?* or *would you . . . ?* in English.

¿Me **podrían aclarar** . . . ? (T. 1, l. 7) *Could you explain . . . ?*

ii Possibility.

. . . **podía provocar** . . . (T. 2, l. 2) *. . . it could cause . . .*
. . . se **puede tomar** sol así . . . (T. 2, l. 5) *. . . one can sunbathe this way . . .*

Note the use of the imperfect in the first example. The conditional **podría** *could*, and the present form **puede** *can*, are equally valid in this context.

iii Allowing and prohibiting, usually translating *may* or *can* in English.

. . . me indicó . . . que no **podía hacer** deporte . . . (T. 3, l. 8) *. . . he told me . . . that I could not do any sport . . .*
¿No **puedo seguir** entrenando? (T. 3, l. 9–10) *Can't I go on training?*
¿**Podemos pasar?** *May we come in?*

iv Ability.

No **pude entenderle**. *I didn't manage to understand him/her.*

The use of the imperfect, No **podía entenderle**, would change the meaning of this sentence into *I couldn't understand him/her.*

e **Deber** *must, ought to, should*, expresses:

i Obligation.

¿ . . . qué **debe hacer**? (T. 1, l. 8) *. . . what must he do?*
. . . los fines de semana siempre **debo jugar** algún partido. (T. 3, l. 3) *. . . at weekends I must always play a game.*
. . . me indicó que **debía seguir** un tratamiento . . . (T. 3, l. 7) *. . . he told me that I should follow a course of treatment . . .*
¿Esto **debe ser** así? (T. 3, l. 9) *Must it be like that?*

Deber is often used in the conditional to mean '*should*' or '*ought to*'.

Deberías ver un médico. *You should/ought to see a doctor.*
Deberías ir con ella. *You ought to go with her.*
No **deberíamos vender** la casa. *We shouldn't sell the house.*

ii Supposition.
Strictly speaking, when expressing supposition, **deber** should be followed by the preposition **de.** Most Spanish speakers, however, will use it without **de.**

Deben (de) ser las seis. *It must be six o'clock.*
Debe (de) estar en casa. *He/she must be at home.*

f **Haber que** *to be necessary*, is an impersonal form, used in the third person singular.

... qué cuidados **hay que tener.** (T. 2, l. 6) *... what precautions it's necessary to take.*
Habrá que venderlo. *It'll be necessary to sell it.*

g **Haber de** *must, to have to*, indicates mild obligation, and is generally uncommon in colloquial speech in Spain. In México, it is used for expressing supposition.

Hemos de terminarlo hoy. (Obligation) *We have to finish it today.*
Ha de haber salido. (Supposition) *He/she must have gone out.*

h **Saber**, followed by the infinitive, means *to know how to.*

No **sé conducir/manejar.** (L. Am.) *I don't know how to drive.*

USING *QUERER* AND *PODER* WITH THE SUBJUNCTIVE

Note that **querer** and **poder** can also be followed by a subordinate clause introduced by **que**, with a verb in the subjunctive (see Chapters 14 and 15). This kind of construction occurs when the subject of the main verb is different from that of the subordinate clause.

... **quisiera que** me **digan** ... (T. 2, l. 5) *... I'd like you to tell me ...*
Puede que lleguen hoy. *It's possible that they may arrive today.*

SABER FOLLOWED BY *QUE*

Saber is followed by **que** when meaning *to know.*

Sé que me ayudarán. *I know they will help me.*

Other points to note in the texts

- Present tense indicative: Text 1: *tiene* (l. 1), *exige* (l. 1), *llega* (l. 2), *suele* (l. 3), *sigue* (l. 3), etc. Text 2: *estoy* (l. 1), *es* (l. 3), *opinan* (l. 4) (see Chapter 1)
- Preterite and imperfect tenses: Text 1: *estábamos desayunando* (l. 4), *cuando quiso pararse se cayó* (l. 5), *el médico dijo que fue* (l. 5), *que se tenía que relajar* (l. 6), etc. Text 2: *fui a la cama* (l. 1), *leí que era malo* (l. 2), *que podía provocar* (l. 2). Text 3: *me sentí muy mal* (l. 4), *me dijo que tenía que hacerme un análisis* (l. 5), *me indicó que debía seguir un tratamiento* (l. 7), etc. (see Chapters 2 and 3)

- *Ser* and *estar*: Text 1: *estábamos desayunando* (l. 4), *fue un simple desmayo* (l. 5–6), *¿qué fue lo que pasó?* (l. 7–8). Text 2: *estoy muy asustada* (l. 1), *era muy malo* (l. 2), *si . . . es real* (l. 3). Text 3: *soy deportista* (l. 1), *como si estuviera débil* (l. 4), *¿Esto debe ser así?* (l. 9) (see Chapter 13)

EXERCISES

1 Correct these sentences.

a Quiero voy a México de vacaciones.
b ¿Cuánto tiempo podemos nos quedamos aquí?
c Debéis habláis con Juan cuanto antes.
d ¿Quieres vienes conmigo?
e Debemos tomamos las cosas con calma.
f Todos los días suele hace dos horas de ejercicio.
g ¿Quién dice que Pepe sabe toca la guitarra?
h No queremos trabajamos más horas por menos dinero.
i Marta no puede sale esta noche.
j Solemos damos un paseo por la tarde antes de cenar.

2 Rewrite the following sentences using the verb **soler** or **deber** according to context.

a Normalmente juego un partido de ajedrez después de la cena.
b De costumbre los abuelos echaban la siesta después de comer.
c Es importante que no tomes el sol entre las dos y las seis.
d Por lo general vamos a la piscina dos veces por semana.
e ¿Por qué no pedís ayuda?
f Lo mejor es tomar una aspirina si te duele la cabeza.
g Generalmente tomábamos las vacaciones con los amigos.
h Jorge no sale; supongo que está estudiando.
i Por regla general entrenaba dos veces a la semana.
j Me imagino que está en plena forma con todo el ejercicio que hace.
k Según los expertos, es aconsejable que tomemos cinco porciones de fruta y verdura por día.
l Normalmente nos reunimos en la cafetería al salir del trabajo.

3 **Tener que/hay que/deber**. Complete the following sentences with the most appropriate verb for the context.

a El médico le dijo al marido de Graciela que ________ relajarse.
b ________ tener cuidado con las camas solares.
c No se ________ tomar el sol en exceso.
d Tengo hora con el médico dentro de diez minutos. ________ irme ahora mismo.
e Florencia no ________ usar la cama solar con tanta frecuencia.
f Para encontrar un buen trabajo ________ saber hablar otros idiomas.

g En este país ________ preocuparnos por aprender otros idiomas.

h María ________ estudiar mucho si quiere aprobar los exámenes; ________ estudiar al menos cinco horas diarias.

i ________ reservar mesa en el restaurante Buli con mucha antelación.

j El médico le ha dicho a Patricio que no ________ entrenar tanto.

k ________ darnos prisa; si no perderemos el tren.

l La entrada al museo es gratuita los miércoles; los otros días ________ pagar.

4 Complete the following text with the missing modal verbs **poder**, **deber**, **soler** and **hay que** in the correct forms.

El sol es bueno contra la depresión, favorece la producción de vitamina D y evita infecciones. Pero, tomado en exceso ________ provocar cáncer de piel, del que cada año se diagnostican 200.000 nuevos casos. (. . .) Para aprovechar sus virtudes sin sufrir sus perjuicios, ________ recordar que (. . .) no por tomar mucho el sol acostumbramos más a nuestra piel. "Los rayos de sol son acumulativos," explica la doctora Barbara Gilchrest, dermatóloga de la Universidad de Boston (Estados Unidos). Esto hace que vayan debilitando nuestro sistema defensivo, de modo que el exceso de radiación que proporcionamos al cuerpo ________ pasarnos factura años más tarde, cuando una lesión en la piel llegue incluso a degenerar en melanoma. "No ____ olvidar que ponerse moreno es un acto de defensa de la epidermis frente a la agresión de los rayos ultravioleta," añade la doctora. (. . .) Los problemas ________ aparecer en personas con piel clara que normalmente no toman el sol y que, de repente, lo hacen de manera intermitente e intensa. El mayor riesgo de aparición de melanoma se produce cuando la irradiación solar se recibe en la infancia. La exposición indiscriminada al sol en esta época de la vida ________ ser muy importante.

Revista *Quo*, España

5 Translate the following sentences into Spanish.

a Can you play the guitar?

b We usually spent the morning on the beach.

c Why have you got to go?

d If you want to sunbathe, you should use a good sun cream.

e It must not be forgotten that the sun's rays can be harmful.

f He used to work ten hours a day until the doctor told him that he had to relax.

g To travel on the AVE, you have to book your seats in advance.

h Pepe, you should pay more attention.

i Of course I know how to cook!

j We'll have to get up early tomorrow.

k Do you have to be a good cook to be able to make this dish?

l If you can drive, you could hire a car and travel round the island.

6 When on holiday, think of and write down:

- **a** a thing that you want to do
- **b** a thing that you can do
- **c** a thing that you usually do
- **d** a thing that you should do
- **e** a thing that you have to do
- **f** a thing that has to be done.

Compare and comment on your list with a partner.

7 Roberto Bolaño tells us in the Chapter 1 text that, although he and his wife have a child and share much of their lives, they live under separate roofs.

Write a list, or discuss with others in Spanish, the advantages and disadvantages of having a partner but not living together. Use modal verbs as far as is possible and appropriate.

11 | Passive and impersonal sentences

Text 1

Text 1 warns about the threat posed to coastal areas by population increase, industrial pollution and tourism. The grammar in this text and in Text 2 below focuses on passive sentences, expressed in English through the construction *to be* + the past participle, as in *It is done*, *They will be built*.

Alerta sobre alteración de costas del mundo

De acuerdo con los análisis efectuados por el Instituto Mundial de Recursos, cerca del 30% del territorio adyacente a los ecosistemas costeros del mundo **ha** 5 **sido alterado** o **destruido** debido principalmente a la creciente demanda por terrenos que luego **son destinados** a la construcción de casas, a la industria y a la recreación. Las poblaciones 10 costeras están aumentando y, a medida que se incrementan, la presión sobre los ecosistemas costeros también crece.

Se estima que más de 70 mil productos químicos sintéticos **han sido** 15 **descargados** en los océanos del mundo. Sólo un pequeño porcentaje de ellos **ha sido controlado**, y éste corresponde a aquéllos relacionados con salud humana y no con impacto 20 ecológico.

El organismo señala que, de continuar la permanente modificación o destrucción de esas áreas, **se pondrá** en grave peligro la capacidad de las 25 costas para mantener la biodiversidad, proveer pesca, hogares y negocios y reducir la polución y la erosión.

Diario *La Tercera*, Chile

Text 2

The article which follows looks at the destruction of the Amazon and outlines the plans being established by the Brazilian government to halt and revert the process of destruction.

Al rescate de la Amazonia

La Tierra pierde cada año 11,2 millones de hectáreas de bosque nativo. **Se estima** que cada dos segundos **se pierde** una superficie equivalente a una cancha de fútbol. En cuatro minutos **se habrán destruido** 90 hectáreas de árboles, lo que explica por qué sólo queda vivo el 22% de los bosques originarios del planeta.

La Amazonia no ha estado exenta de la destrucción en serie. El 80% de la madera que **se extrae** de esta zona **se corta** sin permiso. La contribución de los bosques amazónicos a la producción total de madera brasileña ha crecido en dos décadas del 14% al 85%.

Para rescatar esta región de características únicas, que posee el 10% de las especies del mundo, el gobierno de Brasil, con el apoyo del Banco Interamericano del Desarrollo, implementará un proyecto de ecoturismo que pretende el rescate económico, medio-ambiental y social de la región. **Se prevé** la construcción de 21 grandes obras de infraestructura, **se crearán** veinte parques y áreas de protección ambiental. También **se incluye** la capacitación de unos mil residentes que se encargarán de llevar adelante el plan y de recibir a los turistas internacionales. **Se construirán** puertos, ferrocarriles y aeropuertos.

Dentro del plan **se pretende** incluir a toda la comunidad para que los beneficios sean también sociales. Por ejemplo, en la ciudad Presidente Figueredo **se llevará a cabo** una remodelación de las instalaciones de agua potable y de alcantarillado.

Diario *El Metropolitano*, Chile

Passive and impersonal sentences

1 ACTIVE AND PASSIVE SENTENCES

Spanish, like English, has active and passive sentences. A sentence such as **El turismo ha destruido las zonas costeras** (*Tourism has destroyed coastal areas*) is an active sentence, with an active subject, **el turismo**, carrying out the action expressed by the verb.

In **Las zonas costeras han sido destruidas por el turismo** (*Coastal areas have been destroyed by tourism*), the direct object of the active sentence, **las zonas costeras**, has become the subject of what is a passive sentence. The agent performing the action, **el turismo**, occupies a secondary place in a phrase introduced by **por** *by*. The construction with **ser** *to be* + past participle here is similar to the one used in English.

Alternatively, you may use a sentence like **Se han destruido las zonas costeras** (*Coastal areas have been destroyed*), another type of passive sentence, much more common than the one above, introduced by **se**, in which the agent performing the action is not mentioned.

2 PASSIVE SENTENCES WITH *SER* + PAST PARTICIPLE

a The past participle must agree in gender (masculine and feminine) and number (singular or plural) with the noun it refers to.

> . . . cerca del 30% del territorio . . . **ha sido alterado** o **destruido** . . . (T. 1, l. 3–5) *. . . nearly 30% of the territory has been altered or destroyed . . .*
> . . . terrenos que . . . **son destinados** . . . (T. 1, l. 7) *. . . land which . . . is used . . .*

See also **han sido descargados** (T. 1, l. 14–15) *they have been dumped*, **ha sido controlado** (T. 1, l. 17) *it has been monitored.*

b The passive with **ser** is found more frequently in written language. It is uncommon in the spoken language, except in a very formal style, for example a formal speech.

c If the agent performing the action of the verb is important, and you wish to name it, then use the passive with **ser**, e.g. **Ha sido destruido por el hombre** *It has been destroyed by man.*

d English passive sentences such as *I was told he was here, She was asked why she'd done it*, cannot be expressed in Spanish with the construction **ser** + past participle. To convey these ideas use the impersonal third person plural **Me dijeron que** . . . , **Le preguntaron por qué** . . .

3 PASSIVE SENTENCES WITH *SE*

a The verb agrees in number (singular and plural) with the subject.

> . . . **se corta** sin permiso. (T. 2, l. 12–13) *. . . it is cut without permission.*
> **Se construirán** puertos . . . (T. 2, l. 32–33) *Ports will be built . . .*

See also **se habrán destruido** (T. 2, l. 6) *they will have been destroyed*, **se extrae** (T. 2, l. 12) *it is extracted*, **se crearán** (T. 2, l. 27) *they will be built*, **se incluye** (T. 2, l. 28–29) *it is included.*

b Passive sentences with **se** are common in all forms of language.

c Do not use this construction when the agent of the action expressed by the verb needs to be specified. Use the passive with **ser** instead, as in (**c**) above.

4 IMPERSONAL USE OF *SE*

Not all sentences with **se** are passive. **Se** is also used in impersonal sentences, the Spanish equivalent of *one/we/they/people*, ***on*** in French and ***man*** in German. In the text we find:

> . . . **se pretende** incluir . . . (T. 2, l. 35) *. . . they hope to include . . .*
> **Se estima** . . . (T. 1, l. 13; T. 2, l. 3) *It is estimated . . .*
> **Se prevé** . . . (T. 2, l. 25) *They are planning . . .*

For the use of **se** as an object pronoun in place of **le**, **les**, see Chapter 25. For the use of **se** with reflexive verbs, see Chapter 12.

5 OTHER IMPERSONAL SENTENCES

Impersonal sentences can also be formed by using one of the following devices:

a **Tú** form of the verb:

Tienes que estar muy alerta. *You have to/one has to be very alert.*

b Third person plural of the verb:

Dicen que el conflicto empeorará. *They say the conflict will get worse.*

c **Uno**

Uno tiene que estar muy seguro. *One has to be very sure.*

d **La gente**

La gente no sabe lo que dice. *People don't know what they say.*

Other points to note in the texts

- Future tense: Text 1: *pondrá* (l. 23). Text 2: *habrán* (l. 6), *implementará* (l. 22), *se crearán* (l. 27), *se encargarán* (l. 30), *se construirán* (l. 32–33), *se llevará a cabo* (l. 39) (see Chapter 6)
- Perfect tense: Text 1: *ha sido alterado* (l. 4–5), *han sido descargados* (l. 14–15), *ha sido controlado* (l. 20). Text 2: *no ha estado exenta* (l. 10), *ha crecido* (l. 14–15) (see Chapter 4)
- Prepositions: There are numerous prepositions in both texts, among these *de, con, por, a*, etc. (see Chapter 28)

EXERCISES

1 Change these sentences from passive to active constructions.

a *La Regenta* fue escrito por Leopoldo Alas.
b El camionero fue interrogado por el policía.
c Los cristales fueron rotos por los chicos.
d El motor ha sido desmontado por Agustín.
e El campeonato no será emitido por Tele-Mundo.
f Estas casas fueron construidas por mi padre.
g La casa de mis sueños será diseñada por mi hermano.
h Los árboles han sido cortados por los agricultores.
i Las fotos fueron tomadas por Fermín.
j Los informes han sido traducidos por una traductora jurada.

2 Change the verb in brackets into the passive form, **ser** with the past participle, to complete these sentences.

a Estos restos incaicos (excavar) ________ el año pasado por un equipo internacional de arqueólogos.

b Los pueblos (repoblar) ________ por familias jóvenes.
c Todos los datos (analizar) ________ antes de publicarlos.
d Mucha gente (invitar) ________ a la inauguración del nuevo teatro.
e Los robots (programar) ________ para tomar fotografías de la superficie de Marte.
f La manifestación del martes pasado (organizar) ________ por los estudiantes.
g La nueva ley (introducir) ________ tras una larga polémica.
h Cada verano grandes áreas de bosque (arrasar) ________ por incendios forestales.
i El gran poeta (encarcelar) ________ a causa de sus ensayos antigubernamentales.
j La película (rodar) ________ en blanco y negro.

3 Rewrite these sentences replacing the passive construction with **ser** with the past participle with **se**.

a La catedral fue construida en el siglo XV.
b Este libro no ha sido traducido al inglés.
c Las películas serán conservadas en cajas metálicas.
d Las estatuas fueron destruidas en el bombardeo.
e La noticia del accidente fue difundida por televisión.
f Los señores fueron convocados para el día veinticuatro.
g Tras la construcción de la autopista, muchos árboles han sido plantados.
h Sin embargo, no reemplazan los árboles que han sido talados.
i Cada vez más libros de la biblioteca son tirados y son triturados.
j Con la reestructuración, serán creados cuatro nuevos puestos de trabajo los cuales serán anunciados en el diario local.

4 Translate the following sentences into Spanish using the passive construction with **se**.

a Twenty parks and conservation areas will be created.
b Ports, railways and airports will be built.
c 80% of the wood which is extracted from this area is cut down without permission.
d Every two seconds, a surface area equivalent to a football pitch is lost.
e In four minutes, 90 hectares of trees will have been destroyed.
f Redevelopment of the drinking water and sewerage systems will be carried out.

5 Translate into Spanish using the third person plural to render the English passive.

a We have not been paid this month.
b I have been given a lot of support.
c They weren't helped very much.
d The cause of the accident was investigated.
e A new cinema is going to open here.
f The lift has been mended.
g Everybody was given the opportunity to take part in the race.
h Alberto was interrogated for four hours.

i The paintings were sold to pay for the renovations.
j I was told I would have to wait till the next day.

6 Rewrite these sentences replacing the passive construction, **ser** with the past participle, with **se** or with the third person plural. Make any other necessary changes.

a El turrón es elaborado en Jijona.
b Una nueva vida extraterrestre será descubierta en un futuro próximo.
c Hoy día muchos libros son fotocopiados y pirateados.
d Una nueva autopista será construida pronto.
e Tras el accidente el conductor fue hospitalizado.
f Las ciudades fueron bombardeadas.
g El alpinista fue rescatado a última hora.
h Los hábitos alimentarios son inculcados durante los primeros años de vida.
i La guía fue distribuida a todas las oficinas de información.
j Una valla de más de ocho metros de altura ha sido levantada alrededor de las instalaciones.

7a Rewrite these sentences using the passive construction **ser** with the past participle.

a Cuando se aprobó la construcción de un complejo turístico en primera línea de la playa, grupos ecológicos empezaron a protestar.
b Años antes, se había clasificado el terreno como zona protegida.
c Luego se declaró la misma zona como urbanizable.
d Se subvencionó la construcción de un hotel de 21 plantas con más de dos millones de euros de las arcas públicas.
e Se vendieron muchos chalés, en su mayoría a extranjeros.
f Se discutió la legalidad de las edificaciones.
g Se denunciaron los efectos ambientales del complejo.
h Se consideró el caso como símbolo de la destrucción del litoral.
i Se obligó a la Administración a frenar la obra.
j Se derrumbó el hotel a medio construir.

7b Compare the sentences you have written with the ones above and consider which passive construction is more appropriate in each case.

8 Complete this report of a robbery by using the verbs below in the correct tense of the passive. Use either **ser** with the past participle or **se** according to which is the most appropriate in the context.

desvalijar amordazar detener atar sustraer perpetrar llevar liberar

Otra vez un comercio en la calle de Enmedio ha sufrido un robo a la hora de cerrar. Según fuentes policiales, sobre las 20.15 del pasado jueves, dos jóvenes entraron en la Óptica Cisne y apuntaron al propietario con una pistola en la cabeza. La víctima ________ al sótano donde ________. También ________ de pies y manos a una silla.

Al ________ por su mujer varias horas después, el propietario, Jesús Valdés, comprobó que ________ la caja y ________ todos los artículos que había en el establecimiento.

El suceso ha sembrado el pánico entre los comerciantes de la localidad ya que es el tercer atraco que ________ en establecimientos comerciales desde principios del mes. Hasta el momento los delincuentes no ________.

9 Below is an outline of a robbery. Add detail to the elements and use **ser** with the past participle, **se** or the third person plural where possible and appropriate to give an account of the incident.

una joyería asaltada • la alarma dada • dos jóvenes corriendo por la calle • dos jóvenes atropellados • alhajas por la calle • llegada de la policía • los jóvenes detenidos y llevados a la comisaría • motivo del asalto desconocido.

12 The reflexive

Text 1

The article which follows looks at the effects of technology in our daily lives through a fictional character. As you read the text, focus attention on the verb forms in bold, which are known as reflexive or pronominal verbs.

El hombre digital

El hombre digital **se despierta** con música. Ha programado su iPod Video para que **se encienda** a las siete y media de la mañana. Hombre de mente sana en cuerpo sano, **se pone** ropa deportiva, toma su iPod más liviano y más práctico para estos efectos, **se** lo **pone** en el brazo y sale a trotar.

De regreso en casa, **se ducha** y, ya vestido, está listo para **irse** a trabajar. **Se sube** a su auto y cuando va conduciendo recibe una llamada. Mira la pantalla en colores del Parrot que **se halla** en la consola, ve que es su jefe, y le contesta a través del micrófono instalado en la cabina. El jefe lo llama para preguntarle si ya va en camino: muy digital será el hombre, pero **se retrasa** como cualquier mortal (. . .)

Cuando llega a su oficina **se instala** en su escritorio y **se da cuenta** de que tiene que hacer algunas llamadas internacionales. Lo hace a través de Skype, el sistema de telefonía por internet que le ahorra – en este caso, le ahorra a su empresa – el costo de la llamada internacional tradicional. Como nuestro hombre digital es algo inquieto, **se pasea** por su despacho mientras habla. No es problema, porque gracias al teléfono inalámbrico Linksys no necesita estar junto a la computadora mientras habla (. . .)

Para su hora de almuerzo, el hombre digital tiene programada una reunión con un cliente al que quiere mostrarle algunas fotografías y, para estar más seguro, **se reúnen** en un café que ofrece Wi Fi gratis a sus clientes. Lleva la pauta de la reunión y las imágenes que debe mostrar en su Palm LifeDrive (. . .)

Aprovechando la cercanía del metro, deja el auto y su *laptop* en la oficina y **se va** escuchando música en su iPod Video, cuyos audífonos originales ha reemplazado por unos

(*Continued*)

de lujo que **se ajustan** perfectamente a la forma de sus orejas.

Después de la reunión vuelve a la oficina y, terminado el día **se sube** a su auto y **se va** a casa. En el camino recibe una llamada de un amigo que **se encuentra** en Londres. Hablan largo, con tranquilidad, pues su amigo está pagando una llamada local: él ha contratado en Inglaterra un número Skype que le permite recibir vía internet llamadas hechas desde cualquier teléfono de Inglaterra con costo de una llamada local para quien marca. Como ha derivado sus llamadas de internet a su teléfono celular, puede recibir la llamada de su amigo en cualquier lugar (. . .)

Adapted from Revista *El Sábado*, Diario *El Mercurio*, Chile

In Peninsular Spanish sale a trotar = sale a hacer footing, su auto = su coche, la computadora = el ordenador, los audífonos = los auriculares, el teléfono celular = el teléfono móvil

Text 2

The increasing tendency among young people to remain in the parental home well into their twenties is the subject of Text 2.

Hasta cuándo los padres "bancan" a los hijos

Rondan los 30 años; muchos son profesionales y tienen trabajo, pero por diversos motivos aún **se resisten** a **independizarse**.

En España **se popularizó** como el síndrome de Peter Pan. En algunos países de América Latina se los bautizó "adultescentes" y en los Estados Unidos también se los llama *kidadults* [. . .]. **Se trata** de un fenómeno social que, con distintas denominaciones, echa raíces y **se extiende** por todo el mundo: los hijos que postergan su independencia y continúan viviendo en la casa de sus padres.

Muchos son profesionales, tienen trabajo y, en algunos casos, también pareja estable. Rondan los 30 años y forman parte de una generación que **se resiste** por algún motivo a cortar definitivamente el cordón umbilical en busca de una autonomía y un espacio propio.

Es el caso de Esteban Abud, un joven de 26 años que, según confesó a La Nación, no tiene ningún apuro por **irse** de la casa donde vive con toda su familia. "Vivo con mi mamá, mi papá y mis hermanos, y como la casa es grande cada uno tiene su intimidad. La mayor parte de mi sueldo la destino al ahorro porque, si tengo que pagar un alquiler en este momento los números no cierran. Antes de **mudarme** tengo otros planes, como un viaje a Europa, por ejemplo."

(*Continued*)

Pero ante este panorama, ¿qué piensan los padres? ¿Hasta cuándo están dispuestos a vivir bajo el mismo
40 techo con sus hijos y asistirlos económicamente? [. . .]

"Yo **me fui** de mi casa cuando **me casé**, a los 25 años – recuerda Esteban Abud padre –. Pero con mi mujer
45 pudimos **comprarnos** una casa y formar una familia siendo muy jóvenes, algo que hoy para nuestros hijos resultaría imposible. Los sueldos promedio de los jóvenes son muy
50 bajos, y el valor de las propiedades está por las nubes. Para vivir solos también hay que tener los recursos para **mantenerse**."

Desde una perspectiva
55 psicoanalítica, Iris Pugliese, codirectora del Centro Psicoanalítico Argentino, los define así: "Hombres y mujeres que no quieren crecer; el problema surge con la negación de
60 superar la etapa de la adolescencia y **resistirse** a afrontar responsabilidades de la vida adulta."

Dijo el padre de Ricardo Sena, un joven profesional de 29 años: "Las
65 cosas eran muy distintas en otra época. Yo **me fui** de mi casa a los 19 años, con un colchón y un bolso de ropa; nada más que eso. En cambio, los chicos ahora están demasiado
70 cómodos; tal vez les cuesta comprender que el esfuerzo también forma parte del aprendizaje. En lugar de alquilar, Lisandro tiene aspiraciones de poder **comprarse** un departamento,
75 y en ese sentido apoyamos su decisión." [. . .]

Perder el nivel de confort garantizado bajo el techo familiar es un riesgo al que estos jóvenes no están
80 dispuestos a **exponerse**. Es el caso de Leandro N. Sánchez, de 28 años, que no quiere sacrificar el nivel de vida que lleva por **irse** a vivir solo. "Con mis viejos **me llevo** muy bien y no
85 hay ningún tipo de conflicto. La verdad es que así estoy muy cómodo; hasta tengo salida independiente a la calle a través del garaje."

Diario *La Nación*, Argentina

In Peninsular Spanish no tener apuro = no tener prisa o urgencia, el departamento = el piso, mis viejos = mis padres, bancar (Argentina) = aguantar, apoyar económicamente

The reflexive

1 USAGE

Verbs such as **dedicarse** *to devote oneself to*, **mantenerse** *to support oneself*, are known as ***reflexive*** or ***pronominal*** verbs because they are accompanied by an object pronoun (see **Forms** below) which refers back to the subject of the verb. The term ***reflexive***, however, is not strictly correct, as this has other uses as well. But you may already be familiar with this label, so it is this one rather than the term ***pronominal***, used in some grammar books, which has been adopted here. The notes below describe the various uses of the reflexive:

a In sentences such as

Pudimos **comprarnos** una casa. (T. 2, l. 45) *We were able to buy ourselves a house.*
Hay que tener los recursos para **mantenerse.** (T. 2, l. 52–53) *One has to have the means to support oneself.*
Tiene aspiraciones de poder **comprarse** un departamento. (T. 2, l. 73–74) *He aspires to buy himself a flat.*
Nos divertimos mucho. *We enjoyed ourselves very much.*
¿**Te hiciste** daño? *Did you hurt yourself?*

usage corresponds to that of English, with the object pronouns **me** *myself,* **nos** *ourselves,* and **te** *yourself,* in these examples, referring back to the ***subject*** of the verb: **yo, nosotros** and **tú,** respectively. All the verbs above can be used without the reflexive pronoun, but then the action would refer not to the subject but to something or someone outside:

Compramos una casa. *We bought a house.*
Apenas podían **mantener** a sus hijos. *They could hardly support their children.*
La película los **divirtió** muchísimo. *The film amused them very much.*
El fumar le **hizo** mucho daño. *Smoking caused him/her a lot of harm.*

b The use of the reflexive may change the meaning of certain verbs. Compare, for example, the meaning of the following verbs from Text 1 with that of the non-reflexive forms. As is the case with other uses of the reflexive below, the reflexive pronoun is not translated in English here.

ponerse (T. 1, l. 5, 7–8) *to put on, to wear*	**poner** *to put, place*
irse (T. 1, l. 10) *to leave*	**ir** *to go*
hallarse (T. 1, l. 14) *to be, be situated*	**hallar** *to find, discover*
reunirse (T. 1, l. 41) *to meet*	**reunir** *to gather, assemble, collect*
encontrarse (T. 1, l. 57) *to be*	**encontrar** *to find*

. . . **se** lo **pone** en el brazo . . . (T. 1, l. 7–8) *. . . he puts it on his arm . . .*
¿Dónde lo **pongo**? *Where shall I put it?*
. . . está listo para **irse** a trabajar. (T. 1, l. 10) *. . . he's ready to leave for work.*
Va a **ir** a la oficina. *He/she is going to the office.*
. . . **se halla** en la consola . . . (T. 1, l. 14) *. . . it's situated on the dashboard . . .*
Hallaron un tesoro escondido. *They discovered a hidden treasure.*
. . . **se reúnen** en un café . . . (T. 1, l. 41–42) *. . . they meet in a café . . .*
Reunió a todos sus amigos. *He/she assembled all his/her friends.*
. . . un amigo que **se encuentra** en Londres. (T. 1, l. 56–57) *. . . a friend who is in London.*
¿Qué tal lo **encuentras**? *How do you find it?*

c Some verbs are used only in their reflexive form, without actually having a reflexive meaning. Among verbs of this kind are **arrepentirse** *to repent, to regret,* **atreverse** *to dare,* **ausentarse** *to stay away, to be absent,* **jactarse** *to boast,* **quejarse** *to complain, to grumble, to moan,* **suicidarse** *to commit suicide.*

No **me arrepiento** de nada. *I don't regret anything.*
¡Cómo **te atreves**! *How dare you!*
Se ausentan a menudo. *They are often absent.*
Luis **se jacta** de hablar muy bien inglés. *Luis boasts of speaking English very well.*
¿De qué **te quejas**? *What are you grumbling about?*
Se suicidó hace justamente un año. *He/she committed suicide exactly a year ago.*

d The reflexive form of certain verbs translates *to get* or *to become* in English. Compare the following pairs of verbs: **aburrirse** *to get bored*, **aburrir** *to bore*, **arreglarse** *to get ready*, **arreglar** *to tidy (up)*, *to fix*, **asustarse** *to become frightened*, **asustar** *to frighten*, **casarse** *to get married*, **casar** *to marry*, **emborracharse** *to become drunk*, **emborrachar** *to get someone drunk*, **ensuciarse** *to get dirty*, **ensuciar** *to soil*, **enfadarse** *to get angry*, **enfadar** *to annoy*, **independizarse** *to become independent*, **independizar** *to make independent.*

Se resisten a **independizarse.** (T. 2, l. 3–4) *They are reluctant to become independent.*
Yo me fui de mi casa cuando **me casé.** (T. 2, l. 42–43) *I left home when I got married.*
Nos aburrimos muchísimo. *We got very bored.*

e The reflexive, used with a verb in the plural, can denote a ***reciprocal*** action. In English, this meaning is usually expressed with phrases such as *one another*, *each other*. Compare the following sentences, in which the second example of each pair corresponds to the reciprocal use.

Lo **vemos** todos los días. *We see him everyday.*
Nos vemos a menudo. *We see each other often.* (reciprocal)
Siempre **mantuvieron** contacto con sus hijos. *They always kept in contact with their children.*
Siempre **se mantuvieron** en contacto. *They always kept in contact with each other.*

Reciprocal meaning can be made clear in Spanish with phrases such as **el uno al otro** or **los unos a los otros** *one another*, or with a word such as **mutuamente**.

Se insultaron el uno al otro/mutuamente. *They insulted each other.*
Nos ayudamos los unos a los otros. *We help one another.*

f The reflexive **se** can be used with a passive meaning, with a verb in the third person singular or plural (see Chapter 11).

Se construyeron en 1998. *They were built in 1998.*
La carta **se envió** por correo electrónico. *The letter was sent by electronic mail.*

g In impersonal sentences, with an indefinite subject, the reflexive **se** is used with a verb in the third person singular (see Chapter 11).

Aquí no **se trabaja** mucho. *People don't work much here.*
¿Por dónde **se va** al aeropuerto? *How does one get to the airport?*

The impersonal **se** is not used where the verb is already accompanied by **se**. The alternative here is to use words such as **la gente** *people*, **uno** *one* or **tú** *you*.

La gente/uno **se divierte** mucho allí. *People have/One has a lot of fun there.*

Se, here, is part of the verb **divertirse** *to enjoy oneself, to have fun*.

h The reflexive is used with certain verbs as an intensifier.

Se leyó todo el libro. *He/She read the whole book.*
Me comí todo lo que había. *I ate up everything there was.*
¡**Bébete** la leche! *Drink up your milk!*

2 FORMS

The infinitive of a reflexive verb has the pronoun **se** added to it, e.g. **irse** (T. 1, l. 10) *to leave*, **independizarse** (T. 2, l. 4), *to become independent*, **resistirse** (T. 2, l. 61) *to be reluctant/unwilling*. The reflexive pronouns show agreement with the subject of the verb. Here is an example:

(yo)	**me** levanto	*I get up*
(tú)	**te** levantas	*you get up*
(usted/él/ella)	**se** levanta	*you get up, he/she gets up*
(nosotros/as)	**nos** levantamos	*we get up*
(vosotros/as)	**os** levantáis	*you get up*
(ustedes/ellos/ellas)	**se** levantan	*you/they get up*

Note that Latin Americans do not use the **vosotros/as** form, as **ustedes** *you* (plural) is used in familiar and polite address. The reflexive pronoun for this will be **se** instead of **os**.

POSITION OF REFLEXIVE PRONOUNS

Like object pronouns (Chapter 25), reflexive pronouns are placed in the following positions:

a Before a *finite verb*, that is, a verb which shows *tense*, *person* and *number*.

. . . para que **se encienda** a las siete y media . . . (T. 1, l. 3–4) *. . . so that it comes on at half past seven . . .*
. . . **se instala** en su escritorio y **se da cuenta** de que . . . (T. 1, l. 21–23) *. . . he sits at his desk and realises that . . .*
Me fui de mi casa a los 19 años. (T. 2, l. 66) *I left home when I was nineteen.*
Con mis viejos **me llevo** muy bien. (T. 2, l. 83–84) *I get on very well with my parents.*

b After the *infinitive*, becoming one word with it.

Antes de **mudarme** tengo otros planes. (T. 2, l. 34–35) *Before I move out I have other plans.*
Con mi mujer pudimos **comprarnos** una casa. (T. 2, l. 44–45) *With my wife we were able to buy ourselves a house.*
Tiene aspiraciones de poder **comprarse** un departamento. (T. 2, l. 73–74) *He'd like to buy himself a flat.*

c After the *gerund* and, as with the infinitive, becoming one word with it.

Enfadándote no conseguirás lo que quieres. *You won't get what you want by getting angry.*
Paseándonos por el parque nos encontramos con Isabel. *While walking in the park we met Isabel.*

d In a construction with a finite verb followed by an infinitive or a gerund, the reflexive pronoun may either precede the finite verb, as in **a** above, or it may be attached to the infinitive or gerund, as in **b** and **c** above.

Con mi mujer pudimos **comprarnos** una casa. (T. 2, l. 44–45) *Or* Con mi mujer **nos** pudimos **comprar** una casa. *With my wife we were able to buy ourselves a house.*
Se va a **dedicar** al cine. Or Va a **dedicarse** al cine. *He/she is going to devote himself/herself to film.*
Nos queremos **casar**. Or Queremos **casarnos**. *We want to get married.*
Se está **duchando**. Or Está **duchándose**. *He/she is having a shower.*
Nos seguimos **viendo**. Or Seguimos **viéndonos**. *We continue to see each other.*

e Attached to the end of positive imperatives.

¡Levántate! *Get up!*
(but No **te levantes**)
Póngase esa camisa. *Put on that shirt.*
(but No **se ponga** esa camisa)

Other points to note in the texts

- Present indicative: Text 1: *se despierta* (l. 1), *se pone* (l. 5), *se ducha* (l. 9), *se halla* (l. 14), *se retrasa* (l. 19), *se instala* (l. 21–22), *se da cuenta* (l. 22–23) etc. (see Chapter 1)
- **Ser** and **estar**: Text 2: *son profesionales* (l. 16), *es el caso de . . .* (l. 24), *la casa es grande* (l. 29–30), *están dispuestos* (l. 39), *siendo muy jóvenes* (l. 46–47), *son muy bajos* (l. 49–50), *está por las nubes* (l. 51), *eran muy distintas* (l. 65), *están demasiado cómodos* (l. 69–70), *estoy muy cómodo* (l. 86), etc. (see Chapter 13)
- Infinitives: Text 1: *sale a trotar* (l. 8), *para irse a trabajar* (l. 10), *para preguntarle* (l. 17), *tiene que hacer* (l. 23), etc. (see Chapter 8)

EXERCISES

1 Complete the following sentences with an appropriate reflexive pronoun.

a Manolo, ¿por qué no ________ has afeitado esta mañana?
b ¡Cómo ________ ensucian los niños cuando juegan!
c Cuando hace calor, no ________ baño; prefiero duchar ________.
d Siento mucho que usted no ________ considere experto en la materia.
e ________ divertíamos tanto que no ________ acordamos de la hora y Raquel ________ enfadó con nosotros.

f No ________ vayan ustedes. Quéden ________, por favor.

g Niños, si no ________ dormís en seguida, mañana no podréis levantar ________.

h – ¿Dónde está Rosario?

– En el cuarto de baño, maquillándo ________.

i – Cuando ________ caíste ¿________ hiciste daño?

– Sí, ________ torcí el tobillo.

j Todos ________ rieron con su chiste menos Eduardo; él ________ limitó a sonreír.

2 Complete these sentences by choosing a verb from the list and putting it into the correct form.

preocuparse	**quejarse**	**fiarse**	**sentarse**	**levantarse**
parecerse	**aburrirse**	**ponerse**	**callarse**	**acostarse**

a Pablo y Pedro son hermanos pero no ________ en nada.

b Cuando suena el despertador lo apago porque no quiero ________.

c Esa gente nunca está contenta; siempre está ________ de algo.

d ¡Cuánto ________ (nosotros) en la clase de religión! El profesor es tan pesado.

e ¿Tienes mucho sueño? ¿A qué hora ________ anoche?

f Si ustedes ________ en ese sofá, estarán más cómodos.

g ¿Por qué ________ usted tanto de su hijo? No le pasará nada.

h ¡Sois tontos! Debéis ________ las botas.

i ¿Quieres ________ de una vez? Tus comentarios no sirven de nada.

j Yo que tú, no ________ de Raimundo; es un mentiroso empedernido.

3 Translate these sentences into Spanish.

a I had an awful time at Carlitos's party.

b First I had an aperitif with Juanjo in the Bar Florida.

c Then, arriving at Carlitos's house, I slipped and fell.

d Carlitos's mother gave me a brandy, and although I don't like it, I drank it.

e I danced for a while and then I fell asleep.

f When I woke up, Juanjo had gone.

g He had got angry with me for falling asleep.

h I didn't feel well so I washed my face with cold water.

i I didn't dare dance again.

j As it was late, I said goodbye to Carlitos's mother and left to go home.

4 Study these sentences and say whether the function of **se** in each one is ***reflexive*** or ***reciprocal***.

a Aunque eran hermanos, se peleaban mucho.

b Roberto y Ana se escribieron durante dos años.

c Muchos de los presos se suicidaron.

d Se cayeron al agua.

e Los amigos se visitaban todos los veranos.
f Se cansaron mucho.
g Se mataron.
h No se querían y por eso se divorciaron.
i Se acomodaron en el sofá y se entretuvieron mandándose mensajes por móvil.
j Hablaban de muchas cosas sin comprometerse en nada.

5 Rewrite these sentences using impersonal **se**.

a Aquí respiramos aire puro.
b Mandas la factura a esta dirección.
c Según lo que dicen, en Escocia beben mucho.
d En España cenan tarde.
e Para hacer la salsa, necesitas un manojo de perejil.
f Hoy en día no leemos tanto.
g Pensamos que vivir en el campo es menos estresante.
h No es posible conseguir todo lo que queremos.
i Estamos muy bien aquí; es un sitio precioso.
j De vez en cuando tomas un descanso para recobrar fuerzas.

6 Write an account of what Alberto did yesterday, incorporating these verbs, and as many more reflexive verbs as your account will take.

levantarse • vestirse • prepararse • reunirse • reírse • enfadarse • irse • sentarse • ducharse • acostarse.

7 Compare and contrast your daily routine with that of *el hombre digital*, including in your response answers to the following questions:

– ¿Cómo te despiertas?
– ¿Qué haces al levantarte?
– ¿Qué cosas siempre llevas encima cuando sales de casa?
– ¿Cuántas veces al día y cómo te comunicas con gente que no está a tu alrededor?
– ¿Qué dispositivos digitales utilizas a lo largo del día y por qué?

For exercises which practise the use of **se** with passive meaning, see Chapter 11. For exercises which practise the use of **se** functioning as an indirect object pronoun, see Chapter 25.

13 *Ser* and *estar*

Text

In an interview, Jorge Ramos, a prominent Mexican journalist and writer living and working in the United States, talked about the growth and increasing influence of the Hispanic population in that country. As you read the text, focus attention on the uses of **ser** and **estar**, the main grammatical point in this unit.

Estados Unidos está en el proceso de convertirse en un país hispano

– *Hay quien dice que la ola latina acaba de estrellarse contra el malecón.*

– No lo creo. Ni el muro en la frontera ni el Ejército van a poder contener la *ola latina*. Este país **está pasando** por un cambio demográfico y cultural muy profundo, aunque haya gente que no lo quiera ver ni aceptar. Estados Unidos **está** en el proceso de convertirse en una nación hispana, les guste o no . . . Lo cierto **es** que ya **es** la segunda nación hispana del mundo, detrás de México, y por delante de España, Argentina y Colombia. Usted y yo no lo veremos, pero en el 2125 se producirá posiblemente el nuevo hito histórico: habrá más hispanos que blancos (de origen anglosajón) en este país.

– *¿No existe el riesgo de un retroceso como ocurrió con otras corrientes migratorias?*

– No, ninguna ley migratoria va a poder frenar lo que **está ocurriendo**. **Sería** ir contra la corriente. El cambio se **está produciendo** desde dentro, con la gente que **está** ya aquí . . . El poder de los latinos **está** en sus números. El crecimiento no **es** cosa de magia: los hispanos se multiplican a razón de tres hijos por familia, frente a dos de media entre los blancos y los afroamericanos. Este país se sigue percibiendo a sí mismo como blanco, pero la realidad **es** muy distinta: cuando se atreva a mirarse al espejo se dará cuenta de que **es** una nación mestiza.

(*Continued*)

¿Cuál **es** *la reacción cuando expone estas ideas ante una audiencia de "gringos"?*
45
– La primera, **es** de enorme sorpresa. No se dan cuenta de la velocidad a la que **está cambiando** todo. Y la segunda reacción **es** de absoluto
50 horror, en el momento en que ven que el país en que crecieron ya no **es** el mismo, que sus vecinos **son** latinos, que en las tiendas hablan español . . . Para hacerse una idea,
55 José **es** ya el nombre más común entre los niños de California, y pronto lo **será** en Texas y en otros estados del sur.

– *¿Qué pasará con el español, ahora*
60 *que han blindado el inglés como lengua "común y unificadora"?*

– El hecho de que tengan que hacer oficial el inglés a estas alturas lo dice todo. Pero éste **es** un país que
65 camina inevitablemente hacia una entidad bilingüe, y eso **es** algo que las leyes no van a poder cambiar. El español no va a **ser** *asimilado* ni va a desaparecer,
70 como ocurrió con el italiano o el alemán. El español **está** aquí para quedarse. Los programas más oídos de radio **son** en este idioma. El español en Estados
75 Unidos **está** muy deformado y se parece más al *spanglish* que al castellano, pero **es** un idioma que se ha vuelto ya totalmente prevalente en
80 partes del país.

Sigo siendo un inmigrante: el acento es mi seña de identidad

– *¿Su nariz sigue apuntando hacia México?*

– Sí, **es** inevitable . . .

– *¿Y no se siente a veces como Ulises,*
85 *anhelando volver a casa?*

– Hay días en que me despierto y no sé de dónde **soy**. Mis sueños siguen **siendo** con la casa en la que me crié en México. Debe de **ser** un trauma
90 de inmigrante . . . En el fondo **estoy** muy desarraigado. Llevo la mitad de mi vida aquí, la mitad allá. En Estados Unidos me siguen diciendo "eh, tú, mexicano, regrésate a tu
95 país". En mi país me ven como el gringo que viene del norte . . . Pero en los últimos años he podido encontrar un cierto equilibrio. Mis dos hijos han nacido aquí: ya no
100 tengo que escoger. Los dos hablan muy bien español, pero **son** norteamericanos. Yo no. Yo sigo **siendo** un inmigrante: mi acento **es** mi seña de identidad.

Diario *El Mundo*, España

Ser and *estar* to be

1 GENERAL

Spanish has two words meaning *to be*, **ser** and **estar**, which are clearly differentiated by native speakers. The generalisation sometimes found in textbooks that **ser** is used to refer to general characteristics and **estar** to temporary states is true only to some extent, and in fact it can be misleading. It seems more appropriate to look at each use separately. The interview above contains several examples of the use of these two verbs. The notes below cover these and other uses not found in the text.

2 USING *SER*

a With nouns.

. . . **es** la segunda nación hispana del mundo . . . (l. 13–14) *. . . it is the second Spanish-speaking country in the world . . .*
El crecimiento no **es** cosa de magia . . . (l. 32) *The increase hasn't happened by magic . . .*
. . . **es** una nación mestiza. (l. 41–42) *. . . it is a racially mixed nation.*
¿Cuál **es** la reacción . . . ? (l. 43) *What is the reaction . . . ?*
. . . sigo **siendo** un inmigrante . . . (l. 102–103) *. . . I'm still an immigrant . . .*
. . . mi acento **es** mi seña de identidad. (l. 103–104) *. . . my accent is the mark of my identity.*

Note also the use of **ser** with nouns denoting occupation or profession.

Es profesora de español. *She's a Spanish teacher.*

b With pronouns.

. . . el país en que crecieron ya no **es** el mismo . . . (l. 51–52) *. . . the country they grew up in is no longer the same . . .*
. . . **es** algo que las leyes no van a poder cambiar. (l. 66–68) *. . . it is something which laws will not be able to change.*
Es ella/él. *It's her/him.*
El dinero **es** mío. *The money is mine.*
¿**Es** este? *Is it this one?*

c With an infinitive.

Sería ir contra la corriente. (l. 27–28) *It would be going against the tide.*
Lo más difícil **fue** subir. *The most difficult thing was to go up.*

d With adjectives.

i Adjectives denoting membership of a group or category, for example, ethnic origin, nationality, religion.

. . . sus vecinos **son** latinos . . . (l. 52–53) *. . . their neighbours are Latin American . . .*
. . . **son** norteamericanos. (l. 101–102) *. . . they are American.*
Somos católicos. *We are Catholic.*

Note that although nationality and religion may not be regarded as permanent, you still need to use **ser**.

ii Adjectives indicating marital status, although **estar** seems to be more common in Spain, especially when the emphasis is on the state of being single, married, etc., rather than on describing someone's marital status.

Es soltero/a. *He/she's single.*
Es divorciado/a. *He/she's divorced.*

See also **3 i** below.

iii Adjectives describing the subject in terms of general attributes, including physical and moral characteristics.

. . . la realidad **es** muy distinta . . . (l. 38–39) *. . . the reality is very different . . .*
. . . **es . . .** mestiza (l. 41–42) *. . . it's . . . racially mixed.*
Es guapa y **es** muy simpática. *She's pretty and she's very nice.*

See also **3 d i** and **ii** below.

iv Adjectives describing the subject in terms of an inherent quality.

La Tierra **es** redonda. *The Earth is round.*

e In the construction **ser** + adjective (+ que).

Sí, **es** inevitable . . . (l. 83) *Yes, it's inevitable . . .*
Es importante estar a la hora. *It's important to be on time.*
Es mejor que lo hagas. *You'd better do it.*

f With a clause.

Lo cierto **es** que . . . (l. 12–13) *The truth is that . . .*
¿Qué **es** lo que quieres? *What is it that you want?*

g With prepositional phrases, many of them introduced by the preposition **de**.

La primera, **es** de enorme sorpresa. (l. 46) *The first is (one) of enormous surprise.*
. . . la segunda reacción **es** de absoluto horror . . . (l. 48–50) *. . . the second reaction is of absolute horror . . .*

Expressions denoting origin, possession and the material something is made of also fall into this category:

. . . no sé de dónde **soy**. (l. 86–87) *. . . I don't know where I am from.*
Ese libro **es** de Ana. *That book belongs to Ana.*
Es de plata. *It's silver.*

h With adverbs of place or time, to say where or when an event is taking place.

La fiesta **es** aquí. *The party is here.*
La reunión **fue** ayer. *The meeting was yesterday.*

i With past participles, to form passive sentences.

El español no va a **ser** asimilado . . . (l. 68–69) *Spanish will not be assimilated . . .*
El edificio **será** demolido. *The building will be demolished.*

For **estar** + past participle see **3 c** below.

j With past participles functioning as adjectives.

Es muy educado/a. *He/she's well-mannered.*
Es una persona muy preparada. *He/she is a very well-educated person.*

k With phrases denoting time, date, price.

Son las tres y media. *It's half past three.*
Mañana **es** domingo. *Tomorrow is Sunday.*
Hoy **es** (el) 20 de abril. *Today is the 20th of April.*
¿Cuánto **es**? *How much is it?*
Son cincuenta euros. *It's fifty euros.*

l To denote identity or existence.

¿Quién **es**? *Who is it?*
Son cuatro. *There are four of them.*

3 USING *ESTAR*

a To indicate position, in a real or figurative sense, and distance.

. . . la gente que **está** ya aquí . . . (l. 29–30) *. . . the people who are already here . . .*
El poder de los latinos **está** en sus números. (l. 30–31) *The power of Latin Americans lies in their numbers.*
El español **está** aquí para quedarse. (l. 71–72) *Spanish is here to stay.*
Está en la plaza, a cinco minutos de aquí. *It's in the square, five minutes from here.*

b With gerunds, to form progressive tenses.

Este país **está pasando** por un cambio demográfico y cultural . . . (l. 6–8) *This country is undergoing a demographic and cultural change . . .*
. . . lo que **está ocurriendo**. (l. 26–27) *. . . what is happening.*
El cambio se **está produciendo** . . . (l. 28–29) *The change is taking place . . .*
. . . **está cambiando** todo. (l. 48) *. . . everything is changing.*

c With past participles, to denote a state which is the result of an action or a process.

El español en Estados Unidos **está** muy **deformado** . . . (l. 74–75) *Spanish in the United States is very deformed . . .*
. . . **estoy** muy **desarraigado**. (l. 90–91) *. . . I'm very rootless.*

For **ser** + past participle, see **2 i** and **j** above.

d With adjectives.

i Denoting, as with past participles above, a state which is the result of a process.

Tu hijo **está** muy grande. *Your child looks very big.*
¡Qué viejo **está**! *How old he looks!*

Compare these examples with:

Tu hijo **es** muy grande. *Your son is very big.* (Regarded as an attribute rather than a state)
¡Qué viejo **es**! *He's very old!* (I hadn't realised how old he was)

ii Showing that a state or condition is regarded as temporary, or implying a change from usual circumstances.

Pablo **está** muy elegante hoy. *Pablo is looking very elegant today.*
Las noches **están** muy frías. *The evenings are very cold.*

Compare these examples with:

Pablo **es** muy elegante. *Pablo is very elegant.* (A general attribute)
Las noches **son** muy frías. *The evenings are* (normally) *very cold.*

See **2 d iii** above.

e With a prepositional phrase.

Estados Unidos **está** en el proceso de convertirse en una nación hispana . . . (l. 10–12)
The United States is in the process of becoming a Hispanic country . . .
Raquel **está** de camarera. *Raquel is working as a waiter.*

f To denote a physical or mental state or condition.

Estoy muy bien, gracias. *I'm very well, thank you.*
Están muy contentos. *They are very happy.*

g To indicate cost, when prices fluctuate.

¿A cuánto/cómo **está** el cambio? *What's the rate of exchange?*
Los tomates **están** caros. *The tomatoes are expensive.* (today or this season)

Compare the second example with:

Los tomates **son** caros. *Tomatoes are* (normally) *expensive.*

h With dates and other expressions of time.

Estamos a 5 de julio/**a** jueves. *It's the 5th of July/It's Thursday.*
Estamos en verano. *It's summer.*

Ser is also correct in this context:

Hoy **es** (el) 25 de diciembre/martes. *Today is the 25th December/Tuesday.*
Es primavera. *It is spring.*

See **2 k** above.

i To indicate marital status.

¿**Está** Vd. casado/a o soltero/a? *Are you single or married?*
Ser is also used in this context, especially in Latin America.

See **2 d ii** above.

j To indicate existence.

También **está** el problema de la discriminación. *There's also the problem of discrimination.*

k On its own.

Laura no **está**. *Laura is not in.*
Ya **está**. *That's it.*
¿Estamos? *Are we agreed?, OK?*
En seguida **está**. *It'll be ready in a moment.*

Changes in meaning with *ser* and *estar*

The meaning of certain words can be affected by the choice between ***ser*** and ***estar***. Here are some examples:

ser aburrido *to be boring*
ser bueno *to be good*
ser decidido *to be resolute*
ser fresco *to be fresh* (of a person); *cheeky*
ser malo *to be bad*
ser nuevo *to be new*
ser tranquilo *to be a quiet person*
ser vivo *to be clever, sharp*

estar aburrido *to be bored*
estar bueno *to be tasty*
estar decidido *to be determined*
estar fresco *to be fresh* (food)
estar malo *to be ill, to be off*
estar nuevo *to seem new*
estar tranquilo *to be calm*
estar vivo *to be alive*

Other points to note in the texts

- Negation: *No lo creo* (l. 14), *Ni el muro en la frontera ni el Ejército* (l. 4–5), *aunque haya gente que no lo quiera ver ni aceptar* (l. 8–10), *les guste o no* (l. 12), *No, ninguna ley migratoria* (l. 25), *No se dan cuenta* (l. 47), *ya no es el mismo* (l. 51–52), *no va a ser asimilado ni va a desaparecer* (l. 68–69), *ya no tengo que escoger* (l. 99–100), *yo no* (l. 102), etc. (see Chapter 27)
- Present subjunctive: *aunque haya gente que no lo quiera ver* (l. 8–9), *les guste o no* (l. 12), *cuando se atreva a mirarse al espejo* (l. 39–40), *el hecho de que tengan que hacer oficial el inglés* (l. 62–63) (see Chapter 14)
- Object pronouns: *No lo creo* (l. 4), *aunque haya gente que no lo quiera ver* (l. 8–9), *les guste o no* (l. 12), *Usted y yo no lo veremos* (l. 16–17), *pronto lo será* (l. 57), *lo dice todo* (l. 63–64) (see Chapter 25)
- The reflexive: *estrellarse* (l. 2), *convertirse* (l. 11), *se producirá . . . el nuevo hito histórico* (l. 17–19), *El cambio se está produciendo* (l. 28–29), *los hispanos se multiplican* (l. 33), *cuando se atreva* (l. 39), *mirarse al espejo* (l. 40), *se dará cuenta* (l. 40–41), *no se dan cuenta* (l. 47), *Para hacerse una idea* (l. 54), *está aquí para quedarse* (l. 71–72), etc. (see Chapter 12)

EXERCISES

1 Use the correct form of **ser** or **estar** to complete the following sentences.

a – ¿________ interesante ese libro?
– No. ________ aburridísimo.

b – ¿Sabes dónde ________ Miguel?
– ________ en el jardín, leyendo.

c – ¿Quién ________ ese chico tan guapo?
– ________ mi amigo Carlos. ________ argentino. Todos los argentinos ________ guapos.

d Las calles de los pueblos blancos ________ estrechas y en verano los balcones ________ repletos de flores.

e Nada ________ fácil en esta vida.

f María y yo ________ contentos de verlos.

g ¿De quién ________ ese bolso? ¿________ tuyo?

h – ¿Quién ________?
– ________ yo.

i Diego ________ de Teruel pero ahora ________ en Valladolid. ________ estudiando filosofía.

j – ¿A cuánto ________ las sardinas?
– Hoy ________ a 3 euros el kilo. ________ muy frescas.

k – ¿De cuándo ________ ese diario?
– ________ de ayer.
– ¿Dónde ________ el de hoy?

l Los obreros ________ en huelga pero ________ una huelga que no les sirve para nada.

m La última vez que Ignacio ________ en La Habana, el Museo de Bellas Artes ________ cerrado por obras.

n Este vestido ________ de seda y ________ carísimo pero el color ________ muy de moda. Voy a comprármelo.

o Cállate, ________ mejor que no hables. ¿No ves que Juan ________ furioso?

2 Fill in the gaps with the correct form of **ser** or **estar**.

a Paco ________ aburrido; el trabajo que hace ________ aburrido.

b Gloria ________ una chica muy guapa pero esta noche ________ más guapa que nunca.

c En este restaurante la comida suele ________ buena; hoy ________ riquísima.

d Mi abuelo no ________ muy mayor pero por lo que le ha pasado ________ bastante viejo.

e Mi tío ________ una persona alegre; ahora ________ muy alegre porque le ha tocado la lotería.

f A Silvia le gusta ________ a la moda aun cuando ________ una moda que no le va.

g Ya sé que Felipe ________ enfermo pero os digo que ahora ________ enfermo de peligro.

h Mira, ya ________ borracho Antonio. ________ que ________ un borracho perdido.

i David ________ un chico muy listo que siempre ________ listo para cualquier cosa.

j No hay duda que esa actriz ________ muy guapa pero en su última película ________ feísima.

3 Write the result of these actions.

a El banco ha abierto.
b Mi gato se ha muerto.
c Se ha enfriado la sopa.
d Los niños han perdido la llave.
e Voy a servir la cena.
f Se prohíbe fumar en este local.
g Hemos reservado la habitación.
h Se ha estropeado el coche.
i Se ha agotado este libro.
j Con tanta edificación, han destruido la costa.

4 Complete these sentences with a progressive tense.

a Estudiar español (ponerse) ________ de moda.
b La población hispana (crecer) ________ a un ritmo más rápido de lo que se pensaba.
c Estados Unidos (convertirse) ________ en un país bilingüe.
d Cuando yo los vi, (estudiar, ellos) ________.
e Pedro (dormir) ________ cuando su mujer lo llamó.
f Arturo es ingeniero de minas pero ahora (trabajar) ________ en una fábrica.
g Últimamente (construirse) ________ muchas casas en el extrarradio.
h Cuando salimos anoche, (llover) ________ a cántaros.
i ¿Qué te pareció esa biografía que (leer) ________?
j Alfonso me dijo que (escribir) ________ un libro sobre sus aventuras en Amazonas; no creo que lo haya terminado.

5 Cross out the incorrect verb.

a Era/estaba fotógrafo pero como su hija era/estaba recién nacida y no quería ser/estar fuera tanto tiempo, era/estaba de técnico en electrodomésticos. Sus suegros no eran/estaban nada contentos. Era/estaba lógico entonces, que al poco tiempo fuera/estuviera divorciado.
b No todo el mundo es/está de acuerdo con que Salvador Dalí es/está uno de los mejores artistas del siglo XX pero es/está el más conocido de los pintores surrealistas. Aunque fue/estuvo un pionero, un revolucionario, muchos se acuerdan de él más por su aparencia estrafalaria y sus declaraciones extravagantes. En una ocasión declaró que la única diferencia entre él y un loco era/estaba que él no era/estaba loco. Su vida fue/estuvo llena de éxitos y controversia pero hacia el final de su vida era/estaba muy solo. Si quieres apreciar su arte, nada mejor que visitar el Teatre-Museu Dalí que es/está en Figueres, Cataluña.

6 Of the following sentences, five are incorrect. Identify them and correct them.

a ¿Usted cree que este sistema es el más seguro?
b Allí es donde vivíamos cuando era niño.
c Nuestro aniversario está en junio.

d El dinero siempre es más seguro en el banco.

e El incendio fue provocado.

f La sopa era muy sosa.

g La fábrica era un edificio imponente que fue demolido el año pasado por estar en malas condiciones.

h Soy sin dinero porque gasté todo lo que tenía en el billete.

i No sé en qué está pensando; las cosas que dice están absurdas.

j Todavía no está muy claro que el Gobierno haya conseguido una mayoría de votos.

7 Translate into Spanish.

a The house was quite far from the station.

b It was late and we were tired when we arrived.

c We are not going to go out because it is raining.

d The streets are very busy today.

e The mirror is broken.

f Do you like this picture? It's not bad, is it?

g It's not good to be so discontented.

h At what time is the concert? It's in the town hall, isn't it?

i The coffee will be cold and Marga will be in a bad mood if you don't come right now.

j The hotel was full, which was a pity.

8 Fill in the gaps with the correct form of **ser** or **estar** to complete the text.

Desde tiempos inmemorables Sevilla ________ un poblado que encanta a todos los que lo visitan. ________ situado en el sur de España a orillas del navegable río Guadalquivir y, además de ________ la capital de Andalucía, ________ la cuarta ciudad de España después de Madrid, Barcelona y Valencia.

Según la leyenda, la ciudad ________ fundada por Hércules, pero los primeros pobladores ________ los iberos que se asentaron en una isla del río. Luego ________ los griegos, los fenecios y los cartaginenses antes de que la población llegara a ________ una de las más importantes del imperio romano.

________ igual de importante durante la época de los musulmanes. Los monumentos emblemáticos, la Giralda, el Alcázar, que ________ coetáneo a la Alhambra de Granada, y la Torre de Oro, ________ de este periodo. Los dos primeros y el Archivo de Las Indias ________ declarados Patrimonio de la Humanidad por la UNESCO en 1987. La Giralda ________ el minarete de la gran mezquita y, junto con el Patio de los Naranjos que da acceso a la catedral, ________ lo único que queda de ese edificio que tras la Reconquista ________ reemplazado por una catedral enorme que solamente ________ superado en dimensiones por los templos de San Pedro del Vaticano y San Pablo de Londres.

Ya ________ demostrado que en la Sala Capitular de la catedral ________ los restos de Cristobal Colón. Tras su descubrimiento del Nuevo Mundo, Sevilla tenía el monopolio del comercio con América y atraía a todo el mundo por ________ una de las ciudades más prósperas de Europa.

Aún durante los últimos dos siglos cuando ________ en decadencia, Sevilla seguía ________ una ciudad cuyo embrujo hechizaba e inspiraba. ________ la ciudad natal de pintores como Velázquez, de numerosos poetas y músicos, y también de toreros. Hay muchos que aseguran que Sevilla ________ la esencia de lo español.

9 You have been asked to contribute to a Spanish magazine by writing an article about your favourite town/city in which you describe its location, its character, the places of interest (where they are in the town and what they are like) and the reasons why you like it.

14 | The present subjunctive

Text

This text considers the frustrations often felt by young university graduates on taking up their first job. The main grammatical point here is the present subjunctive. Read the article and then, with the help of the notes which follow the text, study the way in which the verbs in bold have been used.

¿Para esto estudié tanto?

Con su mejor traje y el estómago apretado, el novato se presenta a tomar posesión de su nuevo puesto de trabajo. Si tiene suerte, puede que alguien
5 lo **salude** y le **indique** dónde sentarse. Pero también es posible que nadie **esté** enterado de su llegada, que la recepcionista lo **mire** con extrañeza y le **pregunte** a quién espera. Es
10 posible que **termine** ocupando algún rincón improvisado, leyendo aburridos documentos para interiorizarse "mientras tanto". Pueden pasar días antes de que alguien lo **introduzca** a su nuevo cargo.
15 Y aunque no **sea** así, sus ilusiones y expectativas tal vez **disminuyan** considerablemente. En las semanas que siguen podrá comprobar la diferencia entre la teoría y la realidad, entre lo que
20 le enseñaron en la universidad y las tareas que tendrá que cumplir. Es común que para comenzar se le **ocupe** en tareas rutinarias, aquéllas que los que llevan más tiempo en la institución
25 ya no están dispuestos a realizar.

Es frecuente que su jefe **sea** una persona con mucha experiencia, pero quizás **tenga** una preparación académica inferior a la suya, y le **sea**
30 difícil entender sus proposiciones. "¿Para esto estudié tanto?" se pregunta el novato y comienza a sentir una leve depresión.

Por otra parte, el joven deberá
35 hacer importantes ajustes en su vida personal. Para muchos no es fácil adquirir esa disciplina. Además, es común que los jóvenes **se casen** cuando ingresan a su primer trabajo o
40 que **se independicen** económicamente de sus padres y **se instalen** por su cuenta o con amigos. De la actitud del joven en este trance dependerá en parte su carrera laboral futura. Si es capaz
45 de sobreponerse a la frustración y enfrentar con entusiasmo esta etapa, es probable que **comience** a recibir poco a poco responsabilidades más interesantes que le **permitan** demostrar sus
50 verdaderas capacidades.

Revista *El Sábado*, Diario *El Mercurio*, Chile

The present subjunctive

1 USAGE

General

Verbs can take different forms depending on how they are used. In Spanish, there are three basic forms of the verb, traditionally referred to as ***moods***: the ***indicative*** mood (all the various tenses covered in this book so far, for example the present tense, the preterite), which is generally used in statements; the ***imperative*** mood, normally used in orders or commands and instructions (Chapter 17); and the ***subjunctive*** mood, generally used in subordinate clauses to refer to events which are unreal or which have not yet taken place, but also found after a number of conjunctions, and in relative and main clauses. Note the contrast between the indicative and the subjunctive in the following sentences.

Llegan mañana. *They are arriving tomorrow.* (a fact, therefore indicative).
Espero que **lleguen** mañana. *I hope they arrive tomorrow.* (not yet a fact, therefore subjunctive)
Aunque **tengo** tiempo, no iré. *Although I have time, I won't go.* (a fact, therefore indicative)
Aunque **tenga** tiempo, no iré. *Even if I have time, I won't go.* (not a fact, therefore subjunctive)
Hay alguien que **habla** español. *There's someone who speaks Spanish.* (a fact, therefore indicative)
¿Hay alguien que **hable** español? *Is there someone who speaks Spanish?* (not a fact, therefore subjunctive)

For more specific uses of the subjunctive and further examples, see the notes below.

In English, the subjunctive, which is very little used, is found in sentences such as *I wish she were here, If I were you.* In Spanish, the subjunctive is very common. Its four main tenses, ***present***, ***imperfect***, ***perfect*** and ***pluperfect***, are found in all forms of language, formal and informal, spoken and written. Of these, the two simple tenses, that is, the present and the imperfect, are by far the most common. Another tense of the subjunctive, the ***future***, constitutes a special case, as this is used very little nowadays, except in very formal written language and in legal documents.

General usage of the subjunctive is much the same for all tenses, so most of the notes below, illustrated here with the present subjunctive, which is the focus of this chapter, will be valid for the other tenses. Tense agreement with the subjunctive, however, is not the same for all subjunctive forms, so before you look at specific usage below, you need to consider the sequence of tenses in which the present subjunctive occurs.

SEQUENCE OF TENSES WITH THE PRESENT SUBJUNCTIVE

The present subjunctive in the subordinate clause is normally dependent on a main clause verb in the present indicative, the future, the perfect or the imperative.

Quiere que lo **haga**. *He/she wants me to do it.*
Les **diré** que te **llamen**. *I'll tell them to call you.*

Me **ha pedido** que le **ayude**. *He's asked me to help him.*
Dile que se **dé** prisa. *Tell him/her to hurry.*

For tense agreement with the imperfect and the pluperfect subjunctive, see Chapters 15 and 16.

Basic uses

a The subjunctive in subordinate clauses.

By far the most frequent general use of the subjunctive is within subordinate clauses introduced by **que** (most examples in the text), e.g. . . . **puede que alguien lo salude** . . . (l. 4–5) . . . *it's possible that someone may greet him* . . . More specifically, the presence of the subjunctive in the subordinate clause is determined by two main factors: one is the nature of the main verb, and the other is the fact that the subject of the main verb and that of the verb in the subordinate clause are different (as in the example above). Among the verbs and expressions calling for the use of the subjunctive in the subordinate clause are the following:

i Verbs and expressions indicating possibility/impossibility, doubt or uncertainty, permission and prohibition, acceptance and agreement, orders or commands, hope, requests and wishes, needs and requirements, recommendation, advice and suggestion, thinking (in negative sentences).

The following sentences from the text are all introduced by verbs expressing possibility:

. . . puede que alguien lo **salude** y le **indique** dónde sentarse . . . (l. 4–5) . . . *maybe someone will greet him and tell him where to sit* . . .
. . . es posible que nadie **esté** enterado . . . (l. 6–7) . . . *it's possible that no one may be aware* . . .
. . . es posible . . . que la recepcionista lo **mire** con extrañeza y le **pregunte** a quién espera. (l. 6–9) . . . *it's possible that the receptionist may look at him in surprise and ask him who he's waiting for.*
Es posible que **termine** ocupando . . . (l. 9–10) *It's possible that he may end up occupying* . . .
. . . es probable que **comience** a recibir poco a poco responsabilidades . . . (l. 46–48) . . . *it's likely that little by little he may start being given responsibilities* . . .

The following examples illustrate the use of the subjunctive with other types of verbs:

Dudo que **vengan**. *I doubt whether they will come.* (doubt or uncertainty)
No le permiten que **fume**. *He/she is not allowed to smoke.* (prohibition)
Él no acepta que ella **trabaje**. *He doesn't agree to her working.* (acceptance or agreement)
Les ordenaré que lo **hagan** de nuevo. *I'll order them to do it again.* (order or command)
Espero que me **ayudes**. *I hope you can help me.* (hope)
Le he pedido que me lo **explique**. *I have asked him/her to explain it to me.* (request)

Quieren que **estemos** con ellos. *They want us to be with them.* (wish)
Necesito que me **acompañéis**. *I need you to accompany me.* (need)
Es imprescindible que **sea** informado. *It's essential that he be informed.* (requirement)
Te recomiendo que lo **compres**. *I recommend that you buy it.* (recommendation)
Me ha aconsejado que **tenga** cuidado. *He/she has advised me to be careful.* (advice)
Te sugiero que lo **devuelvas**. *I suggest you return it.* (suggestion)
No creo que **estén** enterados. *I don't think they are aware of it.* (thinking)

ii Verbs and expressions conveying some kind of emotion, e.g. **alegrarse** *to be glad*, **molestar** *to bother*, **detestar** *to detest, hate*, **gustar** *to like*, **temer** *to fear*.

Me alegro de que me **llames**. *I'm glad you are calling.*
Le molesta que la **interrumpan**. *It bothers her to be interrupted.*
Detesto que me **ignore**. *I hate to be ignored by him/her.*
Les gusta que yo les **escriba**. *They like me to write to them.*
Temo que **sea** verdad. *I'm afraid it may be true.*

iii Impersonal expressions indicating some kind of value judgement, usually associated with the constructions **ser** + adjective, e.g. **es común/frecuente/normal/natural/importante/mejor/injusto**, or **ser** + noun, as in **es una pena/lástima**, both constructions to be followed by a subordinate clause introduced by **que**. This rule also applies to expressions such as **¡qué pena que . . . !**, **¡qué lástima que . . . !**, **¡qué terrible que . . . !**

Es común que para comenzar se le **ocupe** . . . (l. 21–22) *It's common that at the beginning he may be employed . . .*
Es frecuente que su jefe **sea** . . . (l. 26) *It's common for his boss to be . . .*
Además, es común que los jóvenes **se casen** . . . (l. 37–38) *Besides, it's common for young people to marry . . .*
. . . es común . . . que **se independicen** . . . y **se instalen** . . . (l. 38–41) *. . . it's common . . . for them to become independent . . . and to establish themselves . . .*
Es normal que así **sea**. *It's normal for it to be like that.*
Es importante que **vengas**. *It's important that you come.*
Es mejor que **vayamos**. *We'd better go.*
Es una pena/lástima que no **puedan** asistir. *It's a pity they can't attend.*
¡Qué pena/lástima que no **hablen** español! *What a pity they don't speak Spanish!*

b The subjunctive in temporal clauses.
The subjunctive is used after conjunctions indicating time, such as **antes (de) que** *before*, **después (de) que** *after*, **una vez que** *once*, **en cuanto** *as soon as*, **hasta que** *until*, **cuando** *when*, but only when these refer to the future.

Pueden pasar días antes de que alguien lo **introduzca** . . . (l. 13–14) *It may be days before someone introduces him . . .*
Después de que **termine**, me iré a casa. *After I finish, I'll go home.*
En cuanto/Una vez que **lleguen**, llámame. *As soon as/Once they arrive, call me.*

Nos quedaremos aquí hasta que **completemos** el trabajo. *We'll stay here until we complete the work.*
Se lo diré **cuando** la vea. *I'll tell her when I see her.*

The subjunctive is not used when the time expression refers to the past or to a habitual action.

Después de que terminó se fue a casa. *After he/she finished he/she went home.*
Cuando estoy con ella siempre habla de ti. *When I'm with her she always talks about you.*

c The subjunctive after conjunctions of concession and condition.
The subjunctive is used after conjunctions expressing concession and condition in sentences such as the following:

i Concession.

Y **aunque (aun cuando)** no **sea** así . . . (l. 15) *And even if it isn't like that . . .*
Iremos de camping, **a no ser que llueva**. *We'll go camping, unless it rains.*
Viajarán a Sudamérica, **a pesar de que (aunque)** no **tengan** suficiente dinero. *They'll travel to South America, despite the fact that they may not have enough money.*

ii Condition.

Te lo compraré, **siempre que/siempre y cuando** te **portes** bien. *I'll buy it for you, provided you behave well.*
En caso de que lo **necesites**, está en la cocina. *In case/If/Should you need it, it's in the kitchen.*
En caso de que llegue, dígale que volveré pronto. *If he/she arrives, tell him/her that I'll be back soon.*
Te lo prestaré **con tal de que/a condición de que** lo **cuides**. *I'll lend it to you provided/on condition that you take care of it.*

When reference is to a fact rather than to something hypothetical, the indicative and not the subjunctive must be used.

Aunque no es así . . . *Although/Even when it isn't like that . . .*
Viajarán a Sudamérica, a pesar de que no tienen suficiente dinero. *They'll travel to South America, despite the fact that they haven't enough money.*

d The subjunctive after conjunctions of purpose and intention.
The subjunctive is used after conjunctions expressing purpose and intention in sentences such as the following:

Lo traeré **para que/a fin de que** lo **veas**. *I'll bring it so that you can see it.*
Le hablaré muy despacio **de manera/modo/forma que pueda** entenderme bien. *I'll speak to him/her very slowly so he/she can understand me well.*

De manera/modo/forma que *so* may also express consequence, in which case the indicative and not the subjunctive must be used. Compare the last sentence above with the following one:

Siempre le hablo muy despacio de manera/modo/forma que puede entenderme bien.
I always speak to him/her very slowly so he/she can understand me well.

e The subjunctive in relative clauses.
The subjunctive is used in relative clauses when the relative pronoun, e.g. **que**, refers back to something which is non-existent, indefinite or unknown. Otherwise, you must use an indicative verb.

. . . responsabilidades . . . **que** le **permitan** . . . (l. 48–49) *. . . responsibilities which may allow him . . .*
Buscan a alguien **que hable** ruso. *They're looking for someone who can speak Russian.*

Compare the examples above with the following ones:

. . . responsabilidades **que** le **permiten** . . . *. . . responsibilities which (actually) allow him . . .*
Buscan a alguien **que habla** ruso. *They're looking for someone who speaks Russian.*

f The subjunctive in main clauses.

i The subjunctive is used in independent clauses introduced by words such as **quizá(s)**, **tal vez** *perhaps*. With these two words its use is optional, the indicative being used when there is a greater degree of certainty.

A lo mejor, also meaning *perhaps*, always takes an indicative verb.

. . . **tal vez disminuyan** . . . (l. 16) *. . . they may perhaps diminish . . .*
. . . **quizás tenga** . . . (l. 28) *. . . he may perhaps have . . .*

But **A lo mejor disminuyen/tiene** . . .

ii Expressions of wish introduced by **que** or **ojalá (que)** are followed by a verb in the subjunctive.

Que tengas suerte. *I hope you are lucky.*
Ojalá (que) consigas entradas. *I hope you get tickets.*

iii The subjunctive is used as the imperative form for **usted** and **ustedes** and for negative familiar commands (see Chapter 17).

Llámeme mañana. *Call me tomorrow.*
No se lo **digan** a nadie. *Don't tell anyone.*
No se lo **cuentes**. *Don't tell him/her.*
(but **Cuéntaselo**. *Tell him.*)

2 FORMATION

Regular verbs

llamar	**comer**	**vivir**
llam**e**	com**a**	viv**a**
llam**es**	com**as**	viv**as**
llam**e**	com**a**	viv**a**
llam**emos**	com**amos**	viv**amos**
llam**éis**	com**áis**	viv**áis**
llam**en**	com**an**	viv**an**

Note that **-er** and **-ir** verbs have the same endings. Note too that, except for the first person (**yo**), the endings of **-ar** verbs are like those of the present indicative of **-er** verbs, while those in **-er** and **-ir** have endings which are similar to those of the present indicative of **-ar** verbs.

Stem-changing and irregular verbs

To form the present subjunctive of stem-changing and irregular verbs, drop the **-o** from the stem of the first person singular of the present indicative and add the endings of regular verbs. Stem-changing verbs keep the stem of the infinitive in the first and second person plural, as in the present tense. Here are some examples:

infinitive	***1st person pres. indicative***	***present subjunctive***
decir	digo	diga, digas, diga, digamos digáis, digan
querer	quiero	quiera, quieras, quiera, queramos, queráis, quieran
venir	vengo	venga, vengas, venga, vengamos, vengáis, vengan

A few verbs form the present subjunctive in a different way.

infinitive	***present subjunctive***
dar *to give*	dé, des, dé, demos, deis, den
estar *to be*	esté, estés, esté, estemos, estéis, estén
haber *to have*	haya, hayas, haya, hayamos, hayáis, hayan
ir *to go*	vaya, vayas, vaya, vayamos, vayáis, vayan
saber *to know*	sepa, sepas, sepa, sepamos, sepáis, sepan
ser *to be*	sea, seas, sea, seamos, seáis, sean

See also **Irregular verbs** on pages 279–282.

Spelling-changing verbs

Verbs ending in **-car**, **-gar**, **-ger**, **-zar** change their spelling in all persons of the present subjunctive. Among these we find **buscar** *to look for* (**busque**, **busques** . . .), **llegar** *to arrive* (**llegue, llegues** . . .), **recoger** *to pick up* (**recoja, recojas** . . .), **empezar** *to begin, start* (**empiece, empieces** . . .).

For other spelling rules affecting verbs, see page 283.

LATIN AMERICAN USAGE

The present subjunctive forms for **vos**, used in the Río de la Plata area in place of **tú** (see Chapters 1, 17 and 25), are slightly different, with the stress falling on the last syllable: **vos llamés, vos comás, vos vivás**. Stem changes do not apply in this case, e.g. **vos empecés, vos volvás** for **tú empieces, tú vuelvas**, while irregular verbs of more than one syllable simply undergo a shift in stress, e.g. **vos vengás, vos vayás.**

Other points to note in the text

- Direct and indirect object pronouns (third person singular, masculine form): *lo salude* (l. 5), *le indique* (l. 5), *lo mire* (l. 8), *le pregunte* (l. 9), *lo introduzca* (l. 14), *le enseñaron* (l. 20), *se le ocupe* (l. 22), *le sea difícil* (l. 29–31), *le permitan* (l. 49) (see Chapter 25)
- *Por* and *para*: *para* (l. 22, 12, 31, 36), *por* (l. 34, 41) (see Chapter 28)
- Possessives: There are numerous examples in the text, among these *su mejor traje* (l. 1), *inferior a la suya* (l. 29), *sus proposiciones* (l. 30), *sus . . . capacidades* (l. 49–50), etc. (see Chapter 24)
- Adjective agreement and position: There are a number of examples in the text. Note in particular *su mejor traje* (l. 1), *el estómago apretado* (l. 1–2), *su nuevo puesto* (l. 3), *algún rincón improvisado* (l. 10–11), *aburridos documentos* (l. 11–12), *tareas rutinarias* (l. 23), *su carrera laboral futura* (l. 44), etc. (see Chapter 20)

EXERCISES

As you do these exercises, study the sentences carefully and think about their equivalent meanings in English.

1 Put the verb in brackets into the correct form of the present subjunctive.

a No quiero llamar a Juan. Prefiero que tú lo (llamar) ________.
b La madre les prohibe a sus hijos que (jugar) ________ en la calle.
c Le recomendamos que (abrir) ________ una cuenta corriente en el Banco Exterior.
d Me ha pedido que (escribir) ________ una carta a su padre.
e Queremos que usted nos (preparar) ________ los informes cuanto antes.
f Nos sugiere que (hablar) ________ con el gerente.
g Mi padre quiere que (estudiar, yo) ________ derecho pero mi madre prefiere que (ver) ________ mundo.
h Os digo que (dejar) ________ los zapatos allí.
i ¿Quieres que (mirar, nosotros) ________ esto juntos o no?

j El profesor exige a todos sus estudiantes que (hablar) ________ en castellano.

k Les aconsejo a ustedes que no (llegar) ________ tarde.

l Por el momento no quiero que (cerrar, tú) ________ el libro.

2 Link the two phrases to form a complete sentence, making whatever adjustments are necessary.

a Siento mucho	• Gloria no se encuentra bien.
b Nos extraña	• mienten.
c ¿Os molesta	• decimos la verdad?
d Temen	• hay un accidente.
e Está muy contento	• nos conocemos.
f No me sorprende	• lo han pasado bien en México.
g Me alegro	• te dan un aumento de sueldo.
h No creo	• viene Pedro a la hora indicada.
i No le gusta	• su hijo sale con Marta.
j No creo	• este trabajo es muy duro.
k Dudamos	• saben mucho sobre el incidente.
l Odio	• la gente no dice la verdad.

3 In Column B below is a list of recommendations to a new employee. You can link an element from Column A with one from Column B without changing the verb from the infinitive in Column B, but by so doing you are making a general statement. To personalise the advice (It is important that *you* . . .), you need to use the subjunctive. Personalise the advice given by choosing a phrase from Column A to go with one from Column B and write a complete sentence, making the necessary changes and additions. Use the formal form of address: **usted**.

A	B
es importante	**a** proponer nuevas ideas en el trabajo
es aconsejable	**b** aprender o perfeccionar un idioma
es bueno	**c** reconocer tanto sus puntos fuertes como sus puntos débiles
es mejor	**d** esforzarse por hacer siempre bien el trabajo
es necesario	**e** aceptar las críticas sin enfadarse
hace falta	**f** desconectarse del trabajo una vez en casa
es imprescindible	**g** no almorzar en el área de trabajo
es recomendable	**h** acudir a cursillos de especialización
es fundamental	**i** cuidar su aspecto personal
conviene	**j** decir 'no' a un exceso de trabajo
es una buena idea	**k** no llevar trabajo a casa
es lógico	**l** intentar estar al día

4 Put the verb in brackets into the correct form of the present subjunctive.

a Aunque les (costar) ________, es una buena idea que lo (hacer) ________.
b Hablaremos más de esto después de que ustedes (llegar) ________.
c Antes de que nos (servir, ellos) ________ la cena, les enseñaremos las fotos que sacamos el otro día.
d En cuanto yo (saber) ________ algo de sus intenciones, les informaré para que (estar) ________ prevenidos.
e En caso de que ustedes no (venir) ________, yo misma me encargaré de todo.
f Mientras no (haber) ________ inconvenientes, es mejor dejarlo tal como está.
g Tendremos que ponernos en camino muy, muy, temprano, antes de que (salir) ________ el sol.
h Alejandro ha dicho que hasta que no le (pagar, ellos) ________ la mensualidad, no puede apuntarse a la excursión.
i Con tal de que su padre nos (dejar) ________ el coche, podremos costearnos el viaje.
j Cuando (recibir, él) ________ la paga, nos tranquilizaremos.
k Del jefe no hay rastro; a ver si lo vemos antes de que (irse, él) ________ de vacaciones.
l Pues hay que dar con él para que (saber, él) ________ de las determinaciones que hemos tomado.

5 Make meaningful sentences by combining a phrase from Column A with one from Column B.

A	B
a Cuando encuentre trabajo	1 no salen
b Tenemos que terminar esto	2 después de que esté allí un par de meses
c Habla con Pepe	3 hasta hartarte
d Cuando llueve	4 después de casarse
e Nos quedaremos aquí	5 daré una fiesta
f Cuando lleguemos	6 mientras espero
g Van a comprarse una casa	7 podremos descansar
h Todo el mundo lo conocerá	8 mientras haya dinero
i Hago esto	9 antes de irte
j En esa casa comes	10 antes de que venga Pepe

6 Change these sentences so that they express a greater degree of uncertainty.

a No lo entiendo. Tal vez no tengo todos los datos.
b No ha llegado Roberto. Quizás viene mañana.
c Tal vez nos invitan a cenar.
d No nos contesta. Quizás no está en casa.
e Todavía no me ha llamado Alfonso. Quizás me llama esta tarde.
f No quiero decirlo, pero quizás Carmen tiene razón.
g Tal vez es mentira lo que acabas de escuchar.
h Tal vez hay alguien que nos indique el camino.
i No tenemos idea de lo que hay que hacer. Tal vez sabe algo Adolfo.
j Sergio no se encuentra nada bien. Quizás ha comido demasiado.

7 Write the correct form of the verb in brackets.

a Gabriel García Márquez escribió una novela que tituló 'El Coronel no tiene quien le (escribir) ________'.
b No tengo nada que (poder) ________ serviros.
c ¿Conoces a alguien que (dar) ________ clases de violín?
d Necesitamos un piso que (ser) ________ bueno pero barato.
e Cómprate algo que te (gustar) ________.
f Mariana está dispuesta a casarse con cualquiera que se lo (pedir) ________.
g Ya no hay nada en este mundo que me (sorprender) ________.
h Buscamos un libro que (contar) ________ la historia de este lugar.
i Es difícil encontrar a alguien que nos (decir) ________ lo que debemos hacer en estas circunstancias.
j Nos hacen falta unas aclaraciones que nos (ayudar) ________ a tomar una decisión.

8 Fill in the blanks using one of the verbs from the list.

pasar	**aprobar**	**tocar**	**tener**	**ir**
llegar	**haber**	**ser**	**dormir**	**mejorar**

a Necesito la ayuda de Alberto. ¡Ojalá ________ pronto!
b Queremos dejar de trabajar. ¡Ojalá nos ________ la lotería!
c Susana tiene un exámen mañana. ¡Ojalá ________¡
d La niña lleva mucho tiempo llorando. ¡Ojalá se ________ pronto!
e Hace calor y la mochila pesa. ¡Ojalá ________ camas libres en el albergue!
f – El lunes Félix empieza su nuevo trabajo.
– ¡Que ________ suerte!
g – Mañana nos vamos de vacaciones.
– ¡Que lo ________ bien!
h – Tengo una entrevista muy importante.
– ¡Que te ________ bien!
i – Me caso la semana que viene.
– ¡Que ________ muy feliz!
j – Julio no se encuentra bien.
– ¡Que se ________ pronto!

9 Correct these sentences and say in each case why the subjunctive is needed.

a Queremos que Eduardo va a Roma el jueves.
b Espero que están ustedes bien.
c Les rogamos a los señores pasajeros que se abrochan los cinturones de seguridad.
d No conozco a nadie que toca el piano como tú.
e Me pide que le doy mis apuntes.
f No le gusta a la gente que uno tiene éxito.
g Es muy buena idea que visitan la destilería antes de marcharse.

h No vamos a empezar hasta que viene Rodrigo.
i No me extraña que a Paloma no le gusta su trabajo.
j Cuando voy a Madrid ¿quieres que te traigo algo?
k Es imposible que se van ustedes antes de que vuelve mi jefe.
l Aunque tiene dinero, no creo que lo gastará.

10 Translate the following sentences into Spanish.

a I'm sorry you are not well; I hope to see you when you are better.
b I don't think there is anyone here who will help us.
c It's not necessary to see it but it's important for us to know how it works.
d Perhaps he can tell us what's happening before Juan gets back.
e Even if he gets a job, Julio will have to carry on studying.
f Samuel may have more experience but it's not very likely that he has studied as much as you.
g It's natural for Javier to want to leave home the moment he starts earning his living.
h Perhaps he'll look for a flat that's not too expensive or too far from his work.
i She doesn't want to make a speech although her boss may ask her to.
j It's sensible for us to introduce ourselves so that everyone knows who we are.

11 The new employee of the text is a friend of yours and has sent you a rather miserable e-mail. You hasten to cheer him up, commiserating with him but also giving him some suggestions and advice as to what he can do.

Write what you would say to him, using the subjunctive as much as possible to convey your thoughts and feelings, e.g. **siento que, espero que, es lógico que, es posible que, te sugiero que, me parece buena idea que**.

12 Imagine and write down the advice you would give to Michael, who wants to learn a foreign language. Use as much as possible expressions which require the use of the subjunctive, e.g. **te aconsejo que, te recomiendo que, te sugiero que, no creo que, es importante que**.

For more exercises on the use of the subjunctive after conjunctions, see Chapter 29, **Conjunctions**.

15 | The imperfect subjunctive

Text 1

Las quejas de las esposas modernas

Long-established male attitudes in marriage are the subject of this letter, and Text 2 which follows. The problem is presented here through the voice of two women from Mexico, who discuss their relationships. Read through and find out what their complaints are, then go back over the texts again and focus attention on the use of the imperfect and the present subjunctive.

"Mi marido no tolera mis éxitos profesionales"

***Ana Luisa**, licenciada en comunicación, 34 años*

"Tengo cinco años de casada. Luis, mi esposo, es un hombre educado a la antigua y, aunque me duele reconocerlo, macho.

*Nos conocimos en la universidad, donde los dos cursábamos la carrera de comunicación. Solíamos estudiar juntos y le daba mucho gusto que yo **sacara** buenas notas . . . claro, siempre y cuando no **fueran** superiores a las de él. No obstante, lo quería tanto que hasta llegué a cometer errores intencionales para que él no **se sintiera** tan mal. Luis no tolera que yo **sea** más que él. No soporta que yo **gane** más y **tenga** más éxitos. Nuestros pleitos son constantes y mi suegra opina que yo debo dejar el empleo, pues lo único que consigo es que mi marido **se sienta** inferior. En un principio pensé hacerlo, pero amo demasiado mi trabajo. Si lo **hiciera** me arrepentiría .*

*Me gustaría que mi marido **fuera** más participativo, que **se sintiera** más orgulloso de mí y **considerara** mis logros como suyos. Sin embargo, por su manera de ser nos alejamos cada vez más y temo que un día no muy lejano **nos separemos**."*

Text 2

"Mi esposo no colabora conmigo en los quehaceres hogareños"

Lucía, secretaria, 35 años

"Luego de mi matrimonio dejé mi empleo de secretaria porque Alberto, mi marido, me pidió que lo **hiciera**. Pero cuando vino el primer hijo, a veces no teníamos dinero ni para la leche. Alberto aseguraba que todo se arreglaría y quería que yo **siguiera** en la casa. Al llegar el segundo hijo
5 nuestra situación económica se agravó y a regañadientes mi marido aceptó que **regresara** al trabajo.

Los primeros meses fueron terribles. Entraba a las 8 de la mañana y muchas veces me daban las 10 de la noche en la oficina. A Alberto le molestaba que yo **volviera** tarde. Yo me indignaba más porque, pese a
10 la hora y a mi cansancio, aún debía limpiar la casa, cocinar, lavar ropa y plancharla. Nuestra situación económica mejoró, pero yo me sentía agobiada por las presiones laborales, las tareas domésticas, el descuido de mis hijos y los celos de mi marido.

Quiero mucho a Alberto y no deseo perderlo. Si me **dejara** no sé qué
15 haría. Hablé con él y aceptó que **contratáramos** una persona para que me **ayudara** en casa (él jamás lo hará). Además, mi jefe accedió a que yo **saliera** más temprano. Alberto está mucho más complacido."

Both texts from diario *El Universal*, México

The imperfect subjunctive

1 USAGE

General

General usage of the imperfect subjunctive corresponds with that of the subjunctive as a whole, so the uses of the subjunctive outlined in Chapter 14 are also valid here. One important exception is the use of the imperfect subjunctive (and the pluperfect subjunctive) in **si** (*if*) clauses (see below).

There are a number of subjunctive forms in the texts, the majority of them in the imperfect, but a few also in the present. In Text 1, note the use of **sea**, **gane** and **tenga** (l. 8), **se sienta** (l. 10) and **nos separemos**, (l. 15–16).

SEQUENCE OF TENSES WITH THE IMPERFECT SUBJUNCTIVE

Tense agreement with the imperfect subjunctive is different from that of the present subjunctive, so before you look at the notes on usage below, you need to consider the sequence of tenses in which it occurs.

The imperfect subjunctive in the subordinate clause is normally dependent on a main clause verb in some form of the past – imperfect indicative, preterite, pluperfect indicative – or in the conditional.

Me **pedía/pidió/había pedido** que **volviera**. *He/she was asking/asked/had asked me to come back.*
Me **gustaría** que **volviera**. *I'd like him/her/you to come back.*

Basic uses

a Subjunctive in subordinate clauses, with the verb in the main clause expressing:

i Some kind of emotion.

. . . le daba mucho gusto **que** yo **sacara** buenas notas . . . (T. 1, l. 4–5) *. . . he was very pleased that I got good marks . . .*
. . . le molestaba **que** yo **volviera** tarde. (T. 2, l. 8–9) *. . . he was annoyed that I should be late home.*

Contrast the sentences above, in which the main verb is in the *imperfect indicative*, with the following ones, with the verb in the main clause in the *present tense* and that in the subordinate clause in the *present subjunctive.*

Le **da** mucho gusto **que** yo **saque** buenas notas. *He's very pleased that I should get good marks.*
Le **molesta que** yo **vuelva** tarde. *He doesn't like me being late home.*

ii Wishes, wants and requests.

Me gustaría **que** mi marido **fuera** más participativo . . . (T. 1, l. 13) *I wish my husband were more cooperative . . .*
. . . **que se sintiera** más orgulloso de mí . . . (T. 1, l. 13–14) *. . . that he were more proud of me . . .*
. . . y **considerara** mis logros como suyos. (T. 1, l. 14) *. . . and that he considered my achievements as his own.*
. . . me **pidió que** lo **hiciera**. (T. 2, l. 2) *. . . he asked me to do it.*
. . . **quería que** yo **siguiera** en la casa. (T. 2, l. 4) *. . . he wanted me to continue being at home.*

The verb in the main clause, governing the verbs in the subordinate clauses in the first three sentences, is in the *conditional tense*: **me gustaría**.

Compare the above with the following sentence, in which the main verb is in the *present indicative*, with those in the subordinate clauses in the *present subjunctive.*

Me **gusta que** mi marido **sea** participativo, **que se sienta** orgulloso de mí y **considere** . . . *I like my husband being cooperative, being proud of me and that he considers . . .*

iii Acceptance and agreement.

> . . . aceptó **que regresara . . .** (T. 2, l. 6) *. . . he agreed that I should go back . . .*
> . . . **aceptó que contratáramos** una persona . . . (T. 2, l. 15) *. . . he agreed that we should hire a person . . .*
> . . . mi jefe **accedió** a **que** yo **saliera** más temprano . . . (T. 2, l. 16–17) *. . . my boss agreed that I should leave earlier . . .*

For further information on the use of the subjunctive in subordinate clauses, see Chapters 14 and 16.

b Imperfect subjunctive after conjunctions.
Conjunctions used with the imperfect subjunctive are the same as those used with the present subjunctive, as seen in Chapter 14. Which of the two tenses to use will depend on the time reference and the tense of the main verb (see Sequence of tenses with the imperfect subjunctive above, and Sequence of tenses with the present subjunctive in Chapter 14).

i Conjunctions expressing conditions: **siempre y cuando**, **siempre que** *as long as*, **en caso de que** *if, in case*, **con tal de que/a condición de que** *provided that, on condition that, etc.*

> . . . **siempre y cuando** (*or* **siempre que**) no **fueran** superiores a las de él. (T. 1, l. 5–6) *. . . as long as they weren't higher than his.*
> Te dije que **en caso de que** no **estuviera** en casa, le dejaras un recado. *I told you that if he/she wasn't at home, you should leave him/her a message.*
> Aceptamos, **con tal de que/a condición de que** nos **dejaran** tranquilos. *We agreed, on condition that they left us in peace.*

ii Conjunctions expressing purpose and intention: **para que**, **a fin de que**, **con el propósito/objeto de que**, etc.

> . . . **para que** él no **se sintiera** tan mal. (T. 1, l. 7–8) *. . . so that he wouldn't feel so bad.*
> . . . aceptó que contratáramos una persona **para que me ayudara** . . . (T. 2, l. 15–16) *. . . he agreed that we should hire a person to help me . . .*
> Se lo llevé **a fin de que** lo **vieran**. *I took it to them, so that they would see it.*
> Invitamos a ambos, **con el propósito/objeto de que se conocieran**. *We invited both of them, so that they could meet.*

iii Conjunctions expressing concession: **aunque**, **aún cuando**, **a no ser que/a menos que**, etc.

> No le invitaría, **aunque** me lo **pidiera**. *I wouldn't invite him, even if he asked me to.*
> Yo que tú se lo diría, **aunque se molestaran**. *If I were you I would tell them, even if they got annoyed.*
> No la dejaría, **a no ser que/a menos que** me **engañara**. *I wouldn't leave her, unless she cheated on me.*

c The imperfect subjunctive in relative clauses (see Chapter 14).

There are no examples of the imperfect subjunctive in relative clauses in the texts, but the following sentences will illustrate this use.

Buscaban una persona **que** les **ayudara** en casa. *They were looking for a person to help them in the home.*

La empresa necesitaba una empleada **que hablara** español. *The company needed an employee who could speak Spanish.*

d Imperfect subjunctive in **si** *if* clauses.

The imperfect subjunctive occurs in **si** *if* clauses, with the verb in the main clause in the conditional. Note that English uses the simple past in the *if* clause.

Si lo **hiciera** me arrepentiría. (T. 1, l. 12) *If I did it, I'd regret it.*

Si me **dejara** no sé qué haría. (T. 2, l. 14–15) *If he left me, I don't know what I would do.*

In the examples above, the conditions are seen as remote or unlikely to be fulfilled. But the same construction can be used to express conditions which cannot be met:

Si fuera más joven conseguiría trabajo. *If he/she were younger, he/she would get work.*

Contrast the first two examples with the following ones, in which **si** is followed by the present indicative. **Si** cannot be used with the present subjunctive.

Si lo **hago** me arrepentiré. *If I do it, I'll regret it.*

Si me **deja** no sé qué haré. *If he leaves me, I don't know what I'll do.*

See also **si** + pluperfect subjunctive, in Chapter 16.

2 FORMATION

Regular verbs

The imperfect subjunctive is formed from the stem of the third person plural of the preterite tense, to which the endings are added. There are two sets of endings for the imperfect subjunctive, which are interchangeable. Note that **-er** and **-ir** verbs share the same endings.

tomar	**comer**	**vivir**
tom**ara/ase**	com**iera/iese**	viv**iera/iese**
tom**aras/ases**	com**ieras/ieses**	viv**ieras/ieses**
tom**ara/ase**	com**iera/iese**	viv**iera/iese**
tom**áramos/ásemos**	com**iéramos/iésemos**	viv**iéramos/iésemos**
tom**arais/aseis**	com**ierais/ieseis**	viv**ierais/ieseis**
tom**aran/asen**	com**ieran/iesen**	viv**ieran/iesen**

Irregular verbs

Irregular verbs form the imperfect subjunctive in the same way as regular ones, as you will see from these examples:

Infinitive	***Preterite*** (3rd pers. pl.)	***Imperfect subjunctive***
decir *to say*	dijeron	dijera/dijese, dijeras/dijeses . . .
poner *to put*	pusieron	pusiera/pusiese, pusieras/pusieses . . .
tener *to have*	tuvieron	tuviera/tuviese, tuvieras/tuvieses . . .

Other points to note in the texts

- Present subjunctive: Text 1: *no tolera que yo sea* (l. 8), *no soporta que yo gane . . . y tenga* (l. 8–9), *lo único que consigo es que . . . se sienta . . .* (l. 10–11), *temo que . . . nos separemos* (l. 15–16) (see Chapter 14)
- Preterite and imperfect tenses: Text 1: *Nos conocimos* (l. 3), *cursábamos* (l. 3), *Solíamos* (l. 4), *llegué* (l. 7), etc. Text 2: *dejé* (l. 1), *pidió* (l. 2), *vino* (l. 2), *teníamos* (l. 3), etc. (see Chapters 2 and 3)
- Adverbs and adverbial phrases: Text 1: *a la antigua* (l. 2–3), *juntos* (l. 4), *claro* (l. 5), *tanto* (l. 6), *hasta* (l. 6), *tan* (l. 7), *demasiado* (l. 11), etc. (see Chapter 21)
- Conditional: Text 1: *me arrepentiría* (l. 12), *Me gustaría* (l. 13). Text 2: *se arreglaría* (l. 3–4), *no sé qué haría* (l. 14–15) (see Chapter 7)
- Possessives: There are numerous possessives in both texts (see Chapter 24).

EXERCISES

As you do these exercises, study the sentences carefully and think about their equivalent meanings in English.

1 Put the verb in brackets into the imperfect subjunctive.

- **a** Yo no esperaba que Laura me (escribir) ________.
- **b** Les mostramos las fotos porque queríamos que (ver, ellos) ________ la casa.
- **c** No era posible que lo (hacer, nosotros) ________ en el tiempo previsto.
- **d** Nos sorprendió mucho que Paco os (hablar) ________ de tal manera.
- **e** Tuvo que ocultarlo como si (ser) ________ una cosa inadmisible.
- **f** Tenía que darle cuanta información (pedir, él) ________.
- **g** Mandó a su hijo al pueblo para que (ayudar, él) ________ a los abuelos.
- **h** Se marchó sin que nadie (despedirse) ________ de él.
- **i** ¡Ojalá (saber, nosotros) ________ su paradero!
- **j** Puede que (salir, ellos) ________ antes de que (llover) ________.
- **k** No pensaba que me (decir, ella) ________ tal cosa.
- **l** Estuvimos preparados para cuando (llegar, vosotros) ________.

2 Rewrite these sentences in the past.

a A Luis no le gusta que Ana Luisa saque mejores notas que él.
b Ana Luisa no quiere que su marido se sienta inferior a ella.
c Es importante que Luis reconozca los éxitos de su esposa.
d Siendo macho, es lógico que Luis tenga celos.
e Ana Luisa no cree que dejar de trabajar sea la solución.
f Ana Luisa teme que se separen pronto.
g Alberto le prohíbe a Lucía que trabaje fuera de casa.
h Es una pena que los ingresos de Alberto no sean suficientes para mantener a la familia.
i A Luisa le duele que su marido no le dé apoyo.
j No está bien que Alberto no ayude en casa.
k Lucía le exige a Alberto que contraten una persona que haga las tareas domésticas.
l Alberto le dice a Luisa que no trabaje tantas horas.

3 Complete these sentences using the imperfect subjunctive.

a La suegra de Ana Luisa no quería que . . .
b Lucía le pidió a su marido que . . .
c No les gustó a los niños que . . .
d Era importante que . . .
e Era extraño que . . .
f A Lucía no le gustaba que . . .
g Ana Luisa sentía mucho que . . .
h Era insoportable que . . .
i El jefe de Lucía se sorprendió de que . . .
j Luis no toleraba que . . .

4 Translate these sentences into Spanish.

a What did she expect her husband to do?
b She asked him to look after the children.
c In those days it was not normal for women to work.
d Many women did not eat so that their children would not go hungry.
e They lived in that house without anyone knowing that they existed.
f Everyone left before Juan arrived.
g We were very sorry that you (familiar, plural) could not come to the party.
h We didn't believe that nothing would happen and that he would keep his word.
i It wasn't natural for them to behave that way.
j We would like someone to explain to us why they did it.

5 Complete the sentences by putting the verb in brackets into the correct form.

a Preferíamos que (acabar, tú) ________ lo más pronto posible.
b Nos gustaría que (quedarse, vosotras) ________ más tiempo.

c Quisiera que no (ser) ________ así.
d Me gustaría que me (acompañar, tú) ________ cuando vaya a Santiago.
e Claro que les gustaría que (ganar) ________ su equipo pero no lo ven muy probable.
f Aunque me (ofrecer, ellos) ________ un sueldo magnífico, no trabajaría allí.
g Tendrían el éxito asegurado siempre que (jugar) ________ bien.
h Sería mejor que (comportarse) ________ como los adultos que son y no como niños.
i Mientras ellos nos (dejar) ________ en paz, no los molestaríamos.
j Sería conveniente que (encontrarse, vosotros) ________ antes del jueves.

6 Cross out the inappropriate verb in each sentence.

a Si tuve/tuviera tiempo, iría.
b Si fumaras/fumas menos, te sentirías mejor.
c Si podemos/pudiéramos, os ayudaríamos.
d Si dijera/dijo la verdad, estaríamos dispuestos a creerlo.
e Si vinieron/vinieran, les gustaría.
f Si te pide/pidiera dinero, se lo darías.
g Si no vivíais/vivierais tan lejos, os visitaríamos más a menudo.
h Se llevaría mejor con sus colegas, si fuera/fue más amable.
i Iría a la piscina si supe/supiera nadar.
j Ha dicho que si se jubile/jubilara, no tendría lo suficiente como para vivir.

7 Complete these sentences as remote conditions.

Example: Compraría una casa . . .
Compraría una casa si me tocara la lotería.

a Estaríamos más contentos si . . .
b Habría menos contaminación si . . .
c Me enfadaría si . . .
d Haría un recorrido por Sudamérica si . . .
e Sería fantástico si . . .
f Le daría dinero a un/a colega si . . .
g Prescindiríamos del coche si . . .
h No utilizaría el móvil* si . . .
i Llevaría puesto un sombrero si . . .
j El mundo sería mejor si . . .

* *In Latin American Spanish:* **celular.**

8 Imagine that you are one of the protagonists of the texts in this chapter and make a list of how you would like things to be in your life, using the following phrases:

Si fuera . . . me gustaría que . . .   Preferiría que . . .   No querría que . . .

See also Chapter 7, **The conditional**. See Chapter 16, **The pluperfect subjunctive and conditional perfect**, for practice of unfulfilled conditions.

16 | The pluperfect subjunctive and conditional perfect

Text

February 23rd 1981 marked a turning point in Spanish political history. Lieutenant-Colonel Antonio Tejero occupied the Congress building with the intention of overthrowing the government. What would have happened if the *Tejerazo* or *23-F*, as it came to be known, had succeeded? This is the subject of this article. As you read the text, note the way in which Spanish expresses ideas such as *What would have happened if it had . . . ?*, *If it had . . . it would have . . .*

¿Qué habría sucedido si . . . ?

El 23 de febrero de 1981 pasó a la historia de España porque un grupo de militares al mando del teniente coronel Antonio Tejero decidió irrumpir en el Congreso e intentar, pistola en mano, tomarse el poder.

Más de veinte años después, los españoles intentan imaginar qué **habría pasado** si la intentona **hubiese triunfado**. ¿Cómo sería España ahora? ¿**Habría entrado** en la Unión Europea? ¿Quién sería el presidente? Probablemente, las cosas serían muy diferentes si Tejero **se hubiera salido** con la suya.

Aunque resulta difícil determinar el curso que **habrían tomado** los acontecimientos, los analistas políticos coinciden en que escasamente España **habría conseguido** el grado de desarrollo económico que ha alcanzado en los últimos 20 años y menos aún **habría formado** parte de la Unión Europea. Porque si el golpe **se hubiera consolidado** España **habría vuelto** a estar bajo una dictadura militar al menos unos años y eso **habría impedido** su integración en la Europa democrática. El país no **se habría beneficiado** de los fondos para el desarrollo que ha recibido desde mediados de los '80 de sus socios comunitarios y su economía se parecería mucho más a la de países como Argentina.

Las noticias serían también muy diferentes si el golpe **hubiese triunfado**. La mayoría de los españoles cree que si el golpe del 23-F **se hubiera consumado**, muchos de los periódicos que hoy existen no **hubieran visto** la luz, ni tampoco las cadenas de TV privadas, mucho más difíciles de controlar por una dictadura.

De haberse concretado el golpe, **habría cambiado** la historia de España. Gracias al fracaso del 23-F, la democracia se encuentra consolidada y sólo un 20% de los españoles cree que existe algún riesgo de que los militares vuelvan al poder.

Diario *El Mercurio*, Chile

 The pluperfect subjunctive

1 USAGE

a *Si* + pluperfect subjunctive.

The pluperfect subjunctive is used in a construction with **si** *if* and the conditional perfect in the main clause, to express unfulfilled conditions in relation to the past. The text as a whole focuses on the idea that had the coup succeeded, things would have been different. Note the following example:

> . . . qué **habría pasado si** la intentona (de golpe de Estado) **hubiese triunfado** . . . (l. 8–10)
> *. . . what would have happened if the attempted coup had succeeded . . .*

The coup did not succeed, therefore the condition here is an unfulfilled one.
Other sentences in the text express a similar idea. Note the following example in which **haber** takes the **-ra** ending instead of **-se**. In the **si** clause the two forms are interchangeable.

> . . . las cosas serían muy diferentes **si** Tejero **se hubiera salido** con la suya. (l. 13–15)
> *. . . things would be very different if Tejero had had his way.*

The same usage of the pluperfect subjunctive is found in lines 24–25, 37–40.

b Pluperfect subjunctive for conditional perfect.

In conditional sentences such as those above, the **-ra** form of the pluperfect subjunctive can replace the conditional perfect in the main clause, with exactly the same meaning. Note the following example from the text:

> . . . **si** el golpe . . . **se hubiera consumado**, muchos de los periódicos . . . no **hubieran visto la** luz . . . (l. 37–42) *. . . if the coup . . . had succeeded, many of the newspapers . . . would not have been published . . .*

In this sentence, **hubieran visto** and **habrían visto** mean the same. Although the pluperfect subjunctive and the conditional perfect are interchangeable in the main clause, this is not the case in the **si** clause, where only the pluperfect subjunctive can be used.

c *De* + perfect infinitive for *si* + pluperfect subjunctive.

An alternative to the construction **si** + pluperfect subjunctive is the less frequent construction with **de** followed by the perfect infinitive. Compare the following pairs of sentences:

> **Si** (yo) lo **hubiera sabido**, (yo) no **habría/hubiera ido**.
> **De haberlo sabido**, (yo) no **habría/hubiera ido**.
> *If I had known, I wouldn't have gone.*

> **Si hubiéramos tenido** suficiente dinero, **habríamos/hubiéramos comprado** el piso.
> **De haber tenido** suficiente dinero, **habríamos/hubiéramos comprado** el piso.
> *If we'd had enough money, we would have bought the flat.*

The alternative construction with ***de*** + perfect infinitive normally occurs when the subject of the **si** clause and that of the other clause are the same, as in the previous examples, unless a different subject has been made explicit and there is no possibility of ambiguity, as in the examples which follow.

Si se hubiera concretado el golpe, **habría/hubiera cambiado** la historia de España.
De haberse concretado el golpe, **habría/hubiera** cambiado la historia de España. (l. 46–48)
Had the coup succeeded, the history of Spain would have changed.

Si el rey no **hubiera intervenido**, quizá las cosas **habrían/ hubieran sido** diferentes.
De no **haber intervenido** el rey, quizá las cosas **habrían/hubieran sido** diferentes.
If the king had not intervened, perhaps things would have been different.

d Other uses of the pluperfect subjunctive.
Usage of the pluperfect subjunctive outside conditional sentences corresponds to that of the subjunctive as a whole, for example in subordinate clauses, independent clauses, after certain conjunctions (see Chapters 14 and 15). Generally, though, it is less frequent than the present or the imperfect subjunctive. Here are some examples:

Nos habría encantado que te **hubieras quedado** con nosotros unos días. *We would have loved it if you had stayed with us a few days.*
Tal vez habría sido mejor que no se lo **hubieras dicho**. *Perhaps it would have been better if you hadn't told him/her/them.*
Ojalá lo **hubieras oído**. *I wish you had heard it.*
Aunque me lo **hubiera rogado**, yo no habría vuelto con él. *Even if he had begged me, I wouldn't have gone back to him.*
Me pidió que les dejara una nota con el conserje en caso de que todavía no **hubiesen regresado**. *He/she asked me to leave a note with the porter in case they still hadn't got back.*
No creo que lo **hubieran aceptado**. *I don't think they would have accepted it.*
(But: Creo que lo **habrían aceptado**. *I think they would have accepted it.*)

2 FORMATION

The pluperfect subjunctive is formed from the imperfect subjunctive of **haber** followed by the past participle.

	cambiar	comer	salir
hubiera/iese			
hubieras/ieses			
hubiera/iese	**cambiado**	**comido**	**salido**
hubiéramos/iésemos			
hubierais/ieseis			
hubieran/iesen			

SEQUENCE OF TENSES WITH THE PLUPERFECT SUBJUNCTIVE

The pluperfect subjunctive in the subordinate clause is normally dependent on a main clause verb in the preterite, imperfect, conditional, conditional perfect and pluperfect, for example:

No **pensé** que me **hubieran visto**. *I didn't think they would have seen me.*
Sentía mucho que te **hubieses ido**. *He/she was very sorry you had gone.*
No **creyó/creía** que yo lo **hubiera hecho** solo. *He/she didn't believe I had done it on my own.*
Me **habría gustado** que la **hubieras visto**. *I would have liked you to have seen her.*
No me **extrañaría** que ya **se hubiese enterado**. *I wouldn't be surprised if he/she had already found out.*
Me **habría encantado** que **hubiesen venido**. *I would have loved it if they had come.*

The conditional perfect

1 USAGE

The conditional perfect is used in the main clause in unfulfilled conditions (see **a** above) to refer to a hypothetical situation, to what *would have happened* given certain circumstances. There are a number of examples in the text, not all used alongside the **si** clause, which is understood.

. . . qué **habría pasado** si . . . (l. 8–9) *. . . what would have happened if . . .*
¿**Habría entrado** en la Unión Europea? (l. 11–12) *Would it have joined the European Union?*

In conditional sentences such as the above, the conditional perfect has the same meaning as the **-ra** form of the pluperfect subjunctive in the main clause (see **b** above).

. . . qué **hubiera pasado si** . . . *what would have happened if . . .*
¿**Hubiera entrado** en la Unión Europea? *Would it have joined the European Union?*

Note also the use of the conditional perfect in **habrían tomado** (l. 17), **habría conseguido** (l. 20), **habría formado** (l. 23), **habría vuelto** (l. 25), **se habría beneficiado** (l. 29–30), **habría cambiado** (l. 47).

2 FORMATION

The conditional perfect is formed from the conditional of **haber** followed by the past participle.

	cambiar	comer	salir
habría			
habrías			
habría	cambiado	comido	salido
habríamos			
habríais			
habrían			

Other points to note in the text

- Definite article: There are a number of examples in the text, but note particularly *El 23 de febrero* (l. 1), *los españoles intentan* (l. 7–8), *las cosas serían* (l. 13), *si . . . se hubiera salido con la suya* (l. 14–15) (see Chapter 18)
- Finite verb + infinitive: *decidió irrumpir . . . e intentar* (l. 4–5), *intentan imaginar* (l. 8), *habría vuelto a estar* (l. 25–26) (see Chapter 8)
- Verb + preposition: *irrumpir en* (l. 4), *entrado en* (l. 11), *coinciden en* (l. 19), *habría vuelto a* (l. 25), *no se habría beneficiado de* (l. 29–30), *se parecería . . . a* (l. 33–34) (see Chapter 28)

EXERCISES

As you do these exercises, study the sentences carefully and think about their equivalent meanings in English.

1 Put the verb in brackets into the correct form of the pluperfect subjunctive.

a Jacobo no estaba convencido de que le (dar, ellos) ________ las mismas oportunidades que a Fidel.
b Consuelo había deseado que (venir, ellos) ________.
c ¡Ojalá (comprar, él) ________ una casa en el campo! Allí (vivir, nosotros) ________ felices.
d Gastó dinero como si (heredar) ________ una fortuna.
e Aunque (traer, tú) ________ el televisor, no podríamos haber visto el partido.
f Lamentaba que no (ver, nosotros) ________ su nueva película.
g No sabíamos que tú (ganar) ________ un premio.
h No creía que a Guillermo le (pasar) ________ tal cosa; parecía un chico muy sensato.
i No había nada que les (complacer) ________ en aquella época.
j ¡Ojalá (venir, vosotros) ________ ayer! ¡Nos (alegrar, vosotros) ________ un montón!

2 Rewrite the following sentences as in the example.

Example: Todo esto ha pasado porque no me hicisteis caso.
Nada de esto hubiera pasado si me hubierais hecho caso.

a No sabía que llovía tanto y no he traído un impermeable.
b No me quedé y por eso no me encontré con el cineasta.
c No hizo buen tiempo y por eso no salimos de excursión.
d No se lo dije porque no vinieron.
e No acudieron a la cita porque nadie les avisó.
f No te ha salido bien porque no me has hecho caso.
g Joaquín tuvo el accidente porque no miró al retrovisor.
h Como quedó algo de comida de la fiesta, no pasamos hambre.
i No te limpiaron los zapatos porque no los dejaste en la puerta.
j Como no vi a Genoveva, no me enteré de la reunión.

3 Change the phrases underlined to a construction using **de** + perfect infinitive.

- **a** ¡Qué pena que el museo esté cerrado! Si lo hubiéramos sabido, no hubiéramos venido.
- **b** Pepe tardó mucho en hacer el trabajo. Si lo hubiera hecho de otra forma, no hubiera tardado tanto.
- **c** No sabía que estuviste solo en casa ayer. Si me lo hubieras dicho, te hubiera llamado.
- **d** El cónsul no sabía que nuestros visados habían llegado. Si se hubiera dado cuenta, nos hubiera avisado.
- **e** No sabemos lo que hubiera hecho el rey si el golpe de estado se hubiera consolidado.
- **f** Si hubieras seguido mis instrucciones, no te encontrarías ahora en este apuro.
- **g** ¿Sabes una cosa? Si no me hubieras echado una mano, hubieras perdido un amigo.
- **h** ¡Lástima que no nos dijeras nada! Si nos hubieras dicho algo, te hubiéramos prestado el dinero que necesitabas.
- **i** Si hubiera existido una salida, la hubiéramos encontrado.
- **j** ¿Por qué no te pusiste en contacto con el señor Millás? Si le hubieras pedido consejo, te hubieras ahorrado unos disgustos.

4 Translate the following sentences into Spanish.

- **a** If he had time, he would go to the cinema.
- **b** If he had had time, he would have gone to the cinema.
- **c** If I did it, I would regret it.
- **d** If I had done it, I would have regretted it.
- **e** If we were rich, we would take you on a journey.
- **f** If we had been rich, we would have taken you on a journey.
- **g** If they read more books, they would understand much more.
- **h** If they had read more books, they would have understood much more.
- **i** When I saw him, I wouldn't have believed that he was ill.
- **j** Andrea would have come earlier if she hadn't had to wait for Paco.
- **k** You wouldn't have said we could speak to him if he weren't coming.
- **l** If Miguel hadn't gone off at that particular moment, he wouldn't have bumped into Basilio and everything would be different now.

5 Complete the sentences using a pluperfect subjunctive or conditional perfect.

- **a** Si el golpe de estado no hubiera fracasado, . . .
- **b** Si España no hubiera entrado en la Unión Europea, . . .
- **c** Si Cristóbal Colón no hubiera navegado hacia el oeste, . . .
- **d** Si Napoleón hubiera ganado la batalla de Waterloo, . . .
- **e** Si no me hubiera puesto a estudiar español, . . .
- **f** Si hubiera ido al cine anoche en vez de quedarme en casa, . . .
- **g** Si no hubieran dicho que el Titanic no era hundible, . . .
- **h** Si Logie Baird no hubiera inventado la televisión, . . .
- **i** Si los Reyes Magos o Papá Noel me hubieran traido lo que había pedido, . . .
- **j** Si hubiera hecho lo que soñaba con hacer, . . .

17 | The imperative

Text 1

The following article warns about the dangers of excessive exposure to the sun and gives recommendations on how to avoid them. As you read the text, note the way in which formal imperative forms have been used.

El sol, ¿amigo o enemigo?

Que el sol se convierta en un enemigo en la época de las vacaciones sólo depende de usted. Para no iniciar relaciones turbias, no **abuse** de él. El cáncer y el envejecimiento prematuro de la piel son dos consecuencias más que suficientes para intentar evitar esos problemas.

Si desea broncearse y no tener que acudir a un médico **procure** tomar el sol comedidamente, aunque sea en la terraza, antes de salir de vacaciones.

Es fundamental que lo haga progresivamente y muy prudente, al principio. Si no quiere deshidratarse **beba** agua, **muévase** y **báñese** y, aunque ya esté bronceado, **extienda** siempre sobre la piel una capa de crema protectora eficaz.

Si sufre una quemadura solar, **refúgiese** en la sombra y no **vuelva** a echarse aceite o crema solar. Mejor **aplique** un poco de hielo en la zona lesionada y **compre** en la farmacia una crema apropiada. Los médicos aconsejan desconfiar del sol. Por eso, **utilice** un protector con un índice de protección en función de la sensibilidad de su piel. **Aplíquelo** antes de la exposición y **repita** la operación con frecuencia. **Cuídese** de los productos de bronceado solar. Si le provocan picores, no los **utilice** y **vigile** su piel.

Revista *Cambio 16*, España

Text 2

This text looks at job interviews and gives advice on how to approach them. As you read it, note the use of the familiar form of the imperative.

Estrategias para encontrar empleo: la entrevista

- **Prepárala** a fondo. **Consigue** todos los datos que puedas sobre la empresa en cuestión.
- **Acude** a la entrevista relajado/a y sereno/a. **Evita** tomar café. (5)
La presencia, impecable, pero no te **arregles** en exceso.
- No importa si tu interlocutor es más joven o de tu misma edad, **háblale** de usted. (10)
- **Responde** a sus preguntas sin rodeos y **sé** sincero/a. **No te justifiques** nunca.
- **Habla** tranquilo/a, vocalizando, no hay prisa. **Piensa** antes de hablar y **deja** largos intervalos antes de contestar. (15)
- Tu actitud hacia la empresa debe ser positiva. **Deja** claro que tienes ganas de trabajar y muchas ideas que aportar. (20)
- **Argumenta** un cambio de aires antes que hacer el papel de víctima parado/a a quien nadie quiere contratar.
- **No te contradigas** en nada **ni des** explicaciones sobre tu salud, familia, novio/a . . . (25)
- **Habla** de tus aficiones siempre que éstas tengan algo que ver con la actividad de la empresa. **Di** sólo lo necesario. (30)
- **No acabes** tú la entrevista. Cuando concluya, **agradéceles** que te hayan recibido y **muéstrate** encantado de haberles conocido.

Revista *Prima*, España

The imperative

1 USAGE

Verb forms such as **habla** *speak*, **beba** *drink*, **repita** *repeat*, are known as imperative or command forms. The imperative, which is more widely used in Spanish than in English, is found in contexts like the following:

a Recommendations and advice. All the examples in Texts 1 and 2 fall into this category.

b Directions and instructions.

Siga todo recto. *Go straight on.*
Tome una cucharada antes de cada comida. *Take one spoonful before each meal.*

c Commands and prohibition.

> **Haga** lo que digo. *Do as I say.*
> No lo **deje** aquí. *Don't leave it here.*

d Requests.

> **Pásame** la sal, por favor. *Pass the salt, please.*

2 FORMATION

Unlike English, Spanish uses different imperative forms depending on who you are talking to (formal or familiar form) and whether you are speaking to one or more than one person (singular or plural form).

a Formal imperative.
Positive and negative commands for **usted** and **ustedes** are taken from the third person of the present subjunctive (Chapter 14). This is itself formed by removing the -**o** of the first person singular of the present tense indicative, to which the endings are added. This rule applies to all regular verbs and, with a few exceptions, to irregular and stem-changing verbs.

Present indicative (1st person)	***Formal imperative*** (*Vd./Vds.*)
habl**o** *I speak*	habl**e/n** *speak*
beb**o** *I drink*	beb**a/n** *drink*
repit**o** *I repeat*	repit**a/n** *repeat*
teng**o** *I have*	teng**a/n** *have*
dig**o** *I say*	dig**a/n** *say*

Irregular forms and spelling changes

Among irregular forms we find **dé/n** *give* (from **dar**), **esté/n** *be* (from **estar**), **vaya/n** *go* (from **ir**), **sepa/n** *know* (from **saber**), **sea/n** *be* (from **ser**).

Note also spelling changes in verbs ending in -**car**, -**gar**, -**ger**, -**zar**, e.g. **aplicar** *to apply*, **aplique/n**; **pagar** *to pay*, **pague/n**; **coger** *to take, catch*, **coja/n**; **empezar** *to begin, start*, **empiece/n**.

All the examples in Text 1 correspond to the formal imperative.
Note that the negative command is formed by placing **no** before the verb.

> . . . no **abuse** . . . (T. 1, l. 4) *. . . do not abuse . . .*
> . . . **procure** tomar el sol . . . (T. 1, l. 10–11) *. . . try to sunbathe . . .*
> . . . **beba** agua . . . (T. 1, l. 16) *. . . drink water . . .*
> . . . **aplique** un poco de hielo . . . (T. 1, l. 23) *. . . apply some ice . . .*
> . . . **repita** la operación . . . (T. 1, l. 30–31) *. . . repeat the operation . . .*

The use of the formal imperative may sound abrupt in some contexts so, to avoid this, use courtesy forms such as **por favor** *please*, **si es Vd. tan amable** *if you would be so kind*, **si no le importa** *if you don't mind*.

Por favor **tenga** cuidado. *Please be careful.*
Venga aquí un momento, si es Vd. tan amable. *Come here a moment, if you would be so kind.*
Póngalo aquí, si no le importa. *Put it here, if you don't mind.*

In polite requests such as the above, the construction **hacer el favor de** + the infinitive is a useful alternative.

Haga el favor de venir un momento. *Please come here a moment.*
Haga el favor de ponerlo aquí. *Please put it here.*

b Familiar imperative.
Negative familiar commands are taken from the present subjunctive, just as formal commands above, but positive familiar ones have special forms.

Infinitive	***Positive***	***Negative***	
habl**ar**	habl**a**	no habl**es**	(tú)
	habl**ad**	no habl**éis**	(vosotros/as)
respond**er**	respond**e**	no respond**as**	(tú)
	respond**ed**	no respond**áis**	(vosotros/as)
acud**ir**	acud**e**	no acud**as**	(tú)
	acud**id**	no acud**áis**	(vosotros/as)

Note that the **tú** positive imperative derives from the second person singular of the present indicative, without its final **-s**, e.g. **tú hablas** *you speak*, **habla** *speak*. The **vosotros/as** positive command is like the infinitive, but with a final **-d** instead of an **-r**, e.g. **hablar** *to speak*, **hablad** *speak*.

Acude a la entrevista . . . (T. 2, l. 4) *Go to the interview . . .*
Responde a sus preguntas . . . (T. 2, l. 11) *Answer his/her questions . . .*
Habla tranquilo/a . . . (T. 2, l. 14) *Speak in a relaxed way . . .*

Irregular forms

Some verbs form the ***singular positive*** familiar imperative in an irregular way: **di** *say* (from **decir**), **haz** *do, make* (from **hacer**), **ve** *go* (from **ir**), **pon** *put* (from **poner**), **sal** *go out* (from **salir**), **sé** *be* (from **ser**), **ten** *have* (from **tener**), **ven** *come* (from **venir**).

. . . **sé** sincero/a. (T. 2, l. 12) *. . . be sincere.*
Di sólo lo necesario. (T. 2, l. 29–30) *Say only what's necessary.*

See also **Irregular verbs** on pages 279–282.

The ***plural positive*** imperative and ***negative*** commands follow the ***regular*** pattern for familiar forms, e.g. **decid** (for **vosotros/as**), **no digas** (for **tú**), **no digáis** (for **vosotros/as**), from **decir** *to say*.

No te **contradigas** . . . (T. 2, l. 24) *Don't contradict yourself . . .*

LATIN AMERICAN USAGE

Latin Americans do not use the **vosotros/as** form, which is replaced by the **ustedes** form in both formal and familiar address.

Regular familiar imperative forms for **vos**, used in the Río de la Plata area in place of **tú** (see Chapters 1, 14 and 25), are mostly similar, except that the stress falls on the last syllable. Below are the positive and negative forms for **hablar**, **comer** and **partir**:

hablá	**comé**	**partí** (for **parte**)
no hablés	**no comás**	**no partás**

c Command forms including the speaker.
Command forms including the speaker, as in *Let's work*, correspond to the first person plural of the present subjunctive (Chapter 14), e.g. **trabajemos** (from **trabajar**) *let's work*, **comamos** (from **comer**) *let's eat*, **no subamos** (from **subir**) *let's not go up*. When **nos** is added, the final **-s** of the verb is removed, e.g. **bañémonos** *let's bathe*, **vámonos** *let's go*.

PRONOUNS WITH IMPERATIVES

Object and reflexive pronouns precede negative imperatives but are attached to positive ones. In the case of object pronouns, the indirect one must come first. There are a number of examples of this in the texts. Note that an accent may need to be added to the positive form to indicate that the stress remains in the same place.

... **muévase** y **báñese** ... (T. 1, l. 16) *... move and bathe ...*
Aplíquelo antes ... (T. 1, l. 29–30) *Apply it before ...*
Prepárala a fondo. (T. 2, l. 1) *Prepare it thoroughly.*
... no **te arregles** en exceso. (T. 2, l. 6–7) *... don't overdress.*
No **te justifiques** ... (T. 2, l. 12) *Don't justify yourself ...*
Hagámoslo. *Let's do it.*
No lo hagamos. *Let's not do it.*
Decídselo. *Tell him/her.*
No se lo digais. *Don't tell him/her.*

The final **-d** of the **vosotros** form is omitted from reflexive forms:

infinitive	***imperative** (for **vosotros**)*
imaginarse *to imagine*	imaginaos *imagine*
alegrarse *to be glad*	alegraos *be glad*

The above rule does not apply to **irse** *to go, leave*: **idos** *go, leave*.

Use of the infinitive as an imperative

The use of the infinitive as an imperative is often found in formal instructions.

Llamar (for **llame**) al teléfono 91542 2728. *Phone 91542 2728.*
Enviar (for **envíe**) nombre y dirección. *Send name and address.*
Tomar una tableta cada ocho horas. *Take one tablet every eight hours.*

In Peninsular Spanish it is sometimes used in place of the **vosotros** form.

¡**Venir** aquí! for ¡Venid aquí! *Come here!*
¡**Sentarse**! or ¡**Sentaros**! for ¡Sentaos! *Sit down!*
¡**Callaros**! for ¡Callaos! *Be quiet!*

(See also Chapter 8)

Other points to note in the texts

- Prepositions: There are numerous prepositions in both texts, including among others *en, de, para, sobre, con, sin* (see Chapter 28)
- Verb + preposition: Text 1: *se convierta en* (l. 1), *depende de* (l. 3), *no abuse de* (l. 4), *acudir a* (l. 10), *Cuídese de* (l. 31) (see Chapter 28)
- Adverbs: There are numerous adverbs in the texts. In Text 1, note *sólo* (l. 2), *más* (l. 6), *comedidamente* (l. 11), *progresivamente* (l. 14), etc. (see Chapter 21)
- Present subjunctive: Text 1: *que el sol se convierta* (l. 1), *aunque sea* (l. 11), *Es fundamental que lo haga* (l. 13), *aunque ya esté* (l. 17). Text 2: *los datos que puedas* (l. 2), *siempre que éstas tengan* (l. 27–28) (see Chapter 14)

EXERCISES

1 Put the following infinitives into the formal imperative forms (**usted** and **ustedes**), positive and negative.

a pasar ______ ______
b leerlo ______ ______
c oír ______ ______
d sentarse ______ ______
e tener ______ ______
f venir ______ ______
g probarlo ______ ______
h ser ______ ______
i salir ______ ______
j dárselo ______ ______
k marcharse ______ ______
l ponérselas ______ ______

2 Put the following infinitives into the singular familiar imperative form (**tú**), positive and negative.

a mirar ______ ______
b acostarse ______ ______
c aprenderlo ______ ______
d dármela ______ ______
e hacerlo ______ ______
f decirnos ______ ______
g ponérselos ______ ______
h irse ______ ______
i subir ______ ______
j beberlo ______ ______
k guardarla ______ ______
l traerlos ______ ______

3 Put the verbs listed in **2** into the plural familiar imperative form (**vosotros/as**), positive and negative.

4 Change these questions into inclusive command forms, *let's . . .*

a ¿Empezamos? Sí, ________
b ¿Por qué enfadarnos? No ________
c ¿Leemos? Sí, ________
d ¿Nos sentamos? Sí, ________
e ¿Nos acostamos? No, no ________
f ¿Seguimos? Sí, ________
g ¿Ponemos la mesa? Sí, ________
h ¿Volvemos? Sí, ________
i ¿Nos vamos ya? Sí, ________
j ¿Por qué hacemos esto? Pues, no ________

5 Here is some advice on what to do and not do when writing a curriculum vitae. Rewrite the advice using the **tú** form of the imperative.

a Procurar no escribir más de 1 o 2 folios.
b Utilizar frases cortas.
c No usar siglas ni abreviaturas.
d Cuidar la ortografía, sintaxis y signos de puntuación.
e Destacar los aspectos que puedan despertar interés.
f No mentir.
g No escribirlo a mano.
h No mandar una fotocopia del original.
i No incluir una fotografía a no ser que se la haya pedido.
j Recordar firmarlo.

6 **a** This ten-point plan for being environmentally friendly was originally written with the verb in brackets in the first person, future tense. Instead of this, put the verb in brackets into the plural familiar form of the imperative (**vosotros/as)** and make other alterations to the text as and where necessary.

DECÁLOGO

Palabra de forjador ambiental

1. **El respeto ayuda a construir un mundo mejor.** (Ejercer) ________ mi rol de forjador, procurando que todos cuidemos el planeta que compartimos.
2. **El aire limpio es fundamental para una vida sana.** (Procurar) ________ caminar o andar en bicicleta*, en lugar de usar medios de transporte motorizados y contaminantes.
3. **El agua es la cuna de toda forma de vida.** (Ahorrar) ________ la cantidad que uso al ducharme, al lavarme los dientes y la que se pierde en las llaves que gotean.
4. **Los animales y las plantas tienen derecho a vivir mejor.** (Plantar) ________ nuevos árboles y (cuidar) ________ todos los que hay a mi alrededor, en las plazas, parques y calles.
5. **Un ambiente sano está libre de basura.** (Elegir) ________ productos biodegradables y en envases retornables, procurando reducir la cantidad de desechos que genero.
6. **La energía que cuido y ahorro hoy, me será útil mañana.** (Apagar) ________ las luces y televisor que nadie esté usando.
7. **El silencio es valioso y sano.** (Evitar) ________ que se toque la bocina sin necesidad, las alarmas que hacen mucho ruido y el volumen excesivo cuando escucho música.
8. **Mi casa también es parte del planeta.** (Cuidar) ________ que nadie fume dentro de la casa y que usemos combustibles limpios.
9. **La tierra seguirá siendo generosa si sabemos cuidarla.** (Cuidar) ________ los bosques, no (contaminar) ________ las aguas y (proteger) ________ la vida silvestre.
10. **La atmósfera hace posible la vida en la tierra.** (Escoger) ________ siempre los productos que no dañen la capa de ozono.

Diario *El Metropolitano,* Chile

**In Peninsular Spanish* andar en bicicleta = ir en bicicleta, la llave = el grifo

b Think of and write down more points which you could add to this list to raise people's awareness of environmental issues and the part they can play.

7 The following text deals with another environmental issue. Read the text, noticing the use of the infinitive in place of the imperative (see Chapter 8, p. 53), and then replace the infinitives with the plural formal form of the imperative (**ustedes**).

Decálogo del ciudadano silencioso

1. Respetar, en general, el derecho de los demás al silencio y la tranquilidad.
2. Prescindir de alarmas y sirenas, para locales o coches, excesivamente ruidosas o de sonido prolongado.

3. No utilizar la bocina del coche salvo en casos de inminente peligro.
4. No manipular los silenciadores o dispositivos de escape de las motocicletas. Puede aumentar los niveles de ruido en 10 decibelios.
5. Vigilar el estado de los neumáticos y el mantenimiento del motor.
6. Prescindir del coche en trayectos cortos y en recorridos por el centro de las ciudades.
7. Conviene no frecuentar en exceso bares, *pubs* o discotecas que tengan la música alta.
8. Mantener conversaciones en voz baja o moderada, y bajar el volumen de televisores o equipos de música.
9. Respetar el silencio en el entorno e interior de hospitales, colegios, espacios naturales, parques, bibliotecas y otros centros culturales.
10. Exigir leyes y medidas contra el ruido a las autoridades locales: planificación urbanística destinada a prevenir ruidos, aislamiento acústico y térmico en la edificación, zonas peatonales o calzadas con revestimientos porosos que absorben más ruido y lo rebajan entre tres y cinco decibelios.

Revista *El País Semanal*, España

Think of more points which you could add to this list and write them down using the plural formal form of the imperative.

8 Text 1 gives general advice on how to reduce the dangers inherent in sunbathing, but there are more besides, especially relating to children. Imagine you work for a parenting magazine and, as the summer holidays approach, you have been asked to produce a 'decálogo' for parents on how best to protect their children from the harmful rays of the sun. Decide whether you are going to use the formal or informal form of the imperative to address the parents and write down your ten points.

9 Your friend is going for an interview. While Text 2 gives advice on how to behave at an interview, there are also things you should do before you get there, from preparing questions to ask and rehearsing answers to the kind of questions you may be asked, to more practical points like polishing your shoes, cleaning your nails, going to the hairdresser's, not using too much perfume/aftershave. Prepare a list of points for your friend, using the familiar form of the imperative.

Part Two:
Grammar essentials

18 Articles

Text 1

This extract from an article in a Spanish magazine expresses concern over drinking habits among young people in Spain. As you read the text, look at the way in which *articles*, the Spanish equivalent of *the* and *a/an*, have been used.

La España beoda

Por lo menos veintiséis millones de ciudadanos consumen cotidianamente alcohol en este país. España es **una** sociedad alcohólica, y **los** españoles
5 beben, según **los** parámetros europeos, de manera desmedida y creciente. La imagen que muchos visitantes extranjeros se llevan de los españoles es **la** de individuos reunidos
10 multitudinariamente en bares, que sostienen copas en **la** mano. Hay más bares en España que en el resto de toda Europa y éstos no están poblados, precisamente, por bebedores de leche.
15 **La** tendencia a beber es claramente ascendente. En España **el** consumo de alcohol se ha disparado entre **los** adolescentes, **los** jóvenes y **las** mujeres. [. . .] Existe **un** verdadero
20 proceso de alcoholización en **la** juventud.

El consumo de alcohol es más frecuente entre personas con mayor nivel de estudios e ingresos. Entre **los** que
25 tienen estudios medio-superiores se da **una** mayor proporción de bebedores frecuentes [. . .] En **los** hogares **los** chicos toman cerveza como otra costumbre más y se sigue
30 despachando alcohol a **los** menores con toda impunidad.

José P.L. tiene veintidós años, es técnico en electrónica e intenta acudir a diario a Alcohólicos Anónimos. Su
35 caso ilustra el drama **del** alcoholismo en **la** juventud española, porque son muchos **los** casos como **el** suyo. José, que sigue sin abandonar **la** bebida, es alcohólico de fin de semana. Comenzó
40 a beber a **los** diecisiete años para superar cierto problema psíquico. Actualmente, al llegar **el** sábado bebe hasta caer **al** suelo . . .

Revista *Cambio 16*, España

Text 2

On a different theme, the interview in Text 2 considers the importance of Spanish in today's world.

Lo que pesa el español hoy en el mundo

La lengua, ese instrumento poderoso y sutil, vigoroso y delicado, no sólo está para escribir poemas o redactar cartas de amor. También para traer divisas, aumentar exportaciones y generar empleo. Así lo piensan en España, a **la** luz de **las** estadísticas que muestran **la** sorprendente expansión **del** español en **el** mundo. No por nada **un** artículo **del** diario *El País* hablaba **del** "petróleo de **la** lengua".

Como lengua de comunicación internacional, **el** inglés posee **una** primacía indudable. Pero **la** enseñanza **del** español como segunda o tercera lengua está creciendo a pasos agigantados, explica José Luis García Delgado, catedrático de **la** Universidad Complutense, especialista en procesos de industrialización, que hoy se dedica a estudiar **un** "intangible" tan poco tangible como **la** lengua.

– *¿Qué hechos concretos muestran hoy **la** fuerza expansiva **del** español?*

– "Vivimos **un** proceso de ensanchamiento **del** territorio físico y humano **del** español, que se expresa en cuatro ámbitos muy claros. En primer lugar, **el** enérgico avance **del** español como segundo idioma más estudiado en Europa, desplazando **al** francés, **al** alemán, **al** ruso y **al** italiano. Por otra parte, **la** explícita apuesta hispánica de Brasil en **el** terreno lingüístico. En tercer lugar está **la** ascensión **del** español **al** puesto de segunda lengua de Estados Unidos, con varias decenas de millones de hispanohablantes. Finalmente, tenemos **el** despegue **del** español en China, donde se están multiplicando con rapidez **los** requerimientos de su enseñanza."

– *El chino puede convertirse en **una** difícil competencia para **el** español, a **la** hora de escoger **una** segunda o tercera lengua para aprender.*

– "Lo que ha avanzado con mucha fuerza en **el** curso de **los** últimos veinte años es **la** economía china, no **la** lengua china. [. . .] **El** español tiene grandes ventajas frente **al** chino: su carácter de gran lengua internacional, y no circunscrita a **un** solo territorio nacional, y **la** gran uniformidad ortográfica y gramatical de que goza. **El** español es lengua de comunicación internacional, **el** chino no lo es."

– *¿Dónde está hoy **la** demanda más importante de español?*

– "Brasil es **uno** de **los** principales focos. **Los** brasileños quieren liderar

(*Continued*)

el mundo iberoamericano y no lo
65 pueden hacer sin dominar **el** español.
Lo han incorporado como oferta
obligada para **la** enseñanza media y
eso requiere **la** llegada de decenas
de miles de profesores de español.
70 En Estados Unidos, a su vez, **la** gran
minoría hispana muestra **una**
movilidad social ascendente, que
está capitalizando **el** tejido más
influyente y eso genera demanda.
75 Aquí está tal vez **el** gran reto de **la**
difusión internacional **del** español:
apostar por **una** lengua con peso
económico y prestigio intelectual
que hablantes de otras lenguas
80 deseen aprender como segunda
lengua."

– *Pese a todos* ***los*** *índices positivos,* ***la*** *presencia* ***del*** *español en internet sigue débil.*

85 – "Si medimos **el** número absoluto de
usuarios de internet por lengua, **el**
español se sitúa en tercer lugar, tras
el inglés y **el** chino. Esto es **la**
consecuencia **del** gran peso
90 demográfico **del** español. En cambio,
si consideramos **el** número de
páginas web en cada idioma, **el**
español ha evolucionado
favorablemente, pero se sitúa por
95 detrás de idiomas menos hablados,
como **el** japonés, **el** alemán y **el**
francés. Si se considera **la** relación
entre cantidad de páginas y número
de internautas, **la** 'productividad' **del**
100 español en intenet se ve sobrepasada
por lenguas menos difundidas como
el holandés, **el** italiano o **el** rumano.
Estos discretos resultados se
relacionan con **la** baja penetración
105 **del** uso de internet entre **la**
población hispanohablante, y
muestra paralelismos evidentes con
datos como **el** nivel educativo o **el**
ingreso per cápita en **la** comunidad
110 de habla hispana." [. . .]

Diario *El Mercurio*, Chile

1 FORMS

There are two types of articles, *definite* and *indefinite*. In English, the definite article is *the*. Spanish uses four different forms:

	singular	*plural*
masculine	**el**	**los**
feminine	**la**	**las**

Note that **a** + **el** becomes **al**, and **de** + **el** becomes **del**.

. . . desplazando **al** francés, **al** alemán, **al** ruso y **al** italiano (T. 2, l. 32–33) *. . . gaining ground over French, German, Russian and Italian*

. . . la sorprendente expansión **del** español (T. 2, l. 8–9) *. . . the surprising expansion of Spanish*

Note also that Spanish has a neuter form of the definite article, **lo**, but this is not used with nouns. (See 'The neuter form *lo*' below.)

2 USAGE

The Spanish definite article agrees in gender (masculine/feminine) and number (singular/plural) with the noun. **El** and not **la** is used before singular feminine nouns beginning with stressed **a-** or **ha-**: **el arte** *art* (but **las artes**), **el habla** *language, speech*. Spanish and English differ substantially in the way in which they use the definite article, as you will see from the notes and examples below:

a With plural nouns used in a general sense.

los españoles (T. 1, l. 4) *Spaniards*
los jóvenes (T. 1, l. 18) *young people*
las estadísticas (T. 2, l. 7) *statistics*
los brasileños (T. 2, l. 63) *Brazilians*

b With abstract nouns.

la juventud (T. 1, l. 21, 40) *young people*
la expansión (T. 2, l. 8) *expansion*

c With words denoting subjects, sciences, sports, arts, illnesses.

el alcoholismo (T. 1, l. 35) *alcoholism*
el inglés (T. 2, l. 13)
el español (T. 2, l. 45)
los idiomas *languages*
las lenguas *languages*

d With parts of the body, in place of a possessive.

en **la mano** (T. 1, l. 11) *in their hand*

e With days of the week and other expressions of time.

al llegar **el sábado** (T. 1, l. 42) *when Saturday comes*
el 2014 *in 2014*

f With words indicating measure, weight and percentages.

el 30 y **el 39 por cient**o *30 and 39 per cent*

g With age, when there is a relationship between this and a certain event.

Comenzó a beber a **los diecisiete años** . . . (T. 1, l. 39–40) *He started drinking at seventeen . . .*

h In place of a noun, meaning *that/those of, the one/s from/belonging to.* The article must show agreement in number and gender with the noun it refers to.

. . . es **la** de individuos . . . (T. 1, l. 9) *. . . it is that of people . . .*
Entre **los** que tienen . . . (T. 1, l. 24–25) *Among those who have . . .*

i With possessive pronouns. (See Chapter 24.)

. . . los casos como **el** suyo . . . (T. 1, l. 37) *. . . cases like his . . .*

j With singular nouns denoting substances, and names of food, drinks and meals.

La cerveza mexicana es buena. *Mexican beer is good.*
El desayuno es a las 9.00. *Breakfast is at 9.00.*

But:

Bebe cerveza. *He/she drinks beer.*

k With titles and words like **señor**, **señora**, **señorita**, except in direct address.

el señor y **la señora** Díaz *Mr and Mrs Díaz*

l With names of languages, unless the name is preceded by **hablar** *to speak* or **aprender** *to learn*, in which case the article is usually omitted. Text 2 contains a number of examples of this use.

el inglés (T. 2, l. 13) *English*
el español tiene grandes ventajas frente **al** chino (T. 2, l. 51–53) *Spanish has great advantages compared to Chinese.*
idiomas menos hablados, como **el** japonés, **el** alemán y **el** francés (T. 2, l. 95–97) *less widely spoken languages, like Japanese, German and French.*

But note the absence of the article in:

¿Hablas español? *Do you speak Spanish?*
Hablo español y francés. *I speak Spanish and German.*
Estoy aprendiendo español. *I'm learning Spanish.*

Usage, however, often departs from the general rule, as shown by the following examples in which the article is optional:

Habla (**el**) español como si fuera su propia lengua. *He/She speaks Spanish as if it were his/her own language.*
Aprendió (**el**) español hablando con su novia. *He learned Spanish by speaking to his girlfriend.*

m With the names of certain countries, although this use is now mostly optional.

(el) Perú, **(el) Ecuador**, **(la) Argentina**, **(los) Estados Unidos,** but
la India, **el Reino Unido**

n With words denoting colours.

El rojo te va/queda bien. *Red suits you.*

o With infinitives to form nouns. (See Chapter 8.)

El beber demasiado es malo para la salud. *Drinking too much is bad for your health.*

The neuter form *lo*

The neuter form **lo** is used:

a Before adjectives and adverbs as an intensifier.

No sabes **lo** hermoso que es. *You don't know how beautiful it is.*
No te imaginas **lo** bien que está. *You can't imagine how well he/she is.*

b With adjectives, to form abstract nouns.

Lo extraño es que no nos dijo nada. *The strange thing is that he/she didn't tell us anything.*

The indefinite article

1 FORMS

In English, the indefinite article is *a/an*. Spanish has four different forms, with the plural forms translating *some*.

	singular	***plural***
masculine	**un**	**unos**
feminine	**una**	**unas**

2 USAGE

The Spanish indefinite article agrees with the noun in gender (masculine/feminine) and number (singular/plural). Before a singular feminine noun beginning with a stressed **a-** or **ha-**, use **un** instead of **una: un arma** *weapon* (but **las armas**), **un habla** *language, speech*. Usage of the indefinite article in Spanish and English does not differ greatly, but there are a few important points to note:

a Generally, the indefinite article is not used in the construction **ser** + noun, unless the noun is qualified. This rule applies with a number of categories of nouns, such as those denoting nationality, religion, occupation.

. . . es técnico en electrónica . . . (T. 1, l. 32–33) *. . . he's an electronics technician . . .*
Es **un** buen técnico en electrónica. *He's a good electronics technician.*

b The indefinite article is not used after **tal** *such*, **qué** *what*, **medio/a** *half*, **de manera/forma/modo** *in a way*.

. . . **de manera** desmedida y creciente. (T. 1, l. 6) *. . . in an excessive and increasing way.*
Beben de **tal** manera. *They drink in such a way.*
¡**Qué** lástima! *What a pity!*

c The indefinite article is not used before **otro** *another* and **cierto** *certain*, **cien** *a hundred* (except with percentages) and **mil** *a thousand*.

otra costumbre (T. 1, l. 29) *another custom*
cierto problema psíquico (T. 1, l. 41) *a certain psychological problem*

d The indefinite article is omitted with **tener** *to have* and **llevar** *to wear*, when the accompanying noun is used in a general sense. If the noun is qualified, **un** or **una** cannot be omitted.

No tengo coche. *I haven't got a car.*
Tiene **un** coche muy caro. *He/she has a very expensive car.*
Llevaba corbata. *He was wearing a tie.*
Llevaba **una** corbata roja. *He was wearing a red tie.*

Other points to note in the text

- Comparison: Text 1: *más . . . que* (l. 11–12), *más frecuente* (l. 22–23), *con mayor nivel* (l. 23), *una mayor proporción* (l. 26); Text 2: *segundo idioma más estudiado* (l. 30–31), *el tejido más influyente* (l. 73–74), *idiomas menos hablados* (l. 95), *lenguas menos difundidas* (l. 101), (see Chapter 22)
- Adjective agreement and position: Text 1: *una sociedad alcohólica* (l. 3–4), *los parámetros europeos* (l. 5), *visitantes extranjeros* (l. 7–8), *un verdadero proceso* (l. 19–20); Text 2: *instrumento poderoso y sutil , vigoroso y delicado* (l. 1–2), *la sorprendente expansión* (l. 8), *comunicación internacional* (l. 12–13), *pasos agigantados* (l. 16–17), etc. (see Chapter 20)
- Adverbs and adverbial phrases: Text 1: *cotidianamente* (l. 2), *de manera desmedida y creciente* (l. 6), *multitudinariamente* (l. 10), *precisamente* (l. 14), *claramente* (l. 15), *a diario* (l. 34); Text 2: *finalmente* (l. 40), *con rapidez* (l. 42), *favorablemente* (l. 94), etc. (see Chapter 21)
- Prepositions **por** and **para**: Text 1: *por lo menos* (l. 1), *por bebedores de leche* (l. 14); Text 2: *para escribir poemas* (l. 3), *para traer divisas* (l. 4), *no por nada* (l. 9), *por otra parte* (l. 33), *para el español* (l. 45), *para aprender* (l. 47), etc. (see Chapter 28)

EXERCISES

1 Put the appropriate definite article in the blank where necessary.

a Nunca salgo ________ sábados por ________ noche; prefiero ver ________ tele en ________ casa.
b En España se sirve ________ cena más tarde que en ________ países nórdicos.
c Se ha roto ________ pierna.
d A pesar de ________ frío que hacía, no se puso ________ abrigo.
e A Luis lo metieron en ________ cárcel ________ semana pasada.
f Julio no se encuentra bien; está en ________ cama.
g ________ año que viene Gonzalo va a estudiar en ________ universidad de Hamburgo.
h ________ abuela viene ________ fin de semana en ________ tren.

i ________ señores de Cortés vivían en ________ calle Pez.
j ________ veintitantos de marzo en ________ hemisferio norte, empieza ________ primavera.
k Me gusta ________ marisco pero no me gustan ________ aceitunas.
l En Escocia se cultiva ________ cebada para hacer ________ whisky.
m ________ tomates están a 2 euros ________ kilo.
n A Pepe le gusta ________ azul pero mi color preferido es ________ rojo.
o Me gusta más la chaqueta verde que ________ marrón.

2 Translate these sentences into Spanish.

a Alcohol consumption is prevalent among today's youth.
b Women are also drinking more than before.
c Over 40% of young people drink at weekends.
d Beer is a popular drink.
e Ramón, José's best friend, began drinking at the age of twelve.
f Girls now drink as much as boys.
g Measures are being taken to prevent drinks advertising near schools.
h You will not be able to buy alcoholic drinks in shops between 10 p.m. and 8 a.m.
i Doctor Justino León thinks that unemployment causes many problems including alcoholism.
j His colleague, Doctor Maribel Osuna says that idleness shortens life while work and diet lengthen it.
k Statistics show that cycling and swimming are good for your health.
l With the coming of spring, people begin to think about outdoor activities.

3 Rewrite these sentences inserting **lo** in the correct place, then study them for meaning.

a Importante es viajar.
b Hay que ver bonitos que son.
c Mío es mío y suyo es suyo.
d Bueno era que se dio cuenta de mezquina que era Patricia.
e Pepe prefiere picante y yo dulce.
f No nos dimos cuenta de tarde que era.
g Cierto es que el calentamiento global ya es un hecho.
h No estuvimos preparados porque llegaron mucho antes de normal.
i Fácil es criticar pero ¿os dais cuenta de dura que es la vida para los jóvenes?
j Han hecho todo posible para proteger esta zona de la urbanización.

4 Translate these sentences into Spanish.

a You can't imagine how good-looking she is.
b I don't want to tell you how bad the film was.
c The best thing is to wait.

d The interesting bit is coming.
e The difficult bit was not so difficult.
f The easy bit is still to come.
g Do you have any idea what a cheat he is?
h I didn't realise how expensive their tastes are.
i The most expensive thing isn't always the best.
j Amelia doesn't like her husband's propensity for anything ostentatious.

5 Put the appropriate indefinite article in the blank where necessary.

a Fernando era ________ diseñador; era ________ diseñador ingenioso.
b Silvio es ________ nicaragüense; es ________ músico.
c Queremos ________ casa con ________ jardín.
d En el frigorífico sólo hay ________ leche.
e En el frigorífico sólo hay ________ botella de leche.
f Mi abuelo tiene ________ paciencia formidable.
g Dame ________ otro pedazo de pan.
h Hay ________ poema de Machado que es ________ recuerdo de cuando era ________ profesor.
i Los niños cantaban ________ cien veces, ________ mil veces, ________ cien mil veces.
j Antonio no llevaba ________ abrigo cuando salió. Luego, se compró ________ abrigo de piel.
k No tengo ________ coche. Todo el mundo me dice que tengo que comprar ________.
l Este año vamos a Costa Rica; ________ otro año iremos a Guatemala.
m Antes era ________ costumbre llevar ________ vestidos negros a los entierros.
n Rosario es ________ abogada eminente y por eso gana ________ buen sueldo.
o La jefa de Margarita es ________ mujer déspota y de ________ falsedad increíble.

6 Translate into Spanish.

a Paco was a really good engineer.
b A certain young man was asking for you.
c I don't want to repeat such an experience.
d What a noise! We left after half an hour.
e Jules is French, is a doctor and doesn't have a girlfriend.
f And another thing – he always wears a ring.
g Do you have a tie? You'll need one for the reception tonight.
h A year and a half has passed since our last meeting.
i What a pair! One was a pedant and the other was a complete idiot.
j A good book is a real treasure. *One Hundred Years of Solitude* by Gabriel García Márquez is such a book.

7 Insert the appropriate article, definite or indefinite, in the gaps where necessary.

a

________ verano pasado estuvimos ________ días en Buenos Aires, ________ capital de Argentina, con ________ amiga nuestra. ________ domingo, después de tomar ________ desayuno, visitamos ________ barrio de San Telmo donde había ________ mercado con ________ puestos que vendían ________ antigüedades y ________ cosas de ________ segunda mano. También vimos a ________ pareja mayor que bailaba ________ tango y ________ otra pareja más joven que bailaba con ________ público. ________ malo de Buenos Aires era ________ tráfico y por tanto ________ ruido constante, pero es ________ ciudad que nos encantó.

b

________ psicólogos dicen que ________ pesadillas son ________ producto de ________ cerebro agitado. ________ domingo, ________ señorita Méndez había soñado con ________ ave rapaz, ____águila quizás, que la circunvolaba de ________ manera amenazante. ________ lunes entró en ________ instituto donde iba a impartir ________ clases de ________ filosofía. Le habían dicho que ________ aula 24 estaba en ________ ala oeste del edificio pero tras correr y recorrer ________ pasillos sin dar con nadie, tenía ________ sensación de estar en ________ buque fantasma ____*María Celeste*. No había ________ ruido que indicara ________ presencia de ________ alma viviente. Buscaba en ________ bolsa su botella de agua pero ________ agua no la calmaba, y ahora ________ nervios y ________ hambre iban a provocarle ________ desmayo.

c Ejercicio físico es protector de la salud

________ científicos han observado que ________ ejercicio practicado regularmente es ________ fuente de ________ juventud. Aunque sea modesto ________ ejercicio pospone ________ fecha de ________ muerte. Cuando se está en ________ curso de ________ longevidad, es importante practicar suficiente ejercicio físico con ________ regularidad, si es posible diariamente, nos conduce por años a ________ bienestar y a vivir con ________ energía de ________ juventud. Complemento valioso es mantener ________ vida activa, caminando, subiendo ________ escaleras, cuidando de ________ jardines y ________ casa.

Es sabido que ________ ejercicio fortifica ________ corazón, lucha contra ________ obesidad, disminuye ________ presión arterial*, mejora ________ nivel de ________ colesterol y conduce a ________ buen humor.

Se ha observado que ________ ejercicio físico alarga ________ vida por cambios que ocurren en ________ sangre, en su efecto es anticoagulante, fluidifica el medio sanguíneo en beneficio de ________ salud, que circula más fácilmente y está menos propensa al coágulo.

En consecuencia ________ ejercicio practicado regularmente contribuye a evitar ________ ataque cardíaco y ________ accidente vascular cerebral. (. . .)

________ personas físicamente inactivas, de vida sedentaria (. . .) si han tenido ________ ataque cardíaco están en riesgo de tener ________ segundo ataque. (. . .) ________ ejercicio es ________ anticoagulante natural.

Revista *El País,* Uruguay

* *In Peninsular Spanish:* **la tensión arterial**.

8 On the basis of the following information, write a description of María, using the article as and when appropriate.

Nombre: María
Apellidos: González Posada
Fecha de nacimiento: 21.04.84
Domicilio: Santa Ana
País: El Salvador
Actividades y deportes: cine; música; lectura; voleibol; baloncesto
Bebida preferida: cerveza
Plato favorito: arroz con frijoles
Color preferido: amarillo **Mayor cualidad**: generosidad **Mayor defecto**: pereza
Preocupaciones: medio ambiente; protección de animales; pobreza en el mundo

19 | Nouns

Text

This article tells about the discovery in southern Chile of the oldest forest in the world, with **alerces**, *larch trees*, more than 4000 years old. The main grammatical point in this unit is nouns. As you read the text, list them according to their gender (masculine and feminine) and look at the ways in which plurals have been formed.

El bosque más antiguo del planeta

El **bosque** más antiguo de la **Tierra**, con **alerces** que superan los 4.000 **años**, se encuentra en la **Cordillera** de Los **Andes**, a mil **kilómetros** de Santiago de Chile, según un **estudio** efectuado por **científicos** y **ecologistas**. (5)

La **expedición** fue organizada por la **fundación** *Ancient Forest International* y su **objetivo** era explorar las **áreas** naturales vírgenes del **bosque** húmedo templado más austral del **mundo**. (10)

El **grupo**, integrado por 92 **profesionales** visitó nueve **zonas**, a fin de determinar la urgente **necesidad** de preservar **sectores** forestales poco estudiados hasta ahora y que se encuentran bajo fuerte **presión** de la **industria** papelera. (15)

En el **volcán** *Hornopirén*, a 800 **metros** sobre el **nivel** del **mar**, el **ecólogo** chileno Daniel González encontró **alerces** cuya **edad** promedio fue determinada entre 1.600 y 2.000 **años**, sin poder, por **razones** climatológicas, explorar **áreas** más altas. Las diferentes **condiciones** de la **topografía** y el **clima** existentes a mayor **altitud** hacen presumir a los **expertos** que los **alerces** que ahí se encuentran superan los 4.300 **años**. Con **anterioridad** a estas **investigaciones** se consideraba que los **árboles** más antiguos del **planeta** eran los famosos *sequoias gigantes* de California. (20, 25, 30, 35)

La **representante** de *AFI* en Chile dijo que la **institución** tiene **interés** en comprar 200.000 **hectáreas** del **bosque** y destinarlas a un **parque** para la **humanidad** y explicó que por ser éste un **ecosistema** único en el **mundo**, existe a **nivel** internacional mucho **interés** por preservarlo. (40)

Diario *Presencia*, Bolivia

Nouns

1 GENDER

All nouns in Spanish are either masculine or feminine. The following simple rules will help you to differentiate a masculine noun from a feminine one. Study the notes and check how the nouns in the text fit each rule. Then do the same for the section on 'Number' below.

a Most nouns ending in **-o** are masculine and most nouns ending in **-a** are feminine, e.g.

> **el mundo** (l. 12) *world*, **la zona** (l. 14) *zone*.
> But, **el clima** (l. 28), **el planeta** (l. 34) *planet*, **la mano** *hand*.

b Nouns referring to males will be masculine and those referring to females will be feminine. To form the feminine of nouns which refer to people, you normally change **-o** to **-a** or add **-a** to the final consonant, e.g. **el ecólogo/la ecóloga** (l. 22) *ecologist*, **el experto/la experta** (l. 29–30) *expert*, **el doctor/la doctora** *doctor* (but **el/la profesional**). Some nouns have a fixed gender and they may be used to refer to a male or to a female, e.g. **el bebé** (masc.) *baby*, **la persona** (fem.) *person*.

c Some nouns referring to people remain invariable, no matter whether they refer to a man or to a woman. Among these we find those ending in **-ista** and many nouns ending in **-e**, e.g. **el/la ecologista** (l. 6) *ecologist*, **el/la representante** (l. 37) *representative* (but **el jefe/la jefa** *boss*).

d Some nouns have different forms for each sex, e.g. **el yerno** *son-in-law*, **la nuera** *daughter-in-law*, **el padre** *father*, **la madre** *mother*, **el actor** *actor*, **la actriz** *actress*.

e Nouns ending in **-or** and **-aje** and in a stressed vowel are usually masculine, e.g. **el sector** (l. 16) *area*, **el aterrizaje** *landing*, **el alelí** *wallflower*.

f Nouns ending in **-ción**, **-sión**, **-ie**, **-iza**, **-dad**, **-tad**, **-tud**, **-umbre** are usually feminine, e.g. **la expedición** (l. 7) *expedition*, **la pasión** *passion*, **la serie** *series*, **la hortaliza** *vegetable*, **la edad** (l. 23) *age*, **la altitud** (l. 29) *altitude*, **la humanidad** (l. 40–41) *humanity*, **la muchedumbre** *crowd*.

g A number of nouns ending in **-ma** are masculine, but some are feminine, e.g. **el clima** (l. 28) *climate*, **el ecosistema** (l. 42) *ecosystem*, **la forma** *shape*, **la yema** *yolk*.

h The following classes of noun are normally masculine: names of languages (e.g. **el español**), mountains and volcanoes (e.g. **Los Andes** (l. 3), **el volcán *Hornopirén*** (l. 20)), rivers and seas (e.g. **el Amazonas**, **el Pacífico**), substances (e.g. **el oro** *gold*, but **la plata** *silver*), colours (e.g. **el rojo** *red*), days of the week (e.g. **el viernes** *Friday*), points of the compass (e.g. **el sur** *south*), fruit trees (e.g. **el manzano** *apple tree*, but **la manzana** *apple*).

i The following classes of noun are normally feminine: islands (e.g. **las islas Baleares** *the Balearic Islands*), letters of the alphabet (e.g. **la be** *b*).

j Some nouns change meaning according to gender (e.g. **el policía** *policeman*, **la policía** *the police*).

2 NUMBER

a Nouns ending in a vowel normally form the plural by adding **-s**, e.g. **el año/los años** (l. 2) *year/s*.

b Nouns ending in a consonant add **-es**, e.g. **el profesional/los profesionales** (l. 14) *professional/s*, **el sector/los sectores** (l. 16).

c Nouns ending en **-z** change **-z** to **-c** and add **-es**, e.g. **el pez/los peces** *fish*.

d Nouns ending in **-í** and **-ú** add **-es**, e.g. **marroquí/marroquíes** *Moroccan*, **hindú/hindúes** *Hindu*, *Indian* (but **el menú/los menús** *menu/s*).

e Nouns carrying a written accent on the last syllable, lose this in the plural, e.g. **el volcán** (l. 20)/**los volcanes** *volcano/es*, **la razón/las razones** (l. 25) *reason/s*.

f Nouns which end in **-en**, with the stress on the penultimate syllable, gain a written accent in the plural, e.g. **el joven/los jóvenes** *young man/young people*.

g The masculine plural of some nouns may be used to refer to members of both sexes, e.g. **los padres** *parents*, **los hermanos** *brothers and sisters*.

h Some nouns are used in the plural only, e.g. **los alrededores** *outskirts*, **las vacaciones** *holidays*.

i Some nouns with a plural sense function as singular nouns, e.g. **la gente es** . . . *people are* . . .

j A few nouns have the same form for singular and plural, **el análisis/los análisis** *analysis/analyses*, **el miércoles/los miércoles** *Wednesday/s*.

Other points to note in the text

- Superlative: *El bosque más antiguo de la Tierra* (l. 1), *el bosque húmedo templado más austral del mundo* (l. 10–12), *los árboles más antiguos del planeta* (l. 33–34) (see Chapter 22)
- *Por* and *para*: *efectuado por* (l. 5), *organizada por* (l. 7–8), *por razones* (l. 25), *para la humanidad* (l. 40–41), *por ser* (l. 41), *interés por preservarlo* (l. 44) (see Chapter 28)
- Relative pronouns: *alerces que superan* (l. 2), *sectores forestales . . . que* (l. 16–17), *alerces cuya edad* (l. 23), etc. (see Chapter 26)

EXERCISES

While these are not vocabulary exercises, use your dictionary to check meanings of words you are not sure of.

1 Give the gender of the following groups of nouns.

a región; habitación; recepción; manifestación
b moto; foto; bici; mano
c calor; dolor; color; motor
d coraje; garaje; viaje; equipaje
e bondad; sinceridad; amistad; mitad

f jabón; jamón; balcón; pantalón
g jueves; viernes; martes; miércoles
h taxi; avión; camión; tranvía
i costumbre; certidumbre; pesadumbre; muchedumbre
j azul; verde; marrón; gris
k virtud; solicitud; altitud; plenitud
l panadería; ferretería; droguería; heladería
m sacapuntas; sacacorchos; pasamanos; rompeolas
n crisis; tesis; parálisis; diagnosis
o edredón; balón; montón; melocotón
p crema; forma; broma; alarma

2 Although all these nouns end in -**a**, only five are feminine. Identify them.

norma	programa	clima	sistema
tema	pijama	idioma	víctima
problema	síntoma	trama	cima
fantasma	lema	telegrama	enigma
aroma	arma	esquema	diagrama

3 Identify which of the following nouns are <u>not</u> feminine.

calle	serie	bronce	hambre	peine
fraude	aire	nieve	cine	catástrofe
sangre	base	parque	tarde	este
azote	auge	fuente	carne	alambre
cumbre	bigote	ave	superficie	coche

4 Say whether the noun is masculine (m) or feminine (f).

catedral	pan	noche	nariz	planeta
luz	dólar	día	agua	estrés
garaje	ciudad	régimen	lesión	césped
deber	labor	sur	flor	porvenir
valor	énfasis	sol	mes	tarde
virtud	imagen	mapa	cárcel	sed
albaricoque	aire	lunes	niñez	multitud
hambre	caos	altavoz	muelle	automóvil
red	lid	póster	zaguán	riñón
jersey	autocar	carril	combustible	nuez

5 Write these nouns in the plural.

bar ________ lápiz ________
crisis ________ hotel ________

paraguas ________ deber ________
examen ________ origen ________
francés ________ nación ________
altavoz ________ orden ________
mes ________ pie ________
país ________ cuarto de baño ________
análisis ________ miércoles ________
buey ________ ley ________
menú ________ tribu ________
esquí ________ marroquí ________

6 Write these nouns in the singular.

regiones ________ aviones ________
quehaceres ________ ingleses ________
coles ________ jóvenes ________
luces ________ sofás ________
convoyes ________ caracteres ________
records ________ rubíes ________
vírgenes ________ ilusiones ________
violines ________ imágenes ________
peces ________ portavoces ________
patines ________ rehenes ________
alemanes ________ reveses ________
cómplices ________ mártires ________

7 The following list of nouns can be classified into two groups:

a compound nouns which, although they appear plural, can function in the singular or plural, e.g. **el paraguas** (*the umbrella*), **los paraguas** (the umbrellas);
b nouns which function only as plurals.
Distinguish between the two groups by writing the appropriate definite article, singular **el/la** before compound nouns, and **los/las** before plural nouns, in the space provided before each noun.

________ rompecabezas ________ alrededores ________ tinieblas
________ comicios ________ guardaespaldas ________ portaaviones
________ celos ________ bienes ________ prismáticos
________ saltamontes ________ víveres ________ gafas
________ enseres ________ limpiabotas ________ parabrisas
________ pintalabios ________ vacaciones ________ expensas
________ añicos ________ salvavidas ________ cosquillas
________ restos ________ abrelatas ________ cumpleaños
________ cuentacuentos ________ portaequipajes ________ nupcias
________ posavasos ________ cimientos ________ afueras

8 Give the feminine equivalents of these nouns.

a padre ________
b hombre ________
c alcalde ________
d príncipe ________
e macho ________
f toro ________
g héroe ________
h profesor ________
l actor ________
j emperador ________
k poeta ________
l rey ________
m traductor ________
n escritor ________
o caballo ________
p presidente ________

9 Some nouns have a masculine form and a feminine form. What difference in meaning is there between the following nouns?

a el puerto ________ la puerta ________
b el libro ________ la libra ________
c el punto ________ la punta ________
d el pato ________ la pata ________
e el pago ________ la paga ________
f el herido ________ la herida ________
g el tramo ________ la trama ________
h el río ________ la ría ________
i el banco ________ la banca ________
j el naranjo ________ la naranja ________

10 Some nouns have the same form (homonyms) but different meaning according to gender. Say what the meanings of these nouns are.

a el capital ________ la capital ________
b el guía ________ la guía ________
c el mañana ________ la mañana ________
d el orden ________ la orden ________
e el cura ________ la cura ________
f el policía ________ la policía ________
g el frente ________ la frente ________
h el parte ________ la parte ________
i el cometa ________ la cometa ________
j el cólera ________ la cólera ________
k el corte ________ la corte ________
l el pendiente ________ la pendiente ________

20 Adjectives

Text 1

This article tells about the recent discovery in the Peruvian Andes of embalmed mummies, in a site which was probably used for human sacrifice. This text serves to illustrate the use of adjectives, whose function is to identify or describe nouns.

Los incas realizaban sacrificios humanos

El **reciente** hallazgo de **tres** momias **embalsamadas** en un pico **nevado** de la cordillera **andina peruana** abre la posibilidad de una **profunda** investigación **científica** en una región en la que, al parecer, los incas celebraban sacrificios **humanos**.

Las víctimas de estos sacrificios habrían sido jóvenes **vírgenes**, entre los 14 y 16 años, integrantes de culturas **incas** que dominaban la zona **sur** del Perú, según las **primeras** indagaciones.

Al parecer, las jóvenes eran sacrificadas para evitar la erupción de los volcanes y así neutralizar la "ira de la naturaleza". Sus cuerpos están **momificados**, cubiertos por elementos y vestimentas **funerarios** y en **virtual** estado de congelamiento.

Este **sorprendente** descubrimiento pone en evidencia que la cultura **inca** fue la **única** civilización en el mundo que construyó edificaciones a más de **seis mil** metros de altura para realizar rituales **mágico-religiosos**.

Diario *El Universal*, México

Text 2

Text 2 looks at the use of computers in cars and roads. Read the text and study the way in which adjectives have been used.

Automóviles y caminos inteligentes

Dentro de **veinte** o **treinta** años, guiar un vehículo por las **tentaculares** y **congestionadísimas** autopistas de Los Angeles será quizá una diversión, y 5 quien vaya al volante leerá el diario, mirará la televisión o dormirá la siesta.

El automovilista de la **mega** metrópoli **californiana** adquirirá 10 **tanta** libertad, gracias a vehículos y caminos "**inteligentes**" dirigidos por **omnipresentes** y **sofisticados** computadores.

¿Un sueño **futurista** en una ciudad 15 inmersa en el gas de los tubos de escape, donde la bicicleta amenaza con convertirse en el medio de locomoción más **rápido**?

No, ya existe en **gran** parte la 20 tecnología **necesaria** para poner al **inmenso** ejército de las **cuatro** ruedas en un maxi-sistema "**inteligente**" y para aumentar en un 50 por ciento el tránsito **caminero**, evitando los 25 **graves** embotellamientos y reforzando los niveles de seguridad.

Diario *El Universal*, Venezuela

Adjectives

1 AGREEMENT OF ADJECTIVES

a In Spanish, adjectives agree in number (singular and plural) and gender (masculine and feminine) with the noun they qualify, e.g. sacrificios **humanos** (masc./pl.) (T. 1, l. 7) *human sacrifice*, momias **embalsamadas** (fem./pl.) (T. 1, l. 1–2) *embalmed mummies*, **inmenso** ejército (masc./sing.) (T. 2, l. 21) *immense army.*

b If the adjective refers to more than one noun, one of them being masculine, you will need to use the masculine plural form of the adjective:

. . . elementos y vestimentas **funerarios** . . . (T. 1, l. 19) . . . *funerary elements and clothing* . . .

If the nouns are all of the same gender, use the same gender for the adjective.

2 POSITION OF ADJECTIVES

a In Spanish, adjectives usually follow the noun:

pico **nevado** (T. 1, l. 2) *snow-capped mountain*, jóvenes **vírgenes** (T. 1, l. 9) *young virgins*, vehículos y caminos '**inteligentes**' (T. 2, l. 10–11), *'intelligent' vehicles and roads*

This is the normal position for adjectives expressing some form of contrast, even when this contrast is only implied, e.g. **vehículos y caminos 'inteligentes'** *'intelligent' vehicles and roads*, as opposed to ordinary ones.

b Among other adjectives which are normally placed after the noun, we find those referring to science and technology, nationality and origin, colour, shape, substance, religion:

investigación **científica** (T. 1, l. 5) *scientific research*, metrópoli **californiana** (T. 2, l. 9) *Californian metropolis*, cultura **inca** (T. 1, l. 22) *Inca culture*, una camisa **blanca** *a white shirt*, una caja **cuadrada** *a square box*, una sustancia **dura** *a hard substance*, la Iglesia **católica** *the Catholic Church*

c Adjectives which express some form of subjective judgement are often placed before the noun. This position is also used as a device for lending greater force to the meaning of the adjective:

este **sorprendente** descubrimiento (T. 1, l. 21) *this surprising discovery*, las **tentaculares** y **congestionadísimas** autopistas (T. 2, l. 2–3) *tentacular and congested motorways*, **graves** embotellamientos (T. 2, l. 25) *serious traffic jams*

d Among other adjectives which are placed before the noun we find those for cardinal and ordinal numbers and some common words such as **mucho**, **poco**, **otro**, **tanto**, **ambos**:

tres momias (T. 1, l. 1) *three mummies*, **primeras** indagaciones (T. 1, l. 12–13) *first investigations*, **tanta** libertad (T. 2, l. 10) *so much freedom*, **mucho** tráfico *a lot of traffic*, **ambas** personas *both persons.*

e Some adjectives change their meaning depending on whether they precede or follow the noun. Note the meaning of **único** in **la única civilización** (T. 1, l. 23) *the only civilisation*, as opposed to **una civilización única** *a unique civilisation*, and of **gran** in **en gran parte** (T. 2, l. 19) *to a great extent*, as opposed to **una parte grande** *a big part*, denoting size. Among other words of this kind we find the following:

	Preceding	***Following***
antiguo	*former*	*old*
diferentes	*several*	*different*
mismo	*same*	*self*
nuevo	*new, another*	*brand new*
pobre	*poor, miserable*	*poor, impecunious*

3 FEMININE FORMS

a Adjectives ending in **-o** change **-o** to **-a**:

profundo – profunda (T. 1, l. 4) *deep*, **científico – científica** (T. 1, l. 5) *scientific*, **primero – primera** (T. 1, l. 12) *first*

Those ending in a vowel other than **-o** keep the same form, e.g. **reciente** (T. 1, l. 1) *recent*, **sorprendente** (T. 1, l. 21) *surprising.*

b Adjectives of nationality or origin form the feminine with **-a**:

andino – andina (T. 1, l. 3), **peruano – peruana** (T. 1, l. 3), **español – española** *Spanish*, **inglés – inglesa** *English*

Those ending in **-a**, **-i**, **-e** remain unchanged:

el imperio **inca** *the Inca empire*, la cultura **inca** (T. 1, l. 22) *Inca culture*, **marroquí** (m/f) *Moroccan*, **costarricense** (m/f) *Costa Rican*

c Adjectives ending in a consonant, with the exception of those referring to nationality or origin (see **b** above), do not change for the feminine.

Note the phrase **jóvenes vírgenes** (T. 1, l. 9) *young virgins*, where **virgen** can refer to a masculine or a feminine noun.

d Adjectives ending in **-án**, **-ón**, **-ín** and **-or** add **-a**:

holgazán – holgazana *lazy*, **dormilón – dormilona** *sleepyhead*, **parlanchín – parlanchina** *chatty*, **seductor – seductora** *seductive*

Comparative forms remain unchanged, e.g. **mayor** (m/f) *greater.*

e Some adjectives may be joined by a hyphen, in which case only the second one will change for gender and/or number, e.g. **rituales mágico-religiosos** (T. 1, l. 26) *magic-religious rituals.*

4 SHORT FORMS

Grande becomes **gran** before singular masculine and feminine nouns, e.g. **en gran parte** (T. 2, l. 19) *to a large extent*, but **grandes ciudades** *large cities.*

Malo, **bueno**, **primero**, **tercero**, **alguno** and **ninguno** lose the final **-o** before a singular masculine noun, e.g. un **mal/buen día** *a bad/good day*, **algún/ningún problema** *some/no problem.*

5 PLURAL FORMS

a Adjectives that end in an unstressed vowel add -**s**. Most of the adjectives in the texts fall within this category:

momias **embalsamadas** (T. 1, l. 1–2) *embalmed mummies*, sacrificios **humanos** (T. 1, l. 7) *human sacrifices*, caminos '**inteligentes**' (T. 2, l. 11) *'intelligent' roads*

b Adjectives that end in a consonant or a stressed vowel add **-es**:

jóvenes **vírgenes** (T. 1, l. 9) *young virgins*, **tentaculares** . . . autopistas (T. 2, l. 2–3) *tentacular motorways*, inmigrantes **marroquíes** *Moroccan immigrants*

Note that adjectives ending in **-z**, e.g. **feliz** *happy*, change this to **-c** to form the plural.

días **felices** *happy days*

6 INVARIABLE ADJECTIVES

Adjectives which are originally names of things do not change for gender and number:

paredes **naranja** *orange walls*, pantalones **violeta** *violet trousers*

Other points to note in the texts

- *Por* and *para*: Text 1: *para evitar* (l. 15), *cubiertos por elementos* (l. 18–19), *para realizar* (l. 25). Text 2: *por las . . . autopistas* (l. 2–4), *dirigidos por* (l. 12), *para poner* (l. 21), *para aumentar* (l. 24–25) (see Chapter 28)
- Future tense: Text 2: *será* (l. 4), *leerá* (l. 6), *mirará* (l. 6), *dormirá* (l. 7), *adquirirá* (l. 9) (see Chapter 6)
- Ser and *estar*: Text 1: *habrían sido* (l. 9), *eran sacrificadas* (l. 14–15), *están momificados* (l. 17–18), *fue la única civilización* (l. 23) (see Chapter 13)

EXERCISES

1 Complete the texts by putting the appropriate ending to the adjectives.

a Hay restos incaic________ en todos los países andin________ de Sudamérica. Muchos se preguntan cómo fue posible fundar una civilización tan avanzad________ en una región tan montaños________ e inhóspit________. Pero civilizaciones anterior________ a la incaic________ también tenían culturas ric________ e interesante________.

En los Andes las comunicaciones parecen imposible________ pero en los tiempos incaic________ existían dos carreteras principal________ muy buen________ que enlazaban el extrem________ norte del imperio con las regiones sureñ________.

En los templos de Cuzco, la capital del imperio, había adornos y estatuas cubiert________ de oro. Después de su larg________ y peligros________ periplo, los conquistadores español________ llegaron a Cuzco cansad________, hambrient________, y temeros________. Cuando vieron los suntuos________ templos y palacios de los Incas, se quedaron totalmente pasmad________.

b La mujer que dio vida al automóvil fue una intrépid________ mujer aleman________, esposa de Karl Benz, reconocid________ por muchos como el padre del coche.

A principios de 1886, Benz patentó un triciclo motorizad________ y en los meses siguient________ construyó dos vehículos motorizad________ más, pero como estos no recorrieron más que trayectos cort________, no pasaron de ser experimental________ por los cuales nadie mostró interés algun________.

Pronto la familia se encontró en una situación económic________ pésim________ y Benz se sentía muy abatid________. Sin embargo, su mujer no estaba dispuest________ a rendirse. En la madrugada del 15 de agosto de 1888, ayudad________ por sus dos hijos y sin despertar a su marido dormid________, Bertha Ringer, con espíritu valient________ y aventurer________, emprendió su viaje tan históric________ a casa de su madre.

Sin saber bien el camino, hicieron grand________ rodeos por zonas montaños________, siempre guiad________ por nombres de pueblos que les resultaron familiares hasta llegar, con las últim________ luces del día, a su destino.

Mostrándose tan atrevid________ como emprendedor________, Bertha Ringer pudo superar los vari________ problemas mecánic________ inherent________ a un vehículo rudimentari________ que muy poco tenía que ver con las lujos________ berlinas actual________ de Mercedes Benz.

No obstante, los primer________ triciclos fabricad________ por la casa Benz y los nuev________ Mercedes clase S, los más lujos________ y los que llevan los mayor________ avances tecnológic________ de la marca aleman________, comparten una mism________ característica: cada uno en su día fue y es un nuev________ y revolucionari________ medio de transporte.

2 Make the adjective in brackets agree with the noun. You may want to refer to Chapter 18 (**Articles**, 'Usage') before you begin.

- **a** La compañía se llama Aguas (Cordobés) ________.
- **b** El águila (pescador) ________ es un ave (protegido) ________.
- **c** El ala (izquierdo) ________ del partido está en decadencia.
- **d** Tengo un hambre (tremendo) ________.
- **e** Hoy tenemos la clase en el aula (pequeño) ________.
- **f** Vuestra hija es un hada (encantador) ________.
- **g** Todos estos estudiantes son de habla (polaco) ________.
- **h** Vagabundeaba por la ciudad como un alma (perdido) ________.
- **i** Marisol quiere estudiar artes (plásticos) ________ en Castellón.
- **j** El área (metropolitano) ________ de Los Ángeles es muy extendida.

3 Complete the sentences, changing the adjective to agree with the new subject.

- **a** Julio es muy trabajador. Julia es ________.
- **b** El niño es dormilón. Las niñas son ________.
- **c** Es una revista juvenil. Son revistas ________.
- **d** Pepe es parlanchín. Susana es ________.
- **e** María es bastante holgazana. Juanito es ________.
- **f** Feliz cumpleaños. ________ fiestas.
- **g** La profesora es burlona. El profesor es ________.
- **h** Es mi hermano mayor. Son mis hermanos ________.
- **i** Lleva un pantalón azul. Lleva un pantalón y una chaqueta ________.
- **j** Mi amigo es alemán. Mi amiga es ________.
- **k** Lee una novela rosa. Lee novelas ________.
- **l** Compró un libro español. Compró un libro y una revista ________.

4 Cross out the incorrect part of the sentence.

- **a** Fuimos a comer a un italiano restaurante/restaurante italiano.
- **b** El hostal estaba en el tercer/tercero piso.
- **c** Carlos es un muy bueno/buen amigo.
- **d** Si ustedes tienen algún/alguno problema, no dejen de ponerse en contacto con nosotros.
- **e** Viven en una grande casa/una casa grande con playa privada/privada playa.

f Mariano fue el primer/primero en llegar.
g No seas tan mal/mala.
h El diccionario me costó la tercer/tercera parte de mi sueldo.
i Alguno/algún día vendrá a visitarme.
j Nueva York es una grande/gran ciudad cosmopólita.
k El imponente palacio real/real palacio fue obra de Churriaga.
l El primer/primero día no hicimos nada especial.

5 Read this short text and correct the fifteen mistakes in adjective agreement to be found in it.

Burgos, antiguo capital de Castilla, está situado en el norte de España entre Madrid y Santander. Es una ciudad muy histórica y por eso turístico. Su principal monumento es la catedral, una de las más bella y representativa del país. Aquí está enterrado Rodrigo Díaz de Vivar que era un noble de la corte castellano a finales del siglo XI y cuya vida está inmortalizado en "El Cantar de Mío Cid", uno de los poemas épicas más importante de la literatura medieval español.

El poema narra la historia de este héroe desde su destierro forzado de Castilla hasta su muerte en Valencia, y cómo, por sus hazañas guerreros, llegó a ser rico, famoso y poderoso, temido y respetado por sus enemigos, ya moros ya cristianos.

La recién inaugurado Ruta del Cid nos permite seguir los pasos de este guerrero atrevido desde su salida lacrimoso de Burgos cuando, ya en las afueras, se volvió para contemplar por último vez esta ciudad tan hermoso.

6 The following is an extract from a longer magazine article called 'Retrato del nuevo español', about the changing lifestyle of the Spanish male. Fill in each blank with an adjective from the list below.

algunos	**nuevo**	**guapo**	**revolucionario**	**solos**
muchas	**español**	**jóvenes**	**machistas**	**viejos**
nuevo	**mayor**	**buena**	**libre**	

Y por si fuera poco, ha surgido un competidor *con faldas.* La incorporación de la mujer a la actividad fuera de casa ha sido otro elemento (**a**) ________ para el varón (**b**) ________ [. . .] El español en fase de adaptación tiene que tomar conciencia de que es muy difícil mantener (**c**) ________ comportamientos (**d**) ________, tanto en casa como en el trabajo. [. . .]

Afortunadamente el (**e**) ________ español también dispone de (**f**) ________ ratos de ocio. Una (**g**) ________ parte del tiempo (**h**) ________ [. . .] lo invierte en su cuerpo. El (**i**) ________ español quiere estar (**j**) ________ [. . .]. Otra novedad: los hombres suelen ir ahora (**k**) ________ a comprar su ropa [. . .]. Hoy en (**l**) ________ casas de matrimonios (**m**) ________ el vestuario de él ocupa (**n**) ________ espacio que el de ella.

Revista *Tiempo*, España

7 Translate these sentences into Spanish.

a It seems incredible that a civilisation which did not know the wheel could be so advanced, but the Inca civilisation was highly developed in every aspect.

b Their roads, which crossed high mountains and deep valleys, were maintained by a small army of engineers, and so were always in good condition.

c Their famous terraces, which were watered by an extensive system of canals, turned the steep mountainsides into fertile fields.

d Without the help of sophisticated machinery but with perfect technique, they constructed huge buildings of enormous stones.

e Their craftsmen used llama and vicuña wool to weave exquisite cloth, and with gold and silver, they made beautiful and intricate ornaments and jewellery.

f The modern car has little in common with the small, black cars manufactured by Mr Benz and Mr Ford.

g Nowadays, an extensive range of new and used cars enables us to choose a car appropriate to our needs.

h Some cars, like the legendary Volkswagen Beetle, now have modern and efficient engineering but keep the shapes of the original models.

i Competition between motor car manufacturers is fierce, and the big challenge of the designers is to be creative, imaginative and visionary.

j The cars of the future will be clean, that is they will be environmentally friendly, they will be 'intelligent', capable of taking their own decisions, and they will be personalised.

8 Use adjectives to answer these questions.

a ¿Cómo es tu mejor amigo/a?

b En tu opinión, ¿cómo es el español/hispanoamericano típico?

c ¿Cómo sería tu casa ideal?

d ¿Cómo será el coche del futuro?

9 Think of a place you know and like sufficiently well to write a description of it, giving information on, for example: its location, what it is like, the places of interest, facilities . . .

21 | Adverbs

Text 1

The problem of unemployment among young Spanish people is illustrated below through a personal story. The grammar in the text focuses on the use of adverbs, words which provide more information about verbs, adjectives or other adverbs.

Veintiocho años, y en paro

Jaime M. tiene veintiocho años, la carrera de Empresariales, un "master" realizado en una universidad británica, habla y escribe **perfectamente** inglés, habla y escribe **menos perfectamente** francés. Extrovertido, simpático, **últimamente ya no** lo es **tanto. Nunca** ha conseguido un empleo. **No** sabe lo que es trabajar en una oficina, en un despacho, tener un jefe o un compañero con el que compartir problemas. **No** encuentra empleo, **ni siquiera** a tiempo parcial. En unos sitios le exigen experiencia; en otros, creen que con sus títulos merece **más** de lo que le pueden dar, y Jaime M. está desesperado, **total** y **absolutamente** desesperado. Sus padres, que le han apoyado, empiezan a agobiarse al verle en casa. Y aunque otros amigos suyos están **también** sin trabajo y viven **todavía** en la casa familiar porque **no** encuentran salida profesional de ningún tipo, **al cabo del tiempo hasta** los padres de Jaime, **siempre tan** comprensivos, **siempre tan** dispuestos a animarle, **siempre tan** cariñosos, comienzan a mostrarse incómodos por su presencia permanente [. . .]

Si triste es el caso del padre de familia que en la cuarentena se queda en la calle con escasas posibilidades de volver a encontrar un trabajo, tremendo es **también** que nuestros jóvenes no consigan acceder a un empleo y se les venga el tiempo **encima** sin haber conocido lo que es un horario, una mesa de despacho, un taller o un balance. La Formación Profesional ha dado salida a bastantes jóvenes y se ha demostrado una fórmula **bastante** aceptable de colocación, pero **no** cubre las expectativas de aquéllos que desean acceder a unas profesiones de carácter universitario, ni **tampoco** ofrecen la posibilidad de trabajo seguro.

Jaime M., por si les interesa, se encuentra bajo tratamiento psiquiátrico. Sus padres pueden pagarlo. Otros, sin embargo, **no** saben qué hacer para luchar contra la depresión de los hijos que viven con la obsesión de conseguir un primer empleo, tener su casa, formar su familia y, **especialmente**, vivir su propia vida.

Revista *Blanco y Negro*, Diario *ABC*, España

Text 2

On a different theme, Text 2 considers how a select number of words have survived for 15,000 years.

El selecto club de las palabras que han sobrevivido por 15.000 años

Aunque suene **como** una idea de una película de ciencia ficción, si usted tuviera la oportunidad de viajar al pasado y escuchar una conversación de los cazadores recolectores de la última Edad de Hielo es probable que lograse entender el sentido de lo que hablan. ¿La razón? Las frases que ellos utilizaban estaban compuestas por un núcleo de palabras tales **como** "hombre", "mano", "fuego", "escuchar" y varias **más** que han sobrevivido sin cambios durante 15.000 años. A esta conclusión llegó un equipo de expertos liderados por Mark Pagel, profesor de biología evolutiva de la Universidad de Reading, Reino Unido, que logró identificar 23 sustantivos, verbos, adjetivos y adverbios considerados términos "ultra conservados" y que se han mantenido **como** base de los **casi** 700 idiomas que **hoy** existen en el mundo.

Todo un hallazgo, si tomamos en cuenta que hasta **ahora** los investigadores consideraban que las palabras **no** sobreviven **más** de 9.000 años debido a su evolución semántica y erosión fonética. De hecho, los análisis del mismo Pagel señalan que 500 mil idiomas han surgido y desaparecido desde que aparecieron los primeros humanos.

Así es. Y por **más** que pensemos que términos universales y parecidos **como** *pater* (latín) o *padre* (español) pudieran permanecer con el mismo significado con el correr de los siglos por el simple hecho de tener un sonido similar, hasta **ahora** no se había logrado probar **estadísticamente** esa relación. Quentin Atkinson, investigador de la Universidad de Auckland (Nueva Zelanda) y coautor del estudio, cuenta a **Tendencias** que algunos estudios habían intentado afirmar que hubo un ancestro común de todas las lenguas humanas que existió hasta hace 60 mil años, pero había sido imposible pasar **más allá** del factor "casualidad" para explicar la similitud del lenguaje. Hasta **ahora**.

Así como el proyecto Genographic creó un mapa de la migración humana, mediante el análisis del ADN y la reconstrucción de las rutas migratorias de nuestros primeros ancestros, una de las interrogantes en la cabeza de Pagel era si la evolución del lenguaje se comportaba **igual** que la de los genes. El nuevo estudio parece comprobar esta idea: la lista de palabras

(*Continued*)

65 identificadas – que también incluye términos **como** "ceniza", "madre" y "que" – sugiere que hasta hace 15.000 años existía una especie de lengua euroasiática que fue el ancestro común 70 de las lenguas que **hoy** hablan miles de millones de humanos. [. . .]

El equipo de Pagel halló que los 23 términos en la lista de palabras "ultra conservadas" son cognados en cuatro 75 o **más** familias lingüísticas. Pero hay una que se repite en las siete familias: "thou" (tú, pronombre). Los otros pronombres son "yo", "nosotros", "ustedes" y "quién". Los sustantivos 80 son "hombre", "mamá", "mano", "fuego", "corteza", "ceniza" y "gusano". Los adjetivos "eso", "este", "viejo" y "negro". Los verbos que aparecieron son "dar", "escuchar", 85 "sacar", "fluir" y "escupir". Y los adverbios "no" y "qué".

Tendencias, Diario *La Tercera,* Chile

Adverbs

Adverbs are words that add information about verbs, adjectives or other adverbs.

. . . habla y escribe **perfectamente** inglés . . . (T. 1, l. 4) *. . . he speaks and writes English perfectly . . .*
. . . **total** y **absolutamente** desesperado. (T. 1, l. 16–17) *. . . totally and absolutely desperate.*
. . . habla y escribe **menos** perfectamente francés. (T. 1, l. 5–6) *. . . he speaks and writes French less perfectly.*
Aunque suene **como** una idea de una película de ciencia ficción . . . (T. 2, l. 1–2) *Even if it sounds like an idea from a science fiction film . . .*
. . . varias **más** han sobrevivido sin cambios . . . (T. 2, l. 12–13) *. . . several more have survived without changes . . .*

There are many different types and categories of adverbs, as you will see from the notes below, which also cover their use.

1 ADVERBS ENDING IN *-MENTE*

Adverbs can be formed by adding the suffix **-mente** to the feminine singular form of the adjective, e.g. **perfecto** (masculine singular adjective), **perfecta** (feminine singular adjective), **perfectamente** (adverb) (T. 1, l. 4, 5) *perfectly.* Adjectives without a special feminine form simply add **-mente** to the singular form, e.g. **especial** (adjective), **especialmente** (adverb) (T. 1, l. 53) *especially*. Note that the suffix **-mente** corresponds to the English ending *-ly*.

Adverbs ending in **-mente** keep the written accent of the adjective, e.g. **fácil** (adjective), **fácilmente** (adverb) *easily*, **económica** (adjective), **económicamente** (adverb), *economically*, **estadística** (adjective), **estadísticamente** (T. 2, l. 42) *statistically* (adverb).

In a sequence of two or more adverbs of this kind, joined by a conjunction, only the last one carries the ending **-mente**, e.g. **total** y **absolutamente** (T. 1, l. 16–17) *totally and absolutely.*

2 ADVERBIAL PHRASES

Overuse of adverbs in -**mente** is considered clumsy in Spanish. In order to avoid this, use adverbial phrases such as the following, all of them followed by an adjective:

de manera (feminine) **rápida** (for **rápidamente**) *rapidly*
de forma (feminine) **lenta** (for **lentamente**) *slowly*
de modo (masculine) **silencioso** (for **silenciosamente**) *silently*, *quietly*

Note also the use of the preposition **con** followed by a noun:

con tranquilidad (for **tranquilamente**) *quietly*
con astucia (for **astutamente**) *cleverly*, *astutely*
con cuidado (for **cuidadosamente**) *carefully*

There are a large number of adverbial phrases in Spanish, not all related to adjectives, e.g. **a escondidas** *secretly*, **a la fuerza** *by force*, **a oscuras** *in the dark*, **con cautela** *cautiously*, **de costumbre** *usually*, **de memoria** *by heart*, **en cambio** *on the other hand*, **sin cuidado** *carelessly*.

3 SINGLE-WORD INVARIABLE ADVERBS

A large number of adverbs in Spanish are single invariable words unrelated to adjectives, e.g. **luego** *later on*, *then*, **dentro** *inside*, **igual** (T. 2, l. 62) *the same*. For further examples, see 'Categories of adverbs' below.

4 ADJECTIVES USED AS ADVERBS

A small number of adjectives can also function as adverbs, e.g. **rápido**, **duro**, **barato**.

Conduce muy **rápido**. *He/she drives very quickly.*
Trabajaron **duro**. *They worked hard.*
Me lo vendió muy **barato**. *He/she sold it to me very cheaply.*

5 CATEGORIES OF ADVERBS

Adverbs and adverbial phrases can be grouped according to their meaning or the kind of information they provide about the word they modify. Among the different categories we find the following. The examples here include mostly single-word invariable adverbs.

a Adverbs of ***time***, for example **ahora** (T. 2, l. 26, 41, 54) *now*, **antes** *before*, **después** *after*, **siempre** (T. 1, l. 25) *always*, **nunca** (T. 1, l. 7), **jamás** *never*, **hoy** (T. 2, l. 23, 70) *today*, **mañana** *tomorrow*, **ayer** *yesterday*, **aún**, **todavía** (T. 1, l. 21) *still*, *yet*, **recientemente** *recently*, **últimamente** (T. 1, l. 7) *lately*, *recently*, **ya** *already*, **ya no** (T. 1, l. 7) *no longer*, *not . . . any more*, **a menudo** *often*, **a tiempo** *in time*.

b Adverbs *of* ***manner***, such as **así** (T. 2, l. 35) *this way, thus*, **casi** (T. 2, l. 22) *almost*, **bien** *well*, **mal** *badly*, **despacio** *slowly*. Among these we also find a number of adverbs ending in **-mente**, for example **estadísticamente** (T. 2, l. 42) *statistically*, **perfectamente** (T. 1, l. 4, 5) *perfectly*, **totalmente** (T. 1, l. 16–17) *totally*, **absolutamente** (T. 1, l. 17) *absolutely*. Note also, adverbial phrases such as **a mano** *by hand*, **con soltura** *with ease.*

c Adverbs of ***degree***, for example **bastante** (T. 1, l. 41) *quite, enough*, **demasiado** *too (much)*, **más** (T. 1, l. 15, T. 2, l. 12, 28, 51, 75), *more*, **menos** (T. 1, l. 5) *less*, **mucho** *(very) much*, **muy** *very*, **tan** (T. 1, l. 25, 26) *so*, **tanto** (T. 1, l. 7) *so much, as much.*

d Adverbs of ***place***, among them **abajo** *down, below*, **debajo** *underneath*, **arriba** *above*, **encima** *above, on top*, **aquí** *here*, **ahí** *there*, **allí** *there*, **acá** *here*, **allá** (T. 2, l. 52) *there*, **adelante** *forward(s)*, **delante** *in front*, **atrás** *back(wards)*, **detrás** *behind*, **cerca** *near(by)*, **lejos** *far.*

e Adverbs of ***affirmation***, ***negation*** and ***doubt***, for example **sí** *yes*, **claro** *certainly*, **también** (T. 1, l. 20, 34) *also*, **no** (T. 1, l. 8, 11; T. 2, l. 28) *no*, **nada** *nothing*, **tampoco** (T. 1, l. 44) *neither, not . . . either*, **a lo mejor**, **quizá(s)**, **tal vez** *perhaps.*

6 POSITION OF ADVERBS

Adverbs normally adjoin the word they modify, either preceding or following this. With verbs the usual position is after it, but for emphasis an adverb may come before the verb. Compare:

Nunca ha conseguido un empleo. (T. 1, l. 7–8) *He's never got a job.*
No han conseguido **jamás** un empleo. *They've never got a job.*

Note that in the previous English sentences the adverb, *never*, comes between the auxiliary verb *to have* and the participle. In Spanish, an adverb must not split an auxiliary from a participle or an infinitive. So a sentence such as *We're certainly going to do it*, translates in two possible ways: **Por supuesto** que vamos a hacerlo, or Vamos a hacerlo **por supuesto**.

For comparison of adverbs, see Chapter 22.

Other points to note in the text

- Negation: Text 1: *ya no* (l. 7), *nunca* (l. 7), *no sabe* (l. 8), *ni siquiera* (l. 12), *de ningún tipo* (l. 23), *incómodos* (l. 28), *ni tampoco* (l. 44), etc. (see Chapter 27)
- Direct and indirect object pronouns: Text 1: There are a number of examples of third person object pronouns in the text, among these *no lo es* (l. 7), *le exigen* (l. 13), *le pueden dar* (l. 15–16), etc. (see Chapter 25)
- *Ser* and *estar*: Text 1: *ya no lo es* (l. 7), *no sabe lo que es* (l. 8–9), *está desesperado* (l. 16), *están . . . sin trabajo* (l. 20–21); Text 2: *es probable* (l. 6), *estaban compuestas* (l. 9), *así es* (l. 35), etc. (see Chapter 13)
- Perfect tense: Text 1: *nunca ha conseguido* (l. 7–8), *le han apoyado* (l. 18); Text 2: *han sobrevivido* (l. 12–13), *se han mantenido* (l. 21–22) , *han surgido y desaparecido* (l. 32–33), etc. (see Chapter 4)

EXERCISES

1 Correct the sentence by forming an adverb with **-mente** from the word in italics.

a Saben *perfecto* ________ que no podemos alcanzarlos.
b Salimos *inmediato* ________ después de ustedes.
c Si te niegas a someterte a la prueba, quedas *automático* ________ descalificado.
d Se espolvorean las fresas *ligero* ________ de azúcar.
e Cómprame un litro de leche *preferente* ________ desnatada.
f No podía quejarse de él; habló *cortés* ________ y se portó *correcto* ________.
g Es *absoluto* ________ absurdo pensar así.
h El señor Abad habló *franco* ________ y *sincero* ________ y al final de su discurso recibió un gran aplauso.
i José es el empleado ideal: trabaja *rápido* ________ y *concienzudo* ________.
j *Último* ________ se comporta de una manera *completo* ________ rara y atípica.
k Por miedo a pisar minas, los soldados avanzaron *lento* ________ y *prudente* ________.
l Queda *definitivo* ________ prohibido fumar en áreas públicas en este país.

2 Link the adverb to the adverbial phrase with the same meaning.

a obviamente	de costumbre
b tristemente	por último
c finalmente	por lo general
d ciertamente	en efecto
e difícilmente	en secreto
f indudablemente	con tristeza
g habitualmente	con dificultad
h efectivamente	por supuesto
i secretamente	sin duda
j generalmente	por cierto

3 Replace the adverb ending with -**mente** with an adverbial phrase.

a Esto se hace fácilmente.
b ¡No tomes las cosas tan seriamente!
c El perro ladró muy ferozmente.
d No nos podemos quejar; nos recibieron muy amablemente.
e Estamos muy orgullosos de ti. En todo momento te has portado prudentemente.
f Desgraciadamente Pepe perdió todos sus ahorros en la Bolsa y tuvo que vender el piso.
g Estos señores siempre actúan cautelosamente.
h Vanamente intentó convencer a su padre de que no había hecho nada malo.
i Frecuentemente los turistas nos preguntan por qué no hay guías en su lengua.
j Se levantó repentinamente y señaló la puerta.
k Vamos a considerar las cosas separadamente.
l Hay que reconocer que ante la noticia Laura reaccionó razonablemente.

4 Translate the following sentences into Spanish, using both adverbs and adverbial phrases where appropriate.

a The door suddenly opened and in walked Jorge.
b You must pack the vase carefully.
c He generously shared all he had, which was not very much.
d Inés wrote to Rodrigo and he replied immediately with a lovely letter.
e It is undoubtedly a good idea to make the first move.
f It really is a shame that things are the way they are.
g When he was asked the question, Gabriel said dryly: 'I don't know anything about that.'
h During the dictatorship, Felipe entered the country secretly three or four times.
i Generally young people don't leave home any more when they finish their studies.
j The roundabout began to turn slowly at first, then very rapidly.

5 Complete the sentences with one of the adverbs of place given below.

abajo	**adelante**	**ahí**	**allí**	**aquí**
arriba	**atrás**	**cerca**	**debajo**	**delante**
dentro	**detrás**	**encima**	**fuera**	**lejos**

a – ¿Dónde están los servicios?
– Para las señoras, ________. Suba por esas escaleras. Los de los señores, están ________, en el sótano.
b Es curioso pero si a ti no te gustan los gatos, ellos lo saben y siempre se te sientan ________.
c En el coche los padres viajan ________ y los niños ________.
d – ¡Adelante! – gritó el sargento a los reclutas – el cuartel no está ________, está ________, a la vuelta de la esquina.
e – ¿Está el señor García?
– No. Esta semana no está, está ________.
f – ¿Dónde has puesto las macetas que estaban en la terraza?
– ________. Ahora están en el garaje.
g – ¿Quieres que ponga las bolsas ________ en esta mesa?
– No. Ponlas ________ en el rincón.
h – Apártense ustedes. Desde ________ no se aprecia el estilo del pintor. Más ________ se ve mucho mejor el cuadro.
i – ¿Los Blanco viven cerca?
– ¡Qué va! Viven ________, muy ________ de ________.
j – ¡Qué bien se ven las estrellas esta noche! Mira, ¿ves ________ la Cruz del Sur?
k Aunque empezó a nublarse, siguieron ________ hasta llegar al mirador.
l ________ están los López; ellos viven en el cuarto piso y nosotros en el quinto.

6 Complete the sentences with one of the adverbs of time given below.

ahora antes aún ayer mañana nunca siempre hoy

________ Julio estaba desempleado pero ________ trabaja en una hamburguesería. Con todos los estudios que ha hecho ________ pensó que llegaría a esto. ________ pensaba que con los títulos conseguiría un buen empleo, un empleo bien pagado. Pero no está desanimado. ________ le queda la esperanza de que algo mejor le pueda salir y ________ va a mandar su currículo a algunas empresas. Cosa que hizo ________, y que hará ________ también.

7 Complete the sentences with one of the adverbs of degree given below.

bastante demasiado más mucho muy tan tanto

a – Otilia, estás aprendiendo portugués ¿verdad? ¿Qué tal lo hablas?
– ________ mal ya que en realidad no estudio ________. Debo esforzarme ________, la verdad.

b El recuerdo que tengo de María es de cuánto comía. Comía ________ que pensaba que iba a reventarse.

c – ¡Cómo trabaja Consuelo!
– Sí, es verdad. Trabaja ________. De todos nuestros empleados es la que ________ trabaja.
– ¿No cree que trabaja ________?

d – ¿Te acuerdas del profesor de literatura? Hablaba mucho ¿verdad?
– Pues no, no hablaba ________.
– Sí, hombre, sí. Hablaba ________, ________.

e No se puede negar que los jóvenes viven bien.
– Bueno, algunos ________ bien y otros no ________ bien.

8 Translate these sentences into Spanish.

a We shall be leaving early tomorrow.
b Teresa read a lot when she was on holiday.
c It is not at all easy to find a job these days.
d Paco was quite ill when we saw him yesterday.
e The car in front was going so slowly that I almost bumped into it.
f I never discovered his secret, not even when he died.
g First we'll pack our bags, then we'll eat and afterwards we'll get going.
h They are walking too slowly; they'll never arrive.
i He did it quite quickly but he didn't do it badly.
j Don't eat any more and come up here!

For exercises with adverbs expressing affirmation and negation, see Chapter 27; for adverbs expressing possibility, see Chapter 14.

22 Comparison

Text 1

Text 1, an extract from an article in a Spanish magazine, looks at the Mediterranean diet. The grammar here focuses on the use of comparative forms.

La dieta mediterránea

La llamada dieta mediterránea está de moda, aunque hasta hace poco no gozaba de muy buena reputación. Los médicos y nutriólogos han descubierto que en los países mediterráneos la incidencia de enfermedades **es** mucho **menor que** en tierra adentro.

En Madrid convergen todas las dietas autonómicas de España. La dieta de los madrileños es equilibrada y saludable, y **es mejor que** la del resto de capitales comunitarias. No obstante, los madrileños **toman menos** verduras **de** las necesarias y demasiadas proteínas y sal. Como complemento, hay que decir que en Madrid **se come menos** pan y patatas y **más** fruta y pescados **que** en otras partes de España.

Los desayunos que se toman los madrileños **son más ligeros** y se advierte una tendencia a no cocinar por la noche en casa. Uno de cada cinco escolares no desayuna y muchos de los que lo hacen **consumen menos** calorías **de** las aconsejables. Esto acarrea una **menor** capacidad de retentiva y **mayor** dificultad de atención entre los estudiantes.

Revista *Cambio 16*, España

Text 2

Text 2 considers the results of a worldwide survey of people's attitudes towards subjects such as sex, racism, religion, food. The article looks specifically at Latin Americans. Note the use of superlative forms in this text.

Los más apasionados y belicosos del mundo

Los latinoamericanos se consideran felices, caritativos y apasionados, según **la** encuesta interactiva **más grande** que se ha realizado en el mundo, en el sitio web *planetproject.com*. El sondeo lo contestaron 600.000 personas de 231 países del mundo. En América Latina unas 50.000 personas respondieron a la encuesta.

Los datos todavía son preliminares, pero ya muestran tendencias. En América Latina, por ejemplo, los peruanos **son los más tradicionalistas**, con **el** porcentaje **más alto** de la región que piensa que el objetivo del sexo es la procreación. Puerto Rico **es el** país **menos racista**, de acuerdo a su respuesta a la pregunta de si adoptaría un niño de otra raza. El 94 por ciento de los encuestados afirmó que sí.

En religión, los latinoamericanos **son los más creyentes**, siendo Colombia el país del área donde más gente contestó que cree que existe un Ser Superior, seguido de Brasil y México.

En salud hay una diferencia marcada con los asiáticos. Los latinoamericanos piensan que la alimentación **es lo más importante** para la salud, mientras que los asiáticos consideran que es lo espiritual.

Aparte de las diferencias regionales, están las de género. Los hombres piensan en el dinero el doble que las mujeres, pero la mayoría de éstas piensa en el peso corporal diariamente mucho **más que** los hombres. Los hombres **son más tolerantes** con las relaciones sexuales extramatrimoniales **que** las mujeres.

Diario *El Mercurio*, Valparaíso, Chile

Comparison

The word 'comparison' in this context is used with reference to forms such as *(tall)**er***, *more/less . . . than*, *as . . . as*, *not so . . . as*, all of which serve to compare people or things in terms of a specific quality. Expressions such as these, known as ***comparative*** forms, focus on the degree to which the people or things being compared share that quality, e.g. *Maria is tall, Ana is also tall, but Ana is **taller than** Maria.*

To say that the noun being referred to possesses a specific quality in its highest degree, English uses forms such as *the (tall)**est***, *the **most** . . .*, which are known as ***superlative*** forms. The notes below explain how to use these constructions.

1 COMPARATIVE FORMS OF ADJECTIVES

a Comparisons of inequality

Regular forms

Comparisons of inequality, such as *bigger than, more comfortable than, less expensive than* are normally expressed in Spanish with **más** *more*, and **menos** *less*, followed by an adjective and **que** *than*. **Que** *than* and the second element being compared may be omitted when the context is clear.

. . . son **más** ligeros . . . (T. 1, l. 20) *. . . they are lighter . . .*
. . . son **más** tolerantes . . . **que** . . . (T. 2, l. 39–41) *. . . they are more tolerant than . . .*

The two examples above, with **más** *more*, indicate superiority. Inferiority is shown by using **menos** *less*.

Es **menos** interesante **que** el otro. *It is less interesting than the other one.*

Comparisons of inequality can also be expressed with the construction **no tan . . . como** *not as . . . as*, or simply **no tan** followed by the adjective if the context is clear.

No es **tan** bueno **como** el tuyo. *It is not as good as yours.*
No son **tan** sabrosos. *They are not as tasty.*

Note also the use of **no tanto como** *not as much as*.

Es eficiente, pero **no tanto como** Andrés. *He/she is efficient, but not as much as Andrés.*

Irregular forms

Some adjectives have irregular comparative forms:

bueno *good*	**mejor** *better*
malo *bad*	**peor** *worse*
grande *big*	**mayor** *older, bigger, greater* (also **más grande**)
pequeño *small*	**menor** *younger, smaller* (also **más pequeño**)

. . . es . . . **menor que** . . . (T. 1, l. 6–7) *. . . it is smaller than . . .*
. . . es **mejor que** . . . (T. 1, l. 11) *. . . it is better than . . .*
Javier es **mayor que** Álvaro. *Javier is older than Álvaro.*
Cristina es **menor**. *Cristina is younger.*

Mayor and **menor** are not normally used with reference to size, for which **más grande** and **más pequeño** are preferred.

Mi piso es mucho **más grande** que el de Emilio. *My flat is much bigger than Emilio's.*
Ecuador es **más pequeño** que Colombia. *Ecuador is smaller than Colombia.*

b Comparisons of equality

Comparisons of equality are expressed with the construction **tan . . . como** *as . . . as*.

Es **tan** delgado **como** ella. *He is as slim as her.*
Son **tan** grandes **como** los de José. *They are as big as José's.*

2 COMPARISON INVOLVING NOUNS, NUMBERS AND CLAUSES

For comparisons involving nouns, use **más . . . que** and **menos . . . que** for inequality and **tanto/a/os/as . . . como** for equality.

se come **menos** pan y patatas y **más** fruta y pescados **que** . . . (T. 1, l. 16–17) *. . . they eat less bread and potatoes and more fruit and fish than . . .*
Gana **tanto** dinero **como** ella. *He earns as much money as her.*

When reference is to quantity or a number, use **más/menos de** instead of **que**.

. . . **menos** verduras **de** las necesarias . . . (T. 1, l. 13–14) *. . . fewer vegetables than necessary . . .*
. . . **menos** calorías **de** las aconsejables . . . (T. 1, l. 24–25) *. . . fewer calories than is advisable.*
más de una docena *more than a dozen*

Before a clause containing a noun, use **más del/de la/de los/de las que**, depending on the gender of the noun. If there is no noun, use **de lo que**.

Había **más** comida **de la que** esperábamos. *There was more food than we expected.*
Es **más** difícil **de lo que** parecía. *It is more difficult than it seemed.*

3 SUPERLATIVE FORMS

a To convey ideas such as *the biggest*, *the most conservative*, *the least racist*, use the definite article (**el**, **la**, **los** or **las**, or the neuter form **lo**) followed by **más** *most* or **menos** *least* and the corresponding adjective.

. . . **la** . . . **más** grande . . . (T. 2, l. 3–4) *. . . the biggest . . .*
. . . son **los más** tradicionalistas . . . (T. 2, l. 14) *. . . they are the most conservative . . .*
. . . es **el** . . . **menos** racista (T. 2, l. 17–18) *. . . it is the least racist . . .*
. . . es **lo más** importante . . . (T. 2, l. 29–30) *. . . it is the most important thing . . .*

b As above, the irregular forms **mejor, peor, mayor, menor** must be preceded by the definite article.

Este restaurante es **el mejor**. *This restaurant is the best.*
Fue **la peor** experiencia que tuve. *It was the worst experience I had.*
Lo mejor es no decir nada. *The best thing is not to say anything.*
El mayor problema es su precio. *The greatest problem is its price.*
La menor de mis hijas se llama Leonor. *My youngest daughter is called Leonor.*

c Another form of the superlative is that formed with the suffix **-ísimo/-ísima** added to the adjective, with the final vowel being removed.

Es **dificilísimo**. *It is very/extremely difficult.*
Es **carísima**. *It is very/extremely expensive.*

Note spelling changes with adjectives ending in **-co**, **-go**, or **-z**:

seco *dry* **sequísimo** *extremely dry*
largo *long* **larguísimo** *very long*
feliz *happy* **felicísimo** *very happy*

d There are also some special superlative forms:

pobre *poor* **paupérrimo** *extremely poor*
antiguo *old, ancient* **antiquísimo** *very old*

4 COMPARATIVE FORMS OF ADVERS

Adverbs are compared in much the same way as adjectives. Note the following examples:

Habló **más claramente que** nunca. *He/she spoke more clearly than ever.*
Me trataron **menos amablemente**. *They treated me less kindly.*
Corre **más rápido/rápidamente**. *He/she runs faster.*
No actúa **tan bien como** ella. *He doesn't act as well as her.*
Ahora viene **más a menudo**. *Now he/she comes more often.*

The comparative forms of **bien** *well* and **mal** *badly* are **mejor** *better* and **peor** *worse.*

Pepe se comporta **mejor que** Inés. *Pepe behaves better than Inés.*

Other points to note in the texts

- *Ser* and *estar*: Text 1: *está de moda* (l. 1–2), *es mucho menor* (l. 6–7), *es equilibrada* (l. 10), *es mejor* (l. 11), *son más ligeros* (l. 20). Text 2: *son preliminares* (l. 11), *son los más tradicionalistas* (l. 14), *es la procreación* (l. 16–17), etc. (see Chapter 13)
- Impersonal sentences: Text 1: *se come* (l. 16), *se advierte* (l. 20–21) (see Chapter 11)
- Neuter *lo*: Text 2: *lo más importante* (l. 29–30), *lo espiritual* (l. 31–32) (see Chapter 18)
- Definite article used with a possessive value, meaning 'the ones belonging to': Text 1: *es mejor que la del resto de capitales comunitarias* (l. 11–12). Text 2: *aparte de las diferencias regionales, están las de género* (l. 33–34) (see Chapter 18)
- Definite article used with a demonstrative value: Text 1: *muchos de los (aquellos) que lo hacen* (l. 23–24) (see Chapter 18)

EXERCISES

1 Make comparisons of inequality with the following elements. Use **más . . . que** and **menos . . . que**.

a	La cocina francesa	la cocina alemana	sabroso
b	El Hotel Crillón	el Ritz	bueno
c	Los peruanos	los portorriqueños	racista
d	Las mujeres	los hombres	pensar en el dinero

e Los estadounidenses	los españoles	comer pescado
f La sed	el hambre	malo
g Las calles de la ciudad	las del pueblo	ancho
h Los pisos de hoy	los de antaño	pequeño
i Los coches modernos	los antiguos	potente
j Las limas	los limones	agrio

2 **¿Que** or **de**? Complete the sentences, adding other elements where necessary.

a Hay que comer más ________ cinco porciones de fruta por día.
b Anoche David comió más ________ quince albóndigas.
c Las fresas de nuestra tierra son menos grandes pero mucho más dulces ________ las de Huelva.
d Pasamos más tiempo en el pueblo ________ queríamos.
e Roberto gasta más dinero ________ gana.
f Si esta camisa vale más ________ 15 dólares, no me la compro.
g La religión es menos importante para los europeos ________ para los americanos.
h La diferencia entre las dietas era mayor ________ se esperaba.
i Era más viejo ________ parecía.
j Trajo mucho más vino ________ podíamos beber.
k El pobre Ernesto gana mucho menos ________ los que viven con él.
l No quiero comprar más fruta ________ me hace falta.
m Hay un mayor índice de obesidad entre los que no desayunan ________ entre los que desayunan.
n Había menos gente ________ esperaban.
o Comían mucho más ________ lo debido.

3 Translate the bracketed elements into Spanish.

a Comer en una cafetería es (as expensive as) ________ comer en un restaurante.
b Esta fruta es (as good as) ________ parece.
c Ahora los ingleses beben (as much coffee as) ________ té.
d No comemos (as many greens as) ________ debemos.
e Todavía la mujer no tiene (as many opportunities as) ________ el hombre.
f No tienen (as much experience as) ________ ellos.
g Pero el hombre no trabaja (as much as) ________ la mujer en la casa.
h Pedro y Pablo no son (as ambitious as) ________ sus padres.
i Mariana no habla portugués (as well as) ________ su hermana.
j No vamos al cine (as often as) ________ antes.
k María no corre (as fast as) ________ el resto de la clase.
l A ver si esta noche nos acostamos (as late as) ________ anoche.
m Esto no es (as difficult as) ________ parece.
n No tengo (as much luck as) ________ mis amigos.
o Viajar en clase turista no es (as comfortable as) ________ viajar en primera clase.

4 Answer these questions using the superlative formed with the suffix -**ísimo**.

a ¿Son dulces esas naranjas?
b ¿Es rica la paella?
c ¿Es caro ese restaurante?
d ¿Es largo el viaje en autocar?
e ¿Estas joyas son antiguas?
f ¿El lago es profundo?
g ¿Begoña es inteligente?
h ¿Manolo vive cerca?
i ¿Es difícil aprender a tocar el oboe?
j ¿Elena e Inma son simpáticas?

5 Translate the bracketed English into Spanish.

a Hay quienes dicen que la dieta mediterránea es (the best) ________ del mundo.
b Las patatas aportan (the greatest amount) ________ de calorías.
c Según una investigación, los norteamericanos son (the fattest) ________ del mundo.
d El desayuno es (the most important meal) ________ del día.
e Una antigua esclava brasileña es (the oldest woman) ________ del mundo.
f El día 21 de junio es (the longest day) ________ en el hemisferio norte.
g El Aconcagua es (the highest mountain) ________ de los Andes.
h ¿Cuáles son (the most interesting books) ________ que habéis leído?
i ¿Por qué has comprado (the most expensive boots) ________ en la tienda? No son (the best quality) ________.

6 Use comparisons of equality and inequality, and superlatives to form sentences about:

a	Madrid	Buenos Aires	Ciudad de México
b	fútbol	baloncesto	tenis
c	Mercedes	Ferrari	Porsche
d	tren	coche	autobús
e	la fruta	las verduras	la carne

7

a Think of a country you have either visited or know about and write sentences comparing and contrasting it with the country in which you live, mentioning for example: climate, landscape, types of housing, transport, customs and habits.
b Think of two towns or cities and compare and contrast them.

23 | Demonstratives

Text

In an interview, the Colombian writer García Márquez talked about his work. As you read the text, study the way in which demonstratives, the Spanish for words like *this*, *that*, have been used.

El amor es mi único discurso

– *Usted pertenece a la generación que ha usado todo tipo de herramientas para escribir, desde el lápiz al procesador de texto, pasando por la máquina de escribir.*

– Sí, pero no pienso que el ideal del escritor haya variado mucho por **eso**. Tuve suerte de conseguir un procesador de palabras en una época en que estaba a punto de perder el control de mi trabajo creativo. Justo al final de su vida Evelyn Waugh temía que nunca podría volver a escribir una novela porque no podía recordar cada palabra contenida en el manuscrito que estaba escribiendo o la relación entre **esa** palabra y las otras en la novela. No puedo soportar usar el mismo adjetivo dos veces en el mismo libro. El procesador de palabras es muy útil para resolver **ese** tipo de problemas. Pero no puede arreglar la memoria de la narración, **eso** es labor del novelista.

En *El amor y otros demonios* había originalmente un marqués que vuelve a ver a su mujer. Abandoné el personaje, pero el disco duro de mi computador mantuvo cuatro líneas sobre él y **éstas** aparecieron en la versión en español del libro. En otras palabras, dejé un personaje volando en el aire hasta que un lector me lo contó. He corregido personalmente las otras versiones, pero no me percaté de **este** error cuando estaba leyendo las pruebas. Mi memoria como novelista está empezando a fallar.

– *Todo su trabajo ficcional, aparte de una docena de historias breves, está situado en el Caribe.*

– ¿Y por qué ponerlas en algún otro lugar? El Caribe ofrece de todo. Para darle una idea de mis sentimientos acerca de **éste**, puedo contarle un incidente de mi infancia, cuando la gente de mi pueblo estaba buscando

(*Continued*)

el cuerpo de un hombre que se había
50 ahogado. Tomaron una calabaza, le
pusieron una vela y la colocaron en el
río. Me acuerdo perfectamente de
aquella escena. La vela fue llevada por
la corriente, pero de pronto se detuvo
55 y empezó a dar vueltas en círculo: allí
estaba el cuerpo del ahogado. Creo
que hoy el Caribe es un poco como el
lugar donde **aquella** vela se detuvo
después de recorrer todo el lugar.
60 Ofrece de todo.

– *. . . Y epidemias también, dice usted.*

– Siempre me han encantado las
epidemias. Es verdad: está la
epidemia del olvido en *Cien años de*
65 *soledad*, la plaga en *La mala hora*, el
cólera. Lo que debería decirme a mí
mismo es, no más epidemias.

– *¿Y no más amor tampoco?*

– Oh, no, no me canso nunca del amor.
70 **Éste** es la fuerza motriz detrás de mis
libros, mi único argumento, mi única
ideología. Cuando recibí el Premio
Nobel, Isaac Bashevis Singer dijo
que el único elemento que le faltaba a
75 mis libros era el amor. **Eso** fue, sin
duda, una de las más extrañas
observaciones que he escuchado
jamás. Él murió antes de que le
pudiera preguntar qué había querido
80 decir con **eso**. Yo creo firmemente que
el amor es el único discurso en mis
libros.

Diario *La Nación*, Chile

Demonstratives

1 USAGE

Demonstratives are words like *this*, *that*, *these*, *those*, which are used to identify things and to avoid repeating words and ideas already mentioned or understood. In his replies, García Márquez uses this device a number of times. The following notes contain more information about their use.

a As in English, demonstratives can function as adjectives, with an accompanying noun, e.g. **esa** palabra (l. 17) *that word*, **ese** tipo (l. 21–22) *that type*, **este** error (l. 36) *this mistake.*

b Demonstratives may also be used to refer to a noun without mentioning it specifically, just like *this (one)/that (one)* in English, in which case they act as pronouns. Demonstrative pronouns in Spanish required the use of an accent to differentiate these from demonstrative adjectives. But the 2010 ruling on orthography is that the accent on demonstrative pronouns is no longer required. Any text predating this, like the one above, will have accents on the demonstrative pronouns and many publications and individuals continue to use them.

. . . mantuvo cuatro líneas . . . y **éstas** aparecieron . . . (l. 30)   *. . . it kept four lines and these appeared . . .*

. . . no me canso nunca del amor. **Éste** es la fuerza motriz . . . (l. 69–70)   *. . . I never tire of love. This is the driving force . . .*

c Spanish has a set of neuter pronouns – **esto**, **eso**, **aquello** – which do not refer back to a specific noun. English uses the same forms as for adjectives and pronouns. Consider the use of the neuter form **eso** (l. 7, 24) *that*, in the text. In line 7 this refers back to the idea that, in his writing, García Márquez has used different tools, 'ha usado todo tipo de herramientas para escribir'. Consider also:

Eso fue, sin duda, una de las más extrañas observaciones . . . (l. 75–77) *That was, without doubt, one of the strangest comments . . .*
Él murió antes de que le pudiera preguntar qué había querido decir con **eso**. (l. 78–80) *He died before I was able to ask him what he had meant by that.*
¿Qué es **esto**? *What's this?*
Eso no es asunto tuyo. *That's none of your business.*
Aquello ocurrió hace mucho tiempo. *That happened a long time ago.*

2 FORMS

In Spanish, there are three types of demonstratives, with forms which agree in gender and number with the noun they qualify or refer to.

	masculine	***feminine***	
singular	**este**	**esta**	*this, this one*
plural	**estos**	**estas**	*these, these ones*
singular	**ese**	**esa**	*that, that one*
plural	**esos**	**esas**	*those, those ones*
singular	**aquel**	**aquella**	*that, that one (distant)*
plural	**aquellos**	**aquellas**	*those, those ones (distant)*

Neuter forms **esto** *this*, **eso** *that*, **aquello** *that* (distant) are invariable.

Aquel, **aquella**, etc. are used to refer to things which are far from the speaker, whether in space or time, e.g. **aquella escena** (l. 53) *that scene*, **aquella vela** (l. 58) *that candle.* Here, García Márquez is remembering his childhood, so these demonstratives help to establish that distance between the present and a remote past.

Other points to note in the text

- *Por* and *para*: *para escribir* (l. 3), *pasando por* (l. 4), *por eso* (l. 7), *para resolver* (l. 21), *para darle una idea* (l. 44–45), *fue llevada por la corriente* (l. 53–54) (see Chapter 28)
- Preterite tense: *tuve* (l. 8), *abandoné* (l. 27), *mantuvo* (l. 28), *aparecieron* (l. 30), etc. (see Chapter 2)
- Gerund: *escribiendo* (l. 16), *volando* (l. 32), *leyendo* (l. 37), *buscando* (l. 48) (see Chapter 9)
- Direct and indirect object pronouns: *me lo contó* (l. 33–34), *ponerlas* (l. 43), *darle* (l. 45), *contarle* (l. 46), *le pusieron* (l. 50–51), *la colocaron* (l. 51) (see Chapter 25)

EXERCISES

1 Replace the underlined definite article with the correct form of the demonstrative adjective for *this/these.*

- **a** Merece la pena leer la novela.
- **b** ¿Por qué no escribís con los lápices?
- **c** Has usado dos veces el adjetivo en la oración.
- **d** La señora es la esposa del doctor.
- **e** El vino no es muy bueno.
- **f** No nos gustan las flores.
- **g** Los timbales son de Amadito ¿verdad?
- **h** El periodista escribe artículos llenos de humor.
- **i** ¿Crees que les va a gustar el regalo?
- **j** ¿De quién es la bolsa?
- **k** Las fresas saben a cartón.
- **l** ¿Por qué has puesto los vasos aquí?

2 Complete the sentences, using the correct form of the demonstrative adjective or pronoun **ese/esa/esos/esas**.

- **a** Este ordenador* ya está viejo; ________ es más moderno.
- **b** Estos vasos están sucios; ________ están limpios.
- **c** No me gustan estas botas; prefiero ________.
- **d** – ¿Este autobús va a Ribadeo?
  – No, el autobús que va a Ribadeo es ________.
- **e** ¿Va a comprar estas manzanas o ________?
- **f** No se siente en esta silla; siéntese en ________.
- **g** ________ melocotones están verdes.
- **h** ¿Vas a comprarte esta camisa o ________?
- **i** Estos zapatos no son tuyos. Los tuyos son ________.
- **j** Mi primo es ________ chico que está sentado en el sofá.
- **k** No quiero saber más de ________ cosas que no son más que suposiciones tuyas.
- **l** Odiamos ________ clase de persona.

* *In Latin American Spanish:* ***computador*** *(**a**).*

3 Complete the sentences with **aquel/aquella/aquellos/aquellas**.

- **a** ________ días fueron los mejores de mi vida.
- **b** ¿Cuál prefieres: este vestido azul o ________ blanco?
- **c** ________ chicas están riéndose de mí.
- **d** ________ noche no salimos.
- **e** Creo que los López viven en ________ casa.
- **f** No sé cómo soportasteis ________ ruido.

g En ________ tiempos no había agua corriente ni electricidad en el pueblo.
h No compre estas naranjas; ________ son más dulces.
i ________ incidente le marcó para toda la vida.
j No les hagas caso a ________ turistas.
k Como había tanto que ver en ________ zona, decidimos quedarnos unos días más.
l No os recomendaría ________ hotel; no es ni bueno ni barato.

4 Relating **aquí** *(here)* with **este/a/os/as**
ahí *(there)* with **ese/a/os/as**
and **allí** *(over there)* with **aquel/aquella/os/as**
complete the questions with the appropriate demonstrative.

Example: **Ahí** hay un abrigo. ¿De quién es **ese** abrigo?

a Aquí hay un bolígrafo. ¿Es ________ tu bolígrafo?
b Ahí hay un libro. ¿Es ________ tu libro?
c Allí hay unos jardines. ¿Son bonitos ________ jardines?
d Ahí hay una chaqueta. ¿Es tuya ________ chaqueta?
e Aquí hay una carta. ¿Para quién es ________ carta?
f Ahí hay dos chicos. ¿Conoces a ________ chicos?
g Tienes muchos libros aquí. ¿Vas a leer todos ________ libros?
h Allí hay una mesa. ¿Está ocupada ________ mesa?
i Ahí viene un perro. ¿Es tuyo ________ perro?
j Allí a la derecha hay una iglesia. ¿Es románica ________ iglesia?
k Hay un bolso aquí. ¿De quién es ________ bolso?
l Allí está el cuadro que tanto te gusta. ________ cuadro es tu favorito ¿verdad?

5 Translate the bracketed elements into Spanish.

a (This) ________ domingo no puedo salir con la pandilla.
b ¿Cómo se llama (that) ________ chica? Creo que la conozco.
c ¿Te gusta (this) ________ camiseta que acabo de comprarme?
d ¿Qué te parecen (those) ________ zapatos negros con puntos blancos?
e Hay mucho que ver y hacer en (this) ________ sitio.
f (That) ________ casa allí en la esquina es donde vivían mis abuelos.
g (Those) ________ viejos son alemanes que veranean en (this) ________ pueblo.
h (These) ________ bolsas no nos pertenecen. No sabemos de quiénes son.
i No nos gusta que nos digan (these) ________ mentiras.
j Dice que (that) ________ día fue el peor de su vida.
k ¿Cuánto vale una habitación en (that) ________ hotel?
l Quisiera comprarme un coche como (this) ________, pero hasta que no me toque la lotería . . .

6 Translate into Spanish.

a This is not difficult.
b I have read this book before.
c Can I try on these shoes?
d At that precise moment there was no one at home.
e I don't like this at all.
f Those biros write better than these.
g I remember those times perfectly. Those were happy times.
h Why have you left all this here?
i That summer it rained every single day.
j I don't know why they did it that way.
k You have to take that street on the right.
l Do you want to watch this film or not?

24 | Possessives

Text

In an interview, the Spanish soprano Montserrat Caballé talked about herself and her family. As you read the text, focus attention on the Spanish equivalent of words such as *my*, *mine*, *your*, *yours*, which are known as possessives.

Text 1

Entrevista: Montserrat Caballé

– *¿Cómo es* ***su*** *vida familiar? ¿Cómo ha podido compaginarla con* ***su*** *profesión?*

– Creo que ha sido paciencia y mucho amor de **mi** familia. Primero con **mis** padres y **mi** hermano antes de casarme. Me ayudaron muchísimo. **Mi** hermano empezó siendo secretario **mío**, después **mi** "manager". Yo siempre decía "**Mi** barco es un barco que no encontrará puerto," porque nunca llegaba esa función que yo soñaba. **Mi** hermano me dijo: "Durante un año voy a trabajar para ti, y si no consigo llevar a cabo este deseo **tuyo** serás libre de hacer lo que quieras." **Mi** hermano supo desde el principio tener ese sexto sentido para guiar **mi** carrera y así lo hizo. Y así fue también cuando conocí a **mi** esposo, que me enamoré mucho de él, y **mi** hermano me dijo: "Me gustaría tanto verte casada, pero es tan difícil encontrar un buen hombre en la vida. Creo que Bernabé es un hombre muy bueno. No sé si pasarán dos Bernabés por **tu** vida." Yo no tenía dudas, lo que sí tenía era miedo a la responsabilidad y pensar si Bernabé realmente quería casarse conmigo. Me parecía mentira que me quisiera. Aquello me animó mucho y nunca se lo agradeceré bastante. Y Bernabé fue algo maravilloso en **mi** vida. Y es. [. . .] Hemos tenido la suerte de tener dos hijos [. . .]. Yo siempre deseé que se parecieran a **su** padre, que es algo muy especial, y verdaderamente se parecen mucho a él. Ése es el gran triunfo de **mi** vida.

Revista *Blanco y Negro*, Diario *ABC*, España

Text 2

In an interview, the Spanish film director Pedro Almodóvar, talks about the personal significance of *Volver*, a film set in his native La Mancha, and one of the most successful in his career.

Volver es mi película más terapéutica

"La Mancha es sinónimo de **mi** madre," dice y hay sentimientos encontrados cuando menciona la región de *El Quijote*. Cuando Pedro aún no era el gran Almodóvar que es ahora, y sólo se trataba de un niño, acompañaba a Francisca Caballero a lavar ropa cerca del río de **su** villa. Esa imagen es la más apreciada de **su** niñez. La postal que se salva de los malos ratos de **su** vida en un caluroso set de filmación.

"Desde pequeño comprendí que, por lo reaccionario, ese no era un sitio apropiado para ser libre y para desarrollar **mi** verdadera naturaleza. Allí estaban contra la vida, ignoraban la sensualidad y rendían culto a la muerte," dice el director con sorpresiva honestidad. Gracias a *Volver* ha podido reconciliarse con ese pasado. [. . .] "Para mí, lo más importante de este proceso ha sido descubrir que todas las mujeres que me rodearon cuando yo era un niño fueron **mi** verdadera educación, las que realmente me formaron para la vida y **mi** carrera de cineasta," cuenta sobre **su** buena educación. "Mientras los hombres trabajaban lejos, para mí, **mi** madre**, mis** hermanas y **nuestras** vecinas significaban el origen de la ficción, el origen de las historias, por los relatos que comentaban, por los comentarios que hacían."

Y sigue: "siempre tuve claro que yo me quería ir del pueblo. Yo no quería vivir allí. Sin embargo, con esta película y reflexionando sobre estos personajes femeninos, he recuperado la parte más positiva que tuvo ese período de **mi** vida y que fue muy importante para mí y eso lo descubres con la madurez." [. . .] "Todas **mis** películas tienen que ver conmigo, con **mi** modo de ver la vida, con **mi** mentalidad," comenta. "Entonces en esta hay una mayor intimidad, que tiene que ver con el hecho de haber vuelto al lugar donde nací. Te aclaro: con **mis** películas no trato de solucionar **mi** vida, pero esta curiosamente ha tenido un aspecto terapéutico que no tenían las otras." [. . .]

Revista *El Sábado,* Diario *El Mercurio,* Chile

Possessives

1 USAGE

Words like **mi** *my*, **tu** *your* (familiar), **mío** *mine*, **tuyo** *yours* (familiar) are called possessives. Spanish possessives can be grouped into two main categories: ***short forms*** and ***long forms***.

a Short forms can only function as ***adjectives***, always preceding the noun or noun phrase, e.g. **mi** familia *my family* (T. 1, l. 4).

b Long forms can function as ***adjectives***, as the equivalent of English '*of mine/yours/his . . .*':

. . . este deseo **tuyo** . . . (T. 1, l. 14) *. . . this wish of yours . . .*

or as ***pronouns***, normally preceded by the definite article:

¿Me puedes prestar tu teléfono móvil? He dejado **el mío** en casa. *May I borrow your mobile phone? I've left mine at home.*

Teléfono is a masculine noun, hence the use of **el mío**.

c No definite article is needed when the possessive is preceded by the verb **ser** *to be*:

Estas gafas no son **mías**. *These glasses are not mine.*

But note the use of the article in:

Estas gafas no son **las mías**, son **las tuyas**. *These glasses are not mine, they are yours.*

in which the possessive serves to establish a distinction.

2 FORMS

a Short forms

Short forms always agree in number (singular or plural) with the noun they refer to, not with the owner. The first person plural and the second person plural familiar also agree in gender (masculine or feminine).

Singular		***Plural***		
Masc.	*Fem.*	*Masc.*	*Fem.*	
mi	**mi**	**mis**	**mis**	*my*
tu	**tu**	**tus**	**tus**	*your* (of **tú**)
su	**su**	**sus**	**sus**	*his, her, its, your* (of **Vd.**)
nuestro	**nuestra**	**nuestros**	**nuestras**	*our*
vuestro	**vuestra**	**vuestros**	**vuestras**	*your* (of **vosotros/as**)
su	**su**	**sus**	**sus**	*their, your* (of **Vds.**)

Except for **mío** *mine* (T. 1, l. 7) and **tuyo** *yours* (T. 1, l. 14), all the examples in texts 1 and 2 correspond to short forms, that is, to adjectives, e.g. **su vida familiar** (T. 1, l. 1) *your family life*, **mis padres** (T. 1, l. 4–5) *my parents*, **mi hermano** (T. 1, l. 5, 6, 11) *my brother*, **tu vida** (T. 1, l. 25) *your life*, **su niñez** (T. 2, l. 9–10) *his childhood*, **mis hermanas** (T. 2, l. 31–32) *my sisters*, **nuestras vecinas** (T. 2, l. 32) *our neighbours*.

De + subject pronoun to avoid ambiguity

If you need to avoid ambiguity when using **su/sus**, which can mean *his*, *her*, *your*, *their*, you can use forms such as **de él**, **de ella**, **de Vd.**, e.g. **el libro de él** *his book*.

Definite article for possessive

When the relationship between the possessor and the thing possessed is clear, as in **Ricardo vendió el apartamento** *Ricardo sold **his** apartment*, Spanish uses the definite article instead of a possessive adjective.

The possessive adjective is also replaced by the definite article when the possessive relationship is already established by a pronoun:

Clara **se** lavó **las** manos. *Clara washed **her** hands.*
Se **me** quebraron **las** gafas. *I broke **my** glasses.*
Me duelen los pies. ***My** feet ache.*

Possession in these sentences is established by the pronouns **se** and **me**.

b Long forms

Long forms agree in number and gender with the noun they refer to.

Singular		***Plural***		
Masc.	*Fem.*	*Masc.*	*Fem.*	
mío	**mía**	**míos**	**mías**	*mine*
tuyo	**tuya**	**tuyos**	**tuyas**	*yours* (of **tú**)
suyo	**suya**	**suyos**	**suyas**	*his, hers, its, yours* (of **Vd.**)
nuestro	**nuestra**	**nuestros**	**nuestras**	*ours*
vuestro	**vuestra**	**vuestros**	**vuestras**	*yours* (of **vosotros/as**)
suyo	**suya**	**suyos**	**suyas**	*theirs, yours* (of **Vds.**)

There are only two examples of long forms, in Text 1, both functioning as adjectives:

. . . empezó siendo secretario **mío** . . . (T. 1, l. 7) *. . . he started by being my secretary . . .*
. . . si no consigo llevar a cabo este deseo **tuyo** . . . (T. 1, l. 13–14) *. . . if I can't manage to fulfil this dream of yours . . .*

De + subject pronoun to avoid ambiguity

To avoid the ambiguity of **suyo** you can use the construction **de** + subject pronoun:

un amigo **de él** *a friend of his*, instead of
un amigo **suyo** *a friend of his/hers/yours/theirs.*

LATIN AMERICAN USAGE

The familiar form **vuestro** is not used in Latin America, where the short form **su** and the long form **suyo** are used in both formal and familiar address. The use of long forms after prepositional phrases such as **detrás** *behind*, **delante** *in front*, **enfrente** *opposite*, is common in spoken Latin American Spanish, e.g. **detrás mío** *behind me*, instead of **detrás de mí**, **delante nuestro** *in front of us*, instead of **delante de nosotros**.

Other points to note in the text

- Imperfect subjunctive: Text 1: *me parecía mentira que me quisiera* (l. 28–29), *yo siempre deseé que se parecieran a su padre* (l. 34–35) (see Chapter 15)
- Demonstratives: Text 1: *esa función* (l. 10–11), *este deseo* (l. 14), *ese sexto sentido* (l. 16), *ése es el gran triunfo* (l. 37) (see Chapter 23)
- Direct and indirect object pronouns: Text 1: *compaginarla* (l. 2), *me ayudaron* (l. 6), *me dijo* (l. 12), *lo hizo* (l. 17), *me gustaría . . . verte* (l. 20–21), *se lo agradeceré* (l. 30), etc. (see Chapter 25)
- Imperfect: Text 2: *no era el gran Almodóvar* (l. 5), *sólo se trataba de un niño* (l. 6), *acompañaba a Francisca Caballero* (l. 7), *ese no era un sitio apropiado* (l. 14–15), *allí estaban contra la vida* (l. 17), *ignoraban la sensualidad* (l. 17–18), etc. (see Chapter 3)
- Prepositions **para** and **por**: Text 2: *por lo reaccionario* (l. 14), *para ser libre* (l. 15), *para desarrollar* (l. 15–16), *para mí* (l. 22, 31), *para la vida* (l. 27–28), *por los relatos* (l. 34–35), etc. (see Chapter 28).

EXERCISES

1 Rewrite the sentence as in the example, using a possessive adjective.

Example: Tengo una habitación grande. Mi habitación es grande.

a Tengo un escritorio muy viejo.
b Carmen tiene una hermana que es médica.
c Tienes unos amigos muy simpáticos.
d Usted tiene una habitación reservada.
e Tenemos una casa muy moderna.
f Ustedes tienen los billetes en la mesa.
g Tenéis un coche muy cómodo.
h Los estudiantes tienen unas ideas muy buenas.
i Tenemos libros muy interesantes.
j Ustedes tienen una opinión muy mala de Gonzalo.
k Tenemos un jardín grande.
l Santiago tiene un trabajo muy aburrido.
m Vosotros tenéis unas hijas muy majas.
n Tengo chaquetas de piel.
o Tienes un marido maravilloso.

2 Complete the sentences using the possessive pronoun.

a Estos son tus regalos. Estos regalos son ________.
b Este bolso es de Miguel. Es ________.
c Estas son nuestras revistas. Estas revistas son ________.
d Estos son mis pañuelos. Estos pañuelos son ________.
e Aquella maleta es de los señores. Aquella maleta es ________.
f Estos son nuestros juguetes. Estos juguetes son ________.
g Estas son vuestras corbatas. Estas corbatas son ________.
h Este es mi diccionario. Este diccionario es ________.
i La casa la compramos José y yo pero es más ________ que ________.
j Carmen, ¿estos guantes son ________? Porque no son ________.
k El tío Adolfo le prestó a Fernando unos libros ________ para que los leyera.
l Los abuelos nos regalaron ese cuadro así que ahora es ________.

3 Translate the bracketed English to complete the sentences.

a Yo vendo mi apartamento y él vende (his) ________.
b Pedro va en su coche y yo voy en (mine) ________.
c Tu casa es grande pero prefiero (ours) ________.
d Este libro no es de Antonia; (hers) ________ está allí.
e La camiseta de Rosario es verde; (mine) ________ es azul.
f Aquí está mi paraguas. ¿Saben ustedes dónde están (yours) ________?
g Paco, pon tu plato aquí y Marta y Teresa, poned (yours) ________ allí.
h Tus fotos han salido muy bien; (mine) ________ no tan bien.
i Mientras tú vas preparando tus cosas, nosotros vamos preparando (ours) ________.
j Como no tenemos coche y vosotros sí, ¿podemos ir en (yours) ________?
k Toma tu billete y yo me quedo con (mine) ________.
l Tú, ¡vete ya! ¿No ves que estamos hablando de mis problemas, no de (yours) ________?
m Es un asunto muy delicado porque se trata de nuestro dinero y no (theirs) ________.
n A mi madre le han otorgado un premio y a (his) ________ también.
o – Chicos, ¿a qué casa vamos, a (ours) ________ o a (yours) ________?
– No vamos a (yours) ________, (ours) ________ queda más cerca.

4 Possessive or definite article? Translate the following sentences into Spanish.

a She took off her coat and put on her jacket.
b Where have I put my passport?
c Would you give me your telephone number? (**usted**)
d He took his money out of his pocket.
e My stomach aches.
f I liked their flat.
g We talked about our children.
h Have you cut your finger?
i Why didn't he introduce us to his friend?

j He took off his shoes because his feet were hurting him.

k Have you hurt your hand?

l They hung their coats on the pegs in their room.

m His eyes were blue and his hair was blond.

n Open your bag and let me see your things.

o He put his hand into the bag and pulled out his keys.

p They came to see our house but unfortunately we were with our grandparents that day.

5 Complete the following texts by filling in each blank with an appropriate possessive or article.

a Anoche fui a una función pero como ________ coche estaba estropeado, Ricardo me dejó ________. ________ coche es un BMW deportivo que ________ padre le compró para ________ cumpleaños. Desde luego yo no tengo tanta suerte. ________ padre está en paro y yo y ________ hermanos tenemos que trabajar mucho para mantener a ________ padres.

b – María, hija ¿quieres poner ________ zapatos debajo de ________ cama?

– No son ________ zapatos. ________ ya están debajo de ________ cama. Esos zapatos son de Antonio.

– No, no son ________. ________ son marrones y éstos son negros. María ¿de quién serán si no son ________?

c Acabamos de volver de la boda de ________ hija. ¿Quieres ver ________ fotos? Aquí estamos mi esposo y yo con uno de ________ hijos. Y esta es una foto de ________ hija con ________ esposo y unos amigos ________. Y esta es una foto de otra hija ________ con ________ novio.

25 | Personal pronouns

Text

The following is part of an interview with the chairman of 'El Refugio', a society for the prevention of cruelty to animals. As you read it, focus attention on the use of words such as *he/him, we/us, they/them*, etc.

Nacho Paunero: "Maltratar a un animal es delito y es necesario denunciarlo"

– *¿Cómo funciona "El Refugio"?*

– Hay una auténtica red, un ejército oculto de colaboradores que no son socios ni voluntarios, pero que quieren y respetan a los animales. Gente que **los** recoge en la calle, que se preocupa de llevar**los** al veterinario y se gasta su dinero. **Nosotros** somos el eslabón final, la última estación de este viaje de rescate.

– *¿A los españoles* ***nos*** *gusta tener bichos en casa?*

– Casi el 50 por ciento de los hogares españoles alberga algún animal, sobre todo perros, gatos y pájaros. Para **nosotros** no es obligatorio tener animales en casa, lo que sí queremos es que quien **los** tenga **los** trate bien. Queremos que antes de hacerse con uno la gente **lo** piense y **lo** valore.

– *¿Quién* ***le*** *tiene que poner el cascabel al gato de la solución del problema del abandono y el maltrato?*

– Creemos en el ciudadano. La gente quiere que se trate bien a los animales, porque no se puede negar que hay un problema ante el que muchas comunidades, ayuntamientos y hasta el Gobierno no dan soluciones integrales . . .

– *¿Se sigue maltratando a los animales domésticos?*

– Desgraciadamente, sí. Sí se da el caso de que hay personas que tienen a los animales en condiciones infrahumanas, hacinados, malviviendo, atados . . . Para **nosotros**, ésas no son formas de tener a un animal. Un gato o un perro, ¿qué es lo que quieren? Pues,

(*Continued*)

realmente lo que **ellos** quieren es estar pegados a su amo, no separarse de **él** ni un momento. Ver la tele con **él**, sentarse a la mesa, pasear. Un animal doméstico no quiere estar encerrado y atado y que de vez en cuando se **le** eche un poco de comida.

– *¿Con respecto al resto de los países de nuestro entorno, España es poco receptiva hacia los animales?*

– No, de ningún modo. Lo que está claro es que hay personas que utilizan animales para su uso personal, y muchas veces como herramienta, y esas personas, por llamar**las** de alguna manera, **los** maltratan, **los** ahorcan o simplemente **los** abandonan cuando ya no **les** sirven. Pero la mayoría de la gente quiere a los animales y que se hagan cosas en favor de **ellos**.

– *No habrá faltado quien* ***les*** *haya dicho que podrían dedicar su tiempo a las personas.*

– Sí, claro que **nos lo** han dicho, y también es lógico que se **nos** haga ese tipo de apreciación. A nivel de persona, creo que hay un extenso abanico de problemas sociales y cada cual está en su derecho de ver cuál considera prioritario. **Nosotros**, sencillamente, elegimos proteger y defender los animales.

Diario *ABC* (por M. de la Fuente), España

Text 2

The following passage from a short story by the Argentinian writer Julio Cortázar (1914–1984) will serve to illustrate the use of **vos** in the River Plate area.

La salud de los enfermos

– Mira – dijo mamá –, yo creo que habría que escribirle a Alejandro que venga a ver a su tía. Siempre fue el preferido de Clelia, y es justo que venga.

– Pero si tía Clelia no tiene nada, mamá. Si Alejandro no ha podido venir a verte a **vos**, **imaginate**. . . .

– Allá él – dijo mamá –. **Vos escribile** y **decile** que Clelia está enferma y que debería venir a verla.

– ¿Pero cuántas veces te vamos a repetir que lo de tía Clelia no es grave?

– Si no es grave, mejor. Pero no te cuesta nada escribirle.

Le escribieron esa misma tarde y le leyeron la carta a mamá. En los días en que debía llegar la respuesta de Alejandro (tía Clelia seguía bien, pero el médico de

(*Continued*)

Manolita insistía en que
aprovechara el buen aire de la
quinta), la situación diplomática
con el Brasil se agravó todavía más
25 y Carlos le dijo a mamá que no
sería raro que las cartas de
Alejandro se demoraran.
– Parecería a propósito – dijo mamá –.
Ya vas a ver que tampoco podrá
30 venir él.
Ninguno de ellos se decidía a leerle
la carta de Alejandro. Reunidos en
el comedor, miraban al lugar vacío
de tía Clelia, se miraban entre ellos,
35 vacilando.
– Es absurdo – dijo Carlos –. Ya
estamos tan acostumbrados a esta
comedia, que una escena más o
menos . . . .
40 – Entonces **llevásela vos** – dijo Pepa,
mientras se le llenaban los ojos de
lágrimas y se los secaba una vez
más con la servilleta.
– Qué **querés**, hay algo que no anda.
45 Ahora cada vez que entro en su
cuarto estoy esperando una sorpresa,
una trampa, casi.
– La culpa la tiene María Laura – dijo
Rosa –. Ella nos metió la idea en la
50 cabeza y ya no podemos actuar con
naturalidad. Y para colmo tía
Clelia . . . .
– **Mirá**, ahora que lo **decís** se me
ocurre que convendría hablar con
55 María Laura – dijo tío Roque –. Lo
más lógico sería que viniera después
de sus exámenes y le diera a su
madre la noticia de que Alejandro
no va a poder viajar.
60 – ¿Pero a **vos** no te hiela la sangre que
mamá no pregunte más por María
Laura, aunque Alejandro la nombra
en todas sus cartas?
– No se trata de la temperatura de mi
65 sangre – dijo tío Roque –. Las cosas
se hacen o no se hacen, y se acabó.

Julio Cortázar, *La salud de los enfermos* (from the collection *Todos los fuegos el fuego*)

Subject pronouns

1 USAGE

Words such as **yo** *I*, **tú** *you*, **usted** *you* (formal), **él** *he*, etc., are known as subject pronouns. Subject pronouns are not normally needed in Spanish, as the verb ending is usually sufficient to indicate the person this refers to. But there are cases in which they are used:

a To mark a change of subject.

Gente que los recoge en la calle, que se preocupa de llevarlos al veterinario . . . **Nosotros** somos el eslabón final . . . (T. 1, l. 6–9) *People who pick them up in the street, who see about taking them to the vet . . . We are the final link . . .*

Cristina adora a su gato. **Yo** también quiero al mío. *Cristina adores her cat. I love mine too.*

The transition between the first subject – *gente* in the first sentence, *Cristina* in the second – and the subject of the sentence which follows, makes the use of subject pronouns appropriate in this case.

b For emphasis.

> **Nosotros**, sencillamente, elegimos proteger y defender los animales. (T. 1, l. 74–76)
> *We simply choose to protect and defend animals.*
> . . . ¿qué es lo que quieren? Pues, realmente lo que **ellos** quieren . . . (T. 1, l. 42–43)
> *What is it they want? Well, really what they want . . .*

Considering the context, the use of **nosotros** might be said to signal a change of subject, but it is also emphatic, whereas **ellos** is there for emphasis only, as the subject of the preceding sentence is the same.

Now consider the following example:

> Quiere que lo hagas **tú**. *He/she wants **you** to do it.*

The position of **tú** after the verb makes its presence in the sentence even more emphatic than in the alternative position before the verb: Quiere que **tú** lo hagas.

c To avoid ambiguity.
Ambiguity can occur with third person verbs. This can make the use of **él**, **ella**, **usted** and the plural forms **ellos**, **ellas**, **ustedes**, desirable or even necessary where the context does not make the subject clear, as in the following sentence:

> Tiene un perro hermoso. *He/she has/You have a beautiful dog.*

In this example, the use of a subject pronoun will prevent ambiguity:

> **Ella** tiene un perro hermoso. *She has a beautiful dog.*

Ambiguity may also occur between first and third person singular verbs in certain tenses, for example the imperfect or the present subjunctive, where **yo** and **él**, **ella**, **usted** share the same forms.

> Vivía en España. *I/he/she/you used to live in Spain.*
> Carmen quiere que vaya. *Carmen wants me/him/her/you to go.*

But:

> **Él** vivía en España. *He used to live in Spain.*
> Carmen quiere que **yo** vaya. *Carmen wants me to go.*

d On its own, without an accompanying verb.

> – ¿Quién te lo dijo? – **Ella**, le contesté. *– Who told you? – She did, I replied.*
> – Me quedaré en casa. – **Yo** también. *– I'll stay at home. – So will I.*

e As a way of establishing a contrast or comparison.

> **Yo** tengo 30 años. ¿Qué edad tienes **tú**? *I'm 30 years old. How old are you?*

f For politeness.
Usted (usually abbreviated **Vd.**) *you* (formal, sing.) and **ustedes** (usually abbreviated **Vds.**) *you* (formal, pl.) are often used for politeness, even when they are not needed.

Pase **usted**, por favor. *Come in, please.*

2 FORMS

	singular	*plural*
1st person	**yo** *I*	**nosotros/as** *we*
2nd person	**tú** *you* (familiar)	**vosotros/as** *you* (familiar)
3rd person	**usted** *you* (formal)	**ustedes** *you* (formal)
	él *he*, **ella** *she*	**ellos/ellas** *they* (masc./fem.)

¿Tú or *usted*?

Generally speaking, the formal forms **usted** and **ustedes** (and all forms related to these) are used to address people one doesn't know, as well as the elderly and one's superiors. In certain working environments, however, especially in Spain, the current trend in hierarchical relationships points towards informal address.

The familiar forms **tú** and **vosotros/as** are used among friends, equals (for example colleagues or people of the same age), and generally among younger people, even if they haven't met before, including relationships in public services. Within the family, the standard form is the familiar one.

LATIN AMERICAN USAGE AND FORMS

As in Spain, Latin Americans make a distinction between familiar and formal address, but only when addressing one person: **tú** and **usted**. The plural **vosotros/as** and the forms related to this are not used in Latin America. **Ustedes** is used in both formal and familiar address, a feature of speech which is not exclusive to Latin America, as it is also found in the Canaries. Generally speaking, in Latin America the familiar form is less prevalent than in Spain, but usage differs from country to country.

¿De dónde eres (**tú**)? *Where are you from?* (fam., sing.)
¿De dónde es **usted**? *Where are you from?* (formal, sing.)
¿De dónde son **ustedes**? *Where are you from?* (fam./formal, pl.)

Voseo

In the River Plate region, notably Argentina and Uruguay, the subject pronoun **tú** and the prepositional form **ti** are replaced by **vos**, a system known as ***voseo***. **Vos** is also used, though less extensively, in parts of Central America, Colombia, Ecuador and Venezuela. It is also heard in Chile, normally among uneducated speakers. The following examples correspond to Argentinian usage.

Vos escribile y decile . . . (T. 2, l. 8–9) *You write to him and tell him . . .*
Si Alejandro no ha podido venir a verte a **vos** . . . (T. 2, l. 6–7) *If Alejandro has not been able to come and see you . . .*
Pero a **vos** no te hiela la sangre . . . (T. 2, l. 60) *Doesn't it make your blood run cold?*

In the first example **vos** is functioning as a subject pronoun in place of **tú**. In the other two it is a prepositional pronoun, with the same meaning as **ti**.

Vos takes a special form of the verb in the present indicative, in the imperative, and in certain constructions with the present subjunctive.

Vos hablás. (for **Tú hablas**) *You speak.*
Vos comés. (for **Tú comes**) *You eat.*
Vos vivís. (for **Tú vives**) *You live.*

Stem changes do not apply when using **vos**.

Qué **querés** . . . (for Qué **quieres**) (T. 2, l. 44) *What do you want . . .*
. . . ahora que lo **decís** . . . (for ahora que lo **dices**) (T. 2, l. 53) *. . . now that you say it . . .*

In the imperative, there is normally a shift in the stress or even the addition of a syllable in irregular forms.

imaginate (for **imagínate**) (T. 2, l. 7) *imagine*
vos escribile (for **tú escríbele**) (T. 2, l. 8) *you write to him*
llevásela vos (for **llévasela tú**) (T. 2, l. 40) *you take it to her*
mirá (for **mira**) (T. 2, l. 53) *look!*
decile (for **dile**) (T. 2, l. 9) *tell him*
vení (for **ven**) *come!*

Direct object pronouns

1 USAGE

a A direct object is that part of the sentence – a noun or a pronoun – which undergoes the action of the verb in a direct way:

. . . quieren y respetan a **los animales.** (T. 1, l. 5) *. . . they love and respect animals.*
Gente que . . . se gasta **su dinero**. (T. 1, l. 6–8) *People who . . . spend their money.*
Gente que **los** recoge en la calle . . . (T. 1, l. 6) *People who pick them up in the street . . .*
. . . hay personas que utilizan **animales** . . . (T. 1, l. 55–56) *. . . there are people who use animals . . .*
. . . **los** maltratan, **los** ahorcan o simplemente **los** abandonan . . . (T. 1, l. 59–61) *. . . they mistreat them, they hang them, or they simply abandon them . . .*

The direct objects in these sentences are **los animales** *animals*, **su dinero** *their money*, **los** *them*, all affected *directly* by the action of the verb.

b Direct object pronouns may stand for a person, an animal or a thing:

Me invitaron a su fiesta. *They invited me to their party.*
El jefe **te** necesita. *The boss needs you.*
Él **la** quiere mucho. *He loves her very much.*
Mi perro se llama León. **Lo** tengo desde hace un año. *My dog is called León. I've had him for a year.*
Ana tiene un nuevo coche. **Lo** compró muy barato. *Ana has a new car. She bought it very cheaply.*

c **Lo** *you, him, it,* sometimes refers to an idea, but it is not always translated:

Queremos que antes de hacerse con uno la gente **lo** piense y **lo** valore. (T. 1, l. 20–21) *We want people to think about it and to consider it before getting one.*
Sí, claro que nos **lo** han dicho . . . (T. 1, l. 68) *Yes, of course they've told us . . .*
– ¿Sabes dónde está? – No, no **lo** sé. *– Do you know where it is? – No, I don't know.*

2 FORMS

	singular	*plural*
1st person	**me** *me*	**nos** *us*
2nd person	**te** *you* (for **tú**)	**os** *you* (for **vosotros/as**)
3rd person (*masc.*)	**lo** *you* (for **Vd.**), *him, it*	**los** *you* (for **Vds.**), *them*
(*fem.*)	**la** *you* (for **Vd.**), *her, it*	**las** *you* (for **Vds.**), *them*

REGIONAL VARIATIONS

There are some important regional variations in the use of third person direct object pronouns, especially in the masculine forms. The use of **le** instead of **lo** for human males is common in Spain today, in speech as well as in writing, particularly in central and northern Spain, with **lo** being used for things:

Le llevé a casa *I took him home.*
Lo llevé a casa *I took it home.*

While this variation is considered correct, the use of the plural **les** for **los**, also common in the same areas, is sometimes frowned upon by educated speakers, even though its use is becoming more widespread. Most other regions, including Latin America, use **lo** and **los** for human males and for things. Variations in the use of the feminine forms **la** and **las** are less extensive and are generally considered unacceptable.

Note that the plural familiar **os** form is replaced by **los** (masc.) or **las** (fem.) throughout Latin America.

¿**Os** acompaño? *Shall I accompany you?* (Peninsular Spanish)
¿**Los/las** acompaño? *Shall I accompany you?* (Latin American Spanish)

A + él / ella / usted

The ambiguity in a sentence such as **Lo llamaré esta tarde** *I'll call him/you this afternoon*, can be avoided by the use of **a + él/usted: Lo llamaré a él/Vd. esta tarde**.

Indirect object pronouns

1 USAGE

a In a sentence such as **Sí, claro que nos lo han dicho** (T. 1, l. 68), *Yes, of course they have told us*, **lo**, *it*, which is what has been told, is the direct object. **Nos** *us*, which stands for the people who were told something (also affected by the action of the verb, but in an indirect way), is the indirect object. Similarly, in . . . **los abandonan cuando ya no les sirven** (T. 1, l. 61–62) . . . *they abandon them when they are no longer of use to them*, **los** *them* is the direct object and **les** *to them* is the indirect one. Note also the use of the indirect object pronouns **nos, le, les** in:

. . . y que de vez en cuando se **le** eche un poco de comida. (T. 1, l. 48–50) *. . . and that from time to time one gives him some food.*

No habrá faltado quien **les** haya dicho . . . (T. 1, l. 65–66) *There must have been those who have told you . . .*

¿A los españoles **nos** gusta tener bichos en casa? (T. 1, l. 12–13) *Do we Spaniards like to have animals at home?* (Literally, *Is it pleasing to us Spaniards to have animals at home?*)

Note that **gustar** *to like* must be preceded by an indirect object pronoun in phrases like the following: **me** gusta *I like it* (literally, *To me is pleasing*), **te** gusta *you like it* (familiar) (literally, *To you is pleasing*), **le** gusta *he/she likes it/you like it (formal)* (literally, *To him/her/you is pleasing*). So the Spanish construction is the reverse of the English one, with the person *doing the liking* coming first, in the form of an indirect object pronoun.

b In a sentence with two object pronouns, one direct and the other indirect, the indirect object pronoun must come first.

Sí, claro que **nos lo** han dicho . . . (T. 1, l. 68) *Yes, of course they have told us . . .*

– ¿Has comprado una cámara? – No, **me la** han regalado. *– Have you bought a camera? – No, I've been given it.* (literally, *No, to me it they have given.*)

¿Quién **te la** ha dado? *Who has given it to you?* (literally, *Who to you it has given?*)

c **Le** and **les** become **se** before **lo/la/los/las**.

– ¿**Les** dijiste la verdad? – Sí, **se la** dije. *– Did you tell them the truth? – Yes, I told them (it).*

In this sentence **se** stands for **les** *them*.

– ¿**Le** enviaste el paquete? – No, no **se lo** envié. *– Did you send him/her the packet? – No, I didn't send it to him/her.*

In this other example **se** stands for **le** *him* or *her*.

2 FORMS

	singular	*plural*
1st person	**me** *(to) me*	**nos** *(to) us*
2nd person	**te** *(to) you* (for **tú**)	**os** *(to) you* (for **vosotros/as**)
3rd person	**le** *(to) you* (for **Vd.**), *(to) him, her, it*	**les** *(to) you* (for **Vds.**), *(to) them*

REGIONAL VARIATIONS

The use of third person indirect object pronouns presents little variation throughout the Spanish-speaking world. A notable exception is the use of **la** for **le**, in the feminine, in central Spain, especially in Madrid, e.g. **la dije** for **le dije** *I told her*. This usage is considered incorrect by most educated speakers.

Note that the **os** form is replaced by **les** (plural, familiar and formal) throughout Latin America.

Ya **os** he dado bastante dinero. *I've already given you enough money.* (Peninsular Spanish)
Ya **les** he dado bastante dinero. *I've already given you enough money.* (Latin American Spanish)

REDUNDANT PRONOUNS

a Indirect object pronouns

In a sentence such as **¿Quién le tiene que poner el cascabel al gato . . . ?** (T. 1, l. 22–23) *Who has to risk their neck . . . ? (Who has to bell the cat . . . ?)* **el cascabel** *the bell* is the direct object and **el gato** *the cat* is the indirect one. The indirect object pronoun **le** stands for **el gato**, which is named in the sentence, so **le** can be said to be redundant. This use of a redundant pronoun is highly common in Spanish, and it is rarely omitted, except occasionally in formal writing. In the spoken language native speakers would consider its absence as odd. Here are some further examples.

Le dije a María que viniese. *I told Maria to come.*
¿**Les** preguntaste a tus padres? *Did you ask your parents?*
Os pedí a ti y a Paco que no fuerais. *I asked you and Paco not to go.*

The omission of the *redundant* pronoun is not acceptable when the indirect object precedes the verb.

A Agustín, **le** pediré ayuda. *I'll ask Agustín for help.*
A mí, **me** traes una limonada. *Bring me a lemonade.*

b Direct object pronouns

Redundancy also occurs with direct object pronouns, as shown in the following examples:

Yo **la** llamo casi todas las noches, a mi madre. ¿Y tú? *I call my mother almost every night. And you?*

Carmen no **los** ha invitado a su casa, a Pedro y José. *Carmen hasn't invited Pedro and José to her house.*
Yo mismo **las** compré, las manzanas. *I myself bought the apples.*

As with indirect object pronouns above, the direct object pronoun cannot be omitted when the direct object precedes the verb. Compare for example **Yo mismo compré las manzanas** *I myself bought the apples*, in which the direct object pronoun has been omitted, with **Las manzanas las compré yo mismo**, in which the pronoun **las** is obligatory.

POSITION OF DIRECT AND INDIRECT OBJECT PRONOUNS

a Direct and indirect object pronouns are normally placed before the verb:

... lo que sí queremos es que quien **los** tenga **los** trate bien. (T. 1, l. 18–19) *... what we want is that those who have them treat them well.*
¿Quién **le** tiene que poner el cascabel al gato ...? (T. 1, l. 22–23) *Who has to risk their neck ...?*
Sí, claro que **nos lo** han dicho ... (T. 1, l. 68) *Yes, of course they have told us ...*

b With an infinitive, a gerund or a positive imperative, pronouns are attached to the end of the verb, becoming one word with it.

... es necesario denunciar**lo** ... (*title*) *... you have to report it ...*
Gente que ... se preocupa de llevar**los** al veterinario ... (T. 1, l. 6–8) *People who see about taking them to the vet ...*
... y esas personas, por llamar**las** de alguna manera ... (T. 1, l. 58–59) *... and those people, to give them a name ...*
Pensándo**lo** bien, es mejor no decír**selo**. *Thinking it over, we'd better not tell him/her/them.*
Tratándo**los** de esa manera, no conseguirás que te obedezcan. *Treating them that way, you won't get them to obey you.*
Dí**selo**. *Tell him/her/them.*
Lláma**la**. *Call her.*

With negative imperatives, pronouns must precede the verb.

No **se lo** digas. *Don't tell him/her/them.*
No **la** llames. *Don't call her.*

c In a construction with a finite verb followed by an infinitive or a gerund, the object pronoun may be placed before the finite verb or it may be added to the infinitive or gerund.

Los voy a denunciar. OR Voy a denunciar**los**. *I'm going to report them.*
Quieren proteger**lo**. OR **Lo** quieren proteger. *They want to protect him.*
Me está llamando. OR Está llamándo**me**. *He/she is calling me.*
Nos estaban esperando. OR Estaban esperándo**nos**. *They were waiting for us.*

Note that when the pronoun follows the gerund, an accent must be added to this in order to signal that the stress on the gerund remains the same, that is, on the penultimate syllable: lla**man**do, espe**ran**do.

In sentences with verbs such as **gustar**, **agradar**, *to like*, **apetecer**, *to feel like*, which are normally preceded by an indirect object pronoun, any additional pronouns must be added to the infinitive:

Me gusta/agrada llevar**la** al parque. *I like taking her to the park.*
No nos apetece hacer**lo**. *We don't feel like doing it.*

PREPOSITIONAL PRONOUNS

a Pronouns which follow prepositions, known as *prepositional* or *disjunctive pronouns*, are the same as the subject pronouns (see Subject pronouns above), except for **mí** *me* and **ti** *you* (familiar, sing.) and **sí**, which is the reflexive third person form translating *himself/herself/itself, themselves* (for **sí**, refer to **b** and **c** below).

Para **nosotros** no es obligatorio . . . (T. 1, l. 17) *For us, it's not obligatory . . .*
Para **nosotros**, ésas no son formas de . . . (T. 1, l. 39–40) *For us, those are not ways to . . .*
Pues, realmente lo que ellos quieren es . . . no separarse de **él** . . . (T. 1, l. 42–45) *Well, really what they want is . . . not to leave his side . . .*
Ver la tele con **él** . . . (T. 1, l. 45–46) *To watch television with him . . .*
. . . la mayoría de la gente quiere . . . que se hagan cosas en favor de **ellos**. (T. 1, l. 62–64) *. . . the majority of people want . . . things done on their behalf.*
Eso es muy importante para **mí**. *That's very important for me.*
Estaba pensando en **ti**. *I was thinking of you.*

After **entre** *between, among*, **hasta** with the meaning of *even*, **incluso** *even*, **según** *according to*, **excepto**, **salvo, menos**, all three meaning *except*, use subject forms **yo** and **tú** instead of **mí** and **ti**.

Entre **tú** y **yo**. *Between you and me.*
Hasta/incluso **yo** logré entenderlo. *Even I managed to understand it.*
(But: La noticia llegó hasta **mí/ti** a través de un amigo. *The news reached me/you through a friend.*)
Según **tú**, entonces, soy yo el que está equivocado. *According to you, then, it's me who's wrong.*
Vinieron todos, excepto/salvo/menos **tú**. *They all came, except you.*

In Argentina, **ti** and **tú** are normally replaced by **vos**:

Estaba pensando en **vos** (for **ti**). *I was thinking of you.*
Vinieron todos menos **vos** (for **tú**). *They all came, except you.*

b **Con** + **mí/ti/sí** results in the following forms: **conmigo** *with me*, **contigo** *with you* (familiar, sing.), and the much less common **consigo** *with himself/herself*, etc. But **con él/ella/Vd.**, etc. *with him/her/you.*

¿Quieres venir **conmigo**? *Do you want to come with me?*
La vi **contigo**. *I saw her with you.*
Nunca lleva suficiente dinero **consigo**. *He/she never takes enough money with him/her.*

c Other than in the construction with **con** above, the reflexive **sí**, which stands for the reflexive pronoun **se**, meaning *himself/herself/itself/yourself* (formal) and the plural forms *yourselves* (formal)/*themselves*, is used in sentences like the following:

Elena sólo piensa en **sí** misma. *Elena only thinks of herself.*
Están orgullosos de **sí** mismos. *They are proud of themselves.*
Mi padre volvió en **sí** después de unos minutos. *My father regained consciousness after a few minutes.*
Javier no cabía en **sí** de contento. *Javier was beside himself with joy.*

(For the reflexive, see Chapter 12.)

Other points to note in the text

- Prepositions: Text 1: *de colaboradores* (l. 3), *a los animales* (l. 5), *en la calle* (l. 6), *se preocupa de llevarlos* (l. 7), *de este viaje de rescate* (l. 10–11), *para nosotros* (l. 17), *hacerse con uno* (l. 20–21), *ver la tele con él* (l. 45–46), *sentarse a la mesa* (l. 46), etc. (see Chapter 28)
- Adjectives: Text 1: *un ejército oculto* (l. 2–3), *el eslabón final* (l. 9), *la última estación* (l. 9–10), *los hogares españoles* (l. 14–15), *soluciones integrales* (l. 31–32), *condiciones infrahumanas* (l. 37–38), etc. (see Chapter 20)
- Relative pronouns: Text 1: *colaboradores que no son socios . . . pero que quieren* (l. 3–5), *Gente que los recoge . . . que se preocupa* (l. 6–7), *un problema ante el que muchas comunidades* (l. 28–30), *hay personas que tienen a los animales* (l. 36–37), *hay personas que utilizan animales* (l. 55–56) (see Chapter 26)

EXERCISES

1 Fill the gap with a subject pronoun.

a ¿________ vas a hablar con la directora o soy ________ la que tiene que hablar con ________?
b ¿Cuándo vais ________ a Suiza?
c A él le ha gustado esa película mexicana pero a ________ no nos ha gustado nada.
d ¿La tortilla es para ________, señor o es para la señora?
e No sé lo que vamos a hacer porque si ________ no quieren ir, y ________ no podemos, pues, no hay nadie más.
f Señores ¿han dejado todos ________ las llaves en recepción?
g – Basilio dijo que estaba de acuerdo con los planes.
– Y Magdalena, ¿qué dijo ________?
h – ¿Vamos tú, Guillermo y yo a la función?
– Ve ________ si quieres, pero ________ no tengo la menor intención de ir.
– ¿Y Guillermo?
– ________ dirá si va a ir o no.
i Señores, si quieren ________ seguirme, empezaremos la visita al monasterio.
j Este verano queremos visitar las Islas Órcadas. Y ________ ¿qué pensáis hacer?

k Vamos a aclarar una cosa. No son de la misma nacionalidad. ________ es español pero ________ es venezolana.

l Para acabar con esto lo más rápido posible, ________ leo y ________ escribes, ¿vale?

2 Answer the questions using the information provided.

Example: ¿Dónde compró Raúl el poncho? / Argentina. Lo compró en Argentina.

a ¿Cuándo escribió Marta la carta? / viernes

b ¿Viste a los señores Gil? / el lunes pasado

c ¿Dónde compras las flores? / en el mercado

d ¿Conoces al tío de Silvia? / No

e ¿Vendieron las tierras? / Sí

f ¿Llamaste a tu madre? / ayer

g ¿Dónde has puesto mi libro? / en el estante

h ¿Habéis probado la tarta? / todavía no

i ¿Cuándo sacaron las entradas? / anteayer

j ¿Dónde metió Natalia los documentos? / en la caja fuerte

k ¿Quién trajo el vino? / Pepe

l ¿Quién tomó las fotos? / Mi amiga

3 Rewrite these sentences, replacing the bracketed words with the appropriate pronoun.

a Montse regaló un collar (a su madre).

b La señora no dio ninguna respuesta (a mí).

c He preparado un café (para ti).

d Nuestro padre mandó una carta (a ti y a tu hermano).

e El jefe ha explicado el problema (a ustedes).

f Ellos no querían vender las tierras (a nosotros).

g Yo siempre digo la verdad (a usted).

h Tenemos que dar los libros (a los alumnos).

i Hicimos un gran favor (a los señores).

j Javier no quiso prestar su coche (a su hermana).

k Mañana van a enseñar el piso (a nosotros).

l Remedios siente no poder traer un regalo (para vosotros).

4 Rewrite these sentences, replacing the words in italics with appropriate pronouns.

a No me dio *la mano.*

b Marta nos mostró *las fotos.*

c Roberto no os ha hecho *la reserva* ¿verdad?

d No te puedo contar *mis problemas.*

e Me entregaron *el premio.*

f Pepe no quiere darme *las joyas.*

g ¿Por qué no os quiso comprar *las revistas*?

h Federico va a leernos *los poemas*.

i ¿Te pongo *los pendientes* en una cajita?

j Me narró *sus aventuras* con todo detalle.

k Van a ofrecerme *el puesto de trabajo*.

l Han dicho que no os pueden traer *los planos* hasta pasado mañana.

5 Replace the words in italics with appropriate pronouns.

a El guía explicó *la historia a los turistas*.

b La señora no quería vender *las tierras a Andrés y su mujer*.

c Recomendé *el libro a los estudiantes*.

d Carlos va a pedir *las notas a Enrique*.

e No pensaba devolver *el dinero a Rosario*.

f ¿Pasaste *los trabajos a Pedro*?

g Olvidé traer *los periódicos para el abuelo*.

h ¿Les has recomendado *el hotel a tus padres*?

i ¿Por qué no querías dar*le el mensaje a Raimundo*?

j ¿Cuándo *le* dejaste *a María la chaqueta*?

k Tuvimos que llevar*le a Andrés la carpeta*.

l *Les* dieron *las noticias a los padres* anoche.

6 Read the following text and consider how it can be improved with the use of pronouns, then rewrite it using subject and object pronouns as and when appropriate.

Cuando Emilio cumplió los diez años, su madre decidió comprar a Emilio una mascota. Con la mascota Emilio aprendería a ser responsable. Una compañera de trabajo aconsejó a ella que fuera a un refugio y como sabía mucho de perros acompañó a ella para ayudar a ella a escoger la futura mascota de Emilio.

¡Qué emoción sintió Emilio cuando vio al perro en los brazos de su madre! En seguida quería jugar con el perro, pero su madre advirtió a él:

– Este perro no es un juguete, es un ser vivo y tienes que cuidar al perro bien. Voy a explicar a ti lo que tienes que hacer. Primero tienes que dar de comer al perro dos veces al día, luego hay que cepillar al perro a diario y dar al perro un baño cada dos semanas. ¿Entendido?

– Sí, mamá, pero también puedo sacar al perro de paseo ¿no? ¿Ya tiene nombre?

– No, hijo. Puedes dar al perro un nombre, uno que te guste. Y mañana llevamos al perro al veterinario.

Al día siguiente, mientras ponía al perro sus inyecciones, la veterinaria dijo a Emilio:

– ¿Sabes que un perro nunca olvida las lecciones que aprende, así que tienes que educar al perro? Por ejemplo, cuando saques al perro de paseo es muy importante que salgas primero y que el perro siga a ti. El perro tiene que obedecer a ti siempre, así aprende que eres el amo y es tu compañero fiel. Sería una buena idea que te apuntaras a unas clases. ¿Ya tiene nombre?

– Sí, voy a llamar al perro Tintín. A propósito ¿es perro o perra?

7 Complete the text with the appropriate pronoun.

Ramoncito encontró el CD en el rastrillo y ________ compró sin pensar ________ más porque sabía que era mi cumpleaños y ________ compró para ________. Nada más comprar________, vino acá para regalar ________ de modo que llegó tarde a casa y su padre se enfadó con ________ y ________ castigó.

Cuando me enteré, ________ dije al padre que no debería haber ________ hecho porque Ramoncito estaba pensando en ________ y quien tenía la culpa era ________. Pero el padre ________ dijo que no tenía por qué meter ________ en asuntos ajenos y si ________ quería castigar a su hijo, ________ haría.

Volví a casa furiosa y cuando vi que mis hijas estaban en el salón escuchando mi disco, ________ grité:

– ¿Quién ________ ha dado permiso para escuchar esto?

– Calma ________, mamá, – ________ contestaron, – Es una música preciosa. ________ encanta. Siénta ________ y escucha ________. Y otra cosa, ________ hemos preparado la cena así que ________ a descansar.

8 Translate into Spanish.

a Who gave you this watch? Nobody gave it to me; I found it.
b I can't give her the money today, I'll give it to her tomorrow.
c Have you visited them before? Between you and me, they are not very friendly.
d Everybody has given you something except her.
e Children, I'll give you your gloves and you can put them on to go out.
f Sir, Madam, how can I help you?
g Her husband listened to her while she served him his dinner.
h 'I'll invite you for a coffee' is what Ricardo said to us.
i According to him, we are going to be charged 100 euros for this consultation.
j Even if you don't like jazz, he does and so do I. He'll come to the concert with me on Saturday.
k I did what you asked me to with the oranges. I gave them to Carmen's mother.
l I just don't understand why he hasn't given her the ring. She chose it and he went the next day to buy it for her but she hasn't got it yet.

See also Chapter 30, **Word order**, for exercises with redundant pronouns.

26 | Relative pronouns

Text 1

Like many illegal migrants today, who cross the Straits of Gibraltar from North Africa into Europe in improvised **balsas** ***rafts***, prehistoric man may have made a similar crossing a million and a half years ago. This is the subject of the first text, which, like the one below it, focuses on the use of relative pronouns.

El homo erectus, el primer "balsero" del estrecho de Gibraltar

Los africanos **que** ahora se juegan la vida para venir a Europa en embarcaciones precarias no son los primeros **que** han hecho ese viaje. 5 Hace cientos de miles de años, otros africanos, **quienes** son nuestros antecesores, hicieron ese mismo camino y colonizaron Europa, según las teorías de algunos de los 10 paleontólogos **que** han estudiado el tema. Parece probado que los primeros humanos nacieron en Africa, en las fértiles praderas del oriente, desde **las que** se 15 expandieron por Asia y Europa en diferentes oleadas. La mayoría de los paleontólogos ha estado siempre de acuerdo en que esa migración se produjo por Oriente Próximo, 20 exactamente por el valle del Jordán. Pero, el paleontólogo surafricano Phillip Tobias explicó una nueva hipótesis: los homínidos **que** llegaron a Europa no lo habrían hecho por 25 Oriente Próximo sino cruzando el estrecho de Gibraltar, a través **del cual** se adentraron en la Península Ibérica, un viaje **que** habría tenido lugar entre 1,5 y 1,6 millones de años atrás.

Revista *Tiempo*, España

Text 2

Text 2 looks at the wave of young Spanish immigrants seeking work opportunities in Chile.

Cómo viven y quiénes son la nueva oleada de españoles en Chile

Tras el inicio de la crisis económica en España, Chile se ha convertido en el segundo país del mundo donde más ha crecido el número de ibéricos. El aumento en la inmigración está impulsado por jóvenes profesionales de entre 25 y 35 años **que** vienen a Chile a emprender o a buscar empleo. Cuando en 2010 su empresa le ofreció venir a trabajar en su filial chilena, para Esther Mesa (34) la estadía en el país tenía fecha de vencimiento: tres años. Y aunque a las dos semanas la sorprendió el terremoto del 27/F y pensó en regresar, hoy siente que tomó la mejor decisión. "Al principio todos decían que era muy lejos, que no viniera, pero ahora me aconsejan quedarme," cuenta Esther.

La crisis por **la que** atraviesa España está haciendo que cada vez más personas miren nuevos destinos en busca de oportunidades. Un fenómeno **que** reflejó el diario español *ABC* al publicar los resultados de una encuesta **que** muestra que siete de cada diez españoles estarían dispuestos a cambiar su lugar de residencia para poder encontrar trabajo. ¿Los tres principales destinos? Brasil, Alemania y Chile [. . .]

Pero a diferencia de la última gran oleada de españoles **que** desembarcó en territorio nacional huyendo de la guerra civil, **que** en su mayoría fueron obreros especializados o técnicos, ahora se trata de profesionales con más de un título universitario. Jóvenes de entre 25 y 35 años **que** no sólo buscan trabajo, sino ejercer su carrera.

Ignacio Chaparro (32) llegó este año junto a su esposa para montar una consultora de soluciones informáticas. En Madrid quedó una casa de **la que** ya habían pagado el pie. "Debido a la situación económica en España surgió la posibilidad de establecerse acá y decidimos tomarla." Algo similar le pasó a la hematóloga María José García (31), **que** aceptó acompañar a su marido chileno, **quien** llegó al país a instalar la filial de una empresa hispana. No se queja. Actualmente trabaja en el Hospital Clínico de la Universidad Católica. [. . .] Lucy Krell, socia de la empresa de *headhunting* CTPartners, dice que gran parte de los inmigrantes hispanos son profesionales **que** vienen a engrosar las filas de empresas de ingeniería, medicina y minería.

Pero no todos tienen la suerte de llegar con capital o un trabajo asegurado. De hecho, cada vez más son los españoles **que** quieren probar suerte, con disímiles resultados. Ana Turull (28), arquitecta catalana, llegó recién titulada sin ningún contacto y a los tres días ya estaba colaborando en la oficina de Teodoro Fernández.

(*Continued*)

"Tuve mucha suerte. En España me habría demorado más y no hubiera encontrado algo tan bueno," dice.

Un caso parecido es el de la analista
75 de mercado Carolina Yepes (27), **quien** arribó después de terminar un contrato en su natal Valladolid [. . .] "Encontré trabajo a las dos semanas como ingeniera comercial y ya he
80 trabajado en tres empresas acá," cuenta Yepes, **quien** agrega que se ha podido dar el lujo de buscar mejores empleos, algo impensado en España donde todos se aferran al **que** tienen.
85 [. . .]

Tendencias, Diario *La Tercera*, Chile

In Peninsular Spanish la estadía = la estancia, el pie = la entrada, arribar = llegar.

Relative pronouns

1 GENERAL USAGE

a Relative pronouns are words like **que** *who, whom, that, which,* **el/la que**, **el/la cual** *that, whom, which,* **cuyo/a** *whose*, which introduce relative clauses. A relative clause is a group of words which refers back to something previously mentioned in the sentence, a noun or a pronoun, known as the ***antecedent***. In Text 1, line 23, for example, the relative pronoun **que** links the noun **los homínidos** . . . (the antecedent) to the relative clause **llegaron a Europa** . . . *the hominids who arrived in Europe . . .*

b A relative pronoun can be the ***subject*** or ***object*** of the relative clause. In Text 1, lines 1–2, **Los africanos que ahora se juegan la vida** . . . *The Africans who now risk their lives* . . . **que** is functioning as the subject of the relative clause, which refers back to **los africanos**. In Text 2, lines 23–25, . . . **un fenómeno que reflejó el diario español *ABC*** . . . . . . *a phenomenon reflected in the Spanish newspaper ABC* . . . , **que** is the object, a direct object in this case, referring back to **el fenómeno.** In English, the relative pronoun can be omitted when this is the direct object of a relative clause. In Spanish, this cannot be done.

2 QUE *WHO, WHOM, WHICH, THAT*

Que is the most common relative pronoun in Spanish, in the spoken and the written language. It is invariable, and it can refer to people and to things.

. . . los paleontólogos **que** han estudiado . . . (T. 1, l. 9–10) . . . *paleontologists who have studied . . .*

. . . profesionales que vienen a Chile . . . (T. 2, l. 6–8) . . . *professionals who come to Chile . . .*

. . . españoles que quieren probar suerte . . . (T. 2, l. 65–66) . . . *Spaniards who want to try their luck . . .*

... una encuesta que muestra ... (T. 2, l. 25–26) *... a survey which shows ...*
... María José García, que aceptó acompañar a su marido chileno, quien llegó al país ... (T. 2, l. 49–51) *... María José García, who agreed to accompany her Chilean husband, who arrived in the country ...*

In the first four sentences, **que** introduces a ***restrictive clause***, one which restricts the scope of the antecedent. No comma or pause is used between the relative pronoun and the antecedent. In the last example, the clause is ***non-restrictive***. It is there simply to provide more information about the antecedent, so a comma is needed in writing, and a pause in speech. As part of a non-restrictive clause, **que**, in this example, can be replaced by **quien** or **la cual**:

... María José García, **quien/la cual** aceptó acompañar a su marido ...

Que is often used with short prepositions such as **a**, **con**, **de**, **en**, with reference to a non-human antecedent.

el dinero **con que** lo compré *the money I bought it with*
la casa **en que** viví *the house I lived in*

Note that the preposition must come before the relative pronoun, never at the end of the clause, as it can do in English.

3 EL/LA QUE, LOS/LAS QUE, EL/LA CUAL, LOS/LAS CUALES *WHOM, WHICH, THAT*

El/la que is less formal and more frequently used than **el/la cual**.

These forms are often used following prepositions. In Text 1, for example, note **desde las que** (l. 14) *from which*, and **a través del cual** (l. 26) *across which*. In Text 2 we find: **por la que** (l. 20) *through which*, **de la que** (l. 44) *for which*.

These relative pronouns are also used when there is a pause in speech, or a comma in writing, between the antecedent and the relative clause.

Llamamos a la policía, **la que** lo arrestó. *We called the police, who arrested him.*

El que, **los que**, etc. can also mean *he/those who, the one(s) who/which, etc.*

Some proverbs are expressed with this construction.

El que termine primero, puede irse. *He who finishes first, can leave.*
Los que hablan español tendrán más posibilidades. *Those who speak Spanish will have a better chance.*
El que a hierro mata, a hierro muere. (proverb) *He who lives by the sword, dies by the sword.*
El que ríe último ríe mejor. (proverb) *He who laughs last laughs longest.*

4 LO QUE, LO CUAL *WHAT, WHICH*

These are neuter forms, which refer back to an idea, never to a specific noun.

Me escribió Antonio, **lo que** me alegró muchísimo. *Antonio wrote to me, which made me very happy.*

5 QUIEN, QUIENES *WHO, WHOM*

Quien, and its plural form **quienes**, can only refer to people, and its use does not differ much from that of **el que/cual** above. It can function as a subject or as an object pronoun, and it can also follow a preposition.

. . . otros africanos, **quienes** son nuestros antecesores, . . . (subject, T. 1, l. 5–7) *. . . other Africans, who are our ancestors . . .*
. . . su marido chileno, **quien** llegó al país . . . (subject, T. 2, l. 51) *. . . her Chilean husband, who arrived in the country . . .*
Carolina Yepes, **quien** arribó . . . (subject, T. 2, l. 75–76) *Carolina Yepes, who arrived . . .*
Elena, a **quien** admiro mucho, ganó el premio. (object) *Elena, whom I admire very much, won the prize.*
Luis, para **quien** nada es difícil, lo solucionó. *Luis, for whom nothing is difficult, solved it.*

Like **el que**, etc., **quien** and **quienes** are used in initial position to translate expressions like *he who, the one(s) who, those who.*

Quienes están listos pueden comenzar. *Those who are ready can start.*

6 CUYO *WHOSE*

Cuyo can refer to people or things and it must agree in gender (masculine or feminine) and number (singular or plural) with the noun that follows it.

Una situación **cuyas** consecuencias pueden ser desastrosas. *A situation whose consequences can be disastrous.*
La persona en **cuya** casa vivíamos. *The person in whose house we lived.*

Other points to note in the texts

- Preterite tense: Text 1: *hicieron* (l. 7), *colonizaron* (l. 8), *nacieron* (l. 12), *se expandieron* (l. 14–15), etc.; Text 2: *ofreció* (l. 10), *sorprendió* (l. 14), *pensó* (l. 15), *tomó* (l. 16), *reflejó* (l. 24), etc. (see Chapter 2)
- *Por* and *para*: Text 1: *para venir* (l. 2), *por Asia* (l. 15), *por Oriente Próximo* (l. 19), *por el Valle del Jordán* (l. 20); Text 2: *por jóvenes profesionales* (l. 6), *para Esther Mesa* (l. 11), *por la que atraviesa* (l. 20), *para poder encontrar* (l. 28–29), *para montar* (l. 42) (see Chapter 28)
- Adjectives: Text 2: *la crisis económica* (l. 1), *jóvenes profesionales* (l. 6), *su filial chilena* (l. 10–11), *nuevos destinos* (l. 22), *principales destinos* (l. 30), *la última gran oleada* (l. 32–33), etc. (see Chapter 20)

EXERCISES

1 Use a relative pronoun to make one sentence out of two.

a El castillo está en el puerto. Data del siglo XVI.
b Encontramos una pensión. Nos hizo recordar Santo Domingo.

c Una camarera nos sirvió. Era muy antipática.
d Un hombre contestó al teléfono. Me dijo que estabas fuera.
e Te dejé prestada la grabadora. Devuélvemela.
f En octubre te llevé a un restaurante. Ahora está cerrado.
g Aquellos son los vecinos. Me quejo de ellos.
h Me escribió una carta. En la carta me explicó todo.
i La chica fue lesionada. Está en el hospital.
j La mujer era mi amiga Consuelo. La viste ayer.
k ¿Has encontrado la estilográfica? Tu tía escribió novelas con ella.
l El sarampión es una enfermedad peligrosa. Hay que protegerse de ella.

2 Complete the sentences with **que**, **lo que** or **quien**.

a Rosario, a ________ todo el mundo quería, murió el mes pasado.
b Las recepcionistas ________ trabajan en ese hotel son todas muy amables.
c Fue Susana ________ perdió la llave, no yo.
d Las flores ________ mejor crecen aquí son los cardos.
e Han detenido al hombre ________ te dio la paliza.
f El periódico ________ prefiero leer es *El Mundo*.
g El hombre con ________ estabas hablando es el presidente de la junta.
h La chica ________ estuvo conmigo en París se hizo modelo.
i ¿Conoces a ese señor ________ pasa por ahí?
j Es con usted con ________ iré a ver al juez.
k Han detenido a Juanjo, ________ no nos extraña ya que es un sinvergüenza.
l ________ mucho abarca, poco aprieta.

3 Complete the sentences with one of the following prepositions and a relative pronoun.

de	**debajo de**	**en**	**encima de**	**detrás de**
enfrente de	**entre**	**para**	**por**	

a La casa ________ se construye un casino pertenece al Doctor Clarín.
b Si quieres, te dejo el video ________ te hablé anoche.
c Los soportales ________ siempre hay tenderetes son una característica de la ciudad.
d Los pueblos ________ hemos pasado doblan sus poblaciones en verano.
e Esa caja ________ guardo mis cositas me la hizo Rafa.
f En el salón hay un sofá ________ cuelga uno de los primeros cuadros de Miró.
g La compañía ________ trabajé tantos años está en quiebra.
h En la plaza tocaban varios músicos ________ reconoció a su primo Jacobo.
i Ese puente por ________ pasa el río Tormes es peatonal y data de la época romana.
j El edificio ________ Rosario aparcó el coche era la comisaría.
k Tuvimos que forzar la puerta ________ se escondió el niño porque no se abría.
l Estas son las calles ________ pasaron los reyes cuando visitaron el pueblo.

4 Complete the sentences with **que** or **lo que**.

a Todo ________ has hecho está bien.
b Cálmate; no es ________ te imaginas.
c El problema ________ nos enfrentaba no tenía solución.
d César dijo exactamente ________ pensaba, ________ me pareció fatal.
e La señora ________ acaba de salir es la persona ________ hace las esculturas.
f Nico pasó horas y horas chateando, ________ le costó su trabajo.
g La página web ________ creó Marco tiene mil visitantes por día.
h Muchos académicos utilizan la red para acceder a bibliotecas en el extranjero ________ facilita mucho sus investigaciones.
i ________ me molesta es que se dejen encendidos los ordenadores ________ en mi opinión es un derroche de electricidad.
j A ________ no me conformo es que el ordenador ________ no es más que una máquina, nos rija la vida.
k No creíamos nada de ________ nos contó el hombre ________ fue mandado por el ayuntamiento.
l ________ no me has dicho es donde has encontrado el libro ________ llevo años buscando.

5 Complete the sentences with the correct form of the relative pronoun **cuyo**.

a Hoy he hablado con Valentina ________ hermanos acaban de volver del Perú.
b El estudiante ________ madre está enferma no ha venido a clase hoy.
c Ven, quiero presentarte a Teresa ________ padre es el pintor que tanto te gusta.
d Por fin llegamos a conocer al chico ________ bromas nos han divertido tanto.
e ¿Cómo se llama la mujer en ________ casa nos alojamos?
f Un huérfano es un niño ________ padres han muerto.
g Por esta calle hay una casa ________ balcones están siempre repletos de flores.
h "En un lugar de La Mancha, de ________ nombre no quiero acordarme . . ." es la famosísima primera frase de *El Quijote* de Cervantes.
i Cienfuegos fue un personaje histórico ________ vida se va a relatar en la película.
j Acaba de presentarme a sus padres ________ viajes me han impresionado tanto.
k Queremos agradecerle a Rafael sin ________ intervención nos hubiéramos ido a pique.
l Mañana encontraréis al señor ________ poemas acabáis de leer y apreciar.

6 Rewrite these sentences as one, using an appropriate relative pronoun.

a La excavación por paleontólogos y arqueólogos de Atapuerca empezó en los años 70 del siglo XX. Atapuerca está en la sierra de Burgos.
b En Atapuerca se han descubierto fósiles humanos. Los fósiles pertenecen a seis individuos diferentes.
c Los seis individuos podrían haber sido los europeos más antiguos. Sus restos tienen unos 800.000 años de antigüedad.

d No se parecen a otros fósiles humanos encontrados en Europa. Este hecho revoluciona las teorías convencionales sobre la evolución de *Homo sapiens.*

e El equipo investigador le puso a esta nueva especie el nombre de *Homo antecessor.* El significado del nombre en latín es pionero.

f Han usado técnicas geofísicas avanzadas. Estas técnicas han permitido una datación precisa del yacimiento de los fósiles.

g En los huesos de *Homo antecessor* hay marcas. Por estas marcas sabemos que era caníbal.

h Los jóvenes arqueólogos han hecho las tesis. Necesitan ayuda económica para poder seguir trabajando. Su labor es de sumo interés general.

i Hoy en día muchas empresas pequeñas promocionan su comercio en Internet. Una de ellas es Frutafresca.com.

j Es un negocio hortofrutícola familiar de Valencia. Sus propietarios, Fernando y sus hijos Javier y Jorge, no querían dejar de recolectar los cultivos de modo artesanal.

k Por ejemplo, recogen las naranjas en su punto idóneo de maduración. Esto no es habitual en la recogida de la fruta.

l Mientras Fernando y Javier están recolectando, Jorge está manejando un ordenador portátil. En este atiende pedidos de frutas remitidos de comercios, hoteles y restaurantes de todo el país.

m Jorge se encargó de diseñar la página *web.* Ha atraído mucha clientela. Se siente muy orgulloso de ella.

n Un cliente estimado es Lorenzo. La idea de llevar el producto directamente del productor al consumidor le atrae.

o Lorenzo es propietario de una frutería. La frutería se encuentra en pleno centro de Madrid. En esta frutería se vende solamente fruta fresca de la mejor calidad.

p La estrategia de Frutafresca.com es ofrecer una recogida selectiva tan sólo 24 horas antes de que llegue a su destino. Internet permite esta estrategia. Frutafresca.com ha nacido con esta estrategia.

27 | Negation

Text 1

An increasing number of couples are turning to antenatal tests to ensure that they have a healthy child, but medical advance and ethics, once again, seem to clash. This is the main subject of this text, which, like Text 2 below, illustrates ***negation*** in Spanish.

Si usted quiere un hijo perfecto . . .

Recuerdo perfectamente el caso de una chica de 21 años que **no** se hizo **ningún** tipo de prueba porque **no** estaba en el segmento de riesgo y tuvo 5 un niño con síndrome de Down. Pues bien, **no** quisieron **ni** conocerlo. Tanto ella como su compañero, también muy joven, decidieron en veinticuatro horas darlo en adopción. Es cruel, sin duda, 10 pero pasa. Ello pone de relieve el creciente rechazo de las parejas más jóvenes a tener niños con malformaciones.

Los futuros padres desean tener el 15 mayor grado de seguridad con respecto a la salud de sus futuros hijos. Esta tendencia se inscribe dentro de una sociedad muy competitiva, en donde **no** se aceptan las debilidades **ni** las 20 imperfecciones **ni** las dificultades. Todo debe regirse en torno al éxito. Y este factor también ha llegado a la hora de tomar la decisión de tener un hijo.

Las parejas que se consideran sin 25 riesgo para engendrar son aquellas cuyos integrantes **no** alcanzan los treinta años, están sanos, **no** son drogadictos **ni** alcohólicos **ni** padecen alguna enfermedad congénita y llevan 30 un régimen alimenticio equilibrado. Pero aún así, en este fragmento de parejas se están dando casos de niños con malformaciones graves. La ciencia todavía **no** puede explicar por qué.

35 La información adecuada es vital en cualquier prueba de este tipo porque un feto puede tener una dolencia que, operada tras su nacimiento, se supera sin dificultad. Lo que pasa es que **no** 40 siempre los padres reciben la información adecuada o **no** van al centro adecuado. Sí existe una presión social por saber cómo está el feto, pero **no** sólo de los futuros padres **sino** de 45 toda la familia.

Revista *Tiempo*, España

Text 2

Forest fires are turning large areas of the Iberian Peninsula into barren land. The following text gives some practical advice on how to prevent them. As you read the text, note the use of negative forms.

Consejos para evitar incendios

- En verano no hacer **ningún** tipo de fuego en el bosque, **ni siquiera** en las áreas habilitadas para ello.
- (5) **No** fumar en el monte. Las cerillas y colillas, aún cuando se piense que están apagadas, constituyen un grave peligro de incendios.
- **No** dejar basuras, ya que pueden (10) convertirse en combustible fácilmente inflamable.
- Si se encuentra una hoguera, **no** abandonarla hasta cerciorarse de que está completamente apagada.
- (15) **No** abandonar **tampoco** botellas o trozos de vidrio que, por refracción, pueden originar un foco calorífico.
- Cuando se viaja por ferrocarril o por (20) carretera **no** se deben arrojar **nunca** cerillas **ni** colillas encendidas por la ventana.

Revista *Tribuna*, España

Negation

1 NEGATIVE WORDS

Negation in Spanish is expressed through the following words:

no *no, not*
nada *nothing, not anything*
nadie *nobody, no one, not anybody*
nunca *never*
jamás *never*
ninguno *no, not any, none*
ni *nor, not even*
ni . . . ni . . . *neither . . . nor . . .*
ni siquiera *not even*
tampoco *neither, not either*
apenas *hardly, scarcely*

Other negative expressions

de ninguna manera *by no means*
en absoluto *not at all*
en mi vida *never in my life*
en ninguna parte *nowhere*
nunca jamás or **jamás de los jamases** *never ever*
por nada del mundo *for all the world*
¡qué va! *not at all, quite the opposite, of course not!*
todavía no *not yet*
ya no *not any more/longer*

2 USING NEGATIVE WORDS

a *No*

No is the most commonly used negative word.

. . . **no** quisieron . . . (T. 1, l. 6) . . . *they didn't want* . . .
. . . **no** alcanzan los treinta años . . . (T. 1, l. 26–27) . . . *they are not yet thirty* . . .
No fumar . . . (T. 2, l. 5) *Do not smoke* . . . See also Text 2, lines 9 and 15.

b Double negative

Negative words such as **nunca**, **nadie**, **ninguno**, **tampoco**, may follow the verb, in which case another negative word must precede it, resulting in a double negative construction.

. . . **no** se hizo **ningún** tipo de prueba . . . (T. 1, l. 2–3) . . . *she didn't undergo any kind of test* . . .
. . . **no** se deben arrojar **nunca** cerillas . . . (T. 2, l. 19–20) . . . *you must never throw matches* . . .
No abandonar **tampoco** botellas . . . (T. 2, l. 15) *Do not leave bottles either* . . .

More emphasis can be achieved by placing such words before the verb, in a single negative construction.

Ningún tipo de prueba se hizo . . .
Nunca se deben arrojar cerillas . . .
Tampoco (se deben) abandonar botellas . . .

c *Ninguno*

Ninguno can function as an adjective and as a pronoun, agreeing in number and gender with the noun it qualifies or refers to. Its plural form, however, is rarely used nowadays. Before a masculine singular noun, **ninguno** becomes **ningún**, as in **ningún tipo** in Text 1, line 3, and Text 2, line 1, where it is functioning as an adjective. Here are some further examples:

No tienen **ninguna** posibilidad. (adjective) *They haven't any chance.*
– ¿Te gusta alguno? – No, **ninguno**. (pronoun) *– Do you like any? – No, none.*

d *Alguno for ninguno*

Alguno may be used as an adjective, after a noun, with the same meaning as **ninguno**, a construction which is more formal and emphatic.

No vemos solución **alguna**. *We don't see any solution.*

e Negative words in comparison

In comparative sentences, words like **nadie**, **nada**, **nunca**, etc. translate *anyone*, *anything*, *ever*, etc.

Él lo sabe mejor que **nadie**. *He knows it better than anyone.*
Nunca he visto **nada** más absurdo. *I've never seen anything more absurd.*
Llovió más que **nunca**. *It rained more than ever.*

f *Sin/sin que* + negative word

In these constructions with **sin** *without*, negative words such as **nada**, **nadie**, **nunca**, etc., translate *anything*, *anyone*, *ever*, etc.

Sin nada que hacer *Without anything to do*
Sin que nadie lo supiera *Without anyone knowing*
Sin quejarse **nunca** *Without ever complaining*

g *Ni, ni siquiera*

Ni has different meanings. In Text 1, line 6, it is the equivalent of **ni siquiera** *not . . . even.*

. . . no quisieron **ni** conocerlo. *. . . they didn't even want to know him.*

(**Ni siquiera** quisieron conocerlo.) Note also **ni siquiera** in Text 2, lines 2–3.

. . . **ni siquiera** en las áreas . . . *. . . not even in the areas . . .*

In Text 1, lines 19–20, **ni** translates as *or*.

. . . **no** se aceptan las debilidades **ni** las imperfecciones **ni** las dificultades. *. . . weaknesses or imperfections or difficulties are not accepted.*

In Text 1, lines 27–28, **no** . . . **ni** corresponds to the English construction *neither . . . nor.*

. . . **no** son drogadictos **ni** alcohólicos **ni** padecen . . . *. . . they are neither drug addicts nor alcoholics, nor do they suffer from . . .*

h *No . . . sino/no solo . . . sino* (*también*)

These constructions with **sino** *but* are used to indicate contradiction or correction.

No este año **sino** el próximo. *Not this year but the next one.*
. . . **no solo** de los futuros padres **sino** de toda la familia. (T. 1, l. 44–45) *. . . not only from the future parents but from all the family.*

i *Tampoco*

Tampoco is used in negative sentences with the meaning of *not . . . either, neither . . .*

No abandonar **tampoco** botellas . . . (T. 2, l. 15) *Do not leave bottles either . . .*
– No lo sé – Yo **tampoco**. *– I don't know – Neither do I.*

3 NEGATION OF ADJECTIVES

Adjectives may be negated by means of prefixes such as **an-**, **a-**, **des-**, **de-**, **i-**, **in-** (**im-** before **b** or **p**).

anormal *abnormal*
analfabeto *illiterate*
desordenado *untidy*
decrecer *decrease*
ilegal *illegal*
incapaz *incapable*

Adjectives may also be negated by means of words such as **no**, **poco**, **nada**.

países **no desarrollados** *underdeveloped countries*
objetos voladores **no identificados** *unidentified flying objects*
poco atractivo *not very attractive, unattractive*
poco eficaz *not very efficient, inefficient*
nada claro/caro *not at all clear/expensive*

4 MAKING NOUNS NEGATIVE

A few nouns accept the word **no** before them to negate their meaning.

no fumadores *non-smokers*
la **no violencia** *non-violence*
la **no intervención** *non-intervention*

Other points to note in the texts

- *Ser* and *estar*: Text 1: *estaba en el segmento* (l. 4), *es cruel* (l. 9), *son aquéllas* (l. 25), *están sanos* (l. 27), etc. Text 2: *están apagadas* (l. 7), *está . . . apagada* (l. 14) (see Chapter 13)
- Reflexive verbs: Text 1: *no se hizo* (l. 2), *se inscribe* (l. 17), *regirse* (l. 21). Text 2: *convertirse* (l. 10), *cerciorarse* (l. 13) (see Chapter 12)
- Passive and impersonal *se*: Text 1: *no se aceptan las debilidades* (l. 19), *se consideran* (l. 24). Text 2: *aun cuando se piense* (l. 6), *si se encuentra una hoguera* (l. 12), *cuando se viaja* (l. 18), *no se deben arrojar nunca cerillas* (l. 20–21) (see Chapter 11)

EXERCISES

1 Give negative answers to these questions.

a ¿Hay alguien aquí?
b ¿Tienes algo que hacer?
c ¿Habéis ido alguna vez a Acapulco?
d No voy al cine esta noche. ¿Y tú?
e ¿Has visto a alguno de mis compañeros?
f ¿Vas a enseñarme alguno de tus cuadros?
g ¿Quieres té o café?
h ¿Ya tenéis los resultados?
i ¿Ponen algo en el periódico sobre la manifestación?
j ¿Han traído alguna noticia de la expedición?
k ¿Sigues acudiendo a clase de solfeo?
l A Carlos no le gustan las películas de Bigas Luna. ¿Y a ti?

2 Rewrite these sentences in a different way.

a No tenía dinero nunca.
b No acompañaba nadie al concejal.
c En esa tienda no vendían ni bolígrafos.

d No me ayudaron tampoco.
e No viene nunca nadie.
f Federica no entiende nada nunca.
g Yo no entiendo nunca nada tampoco.
h No te lo podría explicar ningún científico.
i ¿Qué hacer si no nos lo explica nadie?
j Aunque vivimos en España, no habla castellano ninguno de mis hijos.
k Las instrucciones no tenían nada que ver con el aparato.
l No entiendo cómo puede ser que no haya acudido nunca a un médico.

3 Complete the sentences using a negative from the list below.

nada	**nadie**	**ni**	**ninguno**
no	**nunca**	**sino**	

a No queremos hablar con ________.
b Salió de allí sin decir ________.
c Todavía ________ se ha presentado ________ oportunidad para decírselo.
d Pepe tiene cara de tonto pero ________ es ________ tonto.
e Porfidio ________ explicó ________ de sus acciones.
f La culpa ________ es del niño ________ de los padres.
g Los chistes de Juanjo ________ tienen ________ de gracia.
h ________ queremos ________ disculpas ________ excusas.
i ________ buscamos la juerga ________ la tranquilidad.
j ________ he visto ________ tan espectacular como los fuegos artificiales de Las Fallas.
k Ya te he dicho que ________ quiero ver a ________.
l ________ tiene ________ más que ofrecer, ________ una cosita más.
m Este año ________ vamos a México de vacaciones ________ a Costa Rica.
n ________ me gustan ________ las aceitunas ________ el vino tinto.

4 Unjumble the words to make meaningful sentences.

a nada • en • nadie • monte • el • dejó
b desviamos • no • del • nos • sendero • nunca
c fumadores • grupo • había • el • no fumadores • en • y
d tiramos • no • ni • ni • sin • colillas • cerillas • apagar
e encendimos • tampoco • hogueras • no
f ningún • del • no • área • fuego • de • hicimos • fuera • indicada • tipo
g el • sabía • fogón • nadie • utilizar • el • en • grupo
h nadie • pasamos • sin • a • el • ver • día
i hizo • llovió • pero • día • bueno • no • muy • tampoco • un
j sino • once • pasadas • a • ocho • volvimos • las • no • las
k un • ninguno • sufrió • de • accidente • nosotros
l tampoco • la • pero • repetir • experiencia • quiere • nadie

5 Translate into Spanish.

a I spent the whole day at home doing nothing.
b Pablito never understands anything.
c He hasn't given me any kind of help.
d What you have written isn't at all clear.
e They don't read the papers or listen to the news on the radio.
f I haven't got the results yet and Jorge hasn't either.
g He went off without saying anything to anyone.
h She did it without any difficulty.
i Elena doesn't write to me any more; she says she hasn't anything to tell me.
j None of these places is far away but none is particularly attractive.
k She hasn't even told Miguel she doesn't want to see him again ever.
l He's going to university, not this year but next.

28 | Prepositions

Text

The following extract from an article by Greenpeace looks at genetically modified crops. As you read the text, note the use of words such as **por**, **para**, **en**, **con**, **de**, known as prepositions.

Ingeniería genética: Frankenstein o el moderno Prometeo

La ingeniería genética está dejando **de** ser – **a** una velocidad alarmante – una técnica **de** laboratorio **para** convertirse **en** un proceso comercial.

5 **En** este proceso, el material genético puede ser transferido **entre** organismos **de** especies no relacionadas, una habilidad que ha sido apropiada **por** la industria, como un método **para** 10 introducir nuevas características **en** las plantas, animales y microorganismos. Se pretende que muchos **de** ellos sean producidos comercialmente **a** gran escala, originando la liberación **al** 15 ambiente **de** organismos vivientes "diseñados".

Esta tecnología ha despertado preocupación **desde** el punto **de** vista científico, socioeconómico y ético. **Por** 20 ejemplo, es posible que se produzcan nuevas plagas y, dado que se trata **de** organismos vivientes, será imposible hacerlos volver **al** laboratorio. Está surgiendo así una nueva manera **de** 25 contaminación: la contaminación genética.

Los impulsores **de** la ingeniería genética, **sin** embargo, están ansiosos **por** convencer **a** la gente **de** que estas 30 preocupaciones son equivocadas y **de** que la tecnología genética resolverá el problema **del** hambre mundial, revolucionando la agricultura **por** ejemplo.

35 Uno **de** los desarrollos más comunes es la producción **de** plantas resistentes **a** herbicidas. **Sin** duda, esto conducirá **a** un mayor uso **de** herbicidas **en** la agricultura, ya que podrán ser 40 aplicados **en** dosis mayores, concentraciones más altas y **con** más frecuencia **sobre** los cultivos modificados genéticamente, puesto que éstos no serían dañados. Asimismo,

(*Continued*)

45 se está utilizando la ingeniería genética **para** desarrollar resistencia **a** insectos y enfermedades.

Frecuentemente, las corporaciones transnacionales consiguen la
50 protección **de** patentes **para** las plantas modificadas **por** ingeniería genética y **para** los métodos utilizados, **para** producirlas **en** países que no son miembros de la OCDE, generando una
55 forma **de** colonialismo genético. Las patentes se utilizan **para** asegurar monopolios **de** importación y **para** controlar la producción local **de** los países **en** desarrollo. Asimismo,
60 numerosas empresas **del** Norte parecen estar usando **a** los países menos desarrollados como campos **de** prueba **para** los cultivos diseñados **con** el fin **de** satisfacer **a** sus mercados **del** Norte.

Greenpeace, Revista *Este país*, México. This article is a summary document *Genetically engineered plants: Releases to the environment and impacts on less developed countries.* A Greenpeace International inventory prepared by Isabelle Meister and Dr. Sue Mayer, November 1994.

Prepositions

Only basic meanings of prepositions are given here.

A

A is one of the most common prepositions in Spanish and has a number of uses and meanings:

a In grammatical constructions:

i Before a direct object denoting people (*personal* **a**) including proper names and pronouns (e.g. **alguien** *someone*), and known animals. This rule also applies to personified nouns as well as collective nouns referring to people.

Note the following examples from the text:

. . . están ansiosos por convencer **a** la gente . . . (l. 28–29) *. . . they are anxious to convince people . . .*
. . . parecen estar usando **a** los países menos desarrollados . . . (l. 60–62) *. . . they seem to be using the less developed countries . . .*

The following contrastive examples may help to understand the use of *personal* **a** more clearly:

Conozco muy bien la ciudad/**a** María. *I know the city/Maria very well.*
Vimos la procesión/**a** un amigo. *We saw the procession/a friend.*

ii Before an indirect object.

Le di el dinero **a** Carlos. *I gave the money to Carlos.*
A Raquel le gusta el tenis. *Raquel likes tennis.*

Note the redundancy in the previous sentences: **le** *to him/her*, but also **a** Carlos/Raquel *to Carlos/Raquel*. (See Redundant pronouns, Chapter 25)

iii In the construction **al** + infinitive.

Al salir del cine vi a José. *On leaving the cinema I saw José.*
Al no tener noticias de él, me preocupé. *As I hadn't had any news from him, I got worried.*

iv With a number of verbs, e.g. **asistir a** *to attend*, **empezar/comenzar a** *to begin*, **ayudar a** *to help*, **jugar a** *to play*.

Empezó a llover. *It started to rain.*
No **asistí a** la reunión. *I didn't attend the meeting.*

b To indicate direction and motion.

. . . volver **al** laboratorio. (l. 23) *. . . come back **to** the laboratory.*
. . . la liberación **al** ambiente . . . (l. 14–15) *. . . the release **into** the atmosphere . . .*
Llegaron **a** Madrid. *They arrived **in** Madrid.*
Doble **a** la izquierda. *Turn left.*

Note that **al** is the combination of **a** + **el**.

c To indicate rate.

. . . **a** una velocidad . . . (l. 2) *. . . **at** a speed . . .*
. . . **a** gran escala . . . (l. 13–14) *. . . **on** a large scale . . .*

d To express position or location and distance.

Está **a** la derecha. *It is **on** the right.*
Sentarse **a** la mesa. *To sit **at** the table.*
Sentarse **al** sol/**a** la sombra. *To sit **in** the sun/shade.*
A unos minutos/metros de aquí. *A few minutes/metres from here.*

e To express time and frequency.

A las seis y media. ***At** half past six.*
Estamos **a** 20 de enero. *It's January the 20th.*
A la semana siguiente. *The following week.*
A mediados/finales de julio. ***In** mid July/**At** the end of July.*
Dos veces **al** día. *Twice a day.*

f To indicate means and manner.

A mano. ***By** hand.*
A pie. ***On** foot.*
Pescado **a** la plancha/**al** vapor. *Grilled/steamed fish.*

g To indicate price or value

Está **a** dos euros la docena/el kilo. *It costs two euros the dozen/kilo.*

Ante

Ante usually translates *before* or *faced with.*

Compareció **ante** el juez. *He/she appeared before the judge.*
Ante una situación así, no sabría qué hacer. *Faced with a situation like this, I wouldn't know what to do.*
Ante el descalabro económico, el presidente renunció. *In view of the economic disaster, the president resigned.*

Antes de means *before* in relation to time.

Antes de las seis. *Before six.*

Bajo, debajo de

Bajo and **debajo de** mean *under*, but the first tends to be used more in a figurative sense and in set phrases, while **debajo de** is normally used in a literal sense.

Las llaves estaban **debajo de** la cama. *The keys were under the bed.*
Bajo ninguna circunstancia. *Under no circumstance.*

Con

The basic meaning of **con** is *with.*

... **con** más frecuencia ... (l. 42–43) *... more frequently ...*
... **con** el fin de ... (l. 63–64) *... in order to ...*
conmigo *with me*
contigo *with you* (fam.)

Contra

Contra normally translates *against.*

Se estrelló **contra** un muro. *He/she crashed against a wall.*

De

De is another very frequent preposition in Spanish, and it has a wide range of uses and meanings, among them *of, in, from, about.* Only the most common meanings are given here.

a As an equivalent of the English construction noun + noun.

... una técnica **de** laboratorio ... (l. 2–3) *... a laboratory technique ...*
... monopolios **de** importación ... (l. 57) *... import monopolies ...*

b With a number of verbs, e.g. **dejar de** *to stop, cease*, **terminar de** *to finish*, **depender de** *to depend on.*

. . . está **dejando de** ser . . . (l. 1–2) . . . *it is ceasing to be . . .*
Han **terminado de** comer. *They've finished eating.*
Depende de ti. *It depends on you.*

c Indicating position.

. . . sus mercados **del** Norte. (l. 64) . . . *its markets* ***in*** *the North.*

d Expressing the idea of possession or belonging to.

. . . la producción local **de** los países en desarrollo . . . (l. 58–59) . . . *local production* ***of*** *developing countries . . .*

e After a noun signalling an agent or an action.

Los impulsores **de** la ingeniería genética . . . (l. 27–28) *The promoters* ***of*** *genetic engineering . . .*
. . . la liberación . . . **de** organismos vivientes . . . (l. 14–15) . . . *the release* ***of*** *living organisms . . .*

f Expressing origin.

Son **de** Córdoba. *They are* ***from*** *Cordoba.*

g In time expressions.

De lunes a viernes/nueve a cinco. *From Monday to Friday/nine to five.*

h Indicating the material something is made of.

Una taza **de** porcelana *A porcelain cup*

i Meaning *about.*

Hablamos **de** muchas cosas. *We spoke* ***about*** *many things.*

Desde

Desde usually translates *from* as well as *since* and *for* in time phrases.

. . . **desde** el punto de vista científico . . . (l. 18–19) . . . ***from*** *a scientific point of view . . .*
Desde ayer. ***Since*** *yesterday.*
Desde hace muchos años. ***For*** *many years.*

En

En is used:

a As the Spanish equivalent of *in*, *on*, *at*, to indicate position.

. . . **en** las plantas . . . (l. 10–11) . . . ***in*** *plants . . .*
. . . **en** países . . . (l. 53) . . . ***in*** *countries . . .*
En la mesa/casa. ***On*** *the table/****At*** *home.*

b In expressions of time.

En diciembre/el año 2013/primavera. ***In*** *December/the year 2013/spring.*

c Means of transport.

En avión/tren/bicicleta. ***By*** *plane/train/****by*** *bike/****on*** *a bicycle.*

d To indicate value.

Lo compré **en** doscientos euros. *I bought it* ***for*** *two hundred euros.*

e With a number of verbs, among them **entrar en** (Latin Americans use **entrar a**) *to go into*, **pensar en** *to think of*, **confiar en** (alguien) *to trust (someone).*

Entró en el despacho y se sentó. *He/she went into the office and sat down.*
¿**En** qué estás **pensando**? *What are you thinking of?*
Rosa no **confía en** nadie. *Rosa doesn't trust anyone.*

Entre

The basic meanings of **entre** are *between* and *among.*

. . . **entre** organismos . . . (l. 6) . . . ***between*** *organisms . . .*
Estaba **entre** tus cosas. *It was* ***among*** *your things.*

Excepto

Excepto is used in similar contexts to *except* in English.

Fueron todos, **excepto** tú. *They all went,* ***except*** *you.*

Hacia

Hacia normally translates *towards*, in sentences like the following:

Iban **hacia** el norte. *They were heading north****wards/towards*** *the north.*
Hacia las tres de la tarde. ***Towards*** *three o'clock in the afternoon.*

Hasta

Hasta indicates limit, both in time, meaning *until*, and space, translating *as far as.*

Hasta las nueve. ***Until*** *nine.*
Hasta el final de la calle. ***As far as*** *the end of the street.*

Para

Para and **por** (below) can be difficult for English speakers, as both can mean *for*, although they have clearly distinctive uses. As a general guideline, it may be useful to remember that **para** can indicate purpose, destination and movement towards, while **por** often expresses cause or reason. The following are more specific uses of **para**:

a To express movement towards.

... **para** convertirse ... (l. 3) ... ***in order to*** *become* ...

b To express purpose.

... **para** introducir nuevas características ... (l. 9–10) ... ***in order to*** *introduce new characteristics* ...
... **para** producirlas ... (l. 52–53) ... ***in order to*** *produce them* ...

c To express destination.

... protección ... **para** las plantas ... (l. 50) ... *protection* ***for*** *plants* ...
... **para** los métodos utilizados ... (l. 52) ... ***for*** *the methods used* ...
Son **para** ti. *They are* ***for*** *you.*

d To indicate direction.

Salieron **para** Cuba. *They left* ***for*** *Cuba.*

e With expressions of time indicating limit, deadline and duration.

Lo quiero **para** mañana/el lunes. *I want it* ***for*** *tomorrow/Monday.*
Queremos una habitación **para** una semana. *We want a room* ***for*** *a week.*

(Most Latin Americans would use **por** in the second example.)

f To express a comparative notion.

Para ser extranjero habla bien. *He/she speaks well for a foreigner.*

Por

Por is used:

a To introduce an agent, e.g. in passive sentences.

... ha sido apropiada **por** la industria ... (l. 8–9) ... *it has been used* ***by*** *industry* ...
... modificadas **por** ingeniería genética (l. 51) ... *modified* ***by*** *genetic engineering* ...

b To indicate cause or reason.

Lo hice **por** ellos. *I did it* ***because of*** *them/****for*** *their* ***sake****.*
Por la lluvia no pudimos salir. *We couldn't go out* ***because of*** *the rain.*

c With expressions of time.

Se fueron **por** la mañana/noche. *They left* ***in*** *the morning/****at*** *night.*

d To indicate movement *through* or *along*.

Pasamos **por** Madrid. *We passed* ***through*** *Madrid.*
Paseamos **por** el río. *We took a walk* ***along*** *the river.*

e To express cost or value.

¿Cuánto pagaste **por** él? *How much did you pay **for** it?*

f To express means.

Por fax/correo electrónico. ***By** fax/electronic mail.*

g To indicate rate.

Por hora/día. ***Per** hour/day.*

Según

Según normally translates *according to* and *depending on.*

Según Aurora, no es verdad. ***According to** Aurora, it is not true.*
Según el tiempo que haga. ***Depending on** what sort of weather we have.*

Sin

Sin means *without.*

Sin duda (l. 37) ***Without** a doubt*

Sobre

Sobre is used to indicate

a Position, with or without actual contact.

. . . **sobre** los cultivos . . . (l. 42) . . . ***over** the crops . . .*
sobre la cómoda ***on** the chest of drawers*

b Approximation in time and space (especially Spain).

sobre las dos/20 kilos ***about/around** two o'clock/20 kilos*

c Subject or topic.

un libro **sobre** la guerra *a book **about** the war*

Tras

Tras *after*, corresponds to a very formal, literary style. In colloquial language, it is replaced by **después de**, with reference to time, and **detrás de**, to refer to space.

tras (**después de**) haber cenado . . . ***after** having dinner . . .*
tras (**detrás de**) la montaña ***behind** the mountain*

Other points to note in the text

- Gerund: *dejando* (l. 1), *surgiendo* (l. 24), *revolucionando* (l. 33), *utilizando* (l. 45), *generando* (l. 54), *usando* (l. 61) (see Chapter 9)
- Passive with *ser* + past participle: *puede ser transferido* (l. 6), *ha sido apropiada* (l. 8), *que . . . sean producidos* (l. 12–13), *podrán ser aplicados* (l. 39–40), *no serían dañados* (l. 44) (see Chapter 11)
- Passive se: *se está utilizando la ingeniería* (l. 45), *las patentes se utilizan* (l. 55–56) (see Chapter 11)
- Present subjunctive: *se pretende que . . . sean* (l. 12), *es posible que se produzcan* (l. 20) (see Chapter 14)

EXERCISES

1 Insert the preposition **a** where necessary.

a Hoy no he visto Juan.
b Solo tengo un hermano.
c Mi madre no le gusta que visite la tía.
d Buscan una secretaria que sepa italiano.
e No oí el profesor.
f Mis tíos les gusta ver sus hijos progresar.
g Pablo quiere mucho Isabel.
h Requieren una chica en la peluquería.
i Llegaron los niños y llamaron Carmen.
j Cuando estuve en Madrid, visité El Prado y también visité Julio y Alejandra.
k Oímos las noticias en la radio y después oímos cantar Montserrat Caballé.
l Susana pegó su hermano menor porque la estaba molestando.

2 Complete the following sentences using one of these prepositions: **de**, **a**, **hasta**, **desde**.

a Salieron ________ casa ________ las ocho ________ la mañana con rumbo ________ Santiago pero no llegaron ________ muy entrada la noche.
b Llamé ________ Perú para decirle que no volvería ________ diciembre.
c El museo quedó cerrado ________ octubre ________ principios ________ mayo.
d Allí venden jamón ________ Teruel ________ 22 euros el kilo. Lo traen ________ las serranías ________ Albarracín.
e Escribió un libro ________ poesías, durmiendo ________ día y escribiendo ________ noche ________ terminarlo.
f ________ tiempo inmemorial ________ la muerte de Patricio, la familia fue ________ ese pueblo ________ veranear.
g Vienen ________ Argentina para asistir ________ la boda ________ su sobrina.
h La piscina no estaba ________ más ________ un kilómetro ________ casa así que siempre íbamos ________ pie.
i Siéntate ________ lado de tu abuelo y háblale ________ tus investigaciones en Bolivia.
j Gire usted aquí ________ la izquierda y vaya ________ el cruce. Siga todo recto y el castillo está ________ dos kilómetros ________ mano derecha.

k Recibí tanto turrón ________ mis amigos españoles que lo estuve comiendo ________ Navidades ________ bien entrado el verano.

l Llevan trabajando ________ finales de agosto y no tienen vacaciones ________ principios de julio; por eso tienen unas ganas tremendas ________ ir ________ un lugar tranquilo ________ descansar.

3 Complete the following sentences using one of these prepositions: **con**, **sin**, **contra**, **según**, **hacia**.

a Te lo haré ________ mucho gusto.

b ________ fuentes oficiales, el choque del avión ________ la torre fue un accidente.

c ________ gran sorpresa mía y ________ la ayuda de nadie, gané el premio.

d Hay que luchar ________ la discriminación para poder mirar ________ el futuro ________ sosiego.

e ________ Pablo, la playa aquí está contaminada; hay que ir más ________ el norte.

f Como ese día no hacía tanto frío, salió ________ sombrero, ________ guantes, ________ nada.

g Vamos a ver. Ustedes se dirigen ________ Tordesillas, ¿verdad?

h Ha decidido montar su propio negocio ________ o ________ la ayuda de su familia.

i Da gusto ver ________ cuánta gana come el niño hoy; ________ su madre, de ordinario come muy poco.

j Paulina odia a Ángel, siempre actúa ________ él y ________ una falta de vergüenza que me deja atónita.

k ________ dicen, Rodrigo lleva años enfadado ________ su hijo; se niega a hablar ________ él y el pobre hijo no entiende qué tiene su padre ________ él.

l El martes día 13, Pedro se dio ________ una escalera que estaba apoyada ________ la pared; por eso anda ahora ________ más precaución.

4 Complete the following sentences with one of these prepositions: **sobre**, **en**, **entre**.

a Alfonso os ha hablado ________ el tema ¿verdad?

b Hubo un incidente ________ el Paseo de la Castellana ________ las cuatro de la tarde.

c No veo ninguna diferencia ________ este bolso y el otro menos ________ el precio.

d ________ Salamanca, el viejo puente ________ el río data de los tiempos romanos.

e ¿Tiene alguna información ________ vuelos a Madrid?

f ¿Quieres poner este cenicero ________ la mesita que está ________ los dos sillones?

g A pesar de llegar tarde, conseguimos localizar a Sofía ________ el público ________ el vestíbulo del teatro.

h Ésta es la habitación que más me gusta porque las ventanas dan ________ la plaza.

i Ha dicho que llegará ________ las tres de la tarde pero como viene ________ coche no nos puede dar una hora exacta.

j Mete esos documentos ________ el archivador así no los pierdo ________ este montón de papeles.

k Esa señora es especialista ________ lingüística y si tuviera que escoger ________ ella y los demás, no dudaría ________ escogerla a ella.

l Ayer asistimos a una conferencia ________ la música ________ la Edad de Oro y nos topamos con José ________ los presentes.

5 Complete the following sentences using one of these prepositions: **ante, bajo, excepto, tras**.

a Me dejó plantado. Estuve tres horas esperándola ________ la lluvia y no llegó.
b Todos fuimos a la fiesta ________ Nicolás que nos dijo que no se encontraba bien.
c ________ tales perspectivas, no era extraño que se deprimiera tanto.
d Menos mal que se repartieron folletos informativos ________ el discurso; fue tan aburrido que me dormí.
e Claro que el niño tiene problemas de comunicación; pasa todo el día ________ la pantalla de televisión.
f Su cuarto siempre parece bien arreglado porque pone todo ________ la cama.
g María me viene a visitar todos los días ________ los domingos.
h Se colocaron uno ________ otro en fila india.
i Ahora resulta difícil imaginar cuánto sufrió el país ________ la dictadura.
j ¡De ninguna manera me pongo yo ________ las órdenes de ese imbécil!
k ________ esta situación tendré que buscar otro empleo.
l ________ una larga reunión que no resolvió nada, se fueron saliendo uno ________ otro.

6 Select the correct preposition.

a Los revolucionarios lucharon *por/para* la igualdad.
b La ley fue aprobada *por/para* el Senado.
c El avión se retrasó dos horas *por/para* la niebla.
d *Por/para* relajarme, doy largos paseos *por/para* la playa.
e Pagó muy poco *por/para* el coche que compró *por/para* su hijo.
f Van a Bolivia *por/para* unos tres meses pero esperan estar de regreso *por/para* Navidad.
g Pili no consiguió el puesto *por/para* no tener conocimientos de inglés.
h Mañana *por/para* la mañana pasaremos *por/para* tu casa *por/para* recogerte.
i Hemos perdido el tren *por/para* tu culpa.
j ¿*Por/para* qué sirve esto? ¿*Por/para* hacer agujeros?
k Acababa de pasar *por/para* debajo del puente cuando la policía lo pilló.
l Me tomaron *por/para* tonto y no querían escucharme.

7 Identify the **five** sentences below which use **por** or **para** incorrectly.

a Para complacer a sus padres estudiaba para médico.
b Lo más rápido será enviar el mensaje por correo electrónico.
c Lo han hecho así para razones que no entiendo.
d Voy para más café.
e Si lo haces por nosotros, no te molestes; no necesitamos tu ayuda.
f Este nuevo juguete es para niños mayores de tres años.
g Siento una profunda admiración para el trabajo de 'Médicos Sin Fronteras'.
h Para Julio lo más importante es el fútbol.
i Por la tarde no hay nadie por las calles porque hace demasiado calor.
j Yo que tú, no pagaría esa cantidad de dinero para unos vaqueros.
k Dicen que el vino tinto es muy bueno por la salud.
l No es de extrañar que se resfriara. Llevaba muy poca ropa para el frío que hacía.

8 Complete the following sentences by supplying the correct preposition to go with the verb.

a No me sorprendo en absoluto ________ que no se acuerden ________ mí.
b ¡La cantidad de gente que sueña ________ ganar la lotería!
c Después de la entrevista con la directora, a Fabián no le quedó más remedio que renunciar ________ puesto.
d Se tarda media hora ________ hacer este trayecto.
e La verdad es que Eva no quiere estar aquí; por eso se queja ________ todo.
f Pepe siempre nos ayudaba ________ preparar las comidas.
g Nos amenazaron ________ despedirnos si no aceptamos el nuevo acuerdo salarial.
h Demasiado tarde me di cuenta ________ que era el famosísimo escritor de novelas negras.
i Dice que no se arrepiente ________ nada en absoluto.
j Fue impresionante ver cómo Sofía se empeñó ________ sacar adelante el negocio.
k Ignoramos por qué se negaron ________ proporcionarnos los datos.
l Cuando los músicos empezaron ________ tocar la sardana, el público se puso ________ bailar.
m Estamos aquí porque María Jesús ha insistido ________ que vengamos.
n ¡Pero cómo ha podido enamorarse ________ ese hombre! Es algo que no acabamos ________ entender.
o Manolo se ha esforzado mucho ________ aprender el chino para poder comunicarse ________ los suegros.
p Trate ________ recordar. Es muy importante que nos diga cuánto sepa.
q Cuando Marta se decide ________ hacer algo, no hay manera de disuadirla.
r El trabajo consiste ________ contestar al teléfono y atender al público.
s Juan no puede prescindir ________ sus cinco tazas de café en el desayuno. ¡Sin ellas no funciona!
t Nos alegramos mucho ________ que hayáis venido. Sin vosotros hubiera sido muy aburrido.

9 Match a Spanish phrase in column A with its English equivalent in column B.

A	B
a con rumbo a	**1** within reach
b al aire libre	**2** with the aim of
c a mano	**3** from door to door
d a la vuelta de la esquina	**4** on the way to
e de puerta en puerta	**5** in the direction of
f camino de	**6** in writing
g al alcance	**7** in the rain
h por escrito	**8** round the corner
i a la sombra	**9** to perfection
j bajo la lluvia	**10** in the shade
k a fuerza de	**11** in favour (of)
l a fin de	**12** by hand
m a favor (de)	**13** by day (during the day)
n de día	**14** in the open air, outdoors
o a la perfección	**15** by (dint of)

10 Complete the texts with suitable prepositions.

1 Agustín es (**a**)________ Madrid pero (**b**)________ septiembre vive (**c**)________ Castellón donde estudia (**d**)________ ser farmacéutico. Comparte un apartamento (**e**)________ Benicasim (**f**)________ su amigo Eduardo. Como Benicasim está (**g**)________ unos 4 kilómetros (**h**) ________ la universidad, los dos chicos van (**i**)________ la Facultad (**j**)________ autobús. Solo tienen clases (**k**)________ la mañana. Dos tardes (**l**)________ semana entrenan (**m**)________ un equipo (**n**)________ baloncesto y los domingos juegan (**o**)________ otro equipo. (**p**)________ su madre, Agustín es un chico muy listo, pero no creo que tome sus estudios muy (**q**)________ serio.

2 (**a**)________ un reportaje del diario *Noticias de China*, la República China apuesta (**b**)________ la ingeniería genética (**c**)________ alimentar al pueblo. Es, (**d**)________ ellos, la única forma (**e**)________ terminar (**f**)________ siempre (**g**)________ el hambre que aflige (**h**)________ millones (**i**)________ sus habitantes.

Un equipo (**j**)________ médicos mandado (**k**)________ el gobierno (**l**)________ zonas rurales ha descubierto un alto porcentaje (**m**)________ niños (**n**)________ enfermedades debilitantes.

(**o**)________ el fin de erradicar estas enfermedades, el gobierno ha puesto en marcha un programa que insiste (**p**)________ la producción (**q**)________ la seguridad. (**r**)________ muchas regiones ya se venden las semillas transgénicas (**s**)________ control y muchas veces producidas (**t**)________ compañías estatales.

29 | Conjunctions

Text

The Spanish writer Ana María Matute remembers her first days at school. Read the text and, as you do so, note the use of the words in bold, which are known as ***conjunctions***.

Lo que aprendí en la escuela

"Las niñas del colegio eran unas brujas asquerosas."

Hasta la primera comunión fui al colegio de monjas San Josep Cluny. 5 Entonces tenía cinco años; recuerdo **que** la monja se quedó estupefacta **porque** yo ya sabía el alfabeto. Me pusieron una medalla de aluminio con un lacito amarillo. ¡Fue la primera **y** 10 última condecoración que me dieron! Yo sabía leer **y** enlazar palabras, era muy tranquila, **pero** hacía preguntas improcedentes; en realidad, era incómoda, **pero** no revoltosa. Siempre 15 última de la clase, no me interesaba estudiar **y** aquellas señoras me parecían unas estúpidas inmensas; cuando un niño se da cuenta de **que** una persona mayor es idiota . . . 20 ¡No hay manera, no les crees! No creía nada de lo que me decían aquellas imbéciles.

Además, no tenía amigos, era tartamuda. ¡Me lo pasé muy mal! 25 Las niñas del colegio eran unas brujas asquerosas. **No obstante** había aspectos en el colegio que sí me gustaban **y** en los cuales despuntaba. Por ejemplo: la geografía **o** la 30 gramática. Odiaba las matemáticas, **pero** es algo que ahora lamento mucho **porque** sé que si me hubieran enseñado bien la aritmética – **porque** entonces no eran matemáticas, **sino** 35 aritmética – a mí me hubiesen encantado. Me acuerdo **que** yo era muy chiquitina, y todavía llevábamos pizarras en las que hacíamos las cuentas. Recuerdo **que** con las 40 lágrimas borraba la pizarrita. ¡**Ni** me lo explicaban bien, **ni** podía resolverlas!

Revista *El País Semanal*, España

Conjunctions

Conjunctions are words such as **y** *and*, **pero** *but*, **porque** *because*, whose function is to link words, groups of words or whole ideas. There are two main types of conjunctions: ***coordinating*** and ***subordinating*** conjunctions.

1 COORDINATING CONJUNCTIONS

Their function is to link words, phrases or clauses of a similar kind. In this group we find **o** (**u** before **o-** and **ho-**) *or*, **y** (**e** before **i-** and **hi-**) *and*, **ni** *neither, nor*, **pero** and **sino** *but.*

a Coordinating conjunctions in the text

. . . la geografía **o** la gramática . . . (l. 29–30) *. . . geography or grammar . . .*
¡Fue la primera **y** última condecoración . . . ! (l. 9–10) *It was the first and last medal . . . !*
¡**Ni** me lo explicaban bien, **ni** podía resolverlas! (l. 40–42) *They neither explained it well, nor could I solve them!*
. . . era muy tranquila, **pero** hacía preguntas improcedentes . . . (l. 11–13) *. . . I was very quiet, but I used to ask improper questions . . .*
. . . entonces no eran matemáticas, **sino** aritmética . . . (l. 34–35) *. . . it wasn't called mathematics then, but arithmetic . . .*

b Using *pero* and *sino*

Note that **pero** and **sino** both translate *but*, but their uses are different. **Sino** is used in a construction with two contrasting elements which are mutually exclusive, the first one negative, the second one positive. The English word *but* translates **sino** in the constructions *not . . . but*, and *not only . . . but also.* Most other uses of *but* in English correspond to **pero** (see also Chapter 27).

No esta semana **sino** la que viene. *Not this week but the next one.*
No uno **sino** dos. *Not one but two.*
No solo aquí **sino también** en España. *Not only here but also in Spain.*

2 SUBORDINATING CONJUNCTIONS

These introduce a subordinate clause, that is, a group of words containing a subject and a verb which is part of a sentence and is dependent on the main clause.

a Subordinating conjunctions in the text

In the text we find: **que**, the most common subordinating conjunction, which, unlike *that* in English, cannot normally be omitted; **porque**, also common, and used in the expression of cause; and **no obstante**, a much less frequent one expressing concession and usually found in formal registers. Note how they have been used:

. . . recuerdo **que** la monja se quedó estupefacta . . . (l. 5–6) *. . . I remember that the nun was astonished . . .*

Me acuerdo **que** yo era muy chiquitina . . . (l. 36–37) *I remember that I was very little . . .*

. . . un niño se da cuenta de **que** una persona mayor es idiota . . . (l. 18–19) *. . . a child realises that an adult is an idiot . . .*

. . . se quedó estupefacta **porque** yo ya sabía el alfabeto. (l. 6–7) *. . . she was astonished because I already knew the alphabet.*

. . . es algo que ahora lamento mucho **porque** sé que . . . (l. 31–32) *. . . it is something I now regret very much because I know that . . .*

No obstante había aspectos en el colegio que sí me gustaban . . . (l. 26–28) *Nevertheless, there were things at school which I did like . . .*

b *Que* in subordinate clauses with a verb in the subjunctive

Que is also the common conjunction in subordinate clauses containing a subjunctive verb (see Chapters 14–16).

Le pedí a Carlos **que** me ayudara. *I asked Carlos to help me.*

Espero **que** lleguen pronto. *I hope they arrive soon.*

For other uses of **que** see **Comparison**, Chapter 22, and **Relative pronouns**, Chapter 26.

c Other common subordinating conjunctions

Here is a list of common subordinating conjunctions, grouped according to usage.

Cause

como *as, since*, **pues** *because, since, for*, **puesto que**, **ya que** *because, since*

Como vive cerca, nos vemos a menudo. *Since he/she lives nearby, we see each other often.*

No salieron, **pues** no tenían dinero. *They didn't go out, because they didn't have any money.*

No la invité, **ya que** no somos amigos. *I didn't invite her since we are not friends.*

Time

antes/después (**de**) **que** *before/after*, **cuando** *when*, **hasta que** *until*, **mientras** (**que**) *while*

Me iré **antes de que** oscurezca. *I'll go before it gets dark.*

Se lo diré **cuando** la vea. *I'll tell her when I see her.*

Nos quedaremos **hasta que** vuelvan. *We'll stay until they come back.*

Condition

a menos que, **a no ser que** *unless*, **con tal de que**, **siempre que** *provided that*, (**en el**) **caso de que** *in case*

A menos que me pida disculpas no le volveré a hablar. *Unless he apologizes I won't speak to him again.*

Se lo prestaré **con tal de que** lo cuide. *I'll lend it to you provided that you look after it.*

Purpose

para que, *in order that, so that*, **de manera/modo/forma que** *so that*, **a fin de que** *so that*

Invitó a su novio **para que** le conociéramos. *She invited her boyfriend so that we could meet him.*

Iremos en taxi **de manera que** lleguemos más rápido. *We'll go in a taxi so that we'll get there quicker.*

Concession

aunque *although*, **a pesar de que** *although*, **sin embargo** *however, nevertheless*

Aunque no habla muy bien español se hace entender. *Although he/she doesn't speak Spanish very well he/she makes him/herself understood.*

A pesar de que él no la quiere, la trata bien. *Although he doesn't love her, he treats her well.*

Consequence

de manera/modo que *so, so that*

No estaban en casa, **de manera que** no pudimos hablar con ellos. *They weren't at home, so we couldn't speak to them.*

Entré sigilosamente, **de modo que** nadie me oyó. *I went in quietly, so that nobody heard me.*

A number of these conjunctions, among them those expressing purpose and condition, require the subjunctive. For more information on this, see Chapters 14 and 15.

Other points to note in the text

- Imperfect and preterite tenses: *fui* (l. 3), *tenía* (l. 5), *se quedó* (l. 6), *sabía* (l. 7), *pusieron* (l. 8), etc. (see Chapters 2 and 3)
- Adverbs: *entonces* (l. 5), *ya* (l. 7), *siempre* (l. 14), *ahora* (l. 31), *bien* (l. 33), *todavía* (l. 37), etc. (see Chapter 21)
- Pluperfect subjunctive: *si me hubieran enseñado* (l. 32–33), *me hubiesen encantado* (l. 35–36) (see Chapter 16)

EXERCISES

1 Insert a coordinating conjunction into the appropriate places in these sentences.

a Jorge Javier han montado su propia compañía.
b ¿Cuál quieres: el negro el azul?
c Los Reyes Católicos se llamaban Fernando Isabel.
d Yo quería que vinieran Cecilia Ignacio no pudieron.
e No vi a Paco a Alejandro.
f Llamé siete ocho veces no había contestación.
g Exportan sus productos a Alemania Italia.
h No sólo vinieron españoles sudamericanos también.

i No creo que vengan que vayan.

j Hizo frío salimos de paseo fuimos al parque.

k Lo oímos no lo vimos.

l Daniel Ignacio corrieron mucho bien el uno el otro ganó un premio.

2 Link an element in Column A with one in Column B to form a sentence.

A	B
a Como es tu cumpleaños	**1** podemos divertirnos.
b La maestra la castigó	**2** pues hace frío.
c Adoptemos el otro plan	**3** no le he dado la noticia.
d Estudiaba contabilidad	**4** pues hay trabajo para todos.
e Puesto que no hay otra	**5** puesto que le encantaban los números.
f Como no me escribe	**6** porque no está dispuesto a trabajar.
g Ya que se ha ido Álvaro	**7** tendremos que seguir esta ruta.
h Ponte el abrigo	**8** te he hecho una tarta.
i Bonifacio no conseguirá nada	**9** ya que han surgido problemas con éste.
j Venid	**10** porque había peleado con Víctor.

3 Turn the two sentences into one, using one of the following conjunctions of time and making any necessary adjustments.

mientras **antes de (que)** **cuando** **hasta que** **después de (que)**

a Leía el periódico. Desayunaba.

b Estamos de vacaciones. Nos gusta hacer algo cultural.

c Tenemos que tener esto terminado. Vuelve el jefe.

d No volveremos al trabajo. El dinero se nos acaba.

e Nos iremos al teatro. Llegan los abuelos.

f No adelgazarás. Sigues tan golosa.

g Hay que pintar la casa. Viene el mal tiempo.

h No me muevo de aquí. Sale Rodrigo Montalbán.

i Nos acostamos. Cenamos.

j Hay que sacar las entradas. Las han vendido todas.

k Jorge va a la panadería por el pan. Nosotros compramos los fiambres.

l Te habrás decidido. Ya será tarde.

4 Complete the sentences using **a pesar de** or **aunque**.

a Lo pasamos bien ________ el mal tiempo.

b Seguimos tomando baños de sol ________ somos conscientes de los riesgos.

c En estas tierras sales ________ llueva.

d Mantuvo la misma postura ________ todo lo que le habían dicho.

e No lo van a contratar ________ sea la persona más idónea.

f Es fuerte ________ ser bajito.

g Siguió con el proyecto ________ las críticas.
h Es importante dar las gracias por un regalo ________ no te guste.
i ________ se jubila a finales de este mes, trabaja con el mismo ahinco que siempre.
j Llegaría al fin de mes sin un céntimo ________ ganara el doble de lo que gana.
k ________ llegar el último, no se desanimó y al año siguiente volvió a correr el maratón.
l Van a declarar la sequía ________ lo mucho que ha llovido últimamente.

5 Translate the words in italics into Spanish.

a Arreglaré el cuarto *in case he comes.*
b Sus cuadros eran buenos *so she sold them all.*
c *Provided that everything is in order,* podéis marcharos.
d Aquí tiene mi teléfono *in case you need it.*
e No iré a la fiesta *unless they send me an invitation.*
f Le mandaron a Sigüenza *so that he would meet Josefa.*
g Sus padres estaban contentos *provided she made progress.*
h Nos explicó el proceso *in such a way that we understood it all.*
i Los juegos se celebrarán el sábado *unless it rains.*
j Os he traído a este museo *so that you see Picasso's 'Guernica'.*
k Visitaremos todos estos sitios *provided we have the time and money.*
l We'll meet at the same time next week *unless you have a prior engagement.*

6 Complete the following extracts (**a**) from this chapter's text, and (**b**) from an interview with the opera singer Plácido Domingo, using the conjunctions given in bold.

ni pero porque que y ya que sino

a Recuerdo ________ la monja se quedó estupefacta ________ yo ya sabía el alfabeto. [. . .] Yo sabía leer ________ enlazar palabras, era muy tranquila, ________ hacía preguntas improcedentes; en realidad, era incómoda ________ no revoltosa. Siempre última de la clase, no me interesaba estudiar ________ aquellas señoras me parecían unas estúpidas inmensas. [. . .] Odiaba las matemáticas, ________ es algo que ahora lamento mucho ________ sé que si me hubieran enseñado bien la aritmética – ________ entonces no eran matemáticas, ________ aritmética – a mí me hubiesen encantado. [. . .] ¡ ________ me lo explicaban bien, ________ podía resolverlas!

b En días normales duermo como ocho horas [. . .] ________ después de una presentación, me es muy difícil. Hoy eran las cinco ________ todavía no podía conciliar el sueño. ________ te quedas excitado, no sólo en el papel, ________ que por la función misma. (*Hablando de donde veranea*) vamos a la playa la mayoría de veces, ________ hemos tratado de que las últimas vacaciones sean siempre en México, ________ mi madre vive allí.

7 Translate the following sentences into Spanish.

a I think we can safely say neither Juan nor José is going to pass the exam.
b And that despite all they have studied during the year.

c We decided they would fetch us should they need us.

d They will give us their support provided we ask for it.

e We stayed in a cheap boarding house so that our money would last longer.

f We'll meet at six, but call me should you not be able to come.

g I'll lend you this book as long as you return it to me when you have finished reading it.

h He said he'd pay me back the money I lent him before I went on holiday, but he didn't.

i I haven't seen Andrés or Enrique today although they said they would be here.

j She says she's happy even though she's poor, as happiness does not depend on money.

k We didn't go out because it wasn't raining but snowing.

l The police arrested him when the plane landed because he was drunk and had been annoying the other passengers.

30 | Word order

Text

The threat of a large meteorite falling on Earth and the actions being taken to prevent a disaster are the subject of this text. The grammar focuses on word order.

A la caza del meteorito

El impacto contra la superficie terrestre de un solo meteorito de un kilómetro de diámetro sería suficiente para devastar el planeta. Científicos de todo el 5 mundo buscan soluciones para prevenir una catástrofe como la que según diversos indicios pudo acabar con el reino de los dinosaurios.

¿Existe alguna probabilidad de que 10 esto ocurra? Los científicos creen que sí, que más que una hipótesis es una amenaza real para la que hay que estar prevenido. Gran Bretaña ha tomado la delantera en la detección de asteroides, 15 pero la NASA no se quiere quedar atrás. **Empieza la caza** del meteorito.

La posibilidad de que un gran cometa o asteroide impacte contra la Tierra dejó de ser ciencia-ficción cuando, en 1994, 20 uno de estos cuerpos chocó contra Júpiter. **¿Por qué en nuestro planeta no puede pasar otro tanto?** Mejor dicho, ya ocurrió. Fue hace 65 millones de años con la caída de un gran cuerpo celeste en 25 la península mexicana de Yucatán, que acabó con la vida de los dinosaurios.

¿Podrá volver a ocurrir algo parecido? El responsable del proyecto de observación de NEOS – objetos celestes 30 cercanos a la Tierra – en el Instituto Astrofísico de Canarias asegura que **la hipótesis en absoluto es desechable**.Y **prevenido quiere ser el Gobierno británico**, que ha apoyado un proyecto 35 científico para la detección de meteoritos. El objetivo: salvar al mundo. “El problema – explica el encargado de NEOS – es que **no sabemos cuál es el problema**. Sabemos que pueden 40 chocar contra la Tierra, pero no sabemos con qué frecuencia ni en qué probabilidad.” **Responder estas preguntas es, precisamente, lo que pretenden los científicos ingleses**.

Diario *16*, España

Word order

1 STATEMENTS

a Spanish is much more flexible than English with regard to word order in sentences. Although the verb usually follows the subject, as it does in English, for emphasis or focus different elements within the sentence can be placed in initial position. This includes the verb, which can precede the subject. Most sentences in the text follow the pattern ***subject*** + ***verb***, but note the following ones where the verb comes first.

Empieza la caza del meteorito. (l. 16) *The hunt for the meteorite begins.*
. . . prevenido quiere ser el Gobierno británico . . . (l. 33–34) *. . . the British Government wants to be prepared . . .*

Both examples above could be rewritten following the pattern ***subject*** + ***verb***, e.g. **La caza del meteorito empieza**, but the emphasis achieved by having the verb in initial position is somewhat lost, at least in writing.

b With short sentences, the tendency is to place the verb before the subject.

Llegó Tomás. *Tomás arrived.*
Murió su madre. *His/her mother died.*

c If the subject is much longer than the verb, again the tendency is to have the verb in initial position.

Respondieron Carmen y su marido, y un par de personas más. *Carmen and her husband, and a couple of other people replied.*

d Within a clause, the verb is normally put before the subject.

. . . lo que pretenden los científicos ingleses. (l. 43–44) *. . . what English scientists intend to do.*

e In statements focusing on more than one element, for example the theme or topic of a conversation and another element one wishes to highlight, the latter may go in final position. Note the following example, in which the object of the sentence (***the topic***) has been placed before the verb, with the final position being reserved for the element we want to emphasise.

La cena (object) la preparó (verb) Raquel (subject). *It was Raquel who prepared dinner.*

Note the redundant pronoun **la** in *la cena* ***la*** *preparó*. This redundancy is obligatory when the object is placed before the verb. (see **Redundant pronouns** in Chapter 25.)

f Adjectives and participles used as adjectives can also be placed, for emphasis, at the beginning of the sentence, as in:

Y **prevenido** quiere ser el Gobierno británico . . . (l. 32–34) *And the British Government wants to be prepared . . .* instead of
El Gobierno británico quiere ser **prevenido** . . . which would be a more neutral position.

g Adverbial phrases can be highlighted by placing them before the verb, as in:

¿Por qué **en nuestro planeta** no puede pasar otro tanto? (l. 21–22), instead of ¿Por qué no puede pasar otro tanto **en nuestro planeta**? *Why could the same not happen again on our planet?*

a more likely position for a longer phrase. Note also the position of **en absoluto** *by no means* in:

. . . asegura que la hipótesis **en absoluto** es desechable. (l. 31–32) *By no means should the hypothesis be discarded.*

h Relative clauses introduced by **lo que** are usually placed, in the spoken language, in initial position:

Lo que más me gusta es . . . *What I like most is . . .*
Lo que pasa es que . . . *What's happening is that . . .*

In line 22 of the text,

. . . **lo que** pretenden los científicos ingleses. *. . . what English scientists are endeavouring (to do).*

has been placed in final position, in order to highlight the centre of interest, in this case the clause **Responder estas preguntas es** . . . *Answering these questions is . . .*

2 QUESTIONS

a In direct questions the verb usually precedes the subject.

¿Existe alguna probabilidad . . . ? (l. 9) *Is there any probability . . . ?*
¿Podrá volver a ocurrir algo parecido? (l. 27) *Could something similar happen again?*

Note also the question introduced by **¿por qué?** in line 21.

b In speech, questions are often signalled through intonation, word order being that of a normal statement.

¿El problema está resuelto? *Is the problem solved?*

c In indirect questions the verb comes before the subject.

. . . no sabemos cuál es el problema. (l. 38–39) *We don't know what the problem is.*

For the position of other grammatical elements such as adjectives, adverbs, object pronouns, see the relevant chapters.

Other points to note in the text

- Present subjunctive: *¿Existe alguna probabilidad de que esto ocurra?* (l. 9–10), *la posibilidad de que . . . impacte* (l. 17–18) (see Chapter 14)
- Prepositions: *para* (lines 3, 5, 12, 35). There are numerous other prepositions in the text (see Chapter 28)

- Modal verbs: *pudo acabar* (l. 7), *hay que estar* (l. 12), *no se quiere quedar* (l. 15), *no puede pasar* (l. 21–22), *podrá volver* (l. 27), *pueden chocar* (l. 39–40) (see Chapter 10)
- *Ser* and *estar*: *sería suficiente* (l. 3), *es una amenaza* (l. 11–12), *estar prevenido* (l. 12–13), *dejó de ser* (l. 18–19), etc. (see Chapter 13)

EXERCISES

1 Rewrite these sentences, beginning with the underlined word.

a Los tíos, los primos y alguna otra persona más vinieron.
b Susana te ha llamado.
c El castillo de Medina del Campo se encuentra a unos dos kilómetros del pueblo.
d Tomar el sol es lo que más les gusta hacer.
e La fresa es la fruta que más se cultiva aquí.
f Nos pusimos en camino al salir el sol.
g Tuve experiencias únicas dando la vuelta al mundo.
h Dice lo mismo hoy que dirá mañana.
i Los mejillones no me gustan.
j No he visto todavía esa película.
k Otra dificultad se presentó más *tarde*.
l Tomamos el autocar a Chihuahua al día siguiente.
m No lo haría yo que tú.
n Muchos inmigrantes vienen a trabajar en los campos freseros.
o Los desempleados y los necesitados viven en este barrio.

2 Study and translate these sentences into English.

a Este coche no me lo compré yo, me lo compró mi padre.
b A estas mujeres las llaman las mujeres de la fresa.
c A ese chico no lo soporto.
d Los geranios los riegas muy poco.
e A mi mejor amiga la conocí en la universidad.
f Todos los libros que veis aquí los vamos a poner en la biblioteca.
g A mi novia le compré un collar de oro.
h A los turistas no les gustó nada el espectáculo.
i A mí me ha dicho el jefe que piensa jubilarse anticipadamente.
j Todas estas labores las llevan a cabo jóvenes voluntarios.
k La información que ustedes buscan se la darán en la oficina de turismo.
l ¿A Felipe le has mandado el paquete ya o se lo vas a entregar en mano?
m A esas señoras estuvimos media hora buscándolas.
n El discurso lo pronunció el señor Márquez y fue muy gracioso.
o El apartamento que teníamos en Ibiza se lo hemos vendido a un vecino.

3 Rewrite these sentences, starting with the underlined object of the verb. Include the necessary object pronoun(s) and make any other changes to the word order that might seem appropriate.

a Sabes muy bien la respuesta.
b Tú dirás la verdad.
c Compré estos libros en el Rastro.
d No vamos a solucionar el problema ahora.
e Vas a encontrar el amor de tu vida cuando menos lo esperas.
f Os darán el dinero el lunes.
g Un colega nos alquiló la casa.
h El profesor de ciencias me explicó la teoría.
i No os va a vender su colección de sellos.
j Te he devuelto ya tu DVD.
k Dieron el primer premio a Conchita.
l Dio ayuda a los que la necesitaban.
m No les dijo nada a los compañeros de trabajo.
n Le pusieron una multa de 500 euros a mi amigo Jaime.
o Le robaron el bolso a María.
p Le entregué el paquete al policía.
q No lo hemos dado a nadie.
r Les concedieron el título a los primeros 20 estudiantes.
s Lo cuenta todo a sus amigos.
t Le entregué los documentos al encargado.

4 Translate these sentences into Spanish, thinking about a possible word order different from the English.

a María is going to the concert as well.
b They have always come here.
c We have to think about the future now and again.
d Finish your work quickly.
e One doesn't do something like that every day.
f It would be difficult to tell the truth here.
g You'll have to look for the truth somewhere else.
h I buy bread from the supermarket sometimes.
i I didn't see her again after that.
j We'll put the passports in the safety deposit box along with the traveller's cheques.
k We can spend the evenings drinking in the pavement cafés.
l She tells me a bit more about her life every day.

5 Read these two texts and identify where you could improve the word order. The first text is about one of the possible reasons for the extinction of dinosaurs; the second text is about the space telescope *Hubble*.

a La extinción en masa se produjo hace millones de años de la mayoría de los dinosaurios que poblaban nuestro planeta. El fenómeno ha siempre fascinado a los científicos y varias hipótesis existen sobre su extinción de las que tres tienen una base en la realidad. La más popular es la hipótesis de la caída de un meteorito. Un meteorito de hecho cayó a una velocidad de hasta 250.000 kilómetros por hora hace unos 65 millones de años y chocó contra la costa del golfo de México. Ocasionó terremotos y maremotos de gran magnitud, lanzando una nube inmensa de polvo y fragmentos de roca a la atmósfera. La materia sólida incandescente provocó graves incendios al volver a la tierra y el polvo impidió la penetración de rayos solares durante meses. Las consecuencias fueron graves para las plantas y los animales. Algunas especies sin embargo sobrevivieron como las aves y los reptiles.

b A pesar del escepticismo de algunos científicos, se lanzó a finales del siglo XX el telescopio espacial *Hubble* que proporcionaría imágenes diez veces más nítidas que las terrestres y que haría posible detectar objetos desconocidos hasta entonces.

Hubo problemas con el telescopio como era de esperar al principio, y eran borrosas las fotografías que transmitió a la NASA. El proyecto sin embargo siguió gracias a los esfuerzos titánicos de unos científicos comprometidos, y el *Hubble* empezó a mandar las imágenes más lejanas del cosmos. En astronomía, cuanto más lejos se apunta el telescopio, más se viaja en el tiempo hacia atrás. Por tanto esas imágenes eran las más antiguas jamás conseguidas.

A los investigadores que tienen acceso a ellas les ha dado muchas sorpresas el estudio de las fotografías, y constantemente tienen que reformular sus teorías sobre la evolución del universo. Se ha resuscitado un interés más general en la exploración espacial además, y aunque no haya señales fiables de momento, puede que encontremos vida fuera de la Tierra algún día.

Consolidation exercises

Text 1

364 días en automóvil

Es de justicia comenzar declarando que el automóvil es una cosa estupenda. Lo malo es que los demás también lo tienen. Y resulta que en una ciudad, por más 5 túneles que se hagan, los automóviles de los demás no caben en las calles.

La dura realidad es que la densidad de población hace físicamente imposible que los desplazamientos se 10 efectúen en automóvil privado. Y aún más imposible que una buena parte de los ciudadanos vivan fuera y entren cada día en su coche privado. Es imprescindible que en toda área urbana 15 haya un sistema de movilidad planificado de forma integral, que permita los desplazamientos en un tiempo, coste y comodidad razonables. En el fondo de todo automovilista hay un 20 usuario potencial del transporte público, esperando que alguien lo saque a la luz.

Brindo dos posibles medidas en favor del transporte público:

a Que cada automovilista lleve visible en 25 el parabrisas su abono de transporte público (lo que permitiría reducir el precio del abono y, a lo mejor, ya que lo han comprado, que prueben a usarlo).

30 **b** Que todos los alcaldes y concejales usen siempre el transporte público para sus desplazamientos y hagan ostentación de ello con cara de satisfacción y continuas 35 manifestaciones de alegría.

Sé que se trata de unas modestísimas contribuciones, pero por algo concreto hay que empezar.

Diario *El País*, España

ANALYSIS

1 As you read the text, identify the verbs which are in the subjunctive mood, and account for their use. (Chapter 14)

2 What is the rule for the formation of the present subjunctive? Of the verbs in subjunctive which you have identified, which one is irregular and what is its infinitive form?

3 Why is the adjective *razonables* (l. 18) plural? (Chapter 20)

4 *Lo malo es que los demás también lo tienen* (l. 2–3). Account for the different uses of *lo* in this sentence. (Chapters 18 and 25)

5 Identify other examples of *lo* as direct object pronoun in the text and say in each case what *lo* refers to.

6 State the function of *se* in *se hagan* (l. 5) and *se efectúen* (l. 9–10). (Chapter 11)

Text 2

In this interview Mario Molina, Nobel Prize winner for chemistry (1995), talks about the ozone layer.

– *¿Cuál es el principal problema que plantea la capa de ozono?*

– La capa de ozono protege la superficie terrestre de radiación ultravioleta. Esta radiación afecta de manera importante a diversos sistemas biológicos, sobre todo a los menos protegidos. Por otra parte, la estructura de la atmósfera depende de la existencia del ozono; por eso nos preocupa que pueda ser dañada.

– *¿Cree que la sociedad en general es consciente del problema?*

– Cada vez más, pero hay que seguir trabajando porque la capa de ozono se está convirtiendo en un queso gruyere. El papel de los periodistas es muy importante para dar cuenta a la sociedad de todos estos factores que poco a poco destruyen el medio ambiente.

– *¿Hay una solución factible?*

– Eliminar la emisión de los compuestos que afectan la capa de ozono – que se usan en refrigeración o en latas de aerosol – y que se pueden sustituir por otros compuestos. Ya se han llevado a cabo diversos acuerdos internacionales para que la producción de estos compuestos nocivos termine. Actualmente, sólo los países en vías de desarrollo continúan produciendo estas sustancias, aunque lo hacen en pequeñas cantidades.

– *¿Cómo afecta el ozono a un ciudadano normal y corriente?*

– Los efectos más directos son las quemaduras y cáncer de piel por exposición al sol. Pero existen también efectos indirectos como los cambios climáticos.

– *¿Qué consejos daría usted a la gente para evitar en lo posible los efectos del ozono?*

– Primero hay que seleccionar lo que se compra, pero sobre todo hacer presión sobre los diferentes gobiernos. Hay que tener conciencia ecológica para que el gobierno se dé cuenta de que es un tema que le importa a la gente y tome medidas.

– *¿Cuál es su previsión para los próximos años?*

– El tema del ozono parece que poco a poco se va resolviendo, pero hay otros problemas muy graves de contaminación global. Uno de ellos es la superpoblación del planeta. Cuando los países desarrollados incrementen sus economías, los cambios serán muy fuertes. Hay demasiada gente e inevitablemente cambiará la manera de vivir. Habrá que conservar energía, por ejemplo, y tomar muchas otras medidas.

Revista *Cambio16*, España

ANALYSIS

1 What Spanish phrase does Mario Molina use to say what must be done to protect the ozone layer? How many times does he use this phrase in his discourse? (Chapter 10)
2 Identify the examples of the gerund in the text and translate them into English. (Chapter 9)
3 *termine* (l. 30) What verb form is this and why is it being used here? Find the other example in the text of the same use of this verb form. (Chapter 14)
4 Why *incrementen* in line 61? (Chapter 14)
5 a Why *pueda* in line 11? (Chapter 14)
  b What type of construction is *ser dañada* (l. 11) and why is the past participle in the feminine form? (Chapter 11)
6 Find the seven occurrences of *se* in the text and account for their use. (Chapters 11 and 12)
7 What is the function of ***lo*** in ... *aunque lo hacen en pequeñas cantidades* (l. 34–35)? (Chapter 25)
8 The text has examples of the infinitive used with modal auxiliary verbs. Find where else the infinitive is used in the text and explain its use. (Chapter 8)
9 Identify the nouns in the text which end in -***a*** but are masculine. (Chapter 19)

Text 3

Trucos para hacer turismo sin arruinarte

- Viaja fuera de las fechas que se consideran temporada alta. Un par de días de diferencia pueden significar precios más baratos.
- (5) Elige agencias especializadas en el destino escogido. Además de conocer todas las tarifas, y acceder a precios más baratos que los mayoristas, te ayudarán a planear mejor el viaje. Las oficinas de turismo de (10) cada país tienen listados de estas agencias.
- Pide los precios por separado si prefieres contratar un paquete turístico (viaje, traslados con guía y alojamiento): a veces la tarifa global (15) oculta que te cobran a precio de oro los transportes del aeropuerto al hotel, y viceversa. En estos casos, ir en taxi te puede salir mucho más económico.
- La fórmula más barata suele ser "avión (20) + alojamiento". Si eres un viajero experimentado y sabes moverte con soltura en otros países, no dudes en contratarla.
- Haz tu reserva con antelación y, para (25) mayor tranquilidad, contrata en la propia agencia un seguro de cancelación del viaje.
- Aprovecha las ofertas de última hora si tienes la suerte de no tener que ajustar (30) tus vacaciones a unas fechas determinadas. Pero ten en cuenta que, contratando una semana antes de salir, difícilmente podrás elegir el destino que más te guste.
- (35) Si quieres hacer un "tour" por varios países, siempre te saldrá más económico contratar un viaje organizado que ir por libre.

Revista *Quo*, España

ANALYSIS

1 Read the advice given in this text and say whether the writer is addressing the reader formally or informally. (Chapter 17)

2 Account for the use of *se* in the first sentence of the text (l. 1). (Chapter 11)

3 In the third 'truco', account for *cobran* in the phrase *a veces la tarifa global oculta que te cobran a precio de oro los transportes del aeropuerto al hotel, y vice versa* (l. 14–17).

4 *. . . difícilmente podrás elegir. . .* (l. 33). What adverbial phrase could replace the adverb *difícilmente* here? Identify the adverbial phrases which have been used in the text. (Chapter 21)

5 *. . . ir en taxi te puede salir mucho más económico* (l. 17–18). Explain each use of the infinitive in this sentence, then reread the text to see if there are further examples of each use. (Chapter 8)

6 What other examples of infinitive use did you find as you reread the text?

7 Rewrite the text using the formal singular form (**usted**) of the imperative and making other adjustments to the text where necessary. (Chapter 17)

Text 4

Margarita lloraba con el rostro oculto entre las manos: lloraba sin gemir, pero las lágrimas corrían silenciosas a lo largo de sus mejillas, deslizándose por entre sus dedos para caer en la tierra, hacia la que había doblado su frente.

Junto a Margarita estaba Pedro, quien levantaba de cuando en cuando
5 los ojos para mirarla, y viéndola llorar, tornaba a bajarlos, guardando a su vez un silencio profundo.

Y todo callaba alrededor y parecía respetar su pena. Los rumores del campo se apagaban; el viento de la tarde dormía y las sombras comenzaban a envolver los espesos árboles del soto.

10 Así transcurrieron algunos minutos, durante los cuales se acabó de borrar el rastro de luz que el sol se había dejado al morir en el horizonte; la luna comenzó a dibujarse vagamente sobre el fondo violado del cielo del crepúsculo y unas tras otras fueron apareciendo las mayores estrellas.

Pedro rompió al fin aquel silencio angustioso, exclamando con voz sorda y
15 entrecortada, como si hablase consigo mismo:

–¡Es imposible . . . , imposible!

Gustavo Adolfo Bécquer, *La Promesa*

ANALYSIS

1 Comment on the main verb tenses used in the passage. (Chapters 2 and 3)

2 Identify the examples of the pluperfect in the text. (Chapter 5)

3 *Junto a Margarita estaba Pedro* (l. 4). Why is the verb *estar* used here? (Chapter 13)

4 If a verb follows a preposition, what form must it take? Find examples in the passage. (Chapter 8)

5 Comment on the function of *se* where it occurs in the passage. (Chapter 12)

6 Find a verb in the subjunctive. What tense is it and why? (Chapter 15)

7 *. . . para mirarla, y viéndola llorar . . .* (l. 5). Justify the position of the object pronouns. (Chapter 25)

8 Comment on the word order of *se acabó de borrar el rastro de luz* (l. 10–11) and *unas tras otras fueron apareciendo las mayores estrellas* (l. 12–13). (Chapter 30)

9 Explain the form of the relative pronoun in *hacia la que había doblado su frente* (l. 3) and *durante los cuales* (l. 10). (Chapter 26)

Text 5

Juan cogió a su mujer como si fuera una muñeca, y le dijo:
– Alma mía, tus sentimientos son de ángel, pero tu razón, allá por esas nubes, se deja alucinar. Te han engañado; te han dado un soberbio timo.
– Por Dios, no me digas eso – murmuró Jacinta, después de una pausa en que
5 quiso hablar y no pudo.
– Si desde el principio hubieras hablado conmigo – añadió el Delfín muy cariñoso – pero aquí tienes el resultado de tus tapujos . . . ¡Ah, las mujeres! Todas ellas tienen una novela en la cabeza, y cuando lo que imaginan no aparece en la vida, que es lo más común, sacan su composicioncita . . . [. . .]
10 Jacinta, anonadada, quería defender su tema a todo trance.
– Juanín es tu hijo, no me lo niegues – replicó llorando.
– Te juro que no . . . ¿Cómo quieres que te lo jure? . . . ¡Ay, Dios mío! Ahora se me está ocurriendo que ese pobre niño es el hijo de la hijastra de Izquierdo. ¡Pobre Nicolasa! Se murió de sobreparto. Era una excelente chica. Su niño tiene, con
15 diferencia de tres meses, la misma edad que tendría el mío si viviese.

Benito Pérez Galdós, *Fortunata y Jacinta*

ANALYSIS

1 Account for the preposition *a* in the first line. (Chapter 28)

2 Find the negative commands in the passage and explain the construction. (Chapter 17)

3 Find in the text where Spanish uses the definite article and English does not. (Chapter 18)

4 Account for the use of the subjunctive in *¿Cómo quieres que te lo jure?* (l. 12). (Chapter 14)

5 *Se murió de sobreparto* (l. 14). What tense is this? In what way is it irregular? Which other common verb is similarly irregular? (Chapter 2)

6 *Te han engañado; te han dado un soberbio timo* (l. 3). Explain why the third person plural is used here and translate the sentence into English. (Chapter 11)

7 *el mío* (l. 15). To what is Juan referring here? (Chapter 24)

8 Find the superlative expression in the text. (Chapter 22)

9 Apart from *como si fuera* (l. 1), find the two 'if' clauses in the text and explain the constructions. (Chapters 15 and 16)

Text 6

No recordaban Abel Sánchez y Joaquín Monegro desde cuándo se conocían. Eran conocidos desde antes de la niñez, desde su primera infancia, pues sus dos sendas nodrizas se juntaban y los juntaban cuando aún ellos no sabían hablar. Aprendió cada uno de ellos a conocerse conociendo al otro. Y así vivieron y se hicieron juntos
5 amigos desde nacimiento, casi más bien hermanos de crianza.

En sus paseos, en sus juegos, en sus otras amistades comunes parecía dominar e iniciarlo todo Joaquín, el más voluntarioso; pero era Abel quien, pareciendo ceder, hacía la suya siempre. Y es que le importaba más no obedecer que mandar. Casi nunca reñían. "¡Por mí, como tú quieras! . . .", le decía Abel a Joaquín, y éste se
10 exasperaba a las veces porque con aquel "¡como tú quieras! . . ." esquivaba las disputas.

– ¡Nunca me dices que no! . . . – exclamaba Joaquín.

– ¿Y para qué? – respondía el otro.

– Bueno, éste no quiere que vayamos al Pinar – dijo una vez aquél, cuando varios
15 compañeros se disponían a dar un paseo.

– ¿Yo? ¡Pues no he de quererlo! . . . – exclamó Abel –. Sí, hombre, sí; como tú quieras. ¡Vamos allá!

Miguel de Unamuno, *Abel Sánchez*

ANALYSIS

1 . . . *sus dos sendas nodrizas se juntaban y los juntaban cuando aún ellos no sabían hablar.* (l. 2–3)

a What is the function of *se* in *se juntaban* and *los* in *los juntaban*? (Chapters 12 and 25)

b Why the use of the subject pronoun *ellos* in this sentence? (Chapter 25)

2 Is the function of *se* in *Aprendió cada uno de ellos a conocerse* . . . (l. 3–4) the same as the example of *se* in the first sentence . . . *desde cuándo se conocían* (l. 1)? (Chapter 12)

3 Account for the form of the conjunction in . . . *dominar e iniciarlo* (l. 6–7). (Chapter 29)

4 *Y es que le importaba más no obedecer que mandar.* (l. 8)

a Account for the use of the infinitives in this sentence. (Chapter 8)

b Study the word order of the clause introduced by *Y es que* and rewrite it with the subject as the first element. Why is the word order used by Unamuno more effective? (Chapter 30)

5 Explain the occurrences of the subjunctive in the text. (Chapter 14)

6 There are two examples of redundant pronouns in the text. Identify them. (Chapter 25)

Keys

Where not stated in the exercises, *you* will be rendered as **tú**.

• Key 1: The present tense

1 **a** saco; llamo **b** estudias; aprendes **c** visitan; vive **d** escribe **e** bailamos; bebemos **f** reciben **g** hablan **h** subís **i** vivimos **j** intentan **k** guardáis **l** trabaja; toca; llega **m** pasamos **n** corre **o** compro; leo; desayuno.

2 **a** dice; conduzco **b** conoces; conozco **c** empieza **d** pensáis **e** oigo; leo; salgo **f** quieres; tienes **g** juega **h** sé; vuelvo **i** dejas; tengo **j** calienta; fríe; añade **k** llueve **l** vienen; dicen; quieren **m** sabes; sigo **n** van; prefieren; piden **o** suelo; duermo.

3 **a** comen **b** pinta **c** nieva **d** pierdes **e** empiezan **f** duerme **g** son **h** va **i** sirve **j** conducen **k** mide **l** consiguen **m** asiste **n** miente **o** abren.

4
- El viernes nos despedimos de María. ¿Qué le regalamos?
- Le gustan las joyas. ¿Le damos unos pendientes?
- Sí, ¿por qué no? La llamo esta noche para decirle que el jueves por la noche hay una fiesta en mi casa.
- ¿Y cuándo compramos los pendientes?
- ¿Lo dejamos para/hasta el miércoles? Tengo que ir a París y no vuelvo hasta el martes.
- Vale. ¿Dónde quedamos/nos encontramos? ¿Delante de la joyería?
- Sí. Te veo allí a las diez.

6
- ¿A qué hora empieza a trabajar y a qué hora termina?
- ¿Come con los actores?
- Para relajarse ¿qué libros lee?
- ¿Qué música escucha?
- ¿Qué programas ve en la televisión?
- ¿Qué deporte hace/practica para mantenerse en forma?

• Key 2: The preterite

1 **a** pasé; salí **b** estudiaste; leiste **c** preparó; bebió **d** entró; cogió **e** viajamos; salimos **f** mandasteis; recibisteis **g** llamaron; subieron **h** encontraron; volvieron. **i** escribió; llamó **j** decidimos **k** intentaron **l** encontraron; aprendieron **m** conociste **n** llegó; perdió **o** alquilé; recorrí.

2 **a** fui; fue **b** supo; hizo **c** anduvimos; anduvimos; pudimos **d** estuvisteis; vinisteis **e** sirvieron; fuimos; dijeron **f** tradujeron; estuvieron **g** compraste; compré; trajo **h** toqué; entré; puse; toqué **i** empecé; empezó; llegué; tomé; me puse; vino; tuve **j** vio; cogió; se puso; consiguió.

3 nació; decidieron; llegaron; fue; nació; adoptó; recibió; incorporó; se convirtió; escribió; salió; llegó; murió; se estrelló.

4 se despertó; quiso; dio; fue; se enfrió; tuvo; se durmió; durmió; se levantó.

5 *This is a model answer.*
Nada más levantarme, me vestí y fui andando al gimnasio. Hice una hora de gimnasia y luego desayuné. Tomé lo de siempre: zumo de naranja, tostadas y café con leche. Fui al baño a lavarme los dientes y tomé un taxi al dentista. No tuve que esperar; el dentista me atendió en seguida y no encontró ninguna caries. A las diez menos cinco llegué al trabajo y a las diez en punto entré en el despacho del jefe de sección para la reunión. Fue una reunión larga pero fructífera. Nos pusimos de acuerdo sobre varios asuntos.
A eso de la una y media bajé al Bar La Flor donde me reuní con Jaime y Susana a tomar el aperitivo. Luego fui al Restaurante La Oficina donde almorcé con Nacho. La comida estuvo muy rica y charlamos y nos reímos mucho Nacho y yo.
A las cuatro y media entré de nuevo en el despacho y trabajé toda la tarde preparando un informe. El tiempo se me fue volando y a las siete y media salí para casa. De repente me acordé del cumpleaños de Adolfo así que le llamé, le deseé un feliz cumpleaños y le invité a tomar unas copas pero él no quiso. Entonces me duché y me arreglé para salir. Primero fui al Bar Gregorio donde tomé unas copas con la pandilla y luego me reuní con M, el amor de mi vida. Cenamos en nuestro restaurante preferido y después decidimos ir al cine. La cena me encantó pero la película no me gustó tanto. Fue un poco aburrida.

6 **a** ¿Adónde fuiste de vacaciones?
b ¿Cuánto tiempo estuviste allí?
c ¿Viajaste solo?
d ¿Cómo viajasteis?
e ¿Dónde os alojasteis?
f ¿Qué hicisteis el primer día?
g ¿Qué sitios visitasteis?
h ¿Salisteis por la noche?
i ¿Qué tiempo hizo?
j ¿Qué compraste?
k ¿Qué tal lo pasaste?

8 *1st paragraph*: nació; sospechaba; iba; Pasó; se dedicaba; trabajaba; fue; transmitió; Tenía; llevaron; iban.
2nd paragraph: se trasladó; gustaba; aprendió; consiguió; se dio cuenta; tenía; Dejó; empezó.
3rd paragraph: trabajaba; decidió; convirtió; vivía; trabajaba; escribía; se acostaba.
4th paragraph: volvió; salió; aparecieron; otorgó; fue; adaptó.
5th paragraph: siguió.

• Key 3: The imperfect

1 eran; vivían; tenía; cultivaba; se ocupaba; hacía; cargaba; se llamaba; iba; vendía; acompañaba; estaban; llevaban.

2 **a** hacía; daba **b** era; llevaba; tocaba **c** trabajaban; charlabas **d** estudiábamos **e** íbamos; llovía **f** veían; se acostaban **g** Sabía; podíamos **h** era; dejaba; quería **i** daba; se reunía **j** íbamos; era **k** ponía; oía; me vestía **l** hacías; practicabas **m** estaban jugando; iban; bajaban **n** era; llevaba; sabía **o** iba; era; contaba.

5 **a** La última vez que vi a Fernando, él estaba buscando trabajo.
b Entramos en el museo porque llovía.
c Cuando conocí a Isabel, tenía el pelo largo y rubio.
d Pedro y yo íbamos por la calle cuando nos topamos con Ana.
e Eran las once de la mañana cuando partieron para Santiago.

f Yo no fui a trabajar porque tenía resaca y me dolía la cabeza.
g Marisa bajaba por la escalera cuando se resbaló y se torció el tobillo. / Cuando Marisa bajaba por la escalera, se resbaló y se torció el tobillo.
h Cuando Jorge llegó a la fiesta, todos estaban borrachos.
i Me duchaba con agua fría cuando hacía mucho calor. / Me duché con agua fría porque hacía mucho calor.
j Cuando estudiaba derecho, Inés compartía piso con tres chicos.

6 **a** En aquellos tiempos las chicas no salían después de las diez.
b Mientras esperaba charlaba conmigo.
c Estábamos muy cansados cuando llegamos.
d No me di cuenta de que estaba enfermo.
e Vivíamos en un pueblo pequeño donde todo el mundo se conocía.
f Todo iba bien hasta que empezó a llover.
g Esperábamos a mi tío por la mañana pero no llegó hasta media tarde.
h Empezábamos a preocuparnos por él así que llamamos a su hija.
i Bajaron del taxi y como la puerta estaba abierta entraron en la casa sin llamar.
j Vicente nos traía una botella de vino cuando/cada vez que nos visitaba.

• Key 4: The perfect

1 **a** hemos entendido **b** han visto **c** ha visitado **d** ha llegado **e** han recibido **f** he podido **g** habéis dicho **h** ha quedado **i** te has esforzado **j** se han despertado.

2 **a** he aprendido **b** has ido **c** ha salido **d** hemos vendido **e** ha llamado **f** se me ha caído **g** han tenido **h** habéis entendido.

3 **a** Siempre hemos ido de vacaciones a España.
b No le han dicho nada a Pili porque no la han visto.
c ¿Por qué no has hecho esto?
d ¿Dónde han puesto las bolsas?
e Todavía no ha vuelto Gonzalo de París.
f No le he escrito a Isabel porque no he tenido tiempo.
g Carlos está muy triste/alterado porque se ha muerto su perro.
h Los vecinos dicen que habéis roto la valla.

4 he hecho; he comprado; he escrito; he envuelto; he puesto; he cambiado; he leído; he podido; he dicho; he dado; he olvidado.

5 **a** has dormido **b** han comido **c** habéis visitado **d** ha ido **e** han pasado **f** ha abierto **g** ha hecho **h** ha llovido **i** he perdido.

• Key 5: The pluperfect

1 **a** habían invitado **b** habíamos repetido **c** habías echado **d** habíais salido **e** había dicho **f** había visto **g** había terminado **h** habían prometido **i** habían contado **j** habían entendido **k** habías estado **l** había terminado **m** se había levantado **n** había vendido **o** había empezado.

2 **a** habían cerrado **b** había ido **c** habíamos visitado; habíamos visto **d** había dicho **e** habían entrado **f** habían robado **g** se había encontrado **h** habían dado **i** habían leído **j** había venido **k** había traído; habíamos dado **l** se había casado **m** se había metido **n** había comunicado **o** habían visto; habían cenado.

3 **a** Estaba contenta porque Roberto me había dado un regalo.
b Lo había envuelto y lo había dejado en mi asiento.
c No le había dicho que era mi cumpleaños.
d Más tarde me dijo que había comprado la pulsera porque le había gustado.
e No había pensado en el precio.
f Cuando llegué a casa, ya se había acostado/se había ido a la cama Amelia.
g Había apagado todo y en la mesa me había dejado un mensaje.
h No se había puesto en contacto con Eduardo porque ella también había estado fuera toda la tarde.
i Sin embargo, había recibido la noticia de que la tía Silvia había muerto.
j Víctor había heredado todo y la tía Silvia no nos había dejado nada.

• Key 6: The future

1 **a** estaré **b** verás **c** saldrá **d** hablaremos **e** jugarán **f** vendrás **g** os agotaréis **h** podré **i** tendrán **j** habrá; practicaremos **k** será; habrá; subirán **l** haremos.

2 **a** haré; será **b** acompañará; será **c** llevaremos; tendré; guiaré; sacará **d** nos alojaremos; intentaremos; bajaremos **e** haré; seguiré; iré; entraré; rezaré; subiré; abrazaré; golpearé; dará **f** volveremos; nos quedaremos; revelará; escribiré; publicaremos **g** saldrá; le pondremos; gustará.

3 **a** ¿Cómo hará el Camino de Santiago?
b ¿Quién lo acompañará?
c ¿Qué llevarán en el globo?
d ¿Dónde se alojarán?
e ¿Qué hará en Santiago?
f ¿Cuánto tiempo se quedarán en Santiago?
g ¿Cuándo saldrá el libro?

4 *This is a model answer.*
El miércoles a las nueve de la mañana, los estudiantes llegarán al Instituto donde los recibirá el director y a continuación visitarán las instalaciones. A las once y cuarto se presentará el grupo de alumnos del Instituto y a las doce y media los estudiantes saldrán del centro para visitar el Ayuntamiento. Comerán en el Ayuntamiento.

El jueves empezarán a las ocho y media y trabajarán toda la mañana. A las doce menos cuarto el grupo de alumnos del Instituto se reunirá con ellos y seguirán trabajando hasta la hora del almuerzo. Comerán en la cantina y por la tarde efectuarán una visita turístico-cultural de la ciudad para conocer los principales monumentos.

Al día siguiente a partir de las diez de la mañana revisarán el proyecto. A las once y media tomarán café y a las doce planificarán las actividades que tendrán que realizar durante el resto del año hasta la próxima reunión. A las dos comerán y tendrán la tarde libre.

El sábado también lo tendrán libre para hacer visitas y realizar compras.

A las ocho y media del domingo se dirigirán al aeropuerto donde tomarán el vuelo de regreso.

5 **1** ejerceré **2** procuraré **3** ahorraré **4** plantaré; cuidaré **5** elegiré **6** apagaré **7** evitaré **8** cuidaré **9** cuidaré; contaminaré; protegeré **10** preferiré.

• Key 7: The conditional

1 **a** podrías **b** podría **c** haría **d** importaría **e** podría **f** permitirían.

2 **a** serían **b** compraría **c** habría **d** serían **e** dolería.

3 **a** participarían; costaría **b** tomaría **c** mediría; sería; vivirían; trabajarían **d** pondría; encontraríamos.

4 **a** estaba; dejarían **b** sabía; contaría **c** prometió; vendría; traería **d** advirtieron; pondrían **e** explicó; tendrían **f** dijeron; tardarían.

5 **a** volvería **b** comprendería **c** se asombraría **d** sufriría **e** llegaría.

• Key 8: The infinitive

1 **a** Fueron a Salamanca para aprender español.
They went to Salamanca to learn Spanish.
b Estoy aquí sin hacer nada.
I'm here doing nothing.
c Al entrar en el salón encendió la luz.
As s/he went into the living room, s/he turned on the light.
d Después de cenar salimos.
After dining, we went out.
e Al llegar, llamaron a sus amigos.
When they arrived, they called their friends.
f Se fue sin decir nada.
S/he went without saying anything.
g Antes de iniciar el programa acudieron al médico.
Before starting the programme, they went to the doctor's.
h Marta compró media docena de huevos para hacer una tortilla.
Marta bought half a dozen eggs to make an omelette.
i Después de visitar el castillo compraron recuerdos.
After visiting the castle, they bought some souvenirs.
j Antes de hablar con Juan leyó la carta.
Before speaking to Juan, s/he read the letter.

2 **a** Siento no poder ayudarte.
b Espera ir a Madrid.
c Inés no quiso seguir con los ejercicios.
d Es muy importante hacer ejercicio.
e Hay que escuchar para aprender.
f No puedo ir al gimnasio porque tengo que trabajar.
g Es imposible ponerse en forma sin hacer ejercicio.
h Quieren comprar un coche para ir a España.
i Marta bajó al supermercado a comprar aceite.
j Ignacio debe tener mucho aguante para poder soportar tanto.

3 **a** Al entrar empezaron a cantar.
b Los oí cantar.
c Lo mejor de vivir aquí es poder ir al teatro.
d Lo peor de vivir en la metrópoli es estar tan lejos del campo.
e La vida en el campo es abrir la ventana y ver, oír y oler la naturaleza.
f Ir al gimnasio es una buena manera de ponerse en forma.
g Es incapaz de dejar de fumar.
h Niega haber ayudado a los ladrones.
i Poder hablar con su hija es su único consuelo.
j Se aburrieron de hacer lo mismo/la misma cosa una y otra vez/de repetir y repetir la misma cosa/lo mismo.

4 **a** No fumar.
b No usar.
c No ducharse antes de las siete.
d No dejar ropa en los vestuarios.
e Apagar las luces antes de medianoche.
f Quitar/recoger la mesa después de comer.
g Fregar/lavar los platos.
h Hacer la cama al llegar.

• Key 9: The gerund

1 **a** durmiendo **b** trabajando **c** corriendo **d** sustituyendo **e** usando **f** bailando **g** viajando **h** estudiando.

2 **a** estuvieron/estaban trabajando **b** está atendiendo **c** estábamos siguiendo **d** se estaba derritiendo/estaba derritiéndose **e** están sirviendo **f** estaban preparándose/se estaban preparando **g** estamos descansando **h** se están riendo/están riéndose **i** estuve bebiendo **j** se está vistiendo/está vistiéndose **k** me estoy poniendo/estoy poniéndome **l** están construyendo.

3 **a** saludando **b** escribiéndome **c** ayudándonos **d** sabiendo **e** leyendo **f** descansando **g** llorando **h** mintiendo **i** saliendo **j** caminando **k** escuchando **l** trabajando.

4 **a** Los agricultores llevan dos años plantando bosques.
The farmers have been planting trees for two years.
b Sofía lleva seis meses yendo al trabajo en autobús.
Sofia has been going to work by bus for six months.
c Los oficinistas llevan año y medio reciclando el papel.
The office workers have been recycling paper for a year and a half.
d Nosotros llevamos mucho tiempo reduciendo nuestro consumo de electricidad.
We have been reducing our electricity consumption for a long time.
e Los ecologistas llevan más de treinta años creando conciencia sobre los peligros que corre el planeta.
The Greens have been raising awareness of the dangers facing the planet for more than thirty years.
f Carlos lleva seis años enseñando francés en la Escuela de Idiomas.
Carlos has been teaching French at the Language School for six years.
g Los campesinos llevan siglos cultivando estas tierras.
The peasants have been farming these lands for centuries.
h Gloria lleva un año ya investigando la desaparición de la abeja.
Gloria has been researching the disappearance of bees for a year now.
i Pepe no lleva mucho tiempo vendiendo relojes.
Pepe hasn't been selling watches for long.
j Este grupo de jóvenes lleva varios años yendo a Guatemala de voluntarios.
This group of young people have been going to Guatemala as volunteers for several years.

5 **a** se está acumulando **b** va mejorando **c** venimos notando **d** acabará destruyendo **e** viene contaminando **f** están instalando **g** seguirán apoyando **h** vamos cambiando **i** acabará dañándose **j** siguen derritiéndose **k** está intensificando; está recalentando **l** van cambiando.

6 **a** anda diciendo **b** vamos aprendiendo **c** sigues fumando **d** andan buscando **e** nos quedamos charlando **f** voy conociendo **g** seguimos tirando **h** iba escribiendo **i** anda buscando **j** siguen pensando **k** venía notando **l** nos quedamos mirando.

7 **a** acabarán/terminarán derritiéndose **b** acusando a los ecologistas de sensacionalismo **c** seguirán aumentando **d** depositando plásticos y latas en una bolsa y tirando las materias orgánicas en otra bolsa **e** consumiendo solo el agua y electricidad necesarias **f** reciclando el vidrio **g** está amenazando a las poblaciones indígenas **h** llevan registrándose las temperaturas.

• Key 10: Modal verbs

1 **a** Quiero ir a México de vacaciones.
b ¿Cuánto tiempo podemos quedarnos aquí?
c Debéis hablar con Juan cuanto antes.
d ¿Quieres venir conmigo?
e Debemos tomar las cosas con calma.
f Todos los días suele hacer dos horas de ejercicio.
g ¿Quién dice que Pepe sabe tocar la guitarra?
h No queremos trabajar más horas por menos dinero.
i Marta no puede salir esta noche.
j Solemos dar un paseo por la tarde antes de cenar.

2 **a** Suelo jugar un partido de ajedrez después de la cena.
b Los abuelos solían echar la siesta después de comer.
c No debes tomar el sol entre las dos y las seis.
d Solemos ir a la piscina dos veces por semana.
e Debéis pedir ayuda.
f Debes tomar una aspirina si te duele la cabeza.
g Solíamos tomar las vacaciones con los amigos.
h Jorge no sale; debe (de) estar estudiando.
i Solía entrenar dos veces a la semana.
j Debe de estar en plena forma con todo el ejercicio que hace.
k Según los expertos, debemos tomar cinco porciones de fruta y verdura por día.
l Solemos reunirnos en la cafetería al salir del trabajo.

3 **a** tenía que **b** hay que **c** debe **d** tengo que **e** debe **f** hay que **g** debemos **h** tiene que; debe **i** hay que **j** debe **k** tenemos que **l** hay que.

4 puede; debemos; puede; hay que; suelen; puede.

5 **a** ¿Sabes tocar la guitarra?
b Solíamos pasar la mañana en la playa.
c ¿Por qué tienes que marcharte?
d Si quieres tomar el sol, debes usar un buen bronceador.
e No hay que olvidar que los rayos solares pueden ser dañinos.
f Solía trabajar diez horas diarias hasta que el médico le dijo que tenía que relajarse.
g Para viajar en el AVE, hay que reservar los asientos con antelación.
h Pepe, debes prestar más atención.
i ¡Claro que sé cocinar!
j Tendremos que madrugar mañana.
k ¿Hay que ser buen cocinero para poder hacer este plato?
l Si sabes conducir, podrías alquilar un coche y recorrer la isla.

6 **a** quiero + infinitive **b** puedo + infinitive **c** suelo + infinitive **d** debo + infinitive **e** tengo que + infinitive **f** hay que + infinitive.

• Key 11: Passive and impersonal sentences

1 **a** Leopoldo Alas escribió *La Regenta*.
b El policía interrogó al camionero.
c Los chicos rompieron los cristales.
d Agustín ha desmontado el motor.
e Tele-Mundo no emitirá el campeonato.

f Mi padre construyó estas casas.
g Mi hermano diseñará la casa de mis sueños.
h Los agricultores han cortado los árboles.
i Fermín tomó las fotos.
j Una traductora jurada ha traducido los informes.

2 **a** fueron excavados **b** han sido repoblados/serán repoblados **c** han sido analizados/fueron analizados **d** fue invitada/ha sido invitada **e** son programados/serán programados **f** fue organizada **g** fue introducida **h** son arrasadas **i** fue encarcelado **j** fue rodada.

3 **a** La catedral se construyó en el siglo XV.
b Este libro no se ha traducido al inglés.
c Las películas se conservarán en cajas metálicas.
d Las estatuas se destruyeron en el bombardeo.
e La noticia del accidente se difundió por televisión.
f Se convocó a los señores para el día veinticuatro.
g Tras la construcción de la nueva autopista, se han plantado muchos árboles.
h Sin embargo, no reemplazan los árboles que se han talado.
i Se tiran y se trituran cada vez más libros de la biblioteca.
j Con la reestructuración se crearán cuatro nuevos puestos de trabajo los cuales se anunciarán en el diario local.

4 *Identify where in Text 2 these sentences have come from and check your translations.*

5 **a** No nos han pagado este mes.
b Me han dado mucho apoyo.
c No les ayudaron mucho.
d Investigaron la causa del accidente.
e Van a abrir un nuevo cine aquí.
f Han arreglado el ascensor.
g A todos les dieron/A todo el mundo le dieron la oportunidad de participar en la carrera.
h Interrogaron a Alberto durante cuatro horas.
i Vendieron los cuadros para pagar la restauración.
j Me dijeron que tendría que esperar hasta el día siguiente.

6 **a** El turrón se elabora/El turrón lo elaboran . . . **b** Se descubrirá/Descubrirán . . . **c** Se fotocopian y piratean/Fotocopian y piratean . . . **d** Se construirá/Construirán . . . **e** Hospitalizaron al . . . /Se hospitalizó al conductor . . . **f** Se bombardearon/Bombardearon . . . **g** Se rescató al . . . /Rescataron al alpinista . . . **h** Los hábitos alimentarios se inculcan . . . **i** Distribuyeron/Se distribuyó la guía . . . **j** Han levantado/Se ha levantado una valla . . .

7a

a Cuando la construcción de un complejo turístico en primera línea de la playa fue aprobada, ...
b Años antes, el terreno fue clasificado . . . .
c Luego la misma zona fue declarada . . . .
d La contrucción de un hotel de 21 plantas fue subvencionada . . . .
e Muchos chalés fueron vendidos . . . .
f La legalidad de las edificaciones fue discutida.
g Los efectos ambientales del complejo fueron denunciados.
h El caso fue considerado . . . .
i La Administración fue obligada . . . .
j El hotel fue derrumbado . . . .

7b The choice of one passive construction over another is often a matter of style. **Ser** and the past participle is as appropriate as **se** in most of the sentences but in **e**, **f**, and **g** the passive construction with **se** is preferable.

8 *1st paragraph*: fue llevada; fue amordazada; fue atada
2nd paragraph: ser liberado; se había desvalijado; se habían sustraído
3rd paragraph: se ha perpetrado; han sido detenidos.

• Key 12: The reflexive

1 **a** te **b** se **c** me; me **d** se **e** nos; nos; se **f** se; se **g** os; os **h** se **i** te; te; me **j** se; se.

2 **a** se parecen **b** levantarme **c** quejándose **d** nos aburrimos **e** te acostaste **f** se sientan **g** se preocupa **h** poneros **i** callarte **j** me fiaría.

3 **a** Me lo pasé fatal en la fiesta de Carlitos.
b Primero me tomé un aperitivo con Juanjo en el Bar Florida.
c Después, al llegar a la casa de Carlitos, me resbalé y me caí.
d La madre de Carlitos me dio un coñac y aunque no me gusta, me lo bebí.
e Bailé un rato y luego me dormí.
f Cuando me desperté, Juanjo se había ido.
g Se había enfadado conmigo por haberme quedado dormido/a.
h No me sentía bien, así que me lavé la cara con agua fría.
i No me atreví a volver a bailar.
j Como ya era tarde, me despedí de la madre de Carlitos y me marché a casa.

4 **a** reciprocal **b** reciprocal **c** reflexive **d** reflexive **e** reciprocal **f** reflexive **g** reciprocal **h** reciprocal; reflexive **i** reflexive; reflexive; reciprocal **j** reflexive.

5 **a** Aquí se respira aire puro. **b** Se manda la factura a esta dirección. **c** Según lo que se dice, en Escocia se bebe mucho. **d** En España se cena tarde. **e** Para hacer la salsa, se necesita un manojo de perejil. **f** Hoy en día no se lee tanto. **g** Se piensa . . . **h** No se puede conseguir todo lo que se quiere. **i** Se está muy bien aquí; . . . **j** De vez en cuando se toma . . .

• Key 13: *Ser* and *estar*

1 **a** es; es **b** está; está **c** es; es; es; son **d** son; están **e** es **f** estamos **g** es; es **h** es; soy **i** es; está; está **j** están; están; están **k** es; es; está **l** están; es **m** estaba; estaba **n** es; es; está **o** es; está.

2 **a** está; es **b** es; está **c** ser; está **d** es; está **e** es; está **f** estar; es **g** está; está **h** está; es; es **i** es; está **j** es; está.

3 **a** El banco está abierto. **b** El gato está muerto. **c** La sopa está fría. **d** La llave está perdida. **e** La cena está servida. **f** Está prohibido fumar . . . **g** La habitación está reservada. **h** El coche está estropeado. **i** Este libro está agotado. **j** La costa está destruida.

4 **a** se está poniendo/está poniéndose **b** está creciendo **c** se está convirtiendo/está convirtiéndose **d** estaban estudiando **e** estaba durmiendo **f** está trabajando **g** se están construyendo **h** estaba lloviendo **i** estabas leyendo **j** estaba escribiendo.

5 **a** *The correct verbs are*: era; era; estar; estaba; estaban; era; estuviera.
b *The correct verbs are*: está; es; es; fue; era; estaba; estuvo; estaba; está.

6 **c** Nuestro aniversario **es** en junio.
d El dinero siempre **está** más seguro en el banco.
f La sopa **estaba** muy sosa.

h Estoy sin dinero . . .
i No sé en qué está pensando; las cosas que dice **son** absurdas.

7 **a** La casa estaba bastante lejos de la estación.
b Era tarde y estábamos cansados cuando llegamos.
c No vamos a salir porque está lloviendo.
d Las calles están muy concurridas hoy.
e El espejo está roto.
f ¿Te gusta este cuadro? No está mal ¿verdad?
g No es bueno/no está bien estar tan descontento.
h ¿A qué hora es el concierto? Es en el Ayuntamiento ¿verdad?
i El café estará frío y Marga estará de mal humor si no vienes ahora mismo.
j El hotel estaba completo lo que fue/era una pena.

8 1st paragraph: es; Está; ser; es.
2nd paragraph: fue; fueron; estuvieron; ser.
3rd paragraph: Fue; es; son; fueron; era; es; fue; ha sido.
4th paragraph: está; están; ser.
5th paragraph: estaba; siendo; Es; es.

• Key 14: The present subjunctive

1 **a** llames **b** jueguen **c** abra **d** escriba **e** prepare **f** hablemos **g** estudie; vea **h** dejéis **i** miremos **j** hablen **k** lleguen **l** cierres.

2 **a** Siento mucho que Gloria no se encuentre bien.
b Nos extraña que mientan.
c ¿Os molesta que digamos la verdad?
d Temen que haya un accidente.
e Está muy contento de que nos conozcamos.
f No me sorprende que lo hayan pasado bien en México.
g Me alegro de que te den un aumento de sueldo.
h No creo que venga Pedro a la hora indicada.
i No le gusta que su hijo salga con Marta.
j No creo que este trabajo sea muy duro.
k Dudamos que sepan mucho sobre el incidente.
l Odio que la gente no diga la verdad.

3 *As there is no one correct way of linking the two parts of the sentence, only the subordinate clause introduced by* **que** *is given.*
a . . . que proponga nuevas ideas en el trabajo.
b . . . que aprenda o perfeccione un idioma.
c . . . que reconozca tanto sus puntos fuertes como sus puntos débiles.
d . . . que se esfuerce por hacer siempre bien el trabajo.
e . . . que acepte las críticas sin enfadarse.
f . . . que se desconecte del trabajo una vez en casa.
g . . . que no almuerce en el área de trabajo.
h . . . que acuda a cursillos de especialización.
i . . . que cuide su aspecto personal.
j . . . que diga 'no' a un exceso de trabajo.
k . . . que no lleve trabajo a casa.
l . . . que intente estar al día.

4 **a** cueste; hagan **b** lleguen **c** sirvan **d** sepa; estén **e** vengan **f** haya **g** salga **h** paguen **i** deje **j** reciba **k** se vaya **l** sepa.

5 **a** 5 **b** 10 **c** 9 **d** 1 **e** 8 **f** 7 **g** 4 **h** 2 **i** 6 **j** 3.

6 **a** Tal vez no **tenga** todos los datos. **b** Quizás **venga** mañana. **c** Tal vez nos **inviten** a cenar. **d** Quizás no **esté** en casa. **e** Quizás me **llame** esta tarde. **f** . . . quizás Carmen **tenga** razón. **g** Tal vez **sea** mentira . . . **h** Tal vez **haya . . .** **i** Tal vez **sepa** algo Adolfo. **j** Quizás **haya comido** demasiado.

7 **a** escriba **b** pueda **c** dé **d** sea **e** guste **f** pida **g** sorprenda **h** cuente **i** diga **j** ayuden.

8 **a** llegue **b** toque **c** apruebe **d** duerma **e** haya **f** tenga **g** paséis **h** vaya **i** seas **j** mejore.

9 **a** Queremos que Eduardo **vaya** a Roma el jueves.
Verb expressing a wish; subject of the verb in the subordinate clause different from the main clause verb.
b Espero que **estén** ustedes bien.
Verb expressing emotion (hope); subject of the verb in the subordinate clause different from the main clause verb.
c Les rogamos a los señores pasajeros que **se abrochen** los cinturones de seguridad.
Verb expressing a request; subject of the verb in the subordinate clause different from the main clause verb.
d No conozco a nadie que **toque** el piano como tú.
Use of the subjunctive after the relative pronoun, which is referring back to someone unknown.
e Me pide que le **dé** mis apuntes.
Verb expressing a request; subject of the verb in the subordinate clause different from the main clause verb.
f No le gusta a la gente que uno **tenga** éxito.
Verb expressing an emotion; subject of the verb in the subordinate clause different from the main clause verb.
g Es muy buena idea que **visiten** la destilería antes de marcharse.
Subjunctive used after 'es muy buena idea que'.
h No vamos a empezar hasta que **venga** Rodrigo.
Subjunctive used after conjunction indicating time in relation to the future; subjects different in main and subordinate clauses.
i No me extraña que a Paloma no le **guste** su trabajo.
Verb expressing an emotion; subject of the verb in the subordinate clause different from the main clause verb.
j Cuando **vaya** a Madrid ¿quieres que te **traiga** algo?
Subjunctive used after conjunction indicating time in relation to the future. Verb expressing a wish; subject of the verb in the subordinate clause different from the main clause verb.
k Es imposible que se **vayan** ustedes antes de que **vuelva** mi jefe.
Subjunctive after 'es imposible que' and used after conjunction indicating time in relation to the future; subjects different in main and subordinate clauses.
l Aunque **tiene/tenga** dinero, no creo que lo **gaste**.
The subjunctive used after 'aunque' expresses possibility/probability rather than certainty; it is used after negative thinking 'no creo que . . .'.

10 **a** Siento que no estés bien; espero verte cuando estés mejor/te hayas mejorado.
b No creo que haya alguien aquí que nos ayude.
c No hace falta verlo pero es importante que sepamos cómo funciona.
d Quizás pueda decirnos qué pasa antes de que vuelva Juan.
e Aunque consiga un trabajo, Julio tendrá que seguir estudiando.
f Puede que Samuel tenga más experiencia pero no es muy probable que haya estudiado tanto como tú.
g Es natural que Javier quiera independizarse en cuanto/tan pronto como empiece a ganarse la vida.
h Quizás busque un piso que no sea muy caro y que no esté muy lejos de su trabajo.

i No quiere pronunciar un discurso aunque su jefe se lo pida.
j Es lógico que nos presentemos para que todos sepan/todo el mundo sepa quiénes somos.

• Key 15: The imperfect subjunctive

Only the **-ra** *form of the imperfect subjunctive is given in the answers.*

1 **a** escribiera **b** vieran **c** hiciéramos **d** hablara **e** fuera **f** pidiera **g** ayudara **h** se despidiera **i** supiéramos **j** salieran; lloviera **k** dijera **l** llegarais.

2 **a** A Luis no le gustaba que Ana Luisa sacara mejores notas que él.
b Ana Luisa no quería que su marido se sintiera inferior a ella.
c Era importante que Luis reconociera los éxitos de su esposa.
d Siendo macho, era lógico que Luis tuviera celos.
e Ana Luisa no creía que dejar de trabajar fuera la solución.
f Ana Luisa temía que se separaran pronto.
g Alberto le prohibió a Lucía que trabajara fuera de casa.
h Era una pena que los ingresos de Alberto no fueran suficientes para mantener a la familia.
i A Luisa le dolía que su marido no le diera apoyo.
j No estaba bien que Alberto no ayudara en casa.
k Lucía le exigió a Alberto que contrataran una persona que hiciera las tareas domésticas.
l Alberto le decía a Luisa que no trabajara tantas horas.

4 **a** ¿Qué esperaba que hiciera su marido?
b Le pidió que cuidara a los niños.
c En aquel entonces no era normal que las mujeres trabajaran.
d Muchas mujeres no comían para que sus hijos no pasaran hambre.
e Vivían en esa casa sin que nadie supiera que existían.
f Todo el mundo salió antes de que llegara Juan.
g Sentimos mucho que no pudierais venir a la fiesta.
h No creíamos que no pasara nada y que cumpliera su palabra/promesa.
i No era natural que se comportaran de aquel modo.
j Quisiéramos que alguien nos explicara por qué lo hicieron.

5 **a** acabaras **b** os quedarais **c** fuera **d** acompañaras **e** ganara **f** ofrecieran **g** jugaran **h** se comportaran **i** dejaran **j** os encontrarais.

6 *The correct verbs are*: **a** tuviera **b** fumaras **c** pudiéramos **d** dijera **e** vinieran **f** pidiera **g** vivierais **h** fuera **i** supiera **j** se jubilara.

• Key 16: The pluperfect subjunctive and conditional perfect

Only the **-ra** *form of the pluperfect subjunctive is given in the answers.*

1 **a** hubieran dado **b** hubieran venido **c** hubiera comprado; hubiéramos vivido **d** hubiera heredado **e** hubieras traído **f** hubiéramos visto **g** hubieras ganado **h** hubiera pasado **i** hubiera complacido **j** hubierais venido; hubierais alegrado.

2 **a** Si hubiera sabido que llovía tanto, me habría/hubiera traído un impermeable.
b Si me hubiera quedado, me habría/hubiera encontrado con el cineasta.
c Si hubiera hecho buen tiempo, habríamos/hubiéramos salido de excursión.
d Se lo habría/hubiera dicho si hubieran venido.

e Habrían/hubieran acudido a la cita si alguien les hubiera avisado.
f Te habría/hubiera salido bien si me hubieras hecho caso.
g Si Joaquín hubiera mirado al retrovisor, no hubiera tenido el accidente.
h Si no hubiera quedado algo de comida de la fiesta, hubiéramos pasado hambre.
i Te hubieran limpiado los zapatos si los hubieras dejado en la puerta.
j Si hubiera visto a Genoveva, me hubiera enterado de la reunión.

3 **a** De haberlo sabido **b** De haberlo hecho de otra forma **c** De habérmelo dicho **d** De haberse dado cuenta **e** de haberse consolidado el golpe de estado **f** De haber seguido mis instrucciones **g** De no haberme echado una mano **h** De habernos dicho algo **i** De haber existido una salida **j** De haberle pedido consejo.

4 **a** Si tuviera tiempo, iría al cine.
b Si hubiera tenido tiempo, habría/hubiera ido al cine.
c Si lo hiciera, me arrepentiría.
d Si lo hubiera hecho, me habría/hubiera arrepentido.
e Si fuéramos ricos, te llevaríamos de viaje.
f Si hubiéramos sido ricos, te habríamos/hubiéramos llevado de viaje.
g Si leyeran más libros, entenderían más.
h Si hubieran leído más libros, habrían/hubieran entendido mucho más.
i Cuando lo vi, no hubiera creído que estaba enfermo.
j Andrea hubiera venido antes si no hubiera tenido que esperar a Paco.
k No hubieras dicho que podríamos hablar con él si no viniera.
l Si Miguel no se hubiera ido/marchado en aquel mismo instante/momento, no hubiera dado/se hubiera encontrado/topado con Basilio y todo sería diferente ahora.

• Key 17: The imperative

1 **a** pase/n; no pase/n **b** léalo/léanlo; no lo lea/n **c** oiga/n; no oiga/n **d** siéntese/siéntense; no se siente/n **e** tenga/n; no tenga/n **f** venga/n; no venga/n **g** pruébelo/pruébenlo; no lo pruebe/n **h** sea/n; no sea/n **i** salga/n; no salga/n **j** déselo/dénselo; no se lo dé/den; **k** márchese/márchense; no se marche/n **l** póngaselas/pónganselas; no se las ponga/n.

2 **a** mira; no mires **b** acuéstate; no te acuestes **c** apréndelo; no lo aprendas **d** dámela; no me la des **e** hazlo; no lo hagas **f** dinos; no nos digas **g** póntelos; no te los pongas **h** vete; no te vayas **i** sube; no subas **j** bébelo; no lo bebas **k** guárdala; no la guardes **l** tráelos; no los traigas.

3 **a** mirad; no miréis **b** acostaos; no os acostéis **c** aprendedlo; no lo aprendáis **d** dádmela; no me la deis **e** hacedlo; no lo hagáis **f** decidnos; no nos digáis **g** ponéoslos; no os los pongáis **h** idos; no os vayáis **i** subid; no subáis **j** bebedlo; no lo bebáis **k** guardadla; no la guardéis **l** traedlos; no los traigáis.

4 **a** empecemos **b** nos enfademos **c** leamos **d** sentémonos **e** nos acostemos **f** sigamos **g** pongámosla **h** volvamos **i** vámonos **j** lo hagamos.

5 **a** Procura **b** Utiliza **c** No uses **d** Cuida **e** Destaca **f** No mientas **g** No lo escribas **h** No mandes **i** No incluyas **j** Recuerda firmarlo.

6a

1. . . . Ejerced vuestro rol de forjador . . .
2. . . . Procurad . . .
3. . . . Ahorrad la cantidad que usáis al ducharos, al lavaros los dientes . . .
4. . . . Plantad . . . y cuidad todos los que hay a vuestro alrededor . . .
5. . . . Elegid . . . procurando reducir la cantidad de desechos que generáis.
6. La energía que cuidáis y ahorráis hoy, os será útil mañana. Apagad . . .

7. . . . Evitad . . . cuando escuchéis música.
8. Vuestra casa . . . Cuidad . . . y que uséis . . .
9. . . . Cuidad . . . no contaminéis . . . y proteged . . .
10. . . . Escoged . . .

7 **1.** Respeten . . . **2.** Prescindan . . . **3.** No utilicen . . . **4.** No manipulen . . . **5.** Vigilen . . . **6.** Prescindan . . . **7.** No frecuenten . . . **8.** Mantengan . . . bajen **9.** Respeten . . . **10.** Exijan . . .

• Key 18: Articles

0 = no article, definite or indefinite, needed.

1 **a** los; la; la; 0 **b** la; los **c** la **d** del; el **e** la; la **f** 0 **g** el; la **h** la; el; 0 **i** los; la **j** el; el; la **k** el; las **l** la; el **m** los; el **n** el; el **o** la.

2 **a** El consumo de alcohol es frecuente entre la juventud de hoy.
b Las mujeres también beben más que antes.
c Más del cuarenta por ciento de los jóvenes bebe los fines de semana.
d La cerveza es una bebida popular.
e Ramón, el mejor amigo de José, empezó a beber a los doce años.
f Ahora las chicas beben tanto como los chicos.
g Se están tomando medidas para prevenir la publicidad de alcohol cerca de los colegios.
h No se podrán comprar bebidas alcohólicas en las tiendas entre las diez de la noche y las ocho de la mañana.
i El doctor Justino León piensa que el paro causa muchos problemas incluído el alcoholismo.
j Su colega, la doctora Maribel Osuna afirma que la ociosidad acorta la vida mientras el trabajo y la dieta la alargan.
k Las estadísticas demuestran que el ciclismo y la natación son buenos para la salud.
l Con la llegada de la primavera, la gente empieza a pensar en actividades al aire libre.

3 **a** Lo importante . . . **b** . . . lo bonitos . . . **c** Lo mío es mío y lo suyo es suyo **d** Lo bueno . . . lo mezquina . . . **e** . . . lo picante . . . lo dulce. **f** . . . de lo tarde . . . **g** Lo cierto es . . . **h** . . . antes de lo normal. **i** Lo fácil . . . lo dura . . . **j** . . . todo lo posible . . .

4 **a** No te imaginas lo guapa que es. **b** No quiero contarte lo mala que era la película. **c** Lo mejor es esperar. **d** Viene lo interesante. **e** Lo difícil no era tan difícil. **f** Lo fácil está por venir. **g** ¿Tienes idea de lo tramposo/engañoso que es? **h** No me di cuenta de lo caros que son sus gustos. **i** Lo más caro no es siempre lo mejor. **j** A Amelia no le gusta la propensión de su marido por lo ostentoso.

5 **a** 0; un **b** 0; 0 **c** una; 0 **d** 0 **e** una **f** una **g** 0 **h** un; un; 0 **i** 0; 0; 0 **j** 0; un **k** 0; uno **l** 0 **m** 0; 0 **n** una; un **o** una; una.

6 **a** Paco era un ingeniero muy bueno. **b** Cierto joven preguntaba por ti. **c** No quiero repetir tal experiencia. **d** ¡Qué ruido! Salimos después de media hora. **e** Jules es francés, es médico y no tiene novia. **f** Y otra cosa – siempre lleva anillo. **g** ¿Tienes corbata? Te hará falta una esta noche para la recepción. **h** Ha pasado año y medio desde nuestro último encuentro. **i** ¡Qué pareja! Uno/a era pedante y el otro/la otra un/a auténtico/a idiota. **j** Un buen libro es un buen/verdadero tesoro. *'Cien años de soledad'* de Gabriel García Márquez es uno de esos libros.

7 **a** el; unos; la; una; el; el; el; un; 0; 0; 0; 0; una; el; 0; el; lo; el; el; una.
b los; las; 0; un; el; la; un; un; 0; el; el; 0/unas; 0; el; el; los; la; el; 0; 0; la; un; la; el; los; el; un.
c los; el; una; 0; el; la; la; el; 0; 0; un; la; la; una; 0; 0; la.
el; el; la; la; el; 0; al.
el; la; la; la.
el; el; el.
las; un; un; el; un.

• Key 19: Nouns

1 *f = feminine; m = masculine*
a f **b** f **c** m **d** m **e** f **f** m **g** m **h** m **i** f **j** m **k** f **l** f **m** m **n** f **o** m **p** f.

2 norma; víctima; trama; cima; arma.

3 bronce; peine; fraude; aire; cine; parque; este; azote; auge; alambre; bigote; coche.

4

catedral (f)	pan (m)	noche (f)	nariz (f)	planeta (m)
luz (f)	dólar (m)	día (m)	agua (f)	estrés (m)
garaje (m)	ciudad (f)	régimen (m)	lesión (f)	césped (m)
deber (m)	labor (f)	sur (m)	flor (f)	porvenir (m)
valor (m)	énfasis (m)	sol (m)	mes (m)	tarde (f)
virtud (f)	imagen (f)	mapa (m)	cárcel (f)	sed (f)
albaricoque (m)	aire (m)	lunes (m)	niñez (f)	multitud (f)
hambre (f)	caos (m)	altavoz (m)	muelle (m)	automóvil (m)
red (f)	lid (f)	póster (m)	zaguán (m)	riñón (m)
jersey (m)	autocar (m)	carril (m)	combustible (m)	nuez (f)

5 bares; lápices; crisis; hoteles; paraguas; deberes; exámenes; orígenes; franceses; naciones; altavoces; órdenes; meses; pies; países; cuartos de baño; análisis; miércoles; bueyes; leyes; menús; tribus; esquíes; marroquíes.

6 región; avión; quehacer; inglés; col; joven; luz; sofá; convoy; carácter; record; rubí; virgen; ilusión; violín; imagen; pez; portavoz; patín; rehén; alemán; revés; cómplice; mártir.

7

el rompecabezas	**los** alrededores	**las** tinieblas
los comicios	**el** guardaespaldas	**el** portaaviones
los celos	**los** bienes	**los** prismáticos
el saltamontes	**los** víveres	**las** gafas
los enseres	**el** limpiabotas	**el** parabrisas
el pintalabios	**las** vacaciones	**las** expensas
los añicos	**el** salvavidas	**las** cosquillas
los restos	**el** abrelatas	**el** cumpleaños
el/la cuentacuentos	**el** portaequipajes	**las** nupcias
el posavasos	**los** cimientos	**las** afueras

8 **a** madre **b** mujer **c** alcaldesa **d** princesa **e** hembra **f** vaca **g** heroína **h** profesora **i** actriz **j** emperatriz **k** poetisa **l** reina **m** traductora **n** escritora **o** yegua **p** presidenta.

9 **a** harbour; door **b** book; pound (money/weight) **c** point/spot; tip/end **d** duck; leg **e** payment; wages **f** injured person; wound **g** section, stretch (e.g. of road, time); plot, weft **h** river; estuary, firth **i** bank; banking **j** orange tree; orange (fruit).

10 **a** capital – money; capital – city **b** guide – person; guide – book **c** future; morning **d** order – arrangement; order – command/religious, military order **e** priest; cure **f** policeman; police force **g** front; forehead **h** report, bulletin; part, section **i** comet; kite **j** cholera; rage, anger **k** cut; court **l** earring; slope.

• Key 20: Adjectives

1 **a** *1st paragraph:* incaic**os**; andin**os**; avanzad**a**; montaños**a**; inhóspit**a**; anterior**es**; incaic**a**; ric**as**; interesant**es**.
2nd paragraph: imposibl**es**; incaic**os**; principal**es**; buen**as**; extrem**o**; sureñ**as**.
3rd paragraph: cubiert**os**; larg**o**; peligros**o**; español**es**; cansad**os**, hambrient**os**; temeros**os**; suntuos**os**; pasmad**os**.

b *1st paragraph:* intrépid**a**; aleman**a**; reconocid**o**.
2nd paragraph: motorizad**o**; siguient**es**; motorizad**os**; cort**os**; experimental**es**; algun**o**.
3rd paragraph: económic**a**; pésim**a**; abatid**o**; dispuest**a**; ayudad**a**; dormid**o**; valient**e**; aventurer**o**; históric**o**.
4th paragraph: grand**es**; montaños**as**; guiad**os**; últim**as**.
5th paragraph: atrevid**a**; emprendedor**a**; vari**os**; mecánic**os**; inherent**es**; rudimentari**o**; lujos**as**; actual**es**.
6th paragraph: primer**os**; fabricad**os**; nuev**os**; lujos**os**; mayor**es**; tecnológic**os**; aleman**a**; mism**a**; nuev**o**; revolucionari**o**.

2 **a** Cordobesas; **b** pescadora; protegida **c** izquierda **d** tremenda **e** pequeña **f** encantadora **g** polaca; **h** perdida; **i** plásticas; **j** metropolitana.

3 **a** trabajadora **b** dormilonas **c** juveniles **d** parlanchina **e** holgazán **f** felices **g** burlón **h** mayores **i** azules **j** alemana **k** rosa **l** españoles.

4 *The correct elements are:*
a restaurante italiano **b** tercer **c** buen **d** algún **e** una casa grande; playa privada **f** el primero **g** mala **h** la tercera **i** algún **j** gran **k** palacio real **l** primer.

5 Burgos, antigu**a** capital de Castilla, está situad**a** en el norte de España entre Madrid y Santander. Es una ciudad muy histórica y por eso turístic**a**. Su principal monumento es la catedral, una de las más bella**s** y representativa**s** del páis. Aquí está enterrado Rodrigo Díaz de Vivar que era un noble de la corte castellan**a** a finales del siglo XI y cuya vida está inmortalizad**a** en "El Cantar de Mío Cid", uno de los poemas épic**os** más importante**s** de la literatura medieval españo**la**.

El poema narra la historia de este héroe desde su destierro forzado de Castilla hasta su muerte en Valencia, y cómo, por sus hazañas guerrer**as**, llegó a ser rico, famoso y poderoso, temido y respetado por sus enemigos, ya moros ya cristianos.

La recién inaugurad**a** Ruta del Cid nos permite seguir los pasos de este guerrero atrevido desde su salida lacrimos**a** de Burgos cuando, ya en las afueras, se volvió para contemplar por últim**a** vez esta ciudad tan hermos**a**.

6 **a** revolucionario **b** español **c** viejos **d** machistas **e** nuevo **f** algunos **g** buena **h** libre **i** nuevo **j** guapo **k** solos **l** muchas **m** jóvenes **n** mayor.

7 **a** Parece increíble que una civilización que no conocía la rueda pudiera ser tan avanzada, pero la civilización Inca fue altamente/sumamente desarrollada en todos los aspectos.
b Sus carreteras que atravesaban/cruzaban montañas altas y valles profundos, fueron mantenidas por un pequeño ejército de ingenieros, y por eso siempre estaban en buenas condiciones.
c Sus terrazas famosas, regadas por un extenso sistema de canales, convirtieron las laderas empinadas de las montañas en campos fértiles.
d Sin la ayuda de maquinaria sofisticada pero con una técnica perfecta, construyeron grandes edificios de piedras enormes.
e Sus artesanos utilizaban la lana de la llama y la vicuña para tejer telas exquisitas, y con el oro y la plata fabricaban ornamentos/adornos y joyas intrincados y bellísimos.
f El coche moderno tiene poco en común con los pequeños coches negros fabricados por el señor Benz y el señor Ford.

g Hoy (en) día una amplia gama de coches nuevos y usados nos permite elegir un coche apropiado para/acorde con nuestras necesidades.
h Algunos coches como el legendario Beetle de Volkswagen, cuentan hoy día/ahora con una mecánica moderna y eficiente pero mantienen las formas de los modelos originales.
i La competencia entre los fabricantes de automóviles/coches es feroz y el gran reto/desafío de los diseñadores es ser creativo, imaginativo y visionario.
j Los coches del futuro serán limpios, es decir respetuosos con el medio ambiente, serán 'inteligentes', capaces de tomar sus propias decisiones y serán personalizados.

• Key 21: Adverbs

1 **a** perfectamente **b** inmediatamente **c** automáticamente **d** ligeramente **e** preferentemente **f** cortésmente; correctamente **g** absolutamente **h** franca y sinceramente **i** rápida y concienzudamente **j** últimamente; completamente **k** lenta y prudentemente **l** definitivamente.

2 **a** por supuesto **b** con tristeza **c** por último **d** por cierto **e** con dificultad **f** sin duda **g** de costumbre **h** en efecto **i** en secreto **j** por lo general.

3 **a** con facilidad **b** tan en serio/con tanta seriedad **c** con ferocidad **d** con mucha/con gran amabilidad **e** con prudencia/de una manera prudente **f** por desgracia **g** con cautela/de una manera cautelosa **h** en vano **i** a menudo/con frecuencia **j** de repente **k** por separado **l** de una manera razonable.

4 **a** De repente/repentinamente/de súbito/súbitamente se abrió la puerta y Jorge entró.
b Hay que empaquetar el florero/jarrón cuidadosamente/con cuidado.
c Compartió generosamente todo lo que tenía, que era poco.
d Inés le escribió a Rodrigo y él respondió/contestó inmediatamente/de inmediato con una carta preciosa.
e Sin duda/indudablemente es una buena idea dar el primer paso.
f De veras/en verdad/verdaderamente es una pena que las cosas sean como son.
g Cuando le hicieron la pregunta, Gabriel dijo secamente: 'No sé nada de eso'.
h Durante la dictadura, Felipe entró clandestinamente/en secreto/secretamente en el país tres o cuatro veces.
i Generalmente/por lo general los jóvenes ya no se marchan de casa cuando terminan los estudios.
j El tiovivo empezó a girar con lentitud/lentamente primero, luego muy rápidamente/vertiginosamente.

5 **a** arriba; abajo **b** encima **c** delante; detrás **d** lejos; cerca/aquí **e** fuera **f** dentro **g** aquí; ahí **h** aquí; atrás **i** lejos; lejos; aquí **j** allí **k** adelante **l** debajo.

6 Antes; ahora; nunca; siempre; aún; hoy; ayer; mañana.

7 **a** bastante/muy; mucho; más **b** tanto **c** mucho; más; demasiado **d** tanto; mucho; demasiado **e** muy/bastante; tan.

8 **a** Mañana saldremos temprano.
b Teresa leyó mucho cuando estuvo de vacaciones.
c Hoy en día no es nada fácil conseguir/encontrar un trabajo/un puesto de trabajo.
d Paco estaba bastante enfermo cuando lo vimos ayer.
e El coche de delante iba tan despacio que por poco/casi choqué con él.
f Nunca descubrí/no descubrí nunca su secreto, ni siquiera cuando se murió.
g Primero haremos las maletas, luego comeremos y después saldremos/nos iremos/nos pondremos en marcha.
h Caminan/andan demasiado lento/lentamente; no llegarán nunca.
i Lo hizo bastante deprisa pero no lo hizo mal.
j ¡No comas más y sube aquí!

• Key 22: Comparison

1 **a** . . . es más sabrosa que . . . **b** . . . es mejor/peor que . . . **c** . . . son más racistas que . . . **d** . . . piensan menos en el dinero que . . . **e** . . . comen menos pescado que . . . **f** . . . es peor que . . . **g** . . . son más anchas que . . . **h** . . . son más pequeños que . . . **i** . . . son más potentes que . . . **j** . . . son menos agrias que . . .

2 **a** de **b** de **c** que **d** del que **e** del que **f** de **g** que **h** de lo que **i** de lo que **j** del que **k** que **l** de la que **m** que **n** de la que **o** de

3 **a** tan caro como **b** tan buena como **c** tanto café como **d** tanta verdura/tantas verduras como **e** tantas oportunidades como **f** tanta experiencia como **g** tanto como **h** tan ambiciosos como **i** tan bien como **j** tan a menudo como **k** tan rápido/deprisa como **l** tan tarde como **m** tan difícil como **n** tanta suerte como **o** tan cómodo como.

4 **a** Son dulcísimas. **b** Es riquísima. **c** Es carísimo. **d** Es larguísimo. **e** Son antiquísimas. **f** Es profundísimo. **g** Es inteligentísima. **h** Vive cerquísimo. **i** Es dificilísimo. **j** Son simpatiquísimas.

5 **a** la mejor **b** la mayor cantidad **c** los más obesos/gordos **d** la comida más importante **e** la mujer más vieja **f** el día más largo **g** la montaña más alta **h** los libros más interesantes **i** las botas más caras; de la mejor calidad.

• Key 23: Demonstratives

1 **a** esta **b** estos **c** este; esta **d** esta **e** este **f** estas **g** estos **h** este **i** este **j** esta **k** estas **l** estos.

2 **a** ese **b** esos **c** esas **d** ese **e** esas **f** esa **g** esos **h** esa **i** esos **j** ese **k** esas **l** esa.

3 **a** aquellos **b** aquel **c** aquellas **d** aquella **e** aquella **f** aquel **g** aquellos **h** aquellas, **i** aquel **j** aquellos **k** aquella **l** aquel.

4 **a** este **b** ese **c** aquellos **d** esa **e** esta **f** esos **g** estos **h** aquella **i** ese **j** aquella **k** este **l** aquel.

5 **a** este **b** esa **c** esta **d** esos/aquellos **e** este **f** aquella **g** esos/aquellos; este **h** estas **i** estas **j** ese/aquel **k** ese/aquel **l** este.

6 **a** Esto no es difícil. **b** He leído este libro antes. **c** ¿Puedo/podría probarme estos zapatos? **d** En ese preciso momento no había nadie en casa. **e** Esto no me gusta nada. **f** Esos/aquellos bolígrafos escriben mejor que estos. **g** Me acuerdo perfectamente de aquellos tiempos. Aquellos eran tiempos felices. **h** ¿Por qué has dejado aquí todo esto? **i** Aquel verano no dejó de llover ni un solo día/llovió todos los días sin excepción. **j** No sé por qué lo hicieron de esa manera/ese modo. **k** Hay que tomar esa calle a la derecha. **l** ¿Quieres ver esta película o no?

• Key 24: Possessives

1 **a** Mi escritorio es muy viejo. **b** Su hermana es médica. **c** Tus amigos son muy simpáticos. **d** Su habitación está reservada. **e** Nuestra casa es muy moderna. **f** Sus billetes están en la mesa. **g** Vuestro coche es muy cómodo. **h** Sus ideas son muy buenas. **i** Nuestros libros son muy interesantes. **j** Su opinión de Gonzalo es muy mala. **k** Nuestro jardín es grande. **l** Su trabajo es muy aburrido. **m** Vuestras hijas son muy majas. **n** Mis chaquetas son de piel. **o** Tu marido es maravilloso.

2 **a** tuyos **b** suyo **c** nuestras **d** míos **e** suya **f** nuestros **g** vuestras **h** mío **i** mía; suya *or vice versa* **j** tuyos; míos **k** suyos **l** nuestro.

3 **a** el suyo **b** el mío **c** la nuestra **d** el suyo **e** la mía **f** los suyos **g** los vuestros **h** las mías **i** las nuestras **j** el vuestro **k** el mío **l** los tuyos **m** del suyo **n** la suya **o** la nuestra; la vuestra; la vuestra; la nuestra.

4 **a** Se quitó el abrigo y se puso la chaqueta. **b** ¿Dónde he puesto el pasaporte? **c** ¿Me da su número de teléfono? **d** Sacó el dinero del bolsillo. **e** Me duele el estómago. **f** Me gustó su piso. **g** Hablamos de los hijos/nuestros hijos. **h** ¿Te has cortado el dedo? **i** ¿Por qué no nos presentó a su amigo/a? **j** Se quitó los zapatos porque le dolían los pies. **k** ¿Te has hecho daño en la mano / ¿Te has lastimado la mano? **l** Colgaron los/sus abrigos en las perchas en su habitación. **m** Sus ojos eran azules y su pelo era rubio. / Tenía los ojos azules y el pelo rubio. **n** Abre el/la/tu bolso/bolsa y déjame ver tus cosas. **o** Metió la mano en la bolsa y sacó las llaves. **p** Vinieron a ver la/nuestra casa pero desgraciadamente/por desgracia ese día estábamos con los abuelos.

5 **a** mi; el suyo; su; su; su; mi; mis; nuestros.
b tus; la; mis; los míos; la; suyos; los suyos; tuyos.
c nuestra; las; nuestros; nuestra; su; suyos; nuestra; su.

• Key 25: Personal pronouns

1 **a** tú; yo; ella **b** vosotros **c** nosotros **d** usted **e** ellos/ustedes; nosotros **f** ustedes **g** ella **h** tú; yo; él **i** ustedes **j** vosotros **k** él; ella **l** yo; tú.

2 **a** La escribió el viernes. **b** Los vi el lunes pasado. **c** Las compro en el mercado. **d** No, no lo conozco. **e** Sí, las vendieron. **f** Ayer la llamé. **g** Lo he puesto en el estante. **h** No, todavía no la hemos probado. **i** Las sacaron anteayer. **j** Los metió en la caja fuerte. **k** Pepe lo trajo. **l** Mi amiga las tomó.

3 **a** Montse le regaló un collar. **b** La señora no me dio ninguna respuesta. **c** Te he preparado un café. **d** Nuestro padre os mandó una carta. **e** El jefe les ha explicado el problema. **f** Ellos no querían vendernos/no nos querían vender las tierras. **g** Yo siempre le digo la verdad. **h** Tenemos que darles los libros. / Les tenemos que dar los libros. **i** Les hicimos un gran favor. **j** Javier no quiso prestarle/le quiso prestar su coche. **k** Mañana nos van a enseñar/van a enseñarnos el piso. **l** Remedios siente no poderos traer/poder traeros un regalo.

4 **a** No me la dio. **b** Marta nos las mostró. **c** Roberto no os la ha hecho ¿verdad? **d** No te los puedo contar. **e** Me lo entregaron. **f** Pepe no quiere dármelas/no me las quiere dar. **g** ¿Por qué no os las quiso comprar/no quiso comprároslas? **h** Federico va a leérnoslos/nos los va a leer. **i** ¿Te los pongo en una cajita? **j** Me las narró con todo detalle. **k** Van a ofrecérmelo. / Me lo van a ofrecer. **l** Han dicho que no os los pueden traer/pueden traéroslos hasta pasado mañana.

5 **a** El guía se la explicó. **b** La señora no quería vendérselas/no se las quería vender. **c** Se lo recomendé. **d** Carlos se las va a pedir/va a pedírselas. **e** No pensaba devolvérselo. **f** ¿Se los pasaste? **g** Olvidé traérselos. **h** ¿Se lo has recomendado? **i** ¿Por qué no querías dárselo/se lo querías dar? **j** ¿Cuándo se la dejaste? **k** Tuvimos que llevársela / Se la tuvimos que llevar. **l** Se las dieron anoche.

6 Cuando Emilio cumplió los diez años, su madre decidió comprar**le** una mascota. Con la mascota **(él)** aprendería a ser responsable. Una compañera de trabajo **le** aconsejó que fuera a un refugio y como sabía mucho de perros **la** acompañó para ayudar**la** a escoger la futura mascota de Emilio.

¡Qué emoción sintió Emilio cuando vio al perro en los brazos de su madre! En seguida quería jugar con **él**, pero su madre **le** advirtió:

– Este perro no es un juguete, es un ser vivo y **(tú)** tienes que cuidar**lo** bien. Voy a explicar**te** lo que tienes que hacer. Primero tienes que dar**le** de comer dos veces al día, luego hay que cepillar**lo** a diario y dar**le** un baño cada dos semanas. ¿Entendido?
– Sí, mamá, pero también puedo sacar**lo** de paseo ¿no? ¿Ya tiene nombre?
– No, hijo. Puedes dar**le** un nombre, uno que te guste. Y mañana **lo** llevamos al veterinario.

Al día siguiente, mientras **le** ponía al perro sus inyecciones, la veterinaria **le** dijo a Emilio:

– ¿Sabes que un perro nunca olvida las lecciones que aprende, así que **(tú)** tienes que educar**lo**? Por ejemplo, cuando **lo** saques de paseo es muy importante que salgas **tú** primero y que **él te** siga. **Él** tiene que obedecer**te** siempre, así aprende que **tú** eres el amo y **él** es tu compañero fiel. Sería una buena idea que te apuntaras a unas clases. ¿Ya tiene nombre?
– Sí, voy a llamar**lo** Tintín. A propósito ¿es perro o perra?

7 *1st paragraph:* lo; pensarlo; lo; mí; comprarlo; regalármelo; él; le/lo.
2nd paragraph: le; haberlo; mí; yo; me; meterme; él; lo.
3rd paragraph: les; os; cálmate; me; nos; siéntate; escúchala; te; tú.

8 **a** ¿Quién te dio este reloj? Nadie me lo dio; lo encontré.
b No puedo darle/no le puedo dar el dinero hoy; se lo daré mañana.
c ¿Los/las has visitado antes? Entre tú y yo, no son muy amables.
d Todos te han dado/todo el mundo te ha dado algo menos ella.
e Niños, os daré los guantes; ponéoslos para salir.
f Señor, señora, ¿en qué puedo ayudarles?
g Su esposo la escuchaba mientras ella le servía la cena.
h 'Os invitaré a un café' es lo que nos dijo Ricardo.
i Según él, nos van a cobrar 100 euros por esta consulta.
j Aunque a ti no te gusta el jazz, a él le gusta/a él sí y a mí también. Él vendrá conmigo/me acompañará al concierto el sábado.
k Hice con las naranjas lo que me pediste. Se las di a la madre de Carmen.
l No llego a entender por qué (él) no le ha dado el anillo (a ella). Lo escogió ella y al día siguiente él fue a comprárselo pero ella todavía no lo ha recibido/no lo tiene.

• Key 26: Relative pronouns

1 **a** El castillo que está en el puerto data del siglo XVI.
b Encontramos una pensión que nos hizo recordar Santo Domingo.
c La camarera que nos sirvió era muy antipática.
d El hombre que contestó al teléfono me dijo que estabas fuera.
e Devuélveme la grabadora que te dejé prestada.
f El restaurante al que te llevé en octubre está cerrado ahora.
g Aquellos son los vecinos de los que me quejo.
h Me escribió una carta en (la) que me explicó todo.
i La chica que fue lesionada está en el hospital.
j La mujer que viste ayer era mi amiga Consuelo.
k ¿Has encontrado la estilográfica con la que tu tía escribió novelas?
l El sarampión es una enfermedad peligrosa de la que hay que protegerse.

2 **a** quien **b** que **c** quien **d** que **e** que **f** que **g** quien **h** que **i** que **j** quien **k** lo que **l** quien.

3 **a** enfrente de la cual **b** del que **c** debajo de los cuales **d** por los que **e** en (la) que **f** encima del cual **g** para la que **h** entre los que **i** debajo del que/cual **j** enfrente/detrás del que/cual **k** detrás de la que **l** por las que.

4 **a** lo que **b** lo que **c** que **d** lo que; lo que **e** que; que **f** lo que **g** que **h** lo que **i** lo que; lo que **j** lo que; que **k** lo que; que **l** lo que; que.

5 **a** cuyos **b** cuya **c** cuyo **d** cuyas **e** cuya **f** cuyos **g** cuyos **h** cuyo **i** cuya **j** cuyos **k** cuya **l** cuyos.

6 **a** La excavación por paleontólogos y arqueólogos de Atapuerca, que está en la sierra de Burgos, empezó en los años 70 del siglo XX.
b En Atapuerca se han descubierto fósiles humanos que pertenecen a seis individuos diferentes.

c Los seis individuos, cuyos restos tienen unos 800.000 años de antigüedad, podrían haber sido los europeos más antiguos.
d No se parecen a otros fósiles humanos encontrados en Europa, lo que revoluciona las teorías convencionales sobre la evolución de *Homo sapiens.*
e El equipo investigador le puso a esta nueva especie el nombre de *Homo antecessor* cuyo significado en latín es pionero.
f Han usado técnicas geofísicas avanzadas que han permitido una datación precisa del yacimiento de los fósiles.
g En los huesos de *Homo antecessor* hay marcas por las que sabemos que era caníbal.
h Los jóvenes arqueólogos que han hecho las tesis y cuya labor es de sumo interés general, necesitan ayuda económica para poder seguir trabajando.
i Una de las empresas pequeñas que hoy en día promocionan su comercio en Internet es Frutafresca.com.
j Es un negocio hortofrutícola familiar de Valencia cuyos propietarios, Fernando y sus hijos Javier y Jorge, no querían dejar de recolectar los cultivos de modo artesanal.
k Por ejemplo, recogen las naranjas en su punto idóneo de maduración, lo que no es habitual en la recogida de la fruta.
l Mientras Fernando y Javier están recolectando, Jorge está manejando un ordenador portátil en el que atiende pedidos de frutas remitidos de comercios, hoteles y restaurantes de todo el país.
m Jorge se encargó de diseñar la página *web* que tanta clientela ha atraído y de la que se siente muy orgulloso.
n La idea de llevar el producto directamente del productor al consumidor es lo que le atrae a Lorenzo, un cliente estimado.
o Lorenzo es propietario de una frutería que se encuentra en pleno centro de Madrid y en la que se vende solamente fruta fresca de la mejor calidad.
p La estrategia de Frutafresca.com, que Internet permite y con la que ha nacido, es ofrecer una recogida selectiva tan sólo 24 horas antes de que llegue a su destino.

• Key 27: Negation

1 **a** No hay nadie. **b** No tengo nada que hacer. **c** No hemos ido nunca/nunca hemos ido. **d** Tampoco voy. / No voy tampoco. **e** No he visto a ninguno de tus compañeros. **f** No voy a enseñarte ninguno de mis cuadros. **g** No quiero ni té ni café. **h** Todavía/Aún no tenemos los resultados. **i** No ponen nada. **j** No han traído ninguna. **k** Ya no. **l** A mí tampoco.

2 **a** Nunca tenía dinero. **b** Nadie acompañaba al concejal. **c** En esa tienda ni vendían bolígrafos. **d** Tampoco me ayudaron. **e** Nunca viene nadie. **f** Federica nunca entiende nada. **g** Yo tampoco entiendo nunca nada. **h** Ningún científico te lo podría explicar. **i** ¿Qué hacer si nadie nos lo explica? **j** Aunque vivimos en España, ninguno de mis hijos habla castellano. **k** Nada tenían que ver las instrucciones con el aparato. **l** No entiendo cómo puede ser que nunca haya acudido a un médico.

3 **a** nadie **b** nada **c** no; ninguna **d** no; nada **e** no; ninguna **f** no; sino **g** no; nada **h** no; ni; ni **i** no; sino **j** no; nada **k** no; nadie **l** no; nada; ni **m** no; sino **n** no; ni; ni.

4 **a** Nadie dejó nada en el monte.
b No nos desviamos nunca del sendero.
c En el grupo había fumadores y no fumadores.
d No tiramos ni colillas ni cerillas sin apagar.
e No encendimos hogueras tampoco.
f No hicimos ningún tipo de fuego fuera del área indicada.

g Nadie en el grupo sabía utilizar el fogón.
h Pasamos el día sin ver a nadie.
i No llovió pero tampoco hizo un día muy bueno.
j No volvimos a las ocho sino pasadas las once.
k Ninguno de nosotros sufrió un accidente.
l Pero nadie quiere repetir la experiencia tampoco.

5 **a** Pasé todo el día en casa sin hacer nada.
b Pablito nunca entiende nada.
c No me ha dado ningún tipo de ayuda.
d Lo que has escrito no está nada claro.
e No/Ni leen los periódicos ni escuchan las noticias en la radio.
f Todavía/Aún no tengo los resultados ni Jorge tampoco.
g Se marchó sin decir nada a nadie.
h Lo hizo sin dificultad/sin dificultad alguna.
i Elena ya no me escribe; dice que no tiene nada que contarme.
j Ninguno de estos lugares está lejos pero ninguno es muy/especialmente atractivo tampoco.
k Ni siquiera le ha dicho a Miguel que no quiere volver a verle nunca jamás.
l No va a la universidad este año sino el año que viene.

• Key 28: Prepositions

1 **a** Hoy no he visto **a** Juan. **c A** mi madre no le gusta que visite **a** la tía. **e** No oí **al** profesor. **f A** mis tíos les gusta ver **a** sus hijos progresar. **g** Pablo quiere mucho **a** Isabel. **i** . . . llamaron **a** Carmen. **j** . . . visité **a** Julio y Alejandra. **k** . . . oímos cantar **a** Montserrat Caballé. **l** Susana pegó **a** su hermano menor . . .

2 **a** de; a; de; a; hasta **b** desde/a; hasta **c** desde; hasta; de **d** de; a; de; de **e** de; de; de; hasta **f** desde; hasta; a; a **g** de/a; a; de **h** a; de; de; a **i** al; de **j** a; hasta; a; a **k** de; desde; hasta **l** desde; hasta; de; a; a.

3 **a** con **b** según; contra **c** con; sin **d** contra; hacia; con **e** según; hacia **f** sin; sin; sin **g** hacia **h** con; sin **i** con; según **j** contra; con **k** según; con; con; contra **l** contra/con; contra; con.

4 **a** sobre **b** en; sobre **c** entre; en **d** en; sobre **e** sobre **f** en/sobre; entre **g** entre; en **h** sobre **i** sobre; en **j** en; entre **k** en; entre; en **l** sobre; en; entre.

5 **a** bajo **b** excepto **c** ante **d** tras **e** ante **f** bajo **g** excepto **h** tras **i** bajo **j** bajo **k** ante **l** tras; tras.

6 **a** por **b** por **c** por **d** para; por **e** por; para **f** por; para **g** por **h** por; por; para **i** por **j** para; para **k** por **l** por.

7 **c** . . . por razones . . . **d** Voy por más café. **g** . . . por el trabajo de . . . **j** . . . por unos vaqueros. **k** . . . para la salud.

8 **a** de; de **b** con **c** al **d** en **e** de **f** a **g** con **h** de **i** de **j** en **k** a **l** a; a **m** en **n** de; de **o** por/en; con **p** de **q** a **r** en **s** de **t** de.

9 **a** 5 **b** 14 **c** 12 **d** 8 **e** 3 **f** 4 **g** 1 **h** 6 **i** 10 **j** 7 **k** 15 **l** 2 **m** 11 **n** 13 **o** 9.

10 **1 a** de **b** desde **c** en **d** para **e** en **f** con **g** a **h** de **i** a **j** en **k** por **l** por **m** con **n** de **o** contra **p** según **q** en.

2 a según **b** por **c** para **d** según **e** de **f** para **g** con **h** a **i** de **j** de **k** por **l** a **m** de **n** con **o** con **p** en **q** sobre **r** en **s** sin **t** por.

• Key 29: Conjunctions

1 **a** Jorge **y** Javier . . . **b** ¿ . . . el negro **o** el azul? **c** . . . Fernando **e** Isabel. **d** . . . Cecilia **e** Ignacio **pero** no pudieron. **e** . . . **ni** a Paco **ni** a Alejandro. **f** . . . siete **u** ocho veces **pero** . . . **g** . . . Alemania **e** Italia. **h** . . . **sino** sudamericanos también. **i** . . . vengan **sino** que vayan. **j** . . . **pero** salimos de paseo **y** . . . **k** Lo oímos **pero** no lo vimos. **l** Daniel **e** Ignacio corrieron mucho **y** bien **pero ni** el uno **ni** el otro . . .

2 **a** 8 **b** 10 **c** 9 **d** 5 **e** 7 **f** 3 **g** 1 **h** 2 **i** 6 **j** 4.

3
- **a** Leía el periódico mientras desayunaba.
- **b** Cuando estamos de vacaciones, nos gusta hacer algo cultural.
- **c** Tenemos que tener esto terminado antes de que vuelva el jefe.
- **d** No volveremos al trabajo hasta que el dinero se nos acabe.
- **e** Nos iremos al teatro después de que/cuando lleguen los abuelos.
- **f** No adelgazarás mientras sigas tan golosa.
- **g** Hay que pintar la casa antes de que venga el mal tiempo.
- **h** No me muevo de aquí hasta que salga Rodrigo Montalbán.
- **i** Nos acostamos después de cenar.
- **j** Hay que sacar las entradas antes de que las hayan vendido todas.
- **k** Jorge va a la panadería por el pan mientras nosotros compramos los fiambres.
- **l** Cuando te hayas decidido, ya será tarde.

4 **a** a pesar del **b** aunque **c** aunque **d** a pesar de **e** aunque **f** a pesar de **g** a pesar de **h** aunque **i** aunque **j** aunque **k** a pesar de **l** a pesar de.

5 **a** en caso de que venga **b** de modo que los vendió todos **c** Siempre que/con tal de que todo esté en orden **d** en el caso de que te haga falta/lo necesite **e** a menos que/a no ser que me envíen una invitación **f** para que conociera a Josefa **g** con tal de que progresara **h** de tal manera que lo entendimos todo **i** a no ser que/a menos que llueva **j** para que veáis el 'Guernica' de Picasso **k** siempre que tengamos tiempo y dinero **l** a no ser que tengas un compromiso previo.

6
- **a** que; porque; y; pero; pero; y; pero; porque; porque; sino; ni; ni.
- **b** pero, y; porque; sino; y; ya que.

7
- **a** Creo que podemos afirmar con toda seguridad que ni Juan ni José va a aprobar el examen.
- **b** Y eso a pesar de todo lo que han estudiado durante el curso/año.
- **c** Decidimos que nos irían a buscar en caso de que nos necesitaran.
- **d** Nos apoyarán/nos darán apoyo siempre que/con tal de que lo pidamos.
- **e** Nos alojamos en una pensión barata para que nos durara más el dinero.
- **f** Quedamos a las seis, pero llámame en caso de que no puedas venir.
- **g** Te dejaré/prestaré este libro siempre que me lo devuelvas cuando hayas terminado de leerlo.
- **h** Dijo que me devolvería el dinero que le dejé/presté antes de que fuera yo de vacaciones, pero no lo hizo.
- **i** No he visto hoy ni a Andrés ni a Enrique aunque dijeron que estarían aquí.
- **j** Dice que es feliz aunque sea pobre, ya que la felicidad no depende del dinero.
- **k** No salimos porque no llovía sino que nevaba.
- **l** Los guardias/policías lo detuvieron cuando aterrizó el avión porque estaba bebido/borracho y había estado molestando a los otros pasajeros.

• Key 30: Word order

1 a Vinieron los tíos, los primos y alguna otra persona más.
b Te ha llamado Susana.
c A unos dos kilómetros del pueblo se encuentra el castillo de Medina del Campo.
d Lo que más les gusta hacer es tomar el sol.
e Aquí la fruta que más se cultiva es la fresa. / Aquí la fresa es la fruta que más se cultiva.
f Al salir el sol nos pusimos en camino.
g Dando la vuelta al mundo tuve experiencias únicas.
h Lo mismo dice hoy que dirá mañana.
i No me gustan los mejillones.
j Todavía no he visto esa película.
k Más tarde se presentó otra dificultad.
l Al día siguiente tomamos el autocar a Chihuahua.
m Yo que tú no lo haría.
n Vienen muchos inmigrantes a trabajar en los campos freseros.
o En este barrio viven los desempleados y los necesitados.

2 a I didn't buy myself this car, my father bought it for me.
b They call these women the strawberry women.
c I can't stand that boy.
d You give geraniums very little water. / You water geraniums very little.
e I met my best friend at university.
f We are going to put all the books you see here in the library.
g I bought my girlfriend a gold necklace.
h The tourists didn't like the show at all.
i The boss has told me that he is thinking of taking early retirement.
j Young volunteers carry out all these jobs.
k You will get/They will give you the information you are looking for in the tourist office.
l Have you sent the parcel to Felipe or are you going to deliver it to him by hand?
m We were looking for those women for half an hour.
n Mr Márquez gave the speech and it was very witty/funny.
o We have sold the apartment we had in Ibiza to a neighbour.

3 a La respuesta la sabes muy bien.
b La verdad la dirás tú.
c Estos libros los compré en el Rastro.
d El problema no lo vamos a solucionar ahora.
e El amor de tu vida lo vas a encontrar cuando menos lo esperas.
f El dinero os lo darán el lunes.
g La casa nos la alquiló un colega.
h La teoría me la explicó el profesor de ciencias.
i Su colección de sellos no os la va a vender.
j Tu DVD te lo he devuelto ya.
k A Conchita le dieron el primer premio.
l A los que lo necesitaban les dio ayuda.
m A los compañeros de trabajo no les dijo nada.
n A mi amigo Jaime le pusieron una multa de 500 euros.
o A María le robaron el bolso.
p El paquete se lo entregué al policía.
q A nadie se lo hemos dado.
r El título se lo concedieron a los primeros 20 estudiantes.
s A sus amigos se lo cuenta todo.
t Los documentos se los entregué al encargado.

4 **a** También va María al concierto. / María también va al concierto.
b Siempre han venido aquí.
c De vez en cuando hay que/tenemos que pensar en el futuro.
d Termina pronto el trabajo.
e Una cosa así no se hace todos los días.
f Aquí decir la verdad sería difícil. / Decir la verdad aquí sería difícil.
g La verdad hay que buscarla/la tendrás que buscar en otra parte.
h A veces compro pan del supermercado.
i Después de eso no la volví a ver. / A ella no la volví a ver después de eso.
j Los pasaportes los guardamos/metemos en la caja de seguridad/la caja fuerte con los cheques de viaje.
k Las noches las podemos pasar tomando copas en las terrazas.
l Cada día me cuenta un poco más de su vida.

5 **a** Hace millones de años se produjo la extinción en masa de la mayoría de los dinosaurios que poblaban nuestro planeta. El fenómeno siempre ha fascinado a los científicos y existen varias hipótesis sobre su extinción de las que tres tienen una base en la realidad. La hipótesis de la caída de un meteorito es la más popular. De hecho hace unos 65 millones de años un meteorito, a una velocidad de hasta 250.000 kilómetros por hora, cayó y chocó contra la costa del golfo de México. Ocasionó terremotos y maremotos de gran magnitud, lanzando a la atmósfera una nube inmensa de polvo y fragmentos de roca. Al volver a la tierra la materia sólida incandescente provocó graves incendios y el polvo impidió la penetración de rayos solares durante meses. Las consecuencias para las plantas y los animales fueron graves. Sin embargo algunas especies como las aves y los reptiles sobrevivieron.

b A finales del siglo XX y a pesar del escepticismo de algunos científicos, se lanzó el telescopio espacial *Hubble* que proporcionaría imágenes diez veces más nítidas que las terrestres, y que haría posible detectar objetos hasta entonces desconocidos.

Como era de esperar, al principio hubo problemas con el telescopio y las fotografías que transmitió a la NASA eran borrosas. Sin embargo, el proyecto siguió gracias a los esfuerzos titánicos de unos científicos comprometidos, y el *Hubble* empezó a mandar las imágenes más lejanas del cosmos. En astronomía, cuanto más lejos se apunta el telescopio, más hacia atrás en el tiempo se viaja. Por tanto esas imágenes/Esas imágenes por tanto eran las más antiguas jamás conseguidas.

El estudio de las fotografías les ha dado muchas sorpresas a los investigadores que tienen acceso a ellas, y tienen que reformular constantemente sus teorías sobre la evolución del universo. Además se ha resucitado un interés más general en la exploración espacial y aunque de momento no haya señales fiables, puede que algún día encontremos vida fuera de la Tierra.

Consolidation exercises key

Analysis 1

1 *por más túneles que se hagan* (l. 4–5): subordinate clause of concession with *por . . . que* requires the subjunctive.
se efectúen (l. 9–10), *vivan; entren* (l. 12); *haya* (l. 15): subjunctive in the subordinate clause as the main clause verb expresses impossibility or necessity.
permita (l. 17), *saque* (l. 21): subjunctive used in a relative clause when the relative pronoun refers back to something indefinite.
lleve (l. 24), *prueben* (l. 28), *usen* (l. 31), *hagan* (l. 32): the verb in the subordinate clause must be subjunctive as the different subject of the main clause verb expresses a wish.

2 Add the endings of the present subjunctive to the stem of the first person singular of the indicative; for **-ar** verbs, add **-e**, **-es**, **-e**, etc., and for **-er** and **-ir** verbs, add **-a**, **-as**, **-a** etc. The irregular present tense subjunctive is *haya* from the verb *haber*.

3 *razonables* is qualifying three nouns so must be in the plural.

4 *Lo malo*: *lo* is used with an adjective to form an abstract noun.
lo: direct object pronoun referring to *el automóvil*.

5 *que alguien lo saque a la luz* (l. 21): *lo* refers to the car owner/potential public transport user.
lo han comprado, que prueben a usarlo (l. 28–29): *lo* refers to *el abono*.

6 ***se*** is used to express the passive.

Analysis 2

1 *Hay que. Hay que seguir trabajando* (l. 14–15), *hay que seleccionar . . . hacer presión* (l. 46–47), *hay que tener conciencia* (l. 48–49), *habrá que conservar* (l. 64–65).

2 *Hay que seguir trabajando*: we must continue working (l. 14–15).
la capa de ozono se está convirtiendo: the ozone layer is becoming (l. 15–16).
los países en vías de desarrollo continúan produciendo: developing countries are still producing (l. 31–33).
El tema del ozono . . . se va resolviendo: the ozone problem is slowly resolving itself (l. 55–56).

3 Present subjunctive after *para que*.
. . . para que el gobierno se dé cuenta . . . y tome medidas (l. 49–52).

4 The subjunctive is required here after a conjunction expressing time (*cuando*) in the future.

5 **a** The subjunctive is used here after the main clause verb expressing an emotion (concern).
b A passive construction *ser + past participle*: the past participle must agree with the noun it refers to, here *la capa de ozono*.

6 *se está convirtiendo* (l. 15–16), *el gobierno se dé cuenta* (l. 50), *se va resolviendo* (l. 56): *se* is a reflexive pronoun.
se usan (l. 25), *se pueden sustituir* (l. 26), *se han llevado a cabo* (l. 27–28): *se* expresses the passive.
se compra (l. 46–47): *se* is the impersonal pronoun.

7 *lo* is a neuter object pronoun referring to the previous clause: *continúan produciendo estas sustancias*.

8 *para dar cuenta* (l. 18), *para evitar* (l. 44): infinitive after a preposition.
Eliminar (l. 23), *la manera de vivir* (l. 64); infinitive functioning as a noun.

9 *sistema; periodista; problema; tema; planeta*.

Analysis 3

1 The writer is addressing the reader in the informal singular form *tú*.

2 Se is used here to avoid a passive construction: *son consideradas*.

3 Again the passive construction *ser + past participle* is avoided, this time by using the third person plural of the verb.

4 *Con dificultad*. Adverbial phrases are: *por separado* (l. 11); *con soltura* (l. 21–22); *con antelación* (l. 24); *por libre* (l. 37–38).

5 *Ir* – the infinitive is functioning as a noun. Similarly: *. . . contratar un viaje organizado que ir por libre*. (l. 37–38).
. . . te puede salir . . . – infinitive after modal verb *poder*. Further examples in the text are: *pueden significar* (l. 3), *suele ser* (l. 19), *sabes moverte* (l. 21), *no tener que ajustar* (l. 29), *podrás elegir* (l. 33), *Si quieres hacer* (l. 35).

6 Infinitive used after prepositions and prepositional phrases: *Además de conocer . . . y acceder* (l. 6–7), *antes de salir* (l. 32).
Infinitive following a verb, sometimes with a preposition: *te ayudarán a planear* (l. 8), *si prefieres contratar* (l. 11–12), *no dudes en contratarla* (l. 22–23).

7 *These are the changes that you should have made to the text.*

- Viaje . . .
- Elija . . . le ayudarán . . .
- Pida . . . si prefiere . . . que le cobran . . . ir en taxi le puede. . . .
- . . . Si es un viajero . . . sabe moverse . . . no dude . . .
- Haga su reserva . . . contrate en la propia agencia . . .
- Aproveche . . . si tiene la suerte de no tener que ajustar sus vacaciones . . . Pero tenga en cuenta . . . difícilmente podrá elegir el destino que más le guste.
- Si quiere hacer un 'tour' . . . siempre le saldrá . . .

Analysis 4

1 First three paragraphs, narrative context with time unspecified: imperfect tense. Paragraphs 4 and 5, actions completed within a time context: preterite tense.

2 *había doblado su frente* (l. 3), *el sol se había dejado* (l. 11).

3 *estar* to state position.

4 Preposition + verb in infinitive. Examples in the text: *sin gemir* (l. 1), *para caer* (l. 3), *para mirarla . . . tornaba a bajarlos* (l. 5), *comenzaban a envolver* (l. 8), *se acabó de borrar* (l. 10), *al morir* (l. 11), *comenzó a dibujarse* (l. 11–12).

5 *se* is functioning as a reflexive pronoun.

6 *como si hablase* (l. 15): imperfect subjunctive after *como si*.

7 Where the verb is in the infinitive form or a gerund, the object pronoun is written on to it.

8 Within a clause, the verb usually goes before the subject; also where the subject is longer than the verb, and for stylistic effect.

9 After a preposition the form of the relative pronoun is *el que*, *el cual* etc., the article being in agreement with the antecedent. Where the preposition is of three syllables or more, *el cual* etc. is the preferred relative pronoun.

Analysis 5

1 The direct object of the verb is a person.

2 *no me digas eso* (l. 4), *no me lo niegues* (l. 11): subjunctive is used for negative commands and the object pronouns precede the verb in the order indirect object, direct object.

3 *las mujeres* (l. 7): collective noun; *la cabeza* (l. 8): English would use a possessive; *la vida* (l. 8–9): abstract noun; *el Delfín* (l. 6): article used before a nickname.

4 Main clause verb expresses a wish with a different subject in the subordinate clause.

5 Preterite of the verb *morir*; *o* becomes *u* in third person singular and plural. *Dormir*: *durmió*; *durmieron*.

6 'You have been deceived, you have been well and truly conned.' This kind of English passive expression is best expressed in Spanish with the third person plural.

7 He is referring to his child.

8 *lo más común* (l. 9).

9 *Si desde el principio hubieras hablado conmigo* (l. 6): the pluperfect subjunctive is used to express an unfulfilled condition in the past – if you had spoken to me (but you did not).
la misma edad que tendría el mío si viviese (l. 15): conditional followed by the imperfect subjunctive in the 'if' clause. The unfulfilled condition relates to present time – the same age as mine would be if he were alive (but he is not).

Analysis 6

1 **a** *se juntaban* – verb used reflexively to mean 'to meet', so se is the reflexive pronoun.
los juntaban – verb used non-reflexively to mean 'to unite, bring together'. *Los* is the direct object pronoun 'them', standing for Abel and Joaquín.
b The subject pronoun is used to make it clear that the subject of *no sabían hablar* is Abel and Joaquín and not their wet nurses.

2 No. In *Aprendió cada uno de ellos a conocerse . . .*, *se* is a reflexive pronoun; in . . . *desde cuándo se conocían*, *se* is reciprocal.

3 'And' *y* becomes e when the following word begins with an *i*.

4 **a** The infinitive forms of the verb are functioning as nouns.
b '. . . no obedecer le importaba más que mandar'.
. . . *le importaba más no obedecer que mandar*. By putting the verb first and keeping the two infinitives *no obedecer* and *mandar*, which are being contrasted, close together, Unamuno focuses our attention on what mattered to Abel, which was not obeying rather than leading; this word order is very effective in telling us quite a bit about Abel's character.

5 . . . *como tú quieras* (l. 9) – Abel is using the subjunctive to say that whatever Joaquín's wishes may be, he will go along with them.
. . . *éste no quiere que vayamos al Pinar* (l. 14) – use of the subjunctive in the subordinate clause because of a change of subject.

6 . . . *parecía dominar e iniciarlo todo Joaquín* (l. 6–7), . . . *le decía Abel a Joaquín* . . . (l. 9).

Irregular and spelling-changing verbs

Irregular verbs

The following list includes only the most common irregular verbs. Only irregular forms are given. Verbs marked with an asterisk are also stem-changing.

abrir *to open*
past participle: abierto

andar *to walk*
preterite: anduve, anduviste, anduvo, anduvimos, anduvisteis, anduvieron
imperfect subjunctive: anduviera, anduvieras, anduviera, anduviéramos, anduvierais, anduvieran

caber *to fit, to be contained*
present indicative: (yo) quepo
preterite: cupe, cupiste, cupo, cupimos, cupisteis, cupieron
future: cabré, cabrás, cabrá, cabremos, cabréis, cabrán
conditional: cabría, cabrías, cabría, cabríamos, cabríais, cabrían
present subjunctive: quepa, quepas, quepa, quepamos, quepáis, quepan
imperfect subjunctive: cupiera, cupieras, cupiera, cupiéramos, cupierais, cupieran

conducir *to drive*
present indicative: (yo) conduzco
preterite: conduje, condujiste, condujo, condujimos, condujisteis, condujeron
present subjunctive: conduzca, conduzcas, conduzca, conduzcamos, conduzcáis, conduzcan
imperfect subjunctive: condujera, condujeras, condujera, condujéramos, condujerais, condujeran
imperative: (Vd.) conduzca, (nosotros) conduzcamos

dar *to give*
present indicative: (yo) doy
preterite: di, diste, dio, dimos, disteis, dieron
present subjunctive: dé, des, dé, demos, deis, den
imperfect subjunctive: diera, dieras, diera, diéramos, dierais, dieran
imperative: (Vd.) dé

decir* *to say*
present indicative: (yo) digo
preterite: dije, dijiste, dijo, dijimos, dijisteis, dijeron

future: diré, dirás, dirá, diremos, diréis, dirán

conditional: diría, dirías, diría, diríamos, diríais, dirían

present subjunctive: diga, digas, diga, digamos, digáis, digan

imperfect subjunctive: dijera, dijeras, dijera, dijéramos, dijerais, dijeran

imperative: (Vd.) diga, (tú) di (nosotros) digamos

gerund: diciendo

past participle: dicho

---

escribir *to write*

past participle: escrito

---

estar *to be*

present indicative: estoy, estás, está, estamos, estáis, están

preterite: estuve, estuviste, estuvo, estuvimos, estuvisteis, estuvieron

present subjunctive: esté, estés, esté, estemos, estéis, estén

imperfect subjunctive: estuviera, estuvieras, estuviera, estuviéramos, estuvierais, estuvieran

imperative: (Vd.) esté

---

haber *to have (auxiliary)*

present indicative: he, has, ha, hemos, habéis, han

preterite: hube, hubiste, hubo, hubimos, hubisteis, hubieron

future: habré, habrás, habrá, habremos, habréis, habrán

conditional: habría, habrías, habría, habríamos, habríais, habrían

present subjunctive: haya, hayas, haya, hayamos, hayáis, hayan

imperfect subjunctive: hubiera, hubieras, hubiera, hubiéramos, hubierais, hubieran

---

hacer *to do, make*

present indicative: (yo) hago

preterite: hice, hiciste, hizo, hicimos, hicisteis, hicieron

future: haré, harás, hará, haremos, haréis, harán

conditional: haría, harías, haría, haríamos, haríais, harían

present subjunctive: haga, hagas, haga, hagamos, hagáis, hagan

imperfect subjunctive: hiciera, hicieras, hiciera, hiciéramos, hicierais, hicieran

imperative: (Vd.) haga, (tú) haz, (nosotros) hagamos

---

ir *to go*

present indicative: voy, vas, va, vamos, vais, van

preterite: fui, fuiste, fue, fuimos, fuisteis, fueron

imperfect indicative: iba, ibas, iba, íbamos, ibais, iban

present subjunctive: vaya, vayas, vaya, vayamos, vayáis, vayan

imperfect subjunctive: fuera, fueras, fuera, fuéramos, fuerais, fueran

imperative: (Vd.) vaya, (tú) ve, (nosotros) vayamos

gerund: yendo

---

oír *to hear*

present indicative: oigo, oyes, oye, oímos, oís, oyen

preterite: (él, ella, Vd.) oyó, (ellos, ellas, Vds.) oyeron *present subjunctive*: oiga, oigas, oiga, oigamos, oigáis, oigan

imperfect subjunctive: oyera, oyeras, oyera, oyéramos, oyerais, oyeran

imperative: (Vd.) oiga, (tú) oye, (nosotros) oigamos

gerund: oyendo

---

poder* *to be able to, can*

preterite: pude, pudiste, pudo, pudimos, pudisteis, pudieron

future: podré, podrás, podrá, podremos, podréis, podrán

conditional: podría, podrías, podría, podríamos, podríais, podrían

imperfect subjunctive: pudiera, pudieras, pudiera, pudiéramos, pudierais, pudieran

---

poner *to put*

present indicative: (yo) pongo

preterite: puse, pusiste, puso, pusimos, pusisteis, pusieron

future: pondré, pondrás, pondrá, pondremos, pondréis, pondrán

conditional: pondría, pondrías, pondría, pondríamos, pondríais, pondrían

present subjunctive: ponga, pongas, ponga, pongamos, pongáis, pongan

imperfect subjunctive: pusiera, pusieras, pusiera, pusiéramos, pusierais, pusieran

imperative: (Vd.) ponga, (tú) pon, (nosotros) pongamos

past participle: puesto

---

querer* *to want, love*

preterite: quise, quisiste, quiso, quisimos, quisisteis, quisieron

future: querré, querrás, querrá, querremos, querréis, querrán

conditional: querría, querrías, querría, querríamos, querríais, querrían

imperfect subjunctive: quisiera, quisieras, quisiera, quisiéramos, quisierais, quisieran

---

saber *to know*

present indicative: (yo) sé

preterite: supe, supiste, supo, supimos, supisteis, supieron

future: sabré, sabrás, sabrá, sabremos, sabréis, sabrán

conditional: sabría, sabrías, sabría, sabríamos, sabríais, sabrían

present subjunctive: sepa, sepas, sepa, sepamos, sepáis, sepan

imperfect subjunctive: supiera, supieras, supiera, supiéramos, supierais, supieran

imperative: (Vd.) sepa, (nosotros) sepamos

---

salir *to go out*

present indicative: (yo) salgo

future: saldré, saldrás, saldrá, saldremos, saldréis, saldrán

conditional: saldría, saldrías, saldría, saldríamos, saldríais, saldrían

present subjunctive: salga, salgas, salga, salgamos, salgáis, salgan

imperative: (Vd.) salga, (tú) sal, (nosotros) salgamos

---

ser *to be*

present indicative: soy, eres, es, somos, sois, son

preterite: fui, fuiste, fue, fuimos, fuisteis, fueron

imperfect indicative: era, eras, era, éramos, erais, eran

present subjunctive: sea, seas, sea, seamos, seáis, sean

imperfect subjunctive: fuera, fueras, fuera, fuéramos, fuerais, fueran

imperative: (Vd.) sea, (tú) sé, (nosotros) seamos

tener* *to have*

present indicative: (yo) tengo

preterite: tuve, tuviste, tuvo, tuvimos, tuvisteis, tuvieron

future: tendré, tendrás, tendrá, tendremos, tendréis, tendrán

conditional: tendría, tendrías, tendría, tendríamos, tendríais, tendrían

present subjunctive: tenga, tengas, tenga, tengamos, tengáis, tengan

imperfect subjunctive: tuviera, tuvieras, tuviera, tuviéramos, tuvierais, tuvieran

imperative: (Vd.) tenga, (tú) ten, (nosotros) tengamos

traer *to bring*

present indicative: (yo) traigo

preterite: traje, trajiste, trajo, trajimos, trajisteis, trajeron

present subjunctive: traiga, traigas, traiga, traigamos, traigáis, traigan

imperfect subjunctive: trajera, trajeras, trajera, trajéramos, trajerais, trajeran

imperative: (Vd.) traiga, (nosotros) traigamos

gerund: trayendo

venir* *to come*

present indicative: (yo) vengo

preterite: vine, viniste, vino, vinimos, vinisteis, vinieron

future: vendré, vendrás, vendrá, vendremos, vendréis, vendrán

conditional: vendría, vendrías, vendría, vendríamos, vendríais, vendrían

present subjunctive: venga, vengas, venga, vengamos, vengáis, vengan

imperfect subjunctive: viniera, vinieras, viniera, viniéramos, vinierais, vinieran

imperative: (Vd.) venga, (tú) ven, (nosotros) vengamos

gerund: viniendo

ver *to see*

present indicative: (yo) veo

imperfect indicative: veía, veías, veía, veíamos, veíais, veían

present subjunctive: vea, veas, vea, veamos, veáis, vean

imperative: (Vd.) vea, (nosotros) veamos

past participle: visto

volver* *to come back*

past participle: vuelto

Spelling-changing verbs

Verbs derived from the ones below and most verbs with similar spelling undergo the same spelling changes. Imperative forms corresponding to the present subjunctive follow the same pattern.

a) **c** changes to **qu** before **e**, e.g. **buscar** *to look for*

Preterite: **busqué**

Present subjunctive: **busque, busques, busque, busquemos, busquéis, busquen**

b) **g** changes to **gu** before **e**, e.g. **llegar** *to arrive*

Preterite: **llegué**

Present subjunctive: **llegue, llegues, llegue, lleguemos, lleguéis, lleguen**

c) **-cer**, **-cir** preceded by a consonant change **c** to **z** before **o** and **a**, e.g. **vencer** *to conquer*

Present indicative: **venzo**

Present subjunctive: **venza, venzas, venza, venzamos, venzáis, venzan**

d) **g** changes to **j** before **o** and **a**, e.g. **coger** *to catch*

Present indicative: **cojo**

Present subjunctive: **coja, cojas, coja, cojamos, cojáis, cojan**

e) Drop **u** before **o** and **a**, e.g. **seguir** *to follow, continue*

Present indicative: **sigo**

Present subjunctive: **siga, sigas, siga, sigamos, sigáis, sigan**

f) **qu** changes to **c** before **o** and **a**, e.g. **delinquir** *to commit an offence*

Present indicative: **delinco**

Present subjunctive: **delinca, delincas, delinca, delincamos, delincáis, delincan**

g) Verbs ending in **guar** change **u** to **ü** before **e**, e.g. **averiguar** *to find out*

Preterite: **averigüé**

Present subjunctive: **averigüe, averigües, averigüe, averigüemos, averigüéis, averigüen**

h) **z** changes to **c** before **e**, e.g. **empezar** *to begin*

Preterite: **empecé**

Present subjunctive: **empiece, empieces, empiece, empecemos, empecéis, empiecen**

Bibliography

Cited works and main works consulted in the preparation of the text are as follows:

Batchelor, R.E. and Pountain, C.J.: *Using Spanish: A guide to contemporary usage.* Cambridge University Press, 2005.

Butt, J.: *Spanish Grammar.* Oxford University Press, 1996.

Butt, J. and Benjamin, C. (4th edition): *A New Reference Grammar of Modern Spanish.* Edward Arnold, London, 2004.

González Hermoso, A., et al. (3rd edition): *Gramática de español lengua extranjera.* Edelsa, Madrid, 1995.

Kattán-Ibarra, J. and Pountain, C.J.: *Modern Spanish Grammar: A practical guide.* Routledge, London, 2003.

Matte Bon, F.: *Gramática comunicativa del español, Tomo I: De la lengua a la idea.* Difusión, Madrid, 2000.

Muñoz, P. and Thacker, M. (2nd edition): *A Spanish Learning Grammar.* Arnold, London, 2006.

Sánchez, A., et al.: *Gramática práctica de español para extranjeros.* Sociedad General Española de Librería, S.A., Madrid, 2005.

Index

www.routledge.com/languages

Companion Website

Spanish Grammar in Context

Companion Website

Spanish Grammar in Context comes with a completely free companion website featuring a generous range of interactive additional exercises. These have been specially designed to provide students with opportunities for further practice and consolidation of their knowledge.

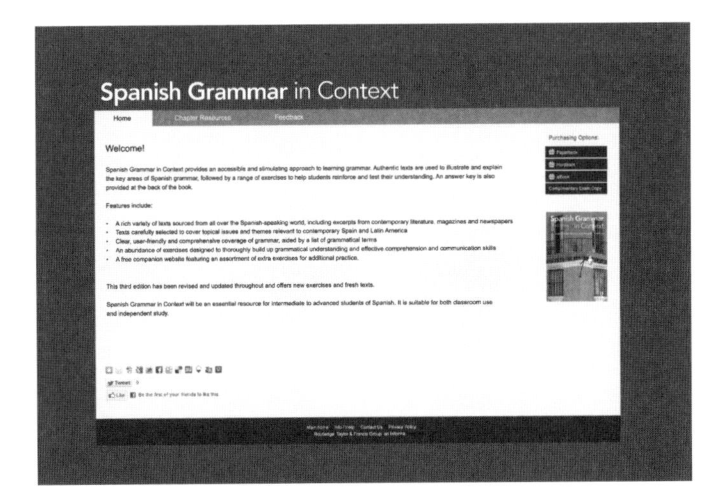

Features include:

- An assortment of "drag and drop", "fill in the gaps", "matching", "true or false" and "multiple choice" exercises to provide variety and active engagement with material.
- A highly user-friendly structure modelled after the organisation of the book, allowing for easy navigation throughout.
- Sample chapters so students can learn on the go.
- A helpful glossary of grammatical terms.

Please find the companion website at **www.routledge.com/cw/Kattan-Ibarra**

Learn more at: www.routledge.com/cw/Kattan-Ibarra